THE OLD TESTAMENT

OUR CALL TO FAITH & JUSTICE

THE OLD TESTAMENT

OUR CALL TO FAITH & JUSTICE

DANIEL SMITH-CHRISTOPHER

AVE MARIA PRESS AVE Notre Dame, Indiana

The Subcommittee on the Catechism, United States Conference of Catholic Bishops, has found this catechetical text, copyright 2013, to be in conformity with the *Catechism of the Catholic Church*.

Nihil Obstat: Reverend Monsignor Michael Heintz, PhD
               Censor Liborum

Imprimatur: Most Reverend Kevin C. Rhoades
               Bishop of Fort Wayne-South Bend

Given at: Fort Wayne, Indiana, on 19 June 2012

The *Nihil Obstat* and *Imprimatur* are official declarations that a book or pamphlet is free of doctrinal or moral error. No implication is contained therein that those who have granted the *Nihil Obstat* or *Imprimatur* agree with its contents, opinions, or statements expressed.

Scripture texts in this work are taken from the *New American Bible with Revised New Testament and Revised Psalms* © 1991, 1986, 1970 Confraternity of Christian Doctrine, Washington, DC, and are used by permission of the copyright owner. All Rights Reserved. No part of the *New American Bible* may be reproduced without permission in writing from the copyright owner.

English translation of the *Catechism of the Catholic Church* for the United States of America copyright © 1994, United States Catholic Conference, Inc.—Libreria Editrice Vaticana. English translation of the *Catechism of the Catholic Church: Modifications from the Editio Typica* copyright © 1997, United States Catholic Conference, Inc.—Libreria Editrice Vaticana.

Theological Consultant:
Hugh R. Page Jr., PhD
Associate Professor of Hebrew Scriptures and Dean of First Year Studies
University of Notre Dame

Catholic Handbook for Faith compiled by Michael Amodei.

Project Editor: Jared Dees

Other references cited as Notes at the end of each chapter.

Engaging Minds, Hearts, and Hands for Faith

An education that is complete is one which the hands and heart are engaged as much as the mind. We want to let our students try their learning in the world and so make prayers of their education.

—Bl. Basil Moreau, Founder of the Congregation of Holy Cross

In this text, you will find:

 intellectually challenging exercises and projects designed to stimulate you to know more about the Old Testament

 presentations and activities that promote a prayerful study of the Scripture and connect you to the Church's liturgy

 stimulating applications that encourage you in service learning and ministry.

Contents

Preface

In Sacred Scripture, the Church constantly finds her nourishment and her strength, for she welcomes it not as a human word, "but as what it really is, the word of God."

Catechism of the Catholic Church, 104

"He saw the writing on the wall." "There was an entire exodus of people leaving the stadium." "It was a flood of Biblical proportions." Phrases like these are heard every day but few people stop to think about where such images and ideas actually come from. We don't seem to know about the Old Testament. Even though it would be difficult to find a Catholic who would not admit the importance of understanding the Bible, the simple fact is that few Catholics (and Christians of all denominations) in the modern world really spend any time reading the Bible for themselves. When they do read the Bible, it is usually not the Old Testament, which is the whole first section and majority of the Bible.

Maybe you know where your "Family Bible" is in your home, but few teens remember the last time they actually read from a Bible. Let's imagine what might have happened if you tried to read it recently. It's a lengthy book with thin, fragile pages and small type. Where would you even start? Let's say you work up some courage, take it down, and in a determined frame of mind, you think "I'm going to *do* it"—and you start reading right from the beginning. That seems logical and the first few chapters aren't bad. The stories of Adam and Eve are interesting and certainly familiar. Then, you hit chapter five of Genesis and you read the following:

> The days of Adam after he became the father of Seth were eight hundred years; and he had other sons and daughters. Thus all the days that Adam lived were nine hundred thirty years; and he died. When Seth had lived one hundred five years, he became the father of Enosh. Seth lived after the birth of Enosh eight hundred seven years, and had other sons and daughters. Thus all the days of Seth were nine hundred twelve years; and he died. When Enosh had lived ninety years, he became the father of Kenan. Enosh lived after the birth of Kenan eight hundred fifteen years, and had other sons and daughters. (Gn 5:4–10)

Suddenly, you feel tired!

Who are these people? Who in the world could live to be eight hundred years old? What's it all about, anyway? You might begin to wonder what people like me see in this stuff. Why are we so fascinated with the Bible that we spend years of our lives reading, studying, writing, and teaching about this book?

Yet, you hold in your hands a ticket to a tremendous journey, which may change your mind forever. I would like to invite you on this journey. You may wonder why I would talk about "traveling" through the Bible. The Bible is not only filled with images of travel but also because you, the reader, will "travel" as you read, learning about new places, ancient languages, archaeological discoveries, wars and peacemaking, family joys, and family tragedies. It seems perfectly appropriate to learn about the Bible by taking a journey with these writings. The last reason I use the image of a "journey" is because the best trips are explorations in which you are transformed by the journey. It is almost impossible to journey into the Bible (or journey *with* the Bible) and not find yourself going through some interesting changes in your point of view as a young person thinking about your future. In this course of study, you will hopefully learn enough to not only want to keep reading the Bible, but actually find yourself, many times, *glued* to the text. It can happen! So, here comes my final warning to you:

Bible reading is addictive. Use with caution!

How do I know? Because I am totally and completely addicted. And I am clearly not the only one. While working in the city of Los Angeles, I have been involved with television and film projects involving the Bible, teaching the Bible to young people and adults, teaching lay leaders of the Church, and even advising Church leaders on issues regarding Scripture. What I have learned from working in the popular media is this: It is a fact that television networks know that if they produce and run "Bible" programs and documentaries, they will pull *very* good ratings. Throughout this course my hope is that you will begin to find out why so many people find Bible study so fascinating.

Like any journey, we will need to make some preparations. In Chapter 1, we will deal with some basic questions many students have posed about the Bible. You may have some other introductory questions of your own. You will also learn that your journey will raise more questions. Hopefully the succeeding chapters will answer some of these as well.

Professor Daniel Smith-Christopher
Loyola Marymount University
Los Angeles, California

Preparing for the Journey:
Basic Information

CHAPTER 1 OUTLINE

- *The many books and stories of the Old Testament help us to see the loving relationship between God and his people throughout history.*

- *It takes the help of the Church and some important skills and resources to accurately interpret the Bible.*

- *The organization of the Old Testament and the history of the Hebrew people shed important light on the scope of Salvation History.*

- *The Church considers the Old Testament the inspired Word of God, useful for study, prayer, and interpretation of the New Testament.*

canon

An official list of books belonging to the Bible, both the Old Testament and New Testament.

deuterocanonical

A term meaning "second canon." Books included in the Catholic Old Testament but not in the Hebrew Bible. These additions are 1 and 2 Maccabees, Judith, Tobit, Baruch, Sirach, Wisdom, and parts of Esther and Daniel.

Tradition

The living transmission of the Church's Gospel message found in the Church's teaching, life, and worship. It is faithfully preserved, handed on, and interpreted by the Church's Magisterium.

The many books and stories of the Old Testament help us to see the loving relationship between God and his people throughout history.

Introduction

An ancient Chinese philosopher named Lao Tzu once said, "A journey of a thousand miles begins with a single step." This wise saying applies to any journey we make in life. It also applies to every course we study. In order to complete the journey successfully, we need to know basic information at the onset. We need to prepare and to gather all the necessary supplies.

Similarly, it is important to prepare before we delve into a serious study of the Bible. Before we can actually start, there are many questions that need answers. If these questions are not answered at least briefly, it is hard to keep our minds on the task. The questions will only keep nagging us. Furthermore, if we don't approach Bible study with the appropriate

background information, we may easily get overwhelmed or sidetracked. We may give up and never complete our journey. Most importantly, we must always keep in mind that the Bible is different from any other book. Since the Bible is the inspired Word of God, it "must be read and interpreted in the sacred spirit in which it was written" (*Dei Verbum*, 12).

So let's begin with some basic preparation and background information. If you have additional questions about the Bible, record them in a notebook or journal.

What Books Make up the Old Testament?

This may seem like a simple question. But actually, it's not. Catholics and other Christians call the first part of their Bible the "Old Testament" in relation to the "New Testament," which has as its central object Jesus Christ (*CCC*, 124). Jews prefer the term "Hebrew Bible" because they do not use the New Testament.

When Jews refer to the "Hebrew Bible" and Christians refer to the "Old Testament," they are basically talking about the same thing; however, there are differences. Catholics include forty-six books of the Old Testament (forty-five if Jeremiah and Lamentations are counted as one book) and twenty-seven books of the New Testament as part of the **canon** of Scripture.

The Old Testament is really a *collection* of books written over the course of a millennium, roughly between 1000 BC and 150 BC. The books were written predominantly in the Hebrew language. The early Church, however, differed with early Judaism in the decision about the canon of the Old Testament. The Church included seven books (1 and 2 Maccabees, Judith, Tobit, Baruch, Sirach, and Wisdom) not

included in the Hebrew Bible that were mostly written in Greek after 300 B.C. These seven books are referred to as **deuterocanonical**—"second canon"—to show that they are not accepted in the Jewish canon. Some of the deuterocanonical books also include additional chapters to older Hebrew books like Daniel and Esther.

At the time of the Protestant Reformation, Martin Luther decided to include only books in the Hebrew Bible. Most Protestant Bibles do print these seven books, but they include them in a separate section. Most Protestants read these books with great interest, and all Christian scholars study them. Nevertheless, to this day, you may hear people speak of "Catholic Bibles" and "Protestant Bibles" because of this very issue.

Who Is God?

In the Old Testament, the God of the Hebrew people has many names. But the most common name is "YHWH" (pronounced yah-way), the name that Moses first heard when he was called to be the liberator of God's people in Egypt (Ex 3). Although there is some uncertainty about the origins of the name, it seems that the name YHWH is constructed from the basic Hebrew verb, "is."

YHWH is usually translated as "I am," but it could also be "I am the God who is" or "I am and will be." Parts of this name YHWH are in many Hebrew personal names like the "iah" in "Isaiah" or "Jeremiah." If these Hebrew names were translated into English, they would sound like Native American names: Isaiah literally means "YHWH saves" or "YHWH is salvation!" and Jeremiah means "YHWH has established."

The non-Hebrew people in the ancient world had their own gods under many different names as well. Baal was the most popular god of the nearby Canaanites. Baal is mentioned in several places in the Old Testament. (More on this later in the journey.)

In some Jewish traditions, the name YHWH is itself considered too sacred to actually pronounce out loud. When reading the Bible, these Jews use "Adonai" (ah-doe-nye) as a replacement. Adonai simply means "Lord." In order to help Jewish readers, most modern Hebrew Bibles have taken the vowel letters from the word "Adonai" and overlaid them on the consonants for YHWH. This strange combination was supposed to remind the reader to say "Adonai." However, when Christian scholars read this in centuries past, they did not know about the tradition, and thought it was a real word—which they pronounced "Jehovah." Jehovah is actually a mistaken reading of the name YHWH. Sometimes when very Orthodox Jews write about God, they even write "G*d" to remind them of the mystery of the sacred name.

Catholics have no custom of not saying the name YHWH out loud. The Church holds that the name "YHWH" expresses God's faithfulness: "despite the faithlessness of men's sin and the punishment it deserves, he keeps 'steadfast love for thousands'" (*CCC*, 211). Church **Tradition** also teaches that the name YHWH reveals that God is "the fullness of Being and of every perfection, without origin and without end" (*CCC*, 213). As revealed to the Hebrews, God's love for us is steadfast, faithful, and constant.

One way to think about the Old Testament is that it contains books about the Hebrew people learning about YHWH over hundreds of years. In other words, God reveals himself through the words of the Old Testament precisely because he *intends and wants to be known by humans*—there are no secrets or hidden tricks. God's very being is Truth and Love. For the ancient Hebrews, they summed up what they knew of God with the name "YHWH." Catholics, too, affirm that part of studying the Bible is remembering that the God of our Faith has revealed himself as YHWH, the God who is. In the fullness of time God revealed himself completely in the sending of his Son, Jesus Christ.

Sharing the Faith

Write a thank-you letter to a person who has taught you about God and Faith.

Knowing the Basic Story Line

Unlike most books, the Old Testament is not one continuous plot divided into episodes or chapters. Instead, what is central to the Old Testament is one loving relationship through history between a people and their God.

It's easy to understand from a human perspective why this relationship would be so important throughout the Old Testament. God created man out of love and calls

"Jesus is Lord!"

(*CCC*, 203–210, 446–451)

One way Jesus and early Christians expressed his divinity was by making connections between the way he described himself and the ways God was named in the Hebrew Scriptures, that is, "YHWH." In John's Gospel there are a series of sayings that include the words "I AM," referring to God's self-identification to Moses in the Old Testament as YHWH, which is translated as "I am." You will probably recognize many of these "I am" statements:

"I am the bread of life." (Jn 6:35, 48)

"I am the light of the world." (Jn 8:12; 9:5)

"I am the good shepherd." (Jn 10:11–14)

"I am the way, the truth, and the life." (Jn 14:6)

Another connection between Jesus and YHWH of the Old Testament is Jesus' identity as "Lord." Since YHWH was a sacred name, *Adonai* was used in its place. Early Christians had the same feelings about the sacredness God's name so they referred to Jesus as Lord. St. Paul quotes an early Christian hymn in his letter to the Philippians that ends with a common early Christian acclamation, "Jesus Christ is Lord!" (Phil 2:11). When the Apostle Thomas recognized the Risen Christ as Jesus, he exclaimed, "My Lord and my God!" (Jn 20:28). In addition, throughout the Gospels Jesus is addressed as "Lord" by those who seek help and healing (Mt 8:2; 14:30; 15:22). "By attributing to Jesus the divine title 'Lord,' the first confessions of the Church's faith affirm from the beginning that the power, honor and glory due to God the Father are due also to Jesus" (*CCC*, 449). To say "Jesus is Lord!" is an expression of the divinity of Christ.

YHWH, Adonai	The Lord Jesus Christ
God is *YHWH*, which is translated "I am" (Ex 3:13–14)	John's "I am" statements (Jn 6:35, 48; Jn 8:12, 9:5; Jn 10:7; Jn 10:11–14; Jn 11:25; Jn 14:6, Jn 15:1, 5)
Adonai, or Lord, was used in place of God's sacred name (Ex 3:15)	"Jesus Christ is Lord!" was a popular early Christian acclamation (Rom 10:9, 1 Cor 12:3, Ph 2:11) Jesus is often addressed as "Lord" (Mt 8:2; 14:30; 15:22)

us all to love. "To love" is the fundamental vocation of being human. This offer of God's love to man can be understood in the context of Christian marriage where the mutual love between a husband and wife "becomes an image of the absolute and unfailing love with which God loves man" (*CCC*, 1604).

Yet, there are ups and downs in any relationship to go along with the wonderful times. Readers of the Old Testament discover that man's relationship with God is not always amiable. The story of the fall of man (Gn 3:1–24) tells of man's disobedience of God. This first **sin** would affect man's relationship with God from that time on. Some first-time readers of the Old Testament are often surprised how the authors of Scripture describe the level of anger that God is said to feel in return to man, especially as expressed through his special messengers called "prophets" (more on them later).

Like all relationships, this divine-human one described in the Old Testament has its dramatic episodes of jealousy and angry disappointment. But perhaps most impressive, the Old Testament also exemplifies moments of moving intimacy, love, compassion, and forgiveness. YHWH, according to the ancient Hebrews, had very human-like qualities. That is not so odd when you think about it. After all, how else can we picture a living God? Our words are never sufficient to entirely portray God, but words are necessary to communicate and to even think about God. The Hebrews wanted to talk to God! They wanted *a relationship*.

Perhaps part of the spell that the Old Testament casts on all those who study it is not unlike the fascination of being in love, with all the wonders provided by the occasional surprises, disappointments, and great joys of romantic relationships. It comes as no surprise that the study of Scripture is compared to "being in love" with "Lady Wisdom" (Prv 3:13–18).

Have you ever received a letter from a loved one? Perhaps a new boyfriend or girlfriend? If so, you take your love letter home and read it and re-read it. You want to "hear" the words of love and affection again and again. For modern Bible study, and our relationship with God, it is as necessary to re-read the previous words spoken between us as it is to continue to find new words to speak and new skills for listening to God today. In short, it is essential to return to the source, which is Scripture.

Section in Review

Quick View

- The Catholic Old Testament is a collection of forty-six books including seven deuterocanonical books.

- The Old Testament contains the story of the Hebrew people learning about God, whose name is "YHWH" and whom they called "Adonai."

- This story of Salvation is about the loving relationship between God and his people.

For Review

1. **Vocabulary**: Use the terms *canon* and *deuterocanonical* to describe the Old Testament in a short paragraph.

2. **Vocabulary**: What does the name "YHWH" mean?

3. **Main Idea**: What is the basic story line of the Old Testament?

Prime Advice

The Book of Deuteronomy records these instructions of the Lord:

> Keep these words that I am commanding you today in your heart. Recite them to your children and talk about them when you are at home and when you are away, when you lie down and when you rise. Bind them as a sign on your hand, fix them as an emblem on your forehead, and write them on the doorposts of your house and on your gates. (Dt 6:6–9 NRSV)

Read Deuteronomy 6:4–5. What is the subject of the Lord's instructions? Make a sign illustrating the heart of the Lord's instruction. After sharing your sign in class, hang it in your room at home to remind you of your ongoing relationship with God.

sin

An offense against God. Sin is a deliberate thought, word, deed, or omission against the eternal law of God.

Magisterium

The teaching authority of the Church concerning issues of faith and morals. The Magisterium consists of the Pope and the college of bishops acting together.

4. **Critical Thinking**: What are the differences between the Hebrew Bible, Catholic Old Testament, and most Protestant Bibles?

For Reflection

In what ways has God's love for you been steadfast, faithful, and constant? Write a short testimony of your Faith to someone younger than you (e.g., a younger sibling, someone in a religious education class, or a scout) in a letter.

It takes the help of the Church and some important skills and resources to accurately interpret the Bible.

How the Church Interprets the Inspired Writings

The Catholic understanding of inspiration is that human authors who were deeply moved by God wrote the Bible. The Church has accepted their writings because through the same wisdom of the Holy Spirit that inspired the original authors, the Church leaders—the Pope and bishops—have also been inspired.

The written Scriptures along with the oral preaching of the Apostles are handed down in the Church through apostolic succession. The living transmission of the message of the Gospel of the Church, accomplished in the Holy Spirit, is called Tradition. The Sacred Scripture and Sacred Tradition are bound closely together, and communicate with one another. Likewise, the task of interpreting God's Word, whether in the form of Scripture or Tradition, is entrusted to the Magisterium. This means that it is the bishops, in communion with the Pope, who can interpret God's Word for each generation. The Church relies equally on Scripture *and* her living Tradition to enrich all people with God's Word. "Both Scripture and Tradition must be accepted and honored with equal sentiments of devotion and reverence" (*Dei Verbum*, 9).

The particular writings of the Bible are valuable and powerful and help in our learning about God and how he builds up his Church. The judgment that these writings are inspired comes from the experience of the Church with these writings. They did not come to the Church pre-packaged and pre-marked: "These are the inspired books." Instead, the Church leaders (Magisterium) read and studied them and came to realize that they were inspired. The Pontifical Biblical Commission wrote: "What characterizes Catholic exegesis is that it deliberately places itself within the living tradition of the Church."

All Catholics can join in the process of understanding the meaning of the Scripture. It is an ongoing process of prayerful dialogue and study. Each succeeding generation raises questions about the Scriptures and keeps the dialogue going. The Preface to the Pontifical Biblical Commission states that the study of the Bible "is never finished; each age must in its own way newly seek to understand the sacred books."

In order for us to interpret Scripture correctly, we must pay attention to both what the human author wanted to say and what the Holy Spirit intended to communicate. To find out the human author's intentions, we must take into account the time and culture, the literary forms of the time, and the manner of speaking and thinking that was current then. Since the Scripture is inspired, they "must be

Our understanding and wisdom of the Scriptures increases over time. And a compassionate God has not abandoned us *only* to the words in the Scriptures. The Holy Spirit continues to lead us through the Church. The Church teaches that there are two senses of Scripture: the literal and the spiritual.

The *literal sense* of Scripture is foundational. It refers to what the actual words directly mean, either in a precise sense (e.g., the narrative of the Passion) or in a figurative sense (e.g., a metaphor or parable).

The *spiritual sense* refers to how the words of Scripture can be signs of something more profound. Understanding the Bible in this way is important for a student of the Old Testament. The spiritual sense has three parts. The allegorical sense helps us understand how some of the events of the Old Testament prefigure Christ; for example, the crossing of the Red Sea symbolizes Christ's victory over death. The moral sense teaches us how to act in a right way. For example, Abraham's faith obliges us to believe in Christ. The anagogical sense (from a Greek word for "leading") helps us to relate what the events of Scripture have to do with our final destiny—Heaven.

It is the task of those who study the Bible to work according to these rules toward a better understanding and explanation of the Scripture. The Magisterium of the Church is ultimately responsible for "watching over and interpreting the Word of God" (*Dei Verbum*, 12).

Learning Some Necessary Skills

Working from the rules listed above, there are several skills that further help to study the Bible. Among these skills is a basic understanding of the original languages in which the Old Testament was written. Many languages were spoken and written in the Ancient Near East during the time of the writing of the Old Testament. Most of the Old Testament was written in Hebrew, but parts were written in Aramaic (a language very close to Hebrew, but more widely spoken among ancient peoples) and some of the later writings were written in Greek. Hebrew and Aramaic are known as "Semitic" languages. There remain a few modern Semitic languages spoken today, including Arabic or Maltese.

The grammar and vocabulary of Hebrew and Semitic languages are similar. Many of the words sound and mean the same thing. For example, the word "peace" is *shalom* in Hebrew and *salaam* in Arabic. Knowing that these

read and interpreted in the sacred spirit in which it was written" (*Dei Verbum*, 12). The Second Vatican Council offered three criteria for interpreting Scripture in the light of the Holy Spirit:

1. Look closely at the content and unity of the whole Scripture.

2. Read the Scripture within "the living Tradition of the whole Church."

3. Be attentive to the analogy of Faith. This means the unity of the truths of Faith among themselves and within the whole context of God's revelation.

What Inspiration Means

God is the author of the Sacred Scripture. But what exactly does that mean? The Bible was not literally penned by God. It did not fall from the sky. Inspiration involves God's inspiring human authors to write the sacred words. Another Christian viewpoint is more literal, holding that the words themselves are inspired. For sake of understanding, examine critically both points of view.

If it is the *authors* who are inspired, then how can we be sure that the person fully and adequately wrote down what should have been written?

If it is merely the *words* that are inspired, then the author's importance diminishes: anybody could have written inspired words accurately—even a young child could have done it! Doesn't it matter that the writer was a spiritual person, deeply in tune with the inspiration of the Holy Spirit? Would we be satisfied to say that they acted like a robot, and just copied words "whispered in their ear" by the Holy Spirit?

Finally, just because someone *says* that a word is from God doesn't make it so! There needs to be some acknowledgement and recognition from the Church. Remember the famous question, "If a tree falls in the forest and nobody hears it, does it make a sound?" In a similar way, how can a word be inspired if nobody hears it, learns from it, and repeats it? The Church is the final part of inspiration.

- Form small groups to debate the meaning of inspiration. Share the conclusions of your group's debate with the rest of the class.

languages are related can help us to understand the culture, context, and wider political and social setting of ancient Hebrew history. In fact, serious students of the Bible learn to read Hebrew, Aramaic, and Greek in order to study the Bible in its original languages.

Of course, most of us do not speak or read these original Biblical languages. We rely on translators to bring the words of the Bible to us. Today there are many different English translations of the Bible. How accurate are they? To understand the answer to this question, you need to ask yourself some analogous questions. For example, why can't scientist No. 1 announce that he has discovered the cure for cancer one day and immediately sell the cure for money the next day? Or, why couldn't scientist No. 2 claim that that there is another planet in our solar system that is beyond Pluto and have her claim immediately accepted? The answer, of course, is that any scientist would have to *prove* their announcement to lots of other scientists! A discovery isn't considered real until *many* people confirm it.

Translation of the Bible is similar. There are literally hundreds of ancient manuscripts of the Bible in Greek, Hebrew, and many other ancient languages, that these translators use to compare to each other. A translation into English is never based on one or two texts in Greek and Hebrew—but *dozens and dozens* of them! It is usually pretty easy to spot single mistakes from one ancient scribe when you have over a hundred other texts of the same passage to compare.

So, not only are there many texts to work with, there are lots of people working on them simultaneously. Biblical scholars—both Catholic and Protestant—meet regularly in conferences, compare notes, argue about their ideas, and suggest new ideas. Bible translations that we use today are the results of years and years of scholarship, learning, debate, and checking. We are learning more all the time, and new discoveries give us more confidence about our translations. The discovery of the Dead Sea Scrolls in 1947–1950, for example, helped Biblical scholars and all Christians tremendously because these scrolls were Hebrew writings of the Bible that were almost 1,000 years *older* than the Hebrew texts we had previously. The Dead Sea Scrolls helped to confirm the previous translations.

The details of Biblical translations are debated. But it would be virtually impossible for someone to suggest a wild translation and get it past all the other translators who are also working on these texts. Take, for example, the *New American Bible*, which is the translation quoted in this text. In 1943, Pope Pius XII issued an encyclical on Scripture studies. He wrote:

We ought to explain the original text which was written by the inspired author himself and has more authority and greater weight than any, even the very best, translation whether ancient or modern. This can be done all the more easily and fruitfully if the knowledge of languages be joined to a real skill in literary criticism of the same text. (*Divino afflante Spiritu*)

The text of the *New American Bible* is a completely new translation taken from the original and the oldest available sacred texts (see Preface to the *New American Bible*, Old Testament). Again, it's important to remember also that the Pope and college of bishops are ultimately responsible for not only determining the validity of a translation, but also of interpreting its words.

Another skill for serious Bible study is knowledge of other ancient writings and how they compare to the Biblical text. A large number of books that have survived from before the time of Jesus, mostly from the Hellenistic and Roman Periods (e.g., 333 BC through about AD 250) are known as the **Pseudepigrapha**. Many such books were discovered in 1945 near Naga Hamdi. These books are of considerable historical, literary, and religious interest for the study of the late Old Testament era and early Christianity. They have long been translated into English and are readily available, and often provide us with an excellent idea of the great diversity in religious thinking in these times.

While there is nothing dangerous or secret about them (although some of them are a bit odd), the Church long ago determined that these writings were not inspired by God and could not be included in either the Old Testament or New Testament canon. It's a good idea to have a strong grounding in the Bible before launching into reading these non-Biblical materials—particularly if you want to appreciate how these other books use Biblical ideas and then go in different directions. As interesting as some of these other books are, they aren't nearly as interesting as the Bible itself. If you become a serious student of the Bible in college, this will be the time to read and analyze them.

The books that are in the canon of the Old Testament and New Testament are historically considered the inspired books of the Bible. To be inspired means that what is written in them is what God wanted to be communicated to humankind. Any interpretation of the Bible must be attentive above all to what God wants to reveal through the sacred authors. What comes from the Spirit is not fully

Psuedepigrapha
Ancient books from the same timeframe as the books of the Bible, especially the New Testament. The Church decided these books were not inspired by God and could not be included in the canon of the Bible.

Two jars that contained the Dead Sea Scrolls.

archaeology
The science of studying material remains of past human life and activities.

artifact
Something created by past humans, usually for a specific purpose (tools, pottery, clothing, etc.).

Finally, for serious study of the Bible, **archaeology** is also of importance. Archaeology is both a science and an art. Imagine digging the remains of a village from Biblical times. What would you find? You might discover the lines of the foundations, perhaps some remnants of building material, possibly some gravesites, and maybe a trash dump with remnants of old broken jars and containers. That is the science part—because that is what you actually see.

What can we learn from this kind of evidence? Here is where science meets art, or in other words, where evidence meets intuition. Sometimes it is difficult to reconstruct in our minds what the buildings actually looked like, how the people lived, and what they did. For example, maybe when this ancient foundation of a village is dug up, archaeologists have many problems trying to identify the name of this particular village. Then they must search for clues.

In the Ancient Near East, it is possible that the name of the village may be found on clay tablets or papyrus scrolls. Or the Bible can help if it refers to a particular village that was in the area of the excavation. Sometimes modern local traditions may help.

Sometimes names are found on **artifacts**. For example, a discovery in Northern Israel from the early 1990s mentioned "The House of David" and an Assyrian royal carving found many decades ago famously pictures Omri, a king of Northern Israel who is mentioned in 1 Kings and 1 Chronicles. Archaeological discoveries that mention Biblical persons or places can confirm their existences, though not everything about the context of the persons or places. Archaeology and Biblical study, therefore, must always be in dialogue, because archaeological discoveries must be interpreted as much as Biblical texts.

understood except by the Spirit's action. Reading the Bible, in short, is not simply an intellectual exercise, but a prayerful one as well. As the *Catechism*, quoting Luke 24:45, reminds us:

> If the Scriptures are not to remain a dead letter, Christ, the eternal Word of the living God, must through the Holy Spirit "open [our] minds to understand the Scriptures." (*CCC*, 108)

Section in Review

Quick View

- Human authors who were inspired by God wrote the Bible.

- The Magisterium—Pope and bishops—interpret God's Word in Scripture and Tradition.

- The Second Vatican Council suggests that when we read Scripture we keep in mind the unity of the whole Scripture, the living Tradition of the whole Church, and unity of the truths of Faith within the whole context of God's Revelation.

- There are two senses of Scripture: the *literal sense* and the *spiritual sense*.

- Accurate and identical translations of the Old Testament from Hebrew, Aramaic, and Greek are challenging, but scholars work together to create accurate translations.

- Various non-canonical books known as the Pseudepigrapha have been discovered to assist in the translation and interpretation of the Old Testament.

- The art and science of archeology offers important assistance to Biblical interpretation.

For Review

1. **Main Idea**: How do Sacred Scripture and Sacred Tradition function together in transmitting God's Word?

2. **Main Idea**: Explain the literal sense and scriptural sense for understanding Scripture.

3. **Main Idea**: What does it mean to say a Biblical book is inspired?

4. **Main Idea**: List and describe three helpful skills needed in the interpretation of Scripture.

5. **Critical Thinking**: What is the ideal relationship between archaeology and Biblical study?

For Reflection

How has a passage from the Old Testament inspired you in your relationship with God? In other words, what do you think God wished to communicate to you through this Bible passage?

The organization of the Old Testament and the history of the Hebrew people shed important light on the scope of Salvation History.

Classifying and Arranging the Old Testament Books

The Jews traditionally divided the books of the Hebrew Bible into three distinct sections:

1. Law (in Hebrew, *Torah*)
2. Prophets (in Hebrew, *Neviim*)
3. Writings (in Hebrew, *Ktuvim*)

The Law consists of the first five books of the Bible: Genesis, Exodus, Leviticus, Numbers, and Deuteronomy. The Prophets are subdivided into the Former Prophets (Joshua, Judges, 1 and 2 Samuel, and 1 and 2 Kings), the Latter Prophets (Isaiah, Jeremiah, Ezekiel), and the Minor Prophets. The Writings include eleven books: Psalms, Proverbs, Job, Canticle of Canticles, Ruth, Lamentations, Ecclesiastes, Esther, Daniel, Ezra/Nehemiah, and Chronicles. If you put together the first letter of the three words in Hebrew, you get the acronym "TaNaK," which is the term often used as shorthand by modern Jews to refer to the Hebrew Bible.

The Old Testament in the *New American Bible* is arranged slightly differently, under Pentateuch (Greek for "five books"), Historical Books, Wisdom Books, and Prophetic Books. The books of the Old Testament are arranged in these categories as follows (with abbreviations):

The Pentateuch

Genesis	Gn
Exodus	Ex
Leviticus	Lv
Numbers	Nm
Deuteronomy	Dt

The Historical Books

Joshua	Jos
Judges	Jgs
Ruth	Ru
1 Samuel	1 Sm
2 Samuel	2 Sm
1 Kings	1 Kgs
2 Kings	2 Kgs
1 Chronicles	1 Chr
2 Chronicles	2 Chr
Ezra	Ezr
Nehemiah	Neh
Tobit	Tb
Judith	Jdt
Esther	Est
1 Maccabees	1 Mc
2 Maccabees	2 Mc

The Wisdom Books

Job	Jb
Psalms	Ps(s)
Proverbs	Prv
Ecclesiastes	Eccl
Song of Songs	Sg
Wisdom	Wis
Sirach	Sir

The Prophetic Books

Isaiah	Is
Jeremiah	Jer
Lamentations	Lam
Baruch	Bar
Ezekiel	Ez
Daniel	Dn
Hosea	Hos
Joel	Jl
Amos	Am
Obadiah	Ob
Jonah	Jon
Micah	Mi
Nahum	Na
Habakkuk	Hb
Zephaniah	Zep
Haggai	Hg
Zechariah	Zec
Malachi	Mal

The most important thing to keep in mind about the arrangement of the books, however, is that the Bible is *not* in chronological order. The first books are *not* necessarily the *oldest* books, and the final books are *not* necessarily the most recently written. Nor is it true that events recorded in the first books all took place before the events in the next books. For example, Leviticus and Deuteronomy both include details about Moses receiving the Ten Commandments. A reader needs to learn about history and the text in order to have a good sense of when a book was written. But there is also the certainty that many books were edited at a later time, or were combinations of other books. For example, the psalms were probably once in shorter collections before being put together to form the large collection that is the Book of Psalms today. (Catholics and Protestants have 150 Psalms; Orthodox Christians have 151 Psalms.)

Some Biblical books even quote books that are not in the Old Testament canon, for example, the "Book of the Kings of Israel" (e.g., 1 Kgs 14:19, 15:31) or the "Book of Jashar" (e.g., Jos 10:13; 2 Sm 1:18). These were likely ancient books that the Biblical authors had in front of them as they were writing their text.

So when were the books of the Old Testament written? The earliest of the Biblical books were based on oral traditions that were first written down either during the time of Solomon (around 950 BC) or perhaps between 900 and 700 BC. The latest books (especially many of the deutercanonical books) were written, probably in Greek, around 150–100 BC.

The reason that the time of Solomon is usually cited is because it is believed that Solomon would have been the first king of Israel who actually had scribes to do some of the writing. Another school of thought is that most of the early writings come from later on—the eighth or seventh centuries BC—when there is more evidence of widespread literacy, and more evidence of royal administrations that would have kept such written records. Ancient writing required institutions, a scribal class, and not merely a few literate persons.

Most certainly, a large portion of the Bible was revised after the fall of Jerusalem in 587 BC. In this case the revision involved adding a revised insight to the original work. The revisions to the inspired texts do not in any way impact their sacredness. Remember, inspiration refers to what God *wanted* recorded in the Bible, including clarifying that message by editors.

To summarize, it continues to be debatable as to when different books of the Bible were actually written, edited, and began to take on the form that we have today. Of course, since many Biblical books were found among the Dead Sea Scrolls, we know that much of the Bible was already in its present form by 100–200 years before the time of Jesus.

Section in Review

Quick View

- The Jews divide the Hebrew Scriptures into three distinct sections, which differs from the way Catholics arrange the book in the *New American Bible*.

- The Old Testament developed over a period of many years, and it is difficult to determine the exact date that books were written and edited.

For Review

6. **Critical Thinking**: How does the Jewish classification of the books of Hebrew Scriptures differ from the way Catholics classify the books of the Old Testament in the *New American Bible*?

7. **Main Idea**: Why is it so difficult to pinpoint when a specific Old Testament book was written?

8. **Main Idea**: Using the timeline on pages 14–15 as a guide, describe the key moments in the history of the Jerusalem Temple.

9. **Critical Thinking**: What are some common struggles that the Hebrew people experienced throughout the history of the Hebrew people depicted on pages 14–15?

For Reflection

Read the Book of Tobit. What message do you think God is giving us regarding relationships (e.g., children and parents, husbands and wives, self and God)?

Ancient Hebrew History:
A BASIC OUTLINE

APPROXIMATELY 1030 BC The beginning of the Monarchy (kings) after the period of the Judges. This is often called the "United Monarchy" because there was, for a time, only one King for all Hebrew peoples: Saul, followed by David, and finally Solomon.

1207–1208 BC Pharaoh Merneptah carved a memorial to his military campaigns in Canaan and mentions the people "Israel." The carving is dated to 1207 or 1208. This is the first use of the word "Israel" in history. Therefore, we know that a people who called themselves "Israel" were in the land at least by 1207–1208.

APPROXIMATELY 1260 BC The exodus of the Hebrew slaves from Egypt under the leadership of Moses. The date of the Exodus cannot be certain, but is usually dated to the reign of Rameses II (1279 –1212 BC).

922 BC The death of Solomon resulted in the division of the Hebrew people into two states (sometimes rivals, sometimes allies) called Judah in the south and Israel in the north.

722 BC The fall of the Northern Kingdom to the invading Assyrians from northwest Mesopotamia (in what is today modern Iraq and Syria).

640–609 BC The Reign of King Josiah. Josiah instituted what scholars call "The Deuteronomic Reforms" (because we think the Laws of Deuteronomy inspired his reform movement), and it is likely that most of the historical writings of the books of Joshua through 2 Kings (six scrolls or books) come from this period as well.

587–586 BC The final defeat of Judah by the Babylonian Empire under King Nebuchadnezzar, who deported many Judean citizens. The Jerusalem Temple built by Solomon was destroyed.

These dates represent important milestones in the history of the Hebrew people. These are especially important to introductory students of the Old Testament, as they will allow you to relate specific books of the Old Testament to specific events and time periods.

539 BC Cyrus the Persian defeats Babylon and allows some of the captive peoples to begin returning to their homelands.

167 BC Antiochus IV (Epiphanes) attempts to unite his territory through forced Hellenism. There was serious oppression of many Jews during this time. As a direct result, the Maccabean resistance breaks out, as described in the Books of Maccabees.

520–515 BC Most probable date for the rebuilding of the destroyed Temple in Jerusalem.

CA 450 BC Approximate time of the missions of Nehemiah and Ezra, Hebrews who traveled back to Palestine from the Persian Diaspora.

CA 64 BC Palestine comes under direct Roman control, although the Romans had been watching events in Palestine for some time before, and occasionally involved themselves in local disputes.

CA 6–4 BC The birth of Jesus.

333 BC Alexander the Great's invasions of Palestine and the Near East—beginning of the influence of Hellenism (Greek culture).

AD 70 The destruction of the second Temple by the Romans and the scattering of the Jerusalem Christians mostly eastward.

The Church considers the Old Testament the inspired Word of God, useful for study, prayer, and interpretation of the New Testament.

How Important Is the Old Testament in the Life of the Church?

This is a very important question for your study of the Old Testament in the context of your course in a Catholic high school. The Church considers the Old Testament "an indispensable part of the Sacred Scripture" (*CCC*, 121). The Old Testament is the true Word of God. The Church has always rejected any idea that the New Testament voided the Old Testament. All of the books of the Old Testament are inspired by God and contain a great amount of teachings on God, wisdom on human life, a treasury of prayers, and a glimpse of the mystery of Salvation. The Old Testament offers a "prefiguration" of what God did in the fullness of time in the Person of his Son, Jesus Christ. This means that Christians also read the Old Testament "in the light of Christ crucified and risen" (see *CCC*, 128–129). This unity between the Old Testament and New Testament is based on **typology**.

As Church Father St. Augustine put it: "The New Testament lies hidden in the Old and the Old Testament is unveiled in the New." Christians read the Old Testament in light of Christ crucified and risen, but also remember that the Old Testament has "its own intrinsic value as Revelation reaffirmed by our Lord himself" (*CCC*, 129). When asked which was the first of all the commandments, Jesus taught those he learned from the Hebrew Scripture (see Mk 12:28–34).

The *Catechism of the Catholic Church* summarizes the importance of the Old Testament to the Church as taught by the Second Vatican Council:

> Indeed, "the economy of the Old Testament was deliberately so oriented that it should prepare for and declare in prophecy the coming of Christ, redeemer of all men." (*CCC*, 122 quoting *Dei Verbum*)

As the Church itself was foreshadowed from the beginning of creation, the Church "was prepared for in a remarkable way throughout the history of the people of Israel and by means of the Old Covenant" (*Lumen Gentium*, 2).

Studying the Old Testament: Some Final Thoughts

A final question to pose as we begin a detailed study of the Old Testament has to do with the nature of the study itself. A first truth must be acknowledged: The books of the Bible have been written under the inspiration of the Holy Spirit. This means that, while God chose

JESUS' BIBLE

It is important to remember that when we read the Old Testament, we are sharing this book with another living faith, Judaism. The faith of the Jews is a viable and living response to God's Revelation in the Old Testament. The Church does not believe, as some Christians unfortunately and wrongly think, that the Jews have been "rejected" or even "cursed" by God. Judaism has a unique relationship to Christianity and Christians ought to affirm Jewish response to God and indeed learn from it as a means of enriching our own faith response to God.

Jesus, after all, and most of the earliest Christians in the first generation of the Church were all Jews. As you study the Old Testament, remember that you are in effect studying "Jesus' Bible"—it was *the* Scripture used by Jesus. We have the benefits of books later written about Jesus and quoting Jesus. But for Jesus himself and his first followers, their "Bible" is what we study in this course.

men as authors, he also instructed them in "writing everything and only those things which he wanted" (*Dei Verbum*, 11). Therefore, because the authors were inspired by the Holy Spirit, the books of the Bible "must be acknowledged as teaching firmly, faithfully, and without error that truth which God wanted put into the sacred writings for the sake of our salvation" (*Dei Verbum*, 11).

Nevertheless, since God speaks in the Scripture through human authors, it is necessary to apply tools of **critical reading** to find out what God wants to communicate with us. What do we mean by "critical" reading of the Bible? First, critical reading does *not* mean finding faults, picking apart, or making disparaging remarks. Rather, in Biblical studies, critical reading simply means very careful examination of all the information that is at hand and thinking it through carefully. To understand the Scriptures, we must try to figure out what the authors wanted to say and what God wanted to reveal in those writings. This means paying special attention to the historical time and the culture in which the writing took place and to the literary styles the author used.

To think "critically" about the Bible, however, is by no means an easy task. This is a book that is not merely a typical human writing. The Bible is the Word of God. The Church teaches that the Word of God is "a light for our path" (a quote from Psalm 119:105), and we must study in faith and prayer to put it in practice. The Scriptures actually guide our sense of conscience and morality. The ability to deal with difficult questions raised by careful analysis is a mark of a mature belief in God, even if it means living with open questions or difficult problems. Be willing to live with questions that you are wondering about. This is a part of becoming a serious student.

If, when you begin to read the Bible, you wonder whether the Adam and Eve stories were religious parables rather than literal history, this is not an evil question. It is not necessary, for example, to believe in *historical* people named Adam and Eve in order to have a deep and abiding faith that God is the author of all creation and that the story is intended to teach profound truth.

The Old Testament remains a primary source for our faith and Catholics do well to take seriously the God who liberates slaves, unseats Kings, speaks through radical prophets, and acts within history. At this stage of your learning, let's concentrate on learning what the Bible is actually talking about, rather than whether or not a Biblical character can be verified historically.

A serious study of the Old Testament will deepen your understanding of God and how he revealed himself over time to humankind. As the fathers of the Second Vatican Council taught:

typology
The study of types of writing that have common traits. Typology in Scripture study involves reading the Old Testament in light of Christ crucified and risen.

critical reading
A number of methods of studying the Bible that aim to discover what God is communicating— both to the people of the Bible and to people today.

And such is the force and power of the Word of God that it can serve the Church as her support and vigor and the children of the Church as strength for their faith, food for the soul, and a pure and lasting font of spiritual life. (*Dei Verbum*, 22)

Section in Review

Quick View

- The Old Testament is the inspired Word of God and not voided by the New Testament.
- "The New Testament lies hidden in the Old Testament and the Old Testament is unveiled in the New."
- Critical reading of the Bible involves the examination of what the authors wanted to say and what God wanted to reveal.

For Review

1. **Main Idea**: How would you describe the relationship between the Old Testament and the New Testament?

2. **Main Idea**: What is critical reading of the Bible? What is the purpose of critical reading?

3. **Critical Thinking**: What are four reasons teens today should study the Bible with critical reading tools?

For Reflection

Read one of the following passages from the Old Testament: Psalm 42:1–12, Sirach 2:1–11, Psalm 139:1–24, or Isaiah 43:1–7. Spend some time in silence, reflecting on the meaning of the passage. Then write your own prayer based on the passage. You will have an opportunity to share your prayer with the class.

Further Reflections

The Old Testament has great value for Christians. The books of the Old Testament should be received and read with reverence. As the fathers of the Second Vatican Council teach:

> Now the books of the Old Testament, in accordance with the state of mankind before the time of salvation established by Christ, reveal to all men the knowledge of God and of man and the ways in which God, just and merciful, deals with men. These books, though they also contain some things which are incomplete and temporary, nevertheless show us true divine pedagogy. These same books, then, give expression to a lively sense of God, contain a store of sublime teachings about God, sound wisdom about human life, and a wonderful treasury of prayers, and in them the mystery of our salvation is present in a hidden way. Christians should receive them with reverence. (*Dei Verbum*, 15)

As to your study of the Old Testament, in summary, there are several important reasons to pursue it:

- The books are divinely inspired.
- The Old Testament is an important part of the liturgy.
- It contains many beautiful prayers.
- It is a powerful witness to God's challenge to live in justice and compassion.

The books of the Old Testament are a testimony to the entire story of our Salvation, including a prophecy of the coming of Jesus Christ, our Redeemer, and an indication of the revolutionary meaning of his coming. The Old Testament is *essential* to a full comprehension of who Jesus is, what he taught, and what he meant in his teachings. For example, understanding the relationship of the prophets to Jesus highlights the power of Jesus' teaching on justice.

Vocabulary Review

Directions: Match the term with the description below.

archaeology   **artifact**   **canon**   **critical reading**   **deuterocanonical**

Magisterium   **Pseudepigrapha**   **Tradition**   **typology**

1. The Church decided that these books were not inspired by God.

2. The teaching authority of the Church, which includes the Pope and college of bishops.

3. A term meaning "second canon," includes books in the Catholic Old Testament that are not in the Hebrew Bible.

4. An official list of books belonging to the Bible.

5. The living transmission of the Church's Gospel message found in the Church's teaching, life, and worship.

6. The science of studying material remains of past human life.

7. Items such as tools, pottery, clothing, etc. that were created in the past.

8. Involves reading the Old Testament in the light of the New Testament.

9. Methods of studying the Bible that aim to discover what God is communicating.

Performance Assessment Project

Imagine that you are a PhD student researching the Old Testament at a Catholic university. You are asked to develop a research proposal for the interpretation of a book in the Old Testament called the First Book of Maccabees. You must answer the following questions within the proposal:

- What type of book is this and when did its events likely take place?

- What documents, books, and tools will you consult to interpret this book?

- What types of people will you contact in the course of your study? Whose research will you consult during your study?

Write a research proposal based on these questions.

Called to Prayer

"Fear not, I am with you;

  be not dismayed; I am your God

I will strengthen you, and help you,

  and uphold you with my right hand of justice."

    —Isaiah 41:10

- **Reflection**: Think of a time when you were afraid. How would these words from God have helped you in that situation?

- **Meditation**: Read the passage over multiple times and choose one word or phrase that particularly jumps out at you today. What meaning does this word or phrase have for you at this moment? Spend a few minutes concentrating on the meaning of this word or phrase.

- **Resolution**: Is there anything in your future that is currently causing you fear and anxiety? Write this Scripture verse somewhere as a reminder that you have no need to be afraid.

Maps for the Journey:
Geographical, Historical, and Literary Context

CHAPTER 2 OUTLINE

■ *Archaeology has made a significant impact on modern understanding of the Old Testament.*

■ *The geography and peoples surrounding the Israelites shed important light on our understanding of the Old Testament.*

■ *The history of God's Chosen People is characterized by a continual lack of political power and dominance by neighboring empires.*

■ *The Old Testament can be divided into five religious literary styles.*

context
The historical, cultural, social, or political circumstances surrounding an event or record.

pictograms
The earliest form of writing in which pictures represented words or ideas.

scribes
People trained to write using the earliest forms of writing before literacy was widespread.

hieroglyphic writing
An ancient form of Egyptian writing, more stylized than pictograms but not based on an alphabet.

Archaeology has made a significant impact on modern understanding of the Old Testament.

Introduction

To analyze something by its **context** involves looking at the circumstances in which it occurs. One of the best ways to understand more about the Old Testament is to put the origins, uses, and interpretations of the books *into context*. For example, Moses's reception of the Ten Commandments must first be understood in the context of the Hebrews' Exodus from Egypt, God's great liberating event that is at the heart of the Old Testament.

Putting the Old Testament into context equates with providing both geographical and historical "maps" for our journey. With the historical context, we can also include the cultural and social factors of the day. For example: What was life like in Palestine in the ancient world? Which groups of people lived in Palestine before the Israelites? What were the important characteristics of the cultures of other people in the Near East? The purpose of this chapter is to shed some light on these kinds of questions.

What is considered the Old Testament Biblical era runs from the decline of the Egyptian and Hittite Empires[1] in roughly 1300–1100 BC until just after the time of Alexander the Great's conquests in the entire region (ca. 333 BC–70 BC). The Exodus of the Israelites from Egypt is typically dated to approximately 1270 BC. As we will see in the chapters that follow, while there is some question about *when* the Bible actually started to be written down, the *events* that the Bible describes are almost entirely confined to roughly this time period: 1300–100 BC. Historically, this is a fairly short period of time. In studying this period of history, it is helpful to examine what happened in Palestine just prior to this time as well.

Archaeology and Biblical Studies

Imagine that you are living hundreds of years in the future. Your house (or what is left of it after being buried in dust and mud over the centuries) has just been uncovered by a group of teenagers studying a unit in archaeology. As they dig in the remains, they stumble upon your room. What will they find? More importantly, what might they be able to tell about you on the basis of what they find? Remember, they will only find those kinds of things that would last for hundreds of years; they will not find paper or clothing, and they will probably not discover any wood products either.

This kind of problem faces archaeologists who are studying the Ancient Near East today. They discover little written material and precious little of anything else.

However, today's archaeologists do have models to emulate. The ancient Israelites were also interested in a kind of archaeology.[2] For example, the Biblical authors presumed that their first readers knew of some interesting locations where events were said to have occurred many years, perhaps even centuries, before the time the books were written. In the Book of Joshua, for example, there is a brief discussion of the destruction of the village Ai. Joshua 8:28 refers to a village in a heap of ruins, adding, "as it remains to this day." At the time the passage was written, it was already a ruin, a site where destroyed remnants were considered to be "evidence" of previous events.

So, in a sense, archaeology is an ancient activity. By the seventeenth century, archaeology had become a romantic endeavor in the mode of the Indiana Jones movies with archeologists unearthing dramatic discoveries. In the twenty-first century, however, archaeology has become more of an exact science, and the *context* of each find is as important as the find. In fact, an artifact is almost totally useless if we don't know the context of its discovery—that is, the approximate level of the dig, other artifacts associated with it, and its location.

Archaeologists can provide clues about the land of Palestine before the arrival of the Israelites. There is very little written about Palestine (also known as "Canaan"), and most of the information comes from digging among the ancient ruins of village locations. When ancient writings *are* discovered, they must be translated. This is one of the major tasks of the modern archaeologist, especially if it is an unknown language. In these cases, translators must be "decoders."

Decoding Ancient Writing

Most scholars date the origins of Ancient Near East writing systems to 3500–3000 BC. Writing emerged in Egypt and Mesopotamia (modern Iraq) at about the same time. It is likely that the earliest forms of writing were **pictograms**. These pictures then evolved slowly to conventional symbols. It wasn't until relatively very late in human history that the Phoenicians (Canaanites) invented a new system of organizing symbols—a designated number of symbols that were used as an alphabet.

Before alphabets were invented **scribes** needed to learn literally hundreds of signs and symbols. That is one reason why literacy was not widespread. A scribe had to train from youth to learn all the signs! Also, early on, only the wealthy could afford to hire scribes. It follows that most of the earliest documents that we have preserved tend to be royal documents (the kings could certainly afford scribes), business documents,

and occasionally military documents. When Biblical archaeologists are lucky, they discover a wealthy temple that could afford to have its religious ideas written down. In those cases, the next task is for the archaeologist to decipher the writings. Archaeologists with an interest in the Bible then determine how many of them actually mention the events or the people of the Bible or religious ideas that may shed light on the Bible in addition to their inherent historical significance in and of themselves.

As mentioned, by the seventeenth century many Western explorers were traveling to the Holy Land. By the nineteenth century, there were several books with illustrations (before photography) of the Holy Land, which sold very well to European Christian readers who were anxious to know more about the "context" of the Bible. These readers wanted to know what places like Jerusalem and Bethlehem looked like.

Luckily, some of these early Western explorers were also serious scientists and scholars. The famous **hieroglyphic writing** of ancient Egypt was finally deciphered in 1822, after Napoleon's invasion of Egypt and the recovery of the Rosetta Stone. The Rosetta Stone featured the same text in two Egyptian languages, including hieroglyphic, and also Greek, allowing

From left to right: Rosetta Stone, Serneptah Stele, and Mesha Inscription

Greek readers to work out the Egyptian translation. From that time on, archaeologists could read ancient Egyptian writings—on stone, on the walls of tombs, from rooms in pyramids—and learn about Egyptian religion and life. Biblical scholars could then compare Egyptian writing with Biblical writings.

By 1846, all of the major ancient languages of the Eastern part of the Near East (Mesopotamia or modern Iran and Iraq) were finally translated. Thus, by the middle of the nineteenth century the two most dominant civilizations of the Biblical era, Egypt and Mesopotamia, were beginning to be understood on a level never previously known.

Personal Archaeology

Go back to thinking about the students digging in the remains of your house hundreds of years from now. What would they learn by digging in houses nearby? Houses in a nearby town? A nearby state? How would that information help them learn about you and your room?

Another ancient writing that has been deciphered is known as the "Mesha Inscription," discovered in 1868. This inscription comes from Moab, one of the rival states of Israel just across the Jordan River. The writing mentions an Israelite king, Omri, albeit in a negative light since Israel and Moab were enemies at the time. However, the reference is but another piece of evidence in piecing together the world in which the Old Testament was created. In the Mesha Inscription, the king of Moab claimed that Moab's God, Chemosh, gave him victory over Israel. Religion and war, sadly, are *both* ancient activities.

Finally, Sir Flanders Petrie made a discovery of an inscription known as the "Merneptah Stele." It was first published in 1897. In the writing, an Egyptian Pharaoh, Merneptah, brags that he

successfully defeated a "people" called "Israel" in a writing that can be dated to roughly 1207 BC. This writing is, in fact, the oldest reference to the Israelites in existence. It doesn't say much, but at least we have a written testimony to a people called Israel. Furthermore, we know that Merneptah was wrong; after all, he claimed to have wiped out the "seed of Israel." Apparently, political exaggerations are not an exclusively modern practice!

You may be wondering if these few references to the Israelites are the only historical evidence outside of the Bible to corroborate their existence. Although there are hundreds of texts that have been translated, and many more that are not yet published, the fact remains that there is *not* a great deal of information about Israel in these vast amounts of writings found among non-Hebrew peoples. These ancient texts tell us about the life and beliefs of the people surrounding the Hebrews, and in some cases; it is easy to see how these other peoples may have influenced the Hebrews (see page 28).

Fortunately, writing is not the only source of information about Biblical times, ruins and artifacts are another major source. What can this kind of evidence tell us?

Other Archaeological Evidence

Modern, scientifically excavated archaeological evidence tells us a great deal about civilizations in the context of the Israelites and the Biblical period.

Archaeological evidence (mostly stone tools) shows that humans have lived in the Palestinian region for over a million years (from the early Paleolithic era). Scientific study revealed that with the end of the final Ice Age in about 10,000 BC, the climate became more hospitable to human existence. The evidence suggests

prehistoric
Refers to events or objects that date to a time before writing developed and written records existed.

DATING THE AGES

Some historians still use the terms "Stone Age," "Bronze Age" (which is divided into early, middle, and late), and "Iron Age" to classify prehistoric artifacts according to successive stages of technological development. The original idea was that metal could be used as a general indicator of human technological innovation, and thus a reliable way to date sites. However, many modern archaeologists have reminded us that this is not a precise science, as older types of materials coexisted with certain new metals. For example, wood plows were used at the same time as bronze or iron ones because some of the new metals were perhaps too expensive or difficult to make for the larger population.

Also, an "Iron Age" doesn't mean everyone was using iron, anymore than the beginning of a "computer age" means that all families have a PC in their homes. Note, for example, that the Old Testament suggests that there was a time when the Israelites did not know how to make iron implements (swords or plows), even though the Philistines had this technology.

the floors of dwellings and human-like and animal figurines suggest a religious life of some kind. Special treatment of skulls at both Jericho and Ain Ghazal also suggest the possibility of some sort of religious practices or observances associated with these burials.[4] Artifacts from other parts of the Near Eastern world were found in Ain Ghazal, suggesting a trading network. Finally, Ain Ghazal reveals the development of pottery that can be dated there to roughly 5,000 BC. In fact, pottery styles are among the most important clues to help archaeologists determine specific dates of finds. In short, human beings lived in this part of the world centuries before the first writings of the Bible.

One of the most important things the tools of the early Israelites can teach us is that the Israelites seemed to have settled in the hills of Palestine, rather than on the coastal plains where larger cities were located. In these terraced hillside villages, they worked with cisterns that kept water available throughout the year. They also used a typically Canaanite form of a collared-rim jar for storage. They lived in a four-pillared house—that is, a typical structure with a second floor (built on beams laid across stone or wood pillars). The people lived on the second floor, but would cook on the ground, and sometimes keep animals on the ground floor as well—especially in cold weather.

In the Near East, civilization began to take other major steps during the fourth millennium BC. Large territories in Egypt and Mesopotamia merged toward common forms of pottery and artifacts, suggesting larger production of materials and populations that were in contact.[5] Cities began to form. These larger urban areas, controlling even larger surrounding territories, were the basis for increased agricultural production and trade and provided the social basis for the beginning of writing.

The largest motivation for writing was not spiritual or religious. Rather, most of the writing samples besides royal documents tended to be business documents or military-related documents. In both Egypt and Mesopotamia, the dominant political systems that arose were centralized monarchies that formed powerful military states. These empires have been described as "giant vacuum cleaners" whose intent was to "suck in" resources by

that humans began to live in groups. By 9,000 BC they were engaged in food production.

Good food production requires water and flat, easily plowed and workable land. Food production allows humans to stay in one location rather than constantly moving to hunt, so it is obviously an important building block for the foundations of a civilization. Large settlements were established near the Tigris and Euphrates rivers in Mesopotamia and the Nile in Egypt. Settlement also creates the conditions for leaving artifacts in one place, which assists archaeologists in making more educated guesses about what life would have been like in those years and in a single location or area.

Two of the most important sites for discovering **prehistoric**[3] artifacts in this part of the world are Jericho, in modern Palestine, and Ain Ghazal, north of Amman, Jordan. In Ain Ghazal, burials have been discovered under military conquest as far as they could manage, and send them to the elite at the centers of power.

Military states, conquest, and political control had gone on for thousands of years by the time the Israelites began to form a nation. Even the "creation myths" of some of these empires reflected domination and control (more information in Chapter 3). Often, these myths suggested that the gods once had to do the work of the fields, but they created human beings to work for them![6] This idea is very different from the creation story told by the Israelites of the one God, YHWH, who is loving and compassionate toward his people.

Section in Review
Quick View

- Placing Old Testament texts in geographical, historical, and cultural context is important for Biblical analysis.

- In some ways, the authors of the Old Testament were interested in archaeology.

- Several important discoveries contributed to the deciphering of Ancient Near East writing and corroborate the existence of the Israelites, including the Rosetta Stone, the Mesha Inscription, and the Merneptah Stele.

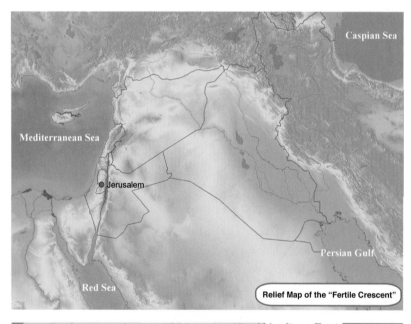

Relief Map of the "Fertile Crescent"

The weather patterns of the entire Near Eastern region have remained fairly constant for the last 10,000 years, but there have been noticeable periods of drought. Overall, the region is warm. Winters can bring temperatures of 50° F in the hills of Palestine, with rainfall averaging about 30 inches. Jerusalem averages a comfortable 77° F in the summer, but it can easily be warmer. Jerusalem actually gets an average rainfall similar to London, but it is not spread out over an entire winter like it is in England.

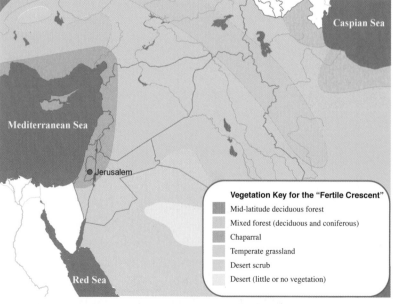

Vegetation Key for the "Fertile Crescent"

- Mid-latitude deciduous forest
- Mixed forest (deciduous and coniferous)
- Chaparral
- Temperate grassland
- Desert scrub
- Desert (little or no vegetation)

Baptism Prefigured in the Old Testament

(*CCC*, 1217–1222)

Water is a rich symbol in both the Old and New Testaments. During the Easter Vigil the Church commemorates the important events in Salvation History that prefigured the mystery of Baptism (*CCC*, 1217). In the Book of Genesis, the Spirit of God "overshadowed" the water, the source of life and fruitfulness (Gn 1:2). The author of the First Letter of Peter attests that the flood waters in the story of Noah's Ark (Gn 7) "prefigured baptism, which saves you now" (1 Pt 3:21). Just as Noah, his family, and the animals were saved on the Ark through the flood, so too are Christians saved from death through water. The most important connection between Baptism and the Old Testament, however, is the experience of freedom from slavery by crossing the Red Sea (Ex 14). Just as the Israelites were freed from slavery in Egypt through the waters of the Red Sea, Christians are saved from slavery to sin by the waters of Baptism. The Israelites also crossed another river, the Jordan River, to enter into the Promised Land (an image of eternal life) just as Christians inherit eternal life through Baptism (*CCC*, 1222).

Water in the Old Testament	Baptism
The Spirit of God hovered over water at creation (Gn 1:2)	The Holy Spirit is present in the waters of Baptism (Mt 3:16, Acts 2:38)
Noah, his family, and the many animals he collected on the Ark were saved through water (Gn 14)	Christians are saved through the waters of Baptism (1 Pt 3:21)
The Israelites found freedom from slavery in Egypt by crossing the Red Sea (Ex 14)	Christians find freedom from slavery to sin through Baptism (Rom 6:1–10)
The Israelites entered the Promised Land by crossing the Jordan River (Jos 3)	Christians enter eternal life through the waters of Baptism (Jn 3:5)

- The ancient Israelites lived in the hill country of Palestine while, in Egypt and Mesopotamia, centralized monarchies formed powerful military states.

For Review

1. **Main Idea**: What years are considered the Old Testament Biblical era? Make a simple timeline covering these dates.

2. **Main Idea**: What is the importance of the Rosetta Stone?

3. **Critical Thinking**: List the archaeological discoveries that have been made at Jericho and Ain Ghazal. What do these findings suggest about the people who lived there?

For Reflection

Make a list of five things in your room at home that archaeologists might find interesting 1,000 years from now. Tell why.

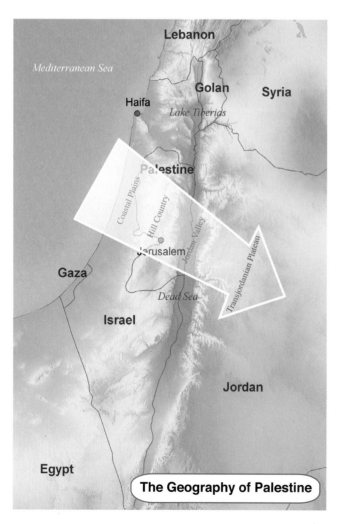

The Geography of Palestine

The geography and peoples surrounding the Israelites shed important light on our understanding of the Old Testament.

The Land of Canaan: At the Center of Civilization

The land of Canaan (later known as Palestine) sat on the coast line between two great centers of ancient civilization: Egypt and Mesopotamia. It was Canaan that God had chosen as a homeland for the Israelites. If you look on a map (see below), you can see that Canaan was really a land bridge between Egypt and Mesopotamia. What do you think it meant for the Israelite nation to arise in a land surrounded by two mighty empires?

Egypt—on the south end of the land bridge—was called a "gift of the Nile" by the Greeks. The agricultural and farming economies of Egypt grew to create vast surpluses. That allowed the Egyptian pharaohs to grow into mighty overlords, mastering vast territories and fashioning weapons for huge armies for conquest and plunder. For example, Egypt was famous for inventing the chariot and equipping vast armies of chariots and infantry. Also, don't forget that the great cultural achievements of the ancient Egyptians (the pyramids, monuments, and temples) were paid for by the masses of people who were forced into labor to make these accomplishments possible—laborers who were both Egyptians and enslaved foreigners.

At the other end of the land bridge east of the Israelites was another fertile land fed by the waters of the Euphrates and Tigris rivers. The land between and around these rivers was known as Mesopotamia ("between the rivers"). Here again, the plentiful supply of fresh water allowed for rich agricultural production, and vast empires arose in Mesopotamia—including the Assyrians and Babylonians. The Persian Empire developed further east.

So, between Egypt to the South and West, and Mesopotamia to the North and East, lay a narrowly habitable land known in Old Testament times as Canaan. We now know this land as Syro-Palestine or Palestine. It includes the territories of Syria, Lebanon, Israel, and Palestine. A closer examination of a map of Palestine reveals more information about the people who lived there in Biblical times.

HEADING TO THE HILLS

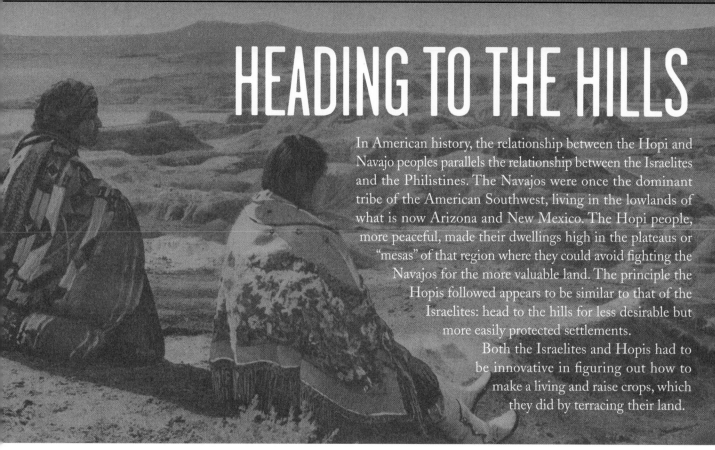

In American history, the relationship between the Hopi and Navajo peoples parallels the relationship between the Israelites and the Philistines. The Navajos were once the dominant tribe of the American Southwest, living in the lowlands of what is now Arizona and New Mexico. The Hopi people, more peaceful, made their dwellings high in the plateaus or "mesas" of that region where they could avoid fighting the Navajos for the more valuable land. The principle the Hopis followed appears to be similar to that of the Israelites: head to the hills for less desirable but more easily protected settlements.

Both the Israelites and Hopis had to be innovative in figuring out how to make a living and raise crops, which they did by terracing their land.

The geography of Palestine runs in zones or strips from North to South. If you flew over Palestine from the Mediterranean Sea (flying from the west and heading east) you would move from the beach toward the inland areas and see below you the following strips or zones:

- **coastal plains** that narrow toward the north of Palestine (near modern Haifa);

- **hill country** that runs like a spine up the "back" of Palestine, and into modern Lebanon, where the hills actually become mountains;

- **Jordan Valley**, a "rift" in the earth that extends all the way from Turkey to Africa. This "rift" is actually the meeting place of the two continental plates of Africa and Asia, and thus is somewhat unstable, which accounts for the frequency of serious earthquakes in Palestine

- **Transjordanian Plateau**, perhaps the best-known regional zone in the ancient period as it contained the "King's Highway," the major North-South trade route of the ancient world.

Finally, after passing over the major geographical zones listed above, you would encounter a vast desert, largely uninhabited—sometimes called the **Syrian Desert**. The Syrian Desert extends all the way to Arabia and down to Yemen on the southern coast. Modern archaeologists have learned that at one time there were occasional settlements and even cities in these vast areas.

Most of the larger ancient cities that were active in Canaan prior to the founding of the Israelites were located on the coastal plains. Travel and farming were easier on the largely level ground there. The Mediterranean Sea is close to this area, and there were some useable ports for shipping. The Jordan River Valley was another populated region with access to water and rich soil for farming.

When the Israelites finally settled in Canaan, they chose neither of these strips or zones. Instead, the Israelites took up residence in the hill country of Palestine because there was little competition for this land. The hill country also afforded natural protection against enemies. A major difficulty to overcome in the hill country was its lack of suitability for farming. The Israelites definitely had to be innovative and resourceful to survive there.

In spite of the willingness of the hill-dwelling peoples to avoid the settlers on the coastal plain and in the Jordan Valley, they were still viewed as competition by the older civilizations. This was the case even when the militarily strong Philistines settled in the coastal plains shortly before Israel came to Canaan. In fact, the name Palestine derives from "Philistine." The Philistines established cities such as Ekron, Ashdod, and Askelon on the coastal plains. When the Israelites did arrive, they settled in the hills perhaps to avoid a battle or simply to establish themselves apart from the other civilizations that were already in place. One of the questions that will be considered as we proceed is whether or not the Israelites were really such "latecomers" to Canaan. After all, the Bible tells of Abraham and his family living in this region at the time of the founding of his people.

The Fertile Crescent: Corridor of Conflict

It is rather clear when you examine a map of Canaan that there is actually a very narrow corridor of fertile land that runs along the Mediterranean coastline and connects the ancient civilizations of Egypt and Mesopotamia. This land bridge between the two great civilizations is part of what is known as the "fertile crescent."

Taking note of this piece of valuable land is a critically important point in Biblical studies. Knowing that the coast road is a major trade route for the ancient world, you begin to see the geographical explanation for the horrendous violence of the Biblical period: *The people of Israel took up residence in the middle of the "land bridge" that connected two great centers of human civilization.* They did not live in a quiet or remote territory, but in the middle of the ancient highways of trade and military transportation. The little area of Palestine that the Israelite tribes settled was blessed with good grapes and olives. However it was cursed to be the main thoroughfare for ancient armies marching north and south, and back and forth, as the Egyptian and Mesopotamian Empires struggled for control of this critical passageway. Israel was literally "caught in the middle" as these two empires struggled to control each other.

The level of violence in these books disturbs many new students of the Old Testament. Understanding the position of the Israelites in Canaan is helpful in understanding why the Old Testament contains so many examples of warfare and retribution. Warfare was all around the Israelites.

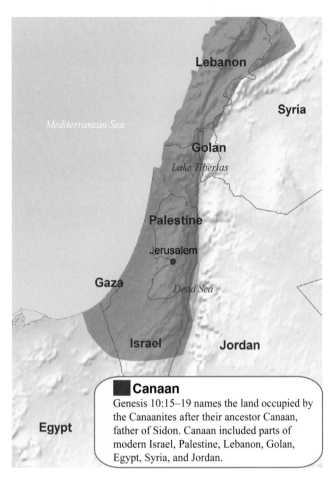

Canaan

Genesis 10:15–19 names the land occupied by the Canaanites after their ancestor Canaan, father of Sidon. Canaan included parts of modern Israel, Palestine, Lebanon, Golan, Egypt, Syria, and Jordan.

Such understanding also helps to explain the Israelites' portrayal of their God YHWH as a warrior. Since the Israelites were not capable of doing much military damage, they held to the belief that their God was a powerful warrior who would protect them. The Israelite peoples would have been intimately familiar with the bottom of every boot that marched through Palestine over the centuries. It is not that the vast empires were all that interested in controlling the Israelites. Rather it was the passageway that they lived on that interested Israel's enemies. To summarize: Geography matters. Context matters. Next, the focus will be on some of the history of the people who lived in the land of Canaan itself.

Before Israel: The Canaanites

Israel arose in the land known to history as "Canaan." This name is used to designate a territory that includes much of modern Israel and Palestine, Lebanon, and the Syrian coastlands, all the way to the beginning of the Sinai Peninsula in the south. There was a civilization in this land for thousands of years before the ancient Israelites formed their state there.

From about 2000 BC to the time of the formation of Israel in 1300–1100 BC, Egypt considered Canaan part of its territory, crucial to Egypt's interests. A major Egyptian trading route ran through Canaan, and the Egyptians also used the seaport in Byblos (now Beirut in Lebanon). However, there were native people living in Canaan, the Canaanites.

The relationship between the Egyptians and the Canaanites was stormy. The Egyptians considered Canaan a rough and unruly land. They often engaged in military activities to maintain their control of Canaanite cities and would bring prisoners-of-war back to Egypt to engage them in forced labor. At other times, when rainfall was scarce in Canaan or when military threats forced them south, Canaanites would immigrate into the northeastern region of Egypt to find water, better land, and work.

For a period of time from roughly 1650 to 1550 BC, a substantial number of the Canaanites invaded and briefly controlled Egypt. This is known as the *Hyksos Period* because the Egyptians called the foreigners *Hyksos*. When the Hyksos were eventually defeated and Egyptians were restored to power, oppression of the Canaanites followed. Some historians suggest that retribution associated with the Hyksos Period provides a possible background to the eventual oppression of the Israelites by the Egyptians. This assumes that the later Israelites had some ancestors from among the Hyksos.

What else is known of the Canaanites? For one, the Canaanites established a strong civilization of their own. Many Caananite cities were quite impressive and powerful, as represented by *Ugarit*, a city located on what is today the Syrian coast, near the modern village of Ras Shamra. The Philistines apparently destroyed the ancient city of Ugarit, perhaps even before the tribes of Israel settled in the land of Canaan further south.

At Ugarit, a number of tablets were discovered that shed light on the religious ideas of the Canaanites. The Canaanites worshipped a variety of gods, including a main god, *El*, who they believed had a wife known as *Asherah* (Asherah is the goddess named in 2 Kings 23:4–7 as one of the pagan gods that the Israelites were not supposed to worship. She was also referred to as the "queen of heaven" in Jeremiah 44:17–25.)

But the most popular god of the Canaanites was the god who brought rain and thus provided for fertile grounds. This god was known as *Baal*. All of the peoples surrounding the Israelites in Canaan worshipped Baal. In the Bible, Baal is often referred to as the most significant rival to YHWH. The most serious warnings in the Old Testament against worshiping other gods were directed at the worship of Baal. The descriptions of Elijah leading the struggle against the worship of Baal in 1 Kings 17–19 (especially chapter 18) represent how serious and competitive the debate was between the Canaanites and Israelites regarding religion.

The Canaanites worshipped their gods in temples administered by various kinds of priests. In fact, the design of these Canaanite temples was exactly the same as the great Temple of Solomon in Jerusalem that was built later. It seems likely that Solomon borrowed from the

One, True, Living God

The Jewish religion grew up amidst several Canaanite religions. Studying some of the Canaanite religious texts is often interesting when compared side-by-side with the Bible. For example, the inspired author of the Psalm 29 may have used the following Ugarit text as a matrix to go well beyond the model to describe the One, True, and Living God.

Note the similarities and differences between the two writings below. Then choose an art medium of your choice to depict God as described in the text from Psalm 29.

Ugaritic Text	Psalm 29:4–6
Baal gave forth his holy voice,	The voice of the Lord is mighty;
Baal repeated the utterance of his lips	the voice of the Lord is majestic.
His holy voice made the earth quake	The voice of the Lord breaks the cedars,
The utterance of his lips the mountains.	the Lord breaks the cedars of Lebanon.
	He makes Lebanon leap like a calf
	and Siron like a young bull.

design of some of the Canaanite temples. The Canaanites offered animal sacrifices to their gods and would sing songs and poems. They would also tell stories of their gods. Some of these stories have survived, found at places such as Ugarit. They tell the tales of Baal in his wars against other gods such as Mot, the god of death, and Yam, the god of the sea.

Because the Israelites lived in such close proximity in time and space with the Canaanites (and some ancestors of the Israelites may have actually been Canaanites), it is understandable that the Bible mentions their myths, poems, and legends. Several of the expressions in Psalm 29 are also found in Canaanite texts written in the fifteenth century BC at Ugarit. For example the text in Psalm 29:7 describes YHWH as a storm God, which is also what Baal was. Consider the thunder and lightning images here:

> The voice of the Lord strikes fiery flames;
>   the voice of the Lord shakes the desert,
>   the Lord shakes the wilderness of Kadesh.
>   (29:7)

The Canaanite religion was also a religion that supported the dominance of the rich and powerful over the majority who were peasants that did not own land. The story of a Canaanite princess, Jezebel (1 Kings 21), who used her influence to steal the land of an Israelite named Naboth, contrasts the justice and equality of YHWH with the privilege and power of the Canaanite gods. For the Israelites to be a member of God's Chosen People meant a commitment to a way of life that emphasized justice and care for others. In fact, many Canaanites converted to the religion of YHWH and called themselves "Israelites" to make it clear they no longer worshipped Baal and Asherah.

Section in Review

Quick View

- Canaan, the Israelites' homeland, sat between the two mighty empires in Egypt and Mesopotamia. This "fertile crescent" was very desirable and often led to conflict between the Israelites and the surrounding powers.

- Of the many geographic strips or zones in Palestine, the Israelites chose to settle in the hill country.

- The Israelites opposed the gods of the Canaanites, but assimilated some of their beliefs and practices into their own religious practices.

For Review

1. **Main Idea**: Describe the geography of Canaan (now Palestine) including the four North-South strips that divide the region.

2. **Main Idea**: What two important civilizations bordered Canaan to the north and to the south?

3. **Critical Thinking**: What were the names of the major gods of the Canaanites? Which was most likely to have appealed to the Israelites? Why?

For Reflection

Look through the Book of Psalms and list descriptions of a compassionate God.

The history of God's Chosen People is characterized by a continual lack of political power and dominance by neighboring empires.

Tracing the History of the Israelites from the Old Testament

Learning about the geography and history of Canaan or Palestine provides us with a large sense of the context of the experience of the Israelites. The nation of Israel arose in a time of great empires among people with their own ancient traditions and civilization, especially the Canaanites. The history of the Israelites parallels much of the Canaanite experience. The Old Testament provides us with another kind of map for our journey, an historical summary of the origins and development of God's Chosen People, the Israelites, and a chance to analyze the literary styles of the Old Testament to learn more about them.

The Book of Genesis traces the origins of the Israelite patriarchs—beginning with Abraham—but not until chapter 12 of the book. The first twelve chapters contain stories about the origins of the world, humans, and varying cultures, often described as the **primeval history**.

The primeval history is followed by descriptions of the first Israelites, including Abraham, Sarah, Isaac, Rebekah, and Jacob and his sons (including Joseph). It is difficult to trace a reliable history of the Israelites using Genesis, as the book was written many years after the events described. It seems best to treat Genesis as a religiously motivated story of the origin of the Hebrew people and their arrangement in "clans" that are named

for figures discussed in the Genesis (e.g. the "twelve tribes" named for the twelve sons of Jacob).

The Genesis stories about the origins of humankind and the Israelite people provided a unifying history for those Canaanites of 1200 to 1000 BC who converted to worship of YHWH. The patriarchal accounts also carry the theme of God's persistent attention to his people, despite the constant failures of the humans represented in these incidents. Genesis will be analyzed in greater depth in Chapter 3.

It is the Book of Exodus that formally introduces the Chosen People. However, the precise date and circumstances of the Exodus from Egypt are difficult to determine from the Old Testament. For example, Exodus 10:28–29 ends by suggesting an "escape" from Egypt, while Exodus 11–12 supports the idea of an "expulsion" of the Jews after a tenth and final "plague" of the death of all Egyptian first-born children.

The Book of Exodus blends the two differing circumstances by portraying Pharaoh as changing his mind and chasing away the Israelites, giving rise to the traditions of the delivery of the Israelites by the sea. But here again, there are two traditions. The first one portrays the Israelites as escaping across slightly muddy marshland that rendered the Egyptian chariots useless (a more natural explanation), and the later edited tradition turned the episode into a miraculous parting of a large body of water likely intended to magnify the theological importance of YHWH's assistance of the Israelites in times of trouble. These differing views show that there were slightly different traditions that were brought together to form the current Book of Exodus.

It is likely that a group of former slaves from Egypt arrived in Canaan about 1250–1230 BC with a religion based in

primeval history
Stories or myths about the origins of the earth, humans, other creatures, languages, and cultures.

the experience of a God who liberated them from Egyptian slavery. This religion, in its early form, is closely associated with Moses. Early Israelite faith was based on:

- a relationship with a God by the name of "YHWH"

- worship in a movable shrine or tent

- basic moral expectations ("laws")

The main feature of this religion was the fact that YHWH was a God who liberated slaves, and was thus a God who spoke to their condition. This religion had an explosive impact upon its arrival in Canaan, and a good number of people who became part of the "Twelve Tribes of Israel" were probably Canaanites who converted to the new religion though they had never been in Egypt with the group that arrived as former slaves.

The conversion to the religion of YHWH, however, was uneven, with a persistent problem of mixing Canaanite and Yahwist religious ideas throughout the era of the Kings of Israel and Judah, from about 1000 BC to the Deuteronomic Reforms of 640–609 BC. There have been a number of recent archaeological discoveries that reveal the extent of **syncretism** (a blending of two or more religious traditions) in this era. For example, prayers inscribed on pieces of clay were found in a small shrine near the Sinai desert that addressed "YHWH" and "his consort/wife Asherah." Such a prayer gives evidence that people were mixing Israelite and Canaanite religious ideas. A close reading of Joshua 24:14–15 seems to reveal that Joshua is addressing a mixed group of people from all over the area. Obviously many people liked what they heard about the religion of Moses, and came to join. Joshua is now telling them to choose if they are joining them or not!

The Bible's condemnation of many of the Israelite and Judean kings who

The inscription on this slab links the Israelite God, YHWH, to the Canaanite Mother Goddess, Asherah.

abandoned pure YHWH worship reveals that the kings often found the conservatism of Canaanite religion more to their liking than the reformist zeal of YHWH worship with its laws of compassionate and equal treatment for all, including care of the poor and the sharing of resources. These kings were severely criticized by the advocates of the worship of YHWH, the prophets. At least two assumptions can be made at this point:

- Worship and living by the laws of YHWH began as a religion among former Egyptian slaves and converted Canaanites.

- This religious movement eventually gained ascendancy late in the monarchy (especially in Josiah's reign). By this time, however, the economic and political fate of the independent nations of Judah and Israel was sealed as subordinate to other nations (e.g., first the Assyrians, next the Babylonians). This religion would lead to the Judaism practiced at the time of Jesus that relied heavily on the belief that God would provide, that God would save the people from their enemies, and that faith meant obedience to God wherever they lived throughout the region.

syncretism
A blending of two or more religious traditions.

Israelite Monarchy

Israelite kings began to rule about 1020 BC. Although tradition holds that Saul was the first king, David was the most significant early leader who managed to unite a diversified people against the immediate threat of the coastal invaders known as Philistines. David also established a capital city, Jerusalem, and extended Israelite political influence across the Jordan into the territories of Ammon, Moab, Edom (in what is largely today the country of Jordan) and northward into Syria.

The son who eventually succeeded David was Solomon. He engaged in further campaigns of consolidation, including the construction of a national Temple modeled on Canaanite temple architecture. But despite Solomon's reputation for diplomacy and "wisdom," the Hebrew tribal leaders and peoples, especially in the northern territory, considered the human toll of his building campaigns oppressive.

Canaan was not a homogeneous environment. Agricultural differences led to social differences that were exacerbated by both labor and taxes—the requirements for Solomon's construction. When Solomon died, the northern peoples broke from the Jerusalem dynasty (a revolt that involved people and territory from ten of the twelve tribes), and established a new Israelite state in 922 BC. The Old Testament refers to the northern state as *Israel* and the southern state as *Judah*. People in Judah later came to be called "Judeans" or "Jews" for short.

Judah continued with leaders who were descendants of King David. Israel was ruled by a succession of monarchs, none of whom was ultimately able to establish a family that could rival the dynasty of King David. It therefore appears that the northern state was unstable. One reason for this was because the prophets in the north (Elisha, for example) would occasionally lead coups by proclaiming that God had chosen a new king—while the old king still sat on the throne! The prophets were constantly involved in politics.

Assyrian and Babylonian Exiles

In the latter half of the eighth century BC, the northern kingdom, Israel, joined a coalition of states in an attempt to resist the increasing pressure of the Assyrian Empire. When Ahaz, the southern king of Judah, refused to join the coalition, the coalition members were determined to force Ahaz's hand and initiated a war. In response, Ahaz called on the massive Assyrian Empire with its brutal legions of soldiers for assistance. Assyria responded with a crushing invasion in the west. The invading Assyrians destroyed the coalition, including the northern state of Israel, in 722 BC.

The Assyrian Empire practiced a military technique that guaranteed conquered territories would never again be able to offer resistance. This technique involved deporting large numbers of the newly conquered population (especially leaders and landowners) and exchanging this body of people with a group taken from another

Just Treatment of Workers

Read and compare 1 Kings 9:22 with 1 Kings 5:27, 1 Kings 11:28, and 1 Kings 12. What clues can you find that Solomon's treatment of workers was oppressive? Next, read the following passage from *Rerum Novarum* ("On the Condition of Workers") by Pope Leo XIII (1891):

> Workers are not to be treated as slaves, justice demands that the dignity of human personality be respected in them . . . gainful occupations are not a mark of shame to man, but rather of respect, as they provide him with an honorable means of supporting life. It is shameful and inhuman, however, to use men as things for gain and to put no more value on them than what they are worth in muscle and energy. (#31)

- Contrast this view of workers with Solomon's view.

- Also, write a journal entry describing what you believe to be the dignity and value of work.

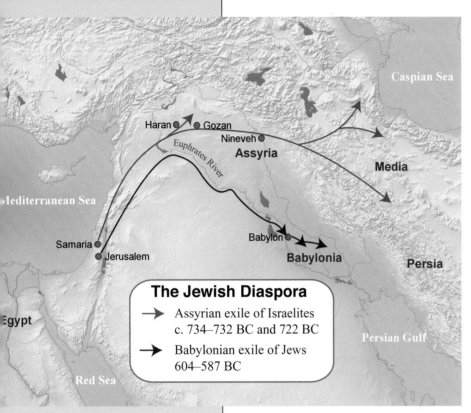

The Jewish Diaspora

→ Assyrian exile of Israelites
c. 734–732 BC and 722 BC

→ Babylonian exile of Jews
604–587 BC

literary production. After the tragic death of Josiah in a campaign against the Egyptians (609 BC), six other historical books were written, beginning with accounts in the Book of Joshua and carrying on to the Babylonian conquest described at the end of 2 Kings.

The Babylonians eventually defeated the Assyrian armies in 609 BC. Next, the Babylonian king Nebuchadnezzar led the Babylonians further south on the Canaanite coastlands, consolidating his control of the area as a buffer zone against the Egyptians. In 597 BC, the young king of Judah, Jehoiachin, surrendered to Nebuchadnezzar. Judah became a vassal state of the Babylonians.

Nebuchadnezzar placed a puppet ruler of his own choosing in Jerusalem. Nebuchadnezzar renamed this man "Zedekiah" (name-changing often symbolized political control), placed him on the throne, and then returned to Babylon with a number of Jewish exiles, including King Jehoiachin. These actions were the beginning of the *Babylonian Exile*, which apparently involved only the upper classes of Jewish society; that is, anyone who might pose an immediate threat to the rule of Babylon—royalty, landowners, military leaders, and even many priests.

In Zedekiah's ten years as token ruler of Judah, he became more ambitious about ruling Judah as an independent state. Zedekiah was encouraged in this bold folly by promises of the neighboring Egyptians for assistance. The prophet Jeremiah bitterly condemned the idea that Egypt would provide any credible assistance in a bid for Jewish independence. When Zedekiah ceased paying taxes to the Babylonians, this was tantamount to a declaration of independence, and it wasn't long before Nebuchadnezzar arrived back in the west with his armies to reassert control.

Diaspora

A group migration or flight away from the homeland into one or more other countries. The word can also refer to people who have maintained their separate identity (often religious, but occasionally ethnic, racial, or cultural) while living in those other countries after the migration.

part of the empire. This exile involved some of the people of the northern kingdom, especially the elite upper classes who might have tried to resist Assyrian authority.

The Assyrian Empire was eventually defeated by the rise of a rival Mesopotamian power based in the southern part of the Tigris-Euphrates basin, the "Babylonians" (so-called because they based themselves in the ancient religious capital of Babylon, near modern-day Baghdad, Iraq).

Between 640–609 BC, that is, between the decline of the Assyrian Empire and the Babylonian ascendancy, Josiah reigned as the king of Judah. Josiah is credited with initiating a major reform among the Hebrews in Judah, centralizing all worship in Jerusalem and restoring a purer form of YHWH worship. His reforms were based on the laws contained in the Book of Deuteronomy, and therefore are referred to as the "Deuteronomic Reform." This reform also inspired further

Jerusalem was destroyed in 587–586 BC after a long siege. Zedekiah's sons were killed. Zedekiah was tortured and taken to Babylon. The Temple was destroyed and Temple furnishings were removed. Large numbers of the population were killed, fled as refugees, or taken captive. This exile was more widespread than ten years before, involving a significant percentage of the population. Estimates vary from 20,000 to more than 70,000 inhabitants of Judah, but the smaller numbers are more likely. Still, 20,000 is a large number of people to forcibly resettle in a foreign land.

The Babylonian Exile represents one of the most decisive changes of destiny for the Jewish people. Perhaps most remarkable of all was that the Judeans not only survived in exile, they reconstructed their faith. When the Persians finally conquered Babylon in 539, the Persian emperor Cyrus allowed Judeans to return to Palestine. Although a sizable Jewish community remained in Babylon, various groups of Judeans returning to Palestine (described in the Book of Ezra) continued to reconstruct the faith, their community, and Temple worship.

Post-Exilic Judean Society

We know very little about post-Exilic Judean society. There are only a few books that are confidently dated to this era, such as the prophetic books Haggai, Zechariah, and Malachi, and the historical books, Ezra and Nehemiah. Notice, also, how short these books are. This lack of information continues to the Hellenistic (Greek) Period, post 333 BC, when we once again begin to have historical literary sources such as the First Book of Maccabees, though it is clearly a partisan perspective on history.

What we can surmise about the post-Exilic period is that the Judeans formed a strong communal and faith identity under the leadership of priests, who emerged as the primary leaders in place of the kings who were descendants of King David. Hopes for a new king from the family of David became the hope for a future age, occasionally inspiring nationalist activity among some Jews in Palestine.

At this time many Jews were still living in a **Diaspora**, that is, in lands other than Palestine that extended from Egypt far into the east beyond Babylon and into Persian territory. For Jews in the Diaspora, their faith was no longer associated with national existence, but with spiritual identity, family practices and diet, and with their ability to resist cultural assimilation. Biblical stories of faithful Jews in foreign lands, such as Daniel, Esther, and Tobit derive from experiences of the Jews in the Diaspora.

From the time of the Babylonian Exile until the twentieth century and the founding of the nation of Israel, with the exception of only a relatively brief time before the Roman occupation in 64 BC, the Jewish people were to remain politically and economically subordinate to non-Jews. This means that both Judaism and Christianity are religions whose roots are to be found in people who either lived in Diaspora or in their own land under the military and political control of outsiders. How does this impact the Bible?

In the Bible, YHWH is the God of the powerless and separated. He is the God who judges the rich and powerful. For the Diaspora or any occupied people, you can understand why these ideas would have considerable meaning. If you keep in mind that virtually all of the Old Testament was written, edited, and arranged by a politically powerless people, then its text takes on a different tone. The focus certainly is not on a vengeful, warring God as many Christians often feel.

Section in Review
Quick View

- Early Israelite faith was based on the relationship with the God who liberated slaves.

- Archaeological discoveries revealed evidence of the syncretism between the Israelite and the Canaanite religions that many kings were criticized by Old Testament prophets for promoting.

- The most prominent kings in the Israelite monarchy were David and Solomon, whose kingdom remained divided after Solomon's death.

- The Northern Kingdom of Israel fell to the Assyrian Empire in 722 BC, and the Southern Kingdom of Judah fell to the Babylonians in 597 BC beginning the Babylonian Exile.

- Little is known about post-exilic Judean society, but it is clear that during this period the leadership of priests grew while the Jewish people waited in anticipation for a new king of a future age.

1. **Main Idea**: Name three basic features of the faith of the early Israelites.

2. **Main Idea**: Give an example of the blending of Canaanite and Yahwist religions.

3. **Critical Thinking**: From what information you have now, which seemed to have the greatest impact on Jewish faith: the Assyrian Exile or the Babylonian Exile? Why?

For Reflection

Write your own prayer of praise to the one, true, living God.

The Old Testament can be divided into five religious literary styles.

Background on Literature Styles of the Bible

If it is true that writing history is never merely a description of events, the recording of Jewish history is surely an excellent example of history written with a clear motive and goal in mind. The main task of the historical writers of ancient Israel was to illustrate their understanding of God, and how God was involved in their lives. In short, the Old Testament was written primarily as religious literature. It was never simply a historical or royal record.

A survey of the various types of literature of the Old Testament offers a good companion to the historical study of Old Testament times and reveals further clues about the God of mercy, compassion, and love.

The Pentateuch

The core of the Old Testament is the Pentateuch, which means "five books." In the Hebrew Bible, these books are called the "Torah," a Hebrew word for "Law." Law is the most prominent feature of the Pentateuch. Virtually all of the religious laws, civil laws, and moral principles of ancient Israel are codified in three collections of laws contained in the first five books.

The earliest of these collections, known as the "Covenant Code," is contained in the Book of Exodus (the laws are roughly chapters 19–24). The Covenant Code was supplemented by the "Deuteronomic Code" of the seventh century B.C. and included in the Book of Deuteronomy. (Deuteronomy means "second law.") The third collection of laws consists mainly of priestly or religious laws that were added by the Jewish priests in the post-Exilic period. These laws can be found mainly in Leviticus. One of the oldest layers of this priestly law is in Leviticus 17–26 (sometimes called the "Holiness Code"). Later commentary and additional laws are found in other parts of Leviticus and Numbers.

The frequent repetition of laws (e.g., the fact that the Ten Commandments are listed twice) is explained by this practice of adding later legal material to the laws from different eras. Interestingly, the supplementation of texts allows modern students to do comparative work on the development of several facets of Jewish life.

Take the development of the treatment of "slaves" or technically what we call "indentured servants." Much can be learned from looking at the different versions of the laws. For example, let's look at the progression of the status of slaves between Exodus 21 (the Covenant Code) and Deuteronomy 15:12–18 (the Deuteronomic Code). While both passages prohibit perpetual slavery, only the latter code specifically delineates the provisions to be provided to released slaves whose debts were paid after seven years, and furthermore prohibits the return of escaped slaves to masters (Dt 23:16). Most impressive of all is the expectation of social justice provided by the priests in Leviticus 25, where the "Jubilee Year" was to provide for the return of all purchased land to the original tribal owners, thus preventing a growing rift between the rich and poor by redistributing the land every fifty years. Law in ancient Israel was both normative and prescriptive. It tended toward what we would call "distributive justice." In other words, there was to be a fair distribution of basic necessities.

Historical Books

Following the Pentateuch, the historical books tell about the history of Israel first as a collection of tribes (the books of Joshua and Judges) and then eventually moving toward existence as a royal state led by a king (1, 2 Sm, and 1, 2 Kgs, much of which is repeated in 1, 2 Chr). The

God as the Author of the Bible

It is accurate to say that God is the author of the Bible, but that is not as simple as it sounds. First, God did not magically pen the Sacred Scripture and then rain the texts down on earth. Nor did God whisper the texts into the ears of the Biblical authors word for word, punctuation and all.

Rather, God *inspired* the authors of Scripture. The authors had the freedom to choose the words they wrote, including the stories and incidents they chose to share. As the Second Vatican Council explained, God chose the authors of the Bible:

> who, all the while he employed them in this task, made full use of their own faculties and powers so that, though he acted in them and by them, it was as true authors that they consigned to writing whatever he wanted written, and no more. (*Dei Verbum*, 11)

Related to this understanding of inspiration is another fact: the Jews of Biblical times, up to and including Jesus, were great storytellers. In reading the Old Testament, we must understand the difference between a story intended to teach a lesson and the description of a historical event, all the while remembering that the text is inspired. God intended for us to read all of it—both history *and* stories.

HAVE YOU SEEN THIS AUTHOR?

For example, the proper response to the fall of man and the flood narrative of the Book of Genesis is to appreciate the religious lessons of moral responsibility, God's care for humanity, and humanity's stubborn resistance. Joining an expedition to find pieces of the "authentic" ark of Noah on Mount Ararat in modern Turkey (to cite one popular example of people who supposedly take the Bible "seriously" by insisting on a literal flood) is not the most appropriate response to the Biblical texts, because it misses their central message and attempts to make these texts into something that they are not—literal history. Sometimes we must use our best judgment to determine the differences between history and story, while some passages are more obvious.

Much of this religion textbook is devoted to looking at the religious meaning of the Old Testament, while providing some brief background on the context of a particular book.

numbers 1 or 2 before the name of book is to be read "first Book of . . ." or "second Book of . . ."

Later historical books tell of the breakup of the kingdom. This breakup included: the disobedience of the kings, the disasters preceding the exiles, and the exiles themselves. The first and second books of Maccabees were written in approximately 100 BC and provide two different views of the Jewish revolt against the Seleucid ruler Antiochus IV and the Hellenistic Greek culture that was imposed during his reign.

Wisdom Books and Psalms

The "Wisdom Books" is a category of the Old Testament that includes the books of Job, Psalms, Proverbs, Ecclesiastes, Song of Songs, Wisdom, and Sirach (Ecclesiasticus). The Wisdom Books consist of poetic religious hymns, stories, and wise advice.

The books of wisdom literature are intended to guide people in learning the lessons of human life. Wisdom literature is not unique to the Bible. In fact, part of the Book of Proverbs is drawn directly from Egyptian wisdom literature (e.g., Prv 22:17–24:22). This is because the main themes of wisdom literature—relationships, diplomacy, watching one's tongue, money and frugality, the dangers of adultery or of strong drink, and the gaining of knowledge—are basic human issues. Wisdom literature includes many observations of the human condition and is an indication of God's respect for human thought in the reality of Faith.

The largest body of religious poetry in the Bible is the Book of Psalms. Ever popular as devotional literature, the psalms were written over a large span of Jewish history. As for the content of the Book of Psalms, there are many different subjects. Some psalms have their origin in the enthronement ceremonies of a king or the celebration of the new year (e.g., Pss 72, 89, 2, and 110). Others, clearly referring to the events of the Exile, reveal a very late origin (e.g., Pss 126, 137). The religious messages of the psalms make it a very popular work.

Prophetic Books

While several of the historical books mention prophets, the largest collection of books of the Old Testament is arranged under a separate category—Prophetic Books—that lists books by the so-called "writing prophets."

It is unfortunate that popular ideas about the prophets tend to focus on the notion that prophets "predict the future." In fact, the main activities of the prophets were:

1. to be *messengers* of God, delivering messages very much like a royal emissary or message runner;

2. to be God's *prosecutor*, that is, delivering judgment on sinful acts that were considered to have violated God's laws given through the tradition of Moses; and

3. to act as tireless *advocates* for the less fortunate of Israelite society—summarized by Jeremiah as "the widow, the orphan, and the foreigner," but called by Amos and Isaiah simply as "the poor."

Any suggestions by the prophets about future events were always in the prior context of these other main activities. The prophets' words were intended for their own time and represented God's continual involvement in history. To suggest that the words of the prophets were for a distant future not only removes the prophets from history (thus misrepresenting the main point of God's involvement in the history of the people), but also invites irresponsible attempts to "interpret" the prophets' words "for the modern times" as if they are hidden predictions.

The prophets' words were feared not because they were cryptic messages for future times, but because they were understood only too well and spoke of real events in the lives of the kings and people who first heard them, and who often did *not* like what they heard.

The prophets of ancient Israel were mysterious and charismatic men and women (yes, there were female prophets, too) who were feared as well as respected. From occasional references in 1 and 2 Samuel, it appears that prophecy had its origins in traveling bands of *charismatics* who would speak out of a self-imposed, trance-like state (see 1 Sm 10:9ff.). In time, however, great prophets became individually noted, and traditions and/or legends sprung up around them. Bands of disciples often were associated with these more noteworthy figures. The best examples of this later development are the accounts of Elijah and Elisha in the historical books (1 Kgs 17–21; 2 Kgs 2–13). Eventually later prophets were remembered as teachers and their sayings were written down.

Each of the prophets is a unique figure with an interesting difference in outlook and perspective, although in the case of some of the shorter books it is hard to determine a perspective on the basis of so little material. The

WHAT ABOUT APOCALYPTIC LITERATURE?

Apocalyptic literature is a type of writing that features highly symbolic visions. The visions are usually described in graphic detail and are accompanied by the narration of an angel or heavenly figure.

Apocalyptic literature became very popular in the Hellenistic (Greek) period and continued to be influential in the Roman period among both Jews and early Christians. Although there are only two major examples of apocalyptic literature in the Bible (Daniel 7–12 and the Revelation of John in the New Testament), many examples of non-Biblical apocalyptic writings have survived from this period. It was obviously a highly popular form of writing.

Apocalyptic literature focused on contemporary events of the day. Apocalyptic visionaries described symbolic visions from God, references to the coming judgment on the oppressive rulers and events of their times. By envisioning God's intervention on behalf of the oppressed, Jewish apocalyptic visions called for an activism of resistance to Greek and Roman culture and rule. The visions of Daniel are attached to stories of Jewish figures in foreign courts that are vindicated for their faithful persistence or, in other words, their spiritual resistance. Indeed, after three months of reading the Bible in a South African jail, Mahatma Gandhi emerged proclaiming Daniel to be "one of the greatest nonviolent resistors in history."

Apocalyptic literature, then, illustrates a central concern of post-Exilic Hebrew faith—maintaining Faith and identity in circumstances of powerlessness and even oppression.

Book of Obadiah, for example, is only twenty-one verses long; Nahum and Malachi are each only three chapters.

The earliest writing prophet was Amos, a somewhat mysterious man, whose prophecies consisted of unrelenting judgment against many nations—not simply Israel and Judah. In fact, the final few verses of the Book of Amos, which offer some hope, may not have been his words, because they sound so uncharacteristically hopeful.

In contrast to Amos, the prophet Hosea used intimate and romanticized images to describe God as a lover and a parent of the people of Israel and to describe his sadness at Israel's disobedience (which Hosea compared to adultery or to rejecting a parent). Hosea even carried his message to the point of giving his children names that were symbolic of God's anger at the people (for example, *Lo-Ammi* means "you are not my people").

About the same time that Hosea and Amos were active in the northern kingdom of Israel, the traditions surrounding the prophet Isaiah began in the south. The Book of Isaiah is a good example of the continued tradition that major prophetic figures can inaugurate. The prophet himself was active from about 740 BC, and his words are largely recalled in chapters 1–39 of the present Book of Isaiah. Chapters 40–55, however, are generally credited to a second, unnamed prophet. This unnamed prophet may have lived at the end of the Babylonian period and the beginning of the Persian period (545–535 BC) and likely witnessed the collapse of Babylon to the Persian empire.

One of the most important images of the Book of Isaiah is the "Suffering Servant." The Suffering Servant passages were deeply influential among early Christians in their struggle for ways to interpret the events and meaning of the Life, Death, and Resurrection of Jesus (see especially Is 42:1–4; 49:1–6; 50:4–9 and 52:13–53:12). Christ himself explained the meaning of his life and death in relation to God's Suffering Servant: "The Son of Man did not come to be served but to serve and to give his life as ransom for many" (Mt 20:28).

The final chapters, 56–66, are thought to have been collected by disciples who inherited the spirit of the great prophet. They may have been writing from Jerusalem and the Diaspora after the exile.

Less openly hopeful, the prophet Jeremiah was a prophet who felt the tragic duty to proclaim to Israel that God ordained the Babylonian Exile. Jeremiah shared the general Deuteronomic perspective that the exilic events were punishment for the rejection of the laws of God during the period of the monarchy. The Book of Jeremiah is composed in two main sections—the poetic sayings of Jeremiah himself, and prose sections of biographical information about Jeremiah. Both sections are attributed to Baruch, a scribe who was a companion of Jeremiah and is featured in the deuterocanonical Book of Baruch.

Ezekiel was a prophet active among the Babylonian exiles. He was given to occasionally bizarre acts to illustrate his prophetic messages. His main concern was to function as the mediator of the exiles spiritual well being. In his great vision (Ez 40–48), the prophet had hopes for a fresh start for the Jews back in Palestine, where land would be divided equally, and the "princes" (he never used the word "King") would have only a fair allotment and never oppress their people again.

The prophet Jeremiah lamenting the destruction of Jerusalem.

Prophetic books continued to be produced in the post-Exilic community as well. The prophet Haggai, for example, was concerned mainly with the restoration of religious life in the post-Exilic community, particularly the importance of rebuilding the Temple. Similarly, Zechariah dealt with issues of faith and practice in the post-Exilic community. The prophets, as will be covered in succeeding chapters of this text, have many surprises in store.

Section in Review

Quick View

- The Pentateuch records numerous religious laws, civil laws, and moral principles of ancient Israel.

- The historical books tell about the development of Israel from a collection of tribes to a royal state and then the breakup of the kingdom.

- The Wisdom Books provide guidance about life in the form of poetry, hymns, stories, and wise advice.

- The Prophetic Books do not contain predictions of the future perse, but provide important messages about justice and judgment to the people of Israel and Judah.

- Although the Book of Daniel is the only example of Old Testament apocalyptic literature, it was clearly a popular genre in post-exilic Jewish writing.

For Review

1. **Main Idea**: List the five major writing styles in the Old Testament. Cite at least one example of each kind of writing.

2. **Main Idea**: What is the main focus of the five books in the Pentateuch?

3. **Main Idea**: Describe three main activities of the prophets.

4. **Critical Thinking**: How do the Wisdom Books differ from the Prophetic Books of the Old Testament?

For Reflection

Choose a current issue at your school, local community, or in the national news. Write a "prophetic" paragraph about it.

Further Reflections

This chapter has presented a sense of the geography and historical context of Canaan (later called Palestine), a quick survey of the history of the Israelite people (later called Jews), and a quick overview of the various kinds of Biblical literature. Learning to put the Old Testament in these areas of context helps us to delve deeper into God's Word and to further apply the lessons of these texts to our Faith.

For example, our Faith tells us that God is the author of Sacred Scripture.

The Bible should be read—not as merely human words—but as the Word of God. As St. Paul wrote to the Thessalonians:

> you received not a human word but, as it truly is, the Word of God, which is now at work in you who believe. (1 Thes 2:13)

God inspired the human authors of the Bible. The human authors had the freedom to choose the words they wrote, and also the discretion of the stories and the incidences that they would include in their texts. Remember, *stories* can be inspired, as well as history or poetry.

The Old Testament was written over a period of many years. The Hebrew Scriptures are contained in the Old Testament.

The Old Testament is oriented to prepare for and declare in prophecy the coming of Jesus Christ.

In no way has the New Testament rendered the Old Testament void. The "Old Covenant has never been revoked" (*CCC*, 121).

Christians hold the Old Testament as the true Word of God.

Vocabulary Review

Directions: Explain how each set of terms is both similar and different.

1. pictograms; hieroglyphic writing
2. primeval history; prehistoric
3. scribes; prophets
4. exile; Diaspora
5. Pentateuch; Torah
6. Baal; YHWH
7. Canaan; Israel
8. Egyptians; Babylonians
9. Historical Books; Prophetic Books
10. Judah; Israel

Performance Assessment Project

You are the producer of a TV documentary about ancient Israel. Create an outline of this documentary that includes a list of scenes with short descriptions about them. Provide samples of the narrator script for each major section of the documentary. Some questions to consider:

- What information will you present and in what order?
- What video reenactments, images, maps, or Scripture verses will you show?
- What scholars will you ask to interview for the documentary and why?

Called to Prayer

Happy are those who do not follow
the counsel of the wicked,
Nor go the way of sinners,
nor sit in company with scoffers.
Rather the law of the Lord is their joy;
God's law they study day and night.
They are like a tree
planted near streams of water,
that yields its fruit in season;
Its leaves never wither;
whatever they do prospers.

But not the wicked!
They are like chaff driven by the wind.
Therefore the wicked will not survive judgment,
nor will sinners in the assembly of the just.
The Lord watches over the way of the just,
but the way of the wicked leads to ruin.

—Psalm 1:1–6

- **Reflection**: What are the consequences of your actions when you choose to follow or not follow the law of the Lord?

- **Meditation**: Choose one phrase from the psalm and apply it to your own life. How does this phrase assist you in the current challenges you are facing?

- **Resolution**: What habits will you need to develop to go the way of the just and avoid the way of the sinners and the wicked? Choose one habit to practice and make a commitment to develop your ability to follow it over time.

Notes

1. The Hittite Empire was in what is today the country of Turkey. Classical historians sometimes call it "Asia Minor."

2. J. Maxwell Miller, "The Ancient Near East and Archaeology," Ch. 15, in *Old Testament Interpretation: Past, Present, and Future*, p. 245–260.

3. Prehistoric technically means "before writing."

4. "In the Beginning," Prologue to *The Oxford History of the Biblical World*, ed. M. Coogan, Oxford University Press: New York, Oxford, 1998: 3–32.

5. Ibid., 22–23.

6. Ibid., 27.

CHAPTER OUTLINE

■ *The Book of Genesis reveals a true history of the Hebrew people through several different texts.*

■ *The two creation accounts within the Book of Genesis reveal essential truths about God and the human person.*

■ *The second creation account tells of humanity's fall from Original Justice into Original Sin.*

■ *The story of the flood and the Tower of Babel actually provide important insights into God's justice rather than his anger.*

■ *The patriarch stories in Genesis provide important clues to the sources of the book and the time period in which it was written.*

■ *God established a covenant with Abraham that was sustained despite some perceived threats.*

■ *The life of the patriarch Jacob is characterized by trickery, reconciliation, and blessings.*

■ *The Joseph narrative chronicles the story of the Hebrew people entering into eventual slavery in Egypt.*

Chapter Three

The Book of Genesis reveals a true history of the Hebrew people through several different texts.

Introduction

Learning about the history of a people is not only about facts and dates. If you think this isn't true, imagine what a future historian might learn about you from the facts of your permanent record:

- date of birth
- place of birth
- schools attended, grades, and dates of graduation
- traffic offenses and any other legal matters

The longer you live, the more facts about your life will become available for public record. But would this information really tell about who you are—the essence of your life? Certainly there would be much more to know about you.

How would a historian find out more about you? How would a historian find out more about your generation and its culture? As an exercise, think, for example, what a future historian might learn about you and your generation and culture from the current movies and television

shows produced as well as fiction books and stories.

The point is that to learn about the history of individuals and societies, we need to listen carefully to their stories. The Book of Genesis contains sacred accounts about the founding of God's People, the Israelites, beginning with the patriarchy of Abraham. But the first eleven chapters of Genesis go beyond the founding of the Israelites; they present accounts of creation.

Genesis 1–11 is not historical in the sense that it includes verifiable names, facts, and dates. The first eleven chapters contain accounts about the origins of the world, humans, the fall of man, and varying cultures, often described as the primeval history.

The first three chapters of Genesis express the truths of creation. From a literary standpoint, these texts may have borrowed from several sources, including **myths** from the ancient Near East. The Israelites—under the inspiration of the Holy Spirit—adapted these lessons to tell how God has been working throughout history in a radical way.

The Book of Genesis also bridges primeval history with information about important people in our religious history. From Genesis 11:27–50:26, we read of our ancestors of Faith, including Abraham (Gn 12–23, 25), Isaac (Gn 24, 25–27), Jacob (Gn 28–35, 49), and Joseph (Gn 37–48, 50).

The ancient Hebrews loved to tell stories. For thousands of years

myths
Symbolic stories that express a spiritual truth or a basic belief about God.

these stories were preserved through *oral traditions*. Writing was difficult during these early times, and most people did not read. For centuries legends, myths, songs, laws, and stories were passed on orally. Eventually the lessons from these oral traditions began to be written down. Much of the Old Testament was written in the tenth century BC. Some of the Book of Genesis may not have been written until the sixth century BC.

Jesus preserved the oral tradition. He was the master storyteller. Many of his stories are so widely known that people of all faiths can and do refer to them. Sometimes people don't even realize they are quoting Jesus. For example,

- A person who does a good deed for another may be called a "good Samaritan";

- the visit of a relative who comes home after a long absence may be referred to as the "return of the prodigal son" and;

- good people are commonly called "the salt of the Earth."

All of these common phrases are taken directly from the stories of Jesus. They have become a part of our day-to-day culture. The stories are powerful and lasting. This chapter offers a tour of the Book of Genesis—texts that tell us about creation and our ancestors of Faith.

Section in Review

Quick View

- Stories often tell more about the history of individuals and societies than the facts and dates.

- The Book of Genesis contains accounts of the origins of the world and the ancestors of Faith.

- Jesus himself was a master storyteller.

For Review

1. **Main Idea**: What kinds of information can we learn about a culture even from stories that are not simply historical reports?

2. **Main Idea**: What two groups of creation accounts appear in the Book of Genesis? List examples of each.

3. **Critical Thinking**: What would centuries of the oral tradition do to the facts and dates of the events in the Book of Genesis? Why wouldn't this affect the divine authority of the book?

For Reflection

Think of two or three things you believe to be true about God and write a short story about your ancestors that reveals those truths.

The two creation accounts within the Book of Genesis reveal essential truths about God and the human person.

God's Creation

Human beings are created with a desire to know their origins, from their personal beginnings or the beginnings of the entire human race. Everyone wants to know how things got started. So did the ancient peoples, including the ancient Hebrews. The Book of Genesis includes *two* creation accounts, not one. The first is the familiar "seven-day creation" account, which runs from Genesis 1:1 through 2:4a (the "a" after the number 4 means the first *half* of verse 4). In this version, creation takes place in six days before God rests on the seventh day, the Sabbath. Also, note that the material God uses for creation is water:

> In the beginning when God created the heavens and the earth, the earth was a formless wasteland, and darkness covered the abyss, while a mighty wind swept over the waters. (Gn 1:1–2)

Also, note, that in this first creation account, humanity is created *at the same time, in the same moment* as male and female. Both man and woman are created in the image of God:

> Then God said: "Let us make mankind in our image, after our likeness. Let them have dominion over the fish of the sea, the birds of the air, and the cattle, and over all the wild animals and

over all the wild animals and all the creatures that crawl on the ground."

> God created man in his image;
>   in the divine image he created him;
>   male and female he created them.
>   (Gn 1:26–27)

In the second creation text in the Book of Genesis (2:4b–25) God's handiwork does not begin out of water, but from the land:

> At the time when the Lord God made the earth and the heavens—while as yet there was no field shrub on earth and no grass of the field had sprouted, for the Lord God had sent no rain upon the earth and there was no man to till the soil. (Gn 2:4b–6)

In this version, the order of creation is different (man, then plants, then animals, whereas in the first account it starts with plants, then animals, then finally man). The second account portrays God as more of a craftsman than did the first creation account: God makes the man out of mud, and actually "breathes life" into him. Life is a rare gift from God—something God did not do with any other part of creation.

The second creation account also mentions Adam and Eve as the names of the first humans, the story of the temptation of eating the fruit of the tree, and the continued population of the world.

So, there are two different creation accounts recorded in Genesis, and thus different sets of ideas, about the beginning of the world in the Old Testament—similar, but not exactly the same. Some who study the Bible believe that the Hebrews had different versions of these events (rather like having more than one version of the life of Jesus in the different Gospels in the New Testament) and included more than one because important things are said in each version.

The Truths of Creation

We can learn much about the nature of God and his intentions for man through the accounts of creation. The Genesis accounts provide clear answers to other related and perpetual questions (*CCC*, 282): Where do we come from? Where are we going? What is our origin? What is our end? Where does everything that exists come from and where is it going?

In more recent times, scientific discoveries have cast more specific light on the details of creation, including the **evolution** of humanity and attempts to pinpoint when and where the first humans appeared on earth. Human intelligence is certainly already capable of finding an accurate answer to these questions. These studies only enhance our appreciation for God, the Creator, whose existence can be known by human reason alone. St. Paul wrote that denial of God is inexcusable because of the light of human reason:

> The wrath of God is indeed being revealed from heaven against every impiety and wickedness of those who suppress the truth by their wickedness. For what can be known about God is evident to them, because God made it evident to them. Ever since the creation of the world, his invisible attributes of eternal power and divinity have been able to be understood and perceived in what he has made. (Rom 1:18–20)

In fact, the questions about creation are so important for human life that God wants to reveal everything that is good about it. God reveals this knowledge to individuals as the mystery of creation was revealed progressively to Israel (*CCC*, 287). The creation of the world and the creation of man and woman was YHWH's first step at forging a **covenant** with Israel. It is easy to understand why the Hebrew Biblical authors addressed creation with two accounts and why these accounts come first in the Bible. As the *Catechism* teaches:

> The inspired authors have placed them at the beginning of Scripture to express in their solemn language the truths of creation— its origins and its end in God, its order and goodness, the vocation of man, and finally the drama or sin and the hope of salvation. (*CCC*, 289)

God's creative actions also reveal several other important truths about him, including:

- God began everything that exists outside of himself, that he alone is the Creator, and that everything that exists in the world depends on God who gives its being (see Gn 1:1).

- God created everything through the eternal Word, his begotten Son, Jesus (see Col 1:16–17).

- Creation is the common work of the Holy Trinity. God the Father made all things "by the Son and the Spirit" (*CCC*, 292 quoting St. Irenaeus). The prologue to the Gospel of John likewise teaches that the Father created everything by his eternal Word, his beloved Son (see Jn 1:1–5, page 56). The Church also professes the Spirit's role as the "giver of life" (see *CCC*, 291). The image of wind ("a mighty wind swept over the waters") in Genesis 1:2 attests to the presence of the Holy Spirit at creation.

God created the world to show his glory and to communicate it. God's perfection is shown through the gifts he offers us, his creations. Human beings are unique because we are made in the image and likeness of God. We are called to share "by knowledge and love" (*CCC*, 356) in God's own life.

The first account of creation also reveals a great deal about the human person. God has created us with both a body and soul. The "soul" refers to the entire human person. It also refers to the innermost, spiritual aspect of man. The human body, too, shares in the image of God because it is intended to be the temple of the Holy Spirit. Also, we are to regard the human body as good and to honor it, since God has created it and will raise it on the last day.

The Beginning of God's Revelation

In the Person and mission of Jesus Christ, God has fully been revealed. But this Revelation was a gradual one through history. The beginning of God's Revelation to man came when he made himself known to our first parents.

God invited Adam and Eve to an "intimate communion with himself and clothed them with resplendent grace and justice" (*CCC*, 54). When Adam and Eve sinned (see page 57), God did not withdraw the Revelation of himself. Rather, he encouraged the human race with the hope of Salvation and the promise of redemption.

God continued to offer a covenant to humanity. The first covenant was made with Noah. God also chose Abraham and formed his people, Israel. After the time of the patriarchs, God freed Israel from slavery in Egypt and established with them the covenant of Mount Sinai. Through Moses, God gave the Israelites his Law so that they would know and worship him as they awaited the Messiah

evolution
The scientific theory which proposes that current forms of life developed gradually out of earlier ones.

covenant
A binding and solemn agreement between human beings or between God and his people, holding each to a particular course of action.

WHAT ELSE DOES THE BIBLE SAY ABOUT CREATION?

There are other discussions of Creation in the Bible besides the Book of Genesis. For example, Psalm 104 praises God the Creator, saying in part:

> How manifold are your works, O Lord!
>   In wisdom you have wrought them all. (v. 24)

The wisdom of Solomon praises God for giving the gift of understanding of the details of creation:

> For he gave me sound knowledge of existing things,
>   that I might know the organization
>   of the universe and its elements,
> The beginning and the end and the midpoints of times,
>   the changes in the sun's course and
>   the variations of the seasons.
> Cycles of years, positions of the stars,
> natures of animals, tempers of beasts,
> Powers of winds and thoughts of men
>   uses of plants, and virtues of roots—
> Such things as are hidden I learned,
>   and such as are plain;
> for Wisdom, the artificer of all,
>   taught me. (Wis 7:17–22)

The prologue of the Gospel of John (1:1–5) also addresses creation:

> In the beginning was the Word,
>   and the Word was with God,
>   and the Word was God.
> He was in the beginning with God.
> All things came to be through him,
>   and without him nothing came to be.
> What came to be through him was life,
>   and the life was the light of the human race;
> the light shines in the darkness,
>   and the darkness has not overcome it.

who would save them from their sins. This ongoing Revelation is the subject of the Old Testament. It serves as a prelude to the New Testament and God's full Revelation in Christ. Though God's Revelation is complete, it is not explicit. It remains the task of the Church, and our own task, to understand its significance over the course of centuries.

Section in Review

Quick View

- The Book of Genesis includes two creation accounts that differ in many respects but reveal important truths about God and humanity.

- The studies and theories of evolution can enhance our appreciation for God.

- God's Revelation began with our first parents and culminated in Christ. Today we continue to understand its significance over time.

For Review

1. **Main Idea**: What is the most important question addressed by the two creation accounts in the Book of Genesis? What answer do these texts provide?

2. **Main Idea**: List some of the differences of the two creation accounts.

3. **Main Idea**: What do God's creative actions reveal about him?

4. **Critical Thinking**: What does being made in the image and likeness of God mean for the way we should treat others?

For Reflection

Write a list of some of the puzzling questions you have about the origins of life and the origins of evil in the world.

The second creation account tells of humanity's fall from Original Justice into Original Sin.

Original Justice and the Fall of Man

Read Genesis 2:4–3:24.

The second creation account teaches us that the first man was created "in friendship with his Creator and in harmony with himself and with the creation around him" (*CCC*, 374). The Church also teaches that Adam and Eve were created in a state of grace known as "Original Justice." The benefits of Original Justice were wonderful, surpassed only by the glory of new creation in Christ. As long as man remained in friendship with God, the gifts of Original Justice would remain, for example:

- There would be no suffering or death.

- Man would be at peace with himself.

- There would be harmony between man and woman.
- There would be peace between Adam and Eve, the first couple, and all of creation.

At the time of creation, our first parents were blessed with the gifts of "self mastery," meaning they had power over lustful desires of the body and covetousness for earthly goods. This deep friendship with God at the time of creation is such that he placed man in a garden (see Gn 2:8). At the time, work was not a burden for man; rather, it was collaboration with God to bring perfection to all of creation.

The second creation account in Genesis describes another reality: the sin of Adam and Eve. With their sin, the harmony of Original Justice intended for humanity would be lost.

Original Sin

As with other events in primeval history, the fall of man described in Genesis 3 uses figurative language but describes an actual "deed that took place *at the beginning of the history of man*" (*CCC*, 390) that reveals with the certainty of faith that all human history is marred by an original, voluntary sin committed by our first parents.

The basic root of sin is man's rejection of God and opposition to his will. The second creation account describes how this first happened. Adam and Eve were tempted to sin by a serpent, a fallen **angel** who was "Satan" or the "devil."

What was the Original Sin? Essentially, it was an abuse of man's freedom. Tempted by the devil, Adam disobeyed God and lacked trust in God's goodness. The Book of Genesis describes the sin as Adam and Eve eating fruit from the forbidden "tree of the knowledge of good and bad" (Gn 2:17, 3:6). All sin, including this Original Sin, is rooted in

disobedience of God. The Original Sin, in essence, is that man *preferred* himself to God. Man was created to be like God in all glory, but instead he chose to be like God but "without God, before God, and not in accordance with God" (*CCC*, 398 quoting St. Maximus the Confessor).

The Original Sin has consequences for all of humanity. Adam and Eve immediately lose the graces of Original Holiness. The harmony of Original Justice is destroyed: human nature is weakened and inclined to sin, man's spiritual control over his body is lost, tensions between men and women are introduced, and the rest of creation (e.g., animals, climate) becomes hostile to humankind. Moreover, "death makes its entrance into human history" (*CCC*, 400).

Yet it is important to note that even after the sin of Adam and Eve, God immediately offered his mercy and the first promise of a Redeemer for the fallen humankind. God said to the serpent:

> I will put enmity between you and the woman
> > and between your offspring and hers;
> He will strike at your head,
> > while you strike at his heel.
> (Gn 3:15)

The woman's offspring is Jesus Christ. The first letter of John teaches: "Indeed, the Son of God was revealed to destroy the works of the devil" (1 Jn 3:8).

Still, sin spread quickly after Adam and Eve. Cain's murder of his brother Abel is a personal sin, which arose from the shared Original Sin of humanity. After the incident (see Gn 4:1–16), God asks Cain to explain himself and tell where his brother is. Cain responds by saying, "I do not know. Am I my brother's keeper?" Sin has caused him to abdicate his responsibility for others, a practice that continues on through each generation.

angel
A spiritual, personal, and immortal creature, with intelligence and free will, who glorifies God and serves as God's messenger. Satan was at first a good angel, but he and other devils became evil through their own choices.

The New Adam

(*CCC*, 411, 504–505, 538–539)

and the New Eve

(*CCC*, 411, 489, 494, 502–507, 511, 726, 975, 2853, 2618)

Many references to the Genesis creation accounts are found in the New Testament. There are connections between Adam and Jesus as well as between Eve and Mary. The relationship between Adam and Jesus is simple. Through Adam, Original Sin and death entered the world. Oppositely, through Christ sanctifying grace and new life was restored. St. Paul described Christ as the Second Adam or New Adam. In the Letter to the Romans he wrote, "for just as through the disobedience of one person the many were made sinners, so through the obedience of the one the many will be made righteous" (5:19).

St. Irenaeus further expands Paul's words by making similar connections between Eve and Mary:

In accordance with this design, Mary the Virgin is found obedient, saying, Behold the handmaid of the Lord; be it unto me according to your word (Luke 1:38). But Eve was disobedient; for she did not obey when as yet she was a virgin . . . having become disobedient, was made the cause of death, both to herself and to the entire human race; so also did Mary, having a man betrothed [to her], and being nevertheless a virgin, by yielding obedience, become the cause of salvation, both to herself and the whole human race." (*Against Heresies*, III, Ch. 2, 4)

Mary is the New Eve who cooperated with the Holy Spirit to bring Christ into the world and people to Christ.

Adam	Jesus Christ (New Adam)
Adam was created without Original Sin (Gn 2:7, 25; 3:6–7)	Jesus was born without Original Sin and remained sinless (Lk 24:47; Rom 5:19; 2 Cor 5:21; Heb 7:26; 1 Jn 3:5)
God breathed life into Adam (Gn 2:7)	Jesus was conceived by the power of the Holy Spirit (Lk 1:35). Jesus gave up his spirit in his last breath on the Cross (Lk 24:46) Jesus breathed the Spirit on his disciples on Pentecost (Jn 20:22)
Eve was created out of the side of Adam (Gn 2:21–23)	Blood and water poured out of the side of Jesus on the Cross symbolizing the Sacraments of Baptism and Eucharist and, therefore, the Church (Jn 19:33)
Adam was tempted to sin by Satan (Gn 3:5)	Jesus resisted temptation by Satan (Lk 4:13)

Eve	Mary (New Eve)
Eve was created without sin (Gn 2:25; 3:6–7)	Mary was born full of grace and without sin (Lk 1:28)
Virgin (Gn 2:25)	Virgin (Lk 1:27, 34)
Tempted by the Serpent, the fallen angel Satan (Gn 3:1–7)	Visited by the angel Gabriel (Lk 1:26)
Disobedience led to Original Sin and death, through her husband Adam (Gn 3:12, 17–19)	Obedience led to Salvation through her Son, Jesus Christ (Lk 1:38)
Eve became mother of all the living (Gn 3:20)	Jesus presented Mary to the Beloved Disciple as the new "mother of the living" (Jn 19:26–27)

The doctrine of Original Sin is an essential truth of the Faith. Without the doctrine of Original Sin, the mystery of Christ is undermined. We come into the world as sinners and need the Salvation that is offered to all through Christ. As the *Exultet* at the Easter vigil proclaims:

> O happy, fault, O necessary sin of Adam,
>   which gained for us so great a Redeemer!

Section in Review

Quick View

- The first humans were created in the state of grace called "Original Justice," which included God's friendship and harmony with themselves and the world around them.

- Although the text of the Fall is written in figurative language, it describes the events that took place at the beginning of history.

- Original Sin is an essential truth of Faith that is linked to the mystery of Christ's redemption.

For Review

1. **Vocabulary**: What is Original Justice?

2. **Main Idea**: Why is the doctrine of Original Sin essential for understanding the mystery of Christ?

3. **Critical Thinking**: Compare the life of Original Justice and our lives after Original Sin. What changed?

For Reflection

Imagine that you are with Adam and Eve in the Garden of Eden. How would your life be different if you were born in Original Justice?

The story of the flood and the Tower of Babel actually provide important insights into God's justice rather than his anger.

Renewal of Life

Read Genesis 6:5–9:17.

God's Revelation was not broken off by the sin of Adam and Eve. In fact, after the fall, God immediately offered the hope of Salvation by promising redemption. At Mass, we hear this reminder:

> Even when he disobeyed you and lost your friendship you did not abandon him to the power of death. . . . Again and again you offered a covenant to man. (*Roman Missal*, Eucharistic Prayer IV, 118)

The covenant God made with Noah is part of the next stage of his Revelation. Noah became the new **ancestor** for humankind. God blessed him and his sons and said to them: "Be fertile and multiply and fill the earth" (Gn 9:1). The covenant with Noah revealed the basic precepts of the law and combated **paganism**, a combination of idol worship (idolatry) and worship of many gods (polytheism). This covenant also called all people—including Gentiles—to relationship with God and remains in force "until the universal proclamation of the Gospel" (*CCC*, 58).

The Literary Nature of the Noah Covenant

The account of Noah and the great flood is the last great story of Genesis 1–11 that details events of primeval history.

The ancient peoples surrounding the Hebrews also had flood legends. One of the most famous is part of

WHY SO MANY FLOOD STORIES?

The Epic of Gilgamesh is one of many flood stories from the ancient world. There are some Biblical scholars who believe that the reason for the many flood stories (including the Genesis story of the Great Flood) relates specifically to an ancient historic event.

One theory of the preponderance of flood legends according to Columbia University geologists is that, as the Ice Age ended and glaciers melted, a wall of seawater surged from the Mediterranean into the Black Sea. During the Ice Age, the geologists argue, the Black Sea was an isolated freshwater lake surrounded by farmland.

Then, according to the theory, about 12,000 years ago, toward the end of the Ice Age, the Earth began growing warmer. Vast sheets of ice that sprawled over the Northern Hemisphere began to melt. Oceans and seas grew deeper as a result. About 7,000 years ago even the Mediterranean Sea swelled. Seawater pushed northward, slicing through what is now Turkey. Funneled through the narrow Bosporus, the water hit the Black Sea with two hundred times the force of Niagara Falls. Each day the Black Sea rose about six inches and coastal farms were flooded. Settlements were discovered in what is today submerged former shorelines of the Black Sea.

Seared into the memories of terrified survivors, the story of the flood was passed down through the generations and eventually became basis for some of the ancient flood stories.[1]

This is a relatively recent theory, and lots of materials are available online and in recent books to assemble more information. Ruins of civilizations are being explored along what is supposed to be the ancient shoreline of the Black Sea to find out if these were the original villages and cities of the flood victims.

- Read and summarize the story of the Great Flood from the notes on verses 6:5–8:22 in the New American Bible.

the great myth cycle of a Mesopotamian poem known as the Epic of Gilgamesh. Many copies of the Epic of Gilgamesh have been found by archaeologists, from as early as 2000 BC in some places and as early as the sixth century BC in other locations. It was obviously an ancient story that was widely known and very popular throughout the region. The Hebrews, too, would have known the story.

While there are similarities between the flood story of the Epic of Gilgamesh and the inspired text of Scripture, the Hebrew story shares how God reveals himself to man and a hint to man's eventual destiny. Here are some of the unique teachings of the Hebrew version:

- Humanity is to be destroyed because they are evil and constantly doing violence to each other.

- Noah is saved because he is a righteous man.

- The Gilgamesh hero takes money on the ark. Noah only takes animals.

- The Hebrew version represents a "second creation story." Noah takes the place of a new "Adam."

Now we understand the wisdom of the Church's interpretation and understanding of elements of this story. The story says that God made an everlasting covenant with Noah and humankind. God intervenes in history and offers his Salvation. This will be an ongoing occurrence through the Old Testament, leading to God's ultimate intervention in history, the incarnation of his son, Jesus Christ, who offers Salvation to all.

ancestor
Any person to whom you are related by blood who comes before you on a family tree.

paganism
The profession of no religion.

The Tower of Babel: More Hope for the World

Read Genesis 11:1–9.

The last of the primeval history events of Genesis 1–11 details how the sin of pride brought into the world by the sin of Adam, increased as an entire city tried to make itself God. The short nine-verse story also has a secondary motive: to show in an imaginative way how the many different languages of the world came to be. This of itself is a hopeful gesture to humankind (see below).

Notice *where* this is taking place. The place is called "Shinar" (vs. 2). This is an ancient term that the Bible often uses for "Babylon" (and thus the play on the name "Babel"). Why is Babylon important? Remember that Babylon was the great Empire that conquered Jerusalem and destroyed Solomon's Temple in 587 BC. This powerful memory of the Hebrews was so great, that "Babylon" passed into history as a symbol for *any* oppressive Empire or state. The New Testament uses Babylon to refer to the Roman Empire (e.g., 1 Pt 5:13; Rv 16:19; 18:2, 10, 21).[2]

Next, consider the second part of the story. One interpretation of the diversity of languages is that God is punishing the people for their sins. However, the unification of all humanity under one language, and putting them all to work to build a great city and tower, would have been good only for the rulers. The scattering of the peoples into different languages would really have been God's *liberation* for most of the people of "Shinar." It is also worth noting that "Shinar" was a word often used in relation to the Babylonian Empire, the conquerors of Jerusalem in 597/587 BC (see Dn 1:2). From this perspective, perhaps the story of the Tower of Babel is intended to point to the folly of these great ancient Empires who thought they could forcibly unite all of humanity under their power, putting them to work on great public projects like their temples and palaces.

Therefore, dividing into different peoples and languages was not punishment, but freedom. Consider the parallel story in Acts 2:5–13. We now can appreciate that each person gathered in Jerusalem at the Pentecost feast heard Peter *in his or her own language*, also a positive development. The Church teaches that God willed the diversity of his creatures and their own particular goodness, their interdependence, and their order. This diversity is deeply celebrated in the liberation of God at the story of the Tower of Babel.

The primeval history stories of Genesis tell us much about the Hebrew people—including what they value about life and their beliefs about YHWH. Here is a summary of some of the things these stories teach us about God and his will:

- God's will is to create a people in his image—both male and female.

- God's will is peace, not violence. Violence is considered sinful in these stories. God creates in peace—it is humans that bring on violence. The Flood story suggests that God was so sickened by human violence that God regretted making humanity.

- God's will is trust and truthfulness—not the lies and deceptions of human beings in their society.

- God's will is care for creation—not destruction and exploitation.

- God's will is joyful diversity—not forced unification

- God is not impressed with how great our human material accomplishments are, but with how we care for each other and also how we care for the created environment.

Section in Review

Quick View

- God's covenant with Noah highlights the importance of God's Law and his intention to establish a covenant with all people.

- Although the flood story in Genesis is similar to Epic of Gilgamesh, it contains important unique teachings.

- The story of the Tower of Babel details the sin of pride, but the historical experiences of the Hebrew people reveal God as a liberator not a punisher.

For Review

1. **Main Idea**: What are some of the unique religious truths expressed in the Hebrew story of Noah and the Flood?

2. **Critical Thinking**: What evidence is there that the story of the Tower of Babel reveals that God liberated rather than punished the people who worked on the tower?

For Reflection

What surprised you the most in the stories you read from the beginning of the Bible? What new information caused you to think differently about human nature or about God?

The patriarch stories in Genesis provide important clues to the sources of the book and the time period in which it was written.

Ancestors of Faith

The structure of Genesis changes with the introduction of the Patriarch Abraham in Genesis 11:27 and continues in the same way through the rest of the book with accounts of other **patriarchs**, Isaac and Jacob, and narrative surrounding Jacob's son, Joseph. While the accounts of the patriarchs are not counted as history in the strict sense, people and events from the time of Abraham onward can be placed in the historical and social setting of the Near East from between 2000 and 1700 BC. These Biblical passages are corroborated by non-Biblical sources.

Abraham is the father of the Chosen People who were called to prepare the way for Christ. At Christ's coming, the Chosen People would be the "root onto which the Gentiles would be grafted, once they came to believe" (see Rom 11:17–18, 24). Abraham, then, is also the "father of all believers."

Why are these accounts of our ancestors of Faith important? Why were they included in the Bible? Why would you tell stories of individual family members as a way of learning about your history? These are only a few of the many interesting

patriarchs
Male rulers, elders, or leaders. The patriarchs of Israel are Abraham, Isaac, and Jacob.

My Family Tree

Research your family history through four generations. Answer: "When did your family's Catholic faith first come to America?"

questions that we must ask when we begin to read the stories of the patriarchs of ancient Israel.

The first thing to notice about Genesis 12–50, besides the fact that it covers a great deal of material, is that this really reads like a collection of short stories. Each of these sections has a clear beginning and a clear ending. When the Bible was divided into chapters and verses from its original manuscripts, it was easy to divide Genesis into chapters, because the stories easily divide into units.

This is the reason that stories about the main characters in Genesis are often referred to as "cycles" of stories: they read very much like a series of short stories all based around prominent central characters which were gathered together into one cycle. When Genesis is looked at in this way, an interesting aspect of the book becomes surprisingly clear. Look at the chapters in which the main characters of Genesis appear. The total chapters are in parentheses:

- Abraham—chapters 12–23, 25 (**13**)
- Isaac—chapters 24, 26–27 (**3**)
- Jacob—chapters 28–35, 49 (**9**)
- Joseph—chapters 37–48, 50 (**12**)

Who are the dominant people in the Book of Genesis? Abraham, certainly, but second to him is Joseph, followed by Jacob. Isaac is more like a transitional figure without a great deal of tradition surrounding his life and adventure. This section of the text focuses most attention on the patriarchs that the authors of Genesis wrote the most about.

It is also important to look at the roles women play in these cycle of stories. Women play a much more significant role in these ancestor stories than they do in many other later portions of the Old Testament.

Dating Ancestor Stories

One way those who closely study the Bible know that the Book of Genesis was written much later than the events it describes is by the phrase "of today" or "to this day" that is included after several of its short lessons. For example:

- He is the ancestor of the Moabites *of today* (Gn 19:37).
- He called it Shibah; hence the name of the city, Beer-sheba, *to this day* (Gn 27:33).

- That is why, *to this day*, the Israelites do not eat the sciatic muscle that is on the hip socket, inasmuch as Jacob's hip socket was struck at the sciatic muscle (Gn 32:32).

This type of phrase is not entirely unique to Genesis. For instance, the Book of Joshua includes similar references, including:

- "[They] piled a great heap of stones over him, which remains *to the present day*" (Jos 7:25b–26).

The phrase "to this day" or something similar indicates that the writer of these words is living at a time much later than the time the stories themselves occurred. The way these stories read, it is almost as if the author is sharing the incident with listeners and then pointing to a heap of stones, or a tree, or to a group of people, and explaining how the story relates to what they see.

There are other interesting phrases in Genesis that suggest that these stories were written down much later than the events they describe. For example, look at these two verses, paying special attention to the part in italic font:

Abram passed through the land as far as the sacred place at Sheckhem, by the terebinth of Moreh. (*The Canaanites were then in the land.*) (Gn 12:6)

The following are the kings who reigned in the land of Edom *before any king reigned* over the Israelites. (Gn 36:31)

These verses sound like they were written long after the events they are describing. In fact, Genesis 36:31 could not have been written before the first king in Israel, and therefore can be no older than roughly 1020 BC, which is hundreds of years (if not a thousand) *after* the times that Abraham may have lived.

Duplication of Ancestor Stories

The ancestor stories provide many clues as to how the authors arranged the particular stories and why certain information was included in the stories.

First of all, we mentioned that they come to us in cycles of short stories. Second, there are a number of these stories that are told twice—in almost the same way. Note, for example, that Abraham tells Sarah to "Tell them you

are my sister" once in Genesis 12:13 and again in Genesis 20:12ff. The same story is used by Isaac regarding his wife Rebekah in Genesis 26:7–11. In another duplication of stories, Abraham sends Hagar into the desert not only in Genesis 16:5–14 but again in 21:8–21.

Sometimes, however, the stories offer differing facts or explanations. One famous example occurs in Genesis 21:31 and 26:33 where there are two *different* explanations for how the village of Beer-Sheba received it's name. In the first it was because Abimelech and Abraham took an oath there. In the latter, the naming had to do with the discovery of water at the location.

What might account for these "double appearances" of stories, or apparent contradictions between them? Simply a literary style? Or did the ancient writers not pay that much attention to such editorial discrepancies? Actually, there is even more to it than that.

Formation and Arrangement of Ancestor Stories

There is strong evidence that these stories were told and re-told over a long period of time. Some of them contain a little explanation as to why a city remains so named or a pile of stones is still in place "to this day" (at least on "the day" that the author told the story). Biblical scholarship has concluded that these were originally oral stories, which were probably passed on by word of mouth long before they were ever written down in the form in which we have them today. This understanding leads us to at least two obvious questions:

- Why have these particular stories been preserved?

- What is important in each of these stories?

Furthermore, these stories were then gathered up in groups which became the cycles or sections in Genesis 12–50. But was there originally more than one group of these stories? There is another mysterious detail to consider—especially regarding the stories told twice.

When there are two versions of the same story, the two different versions always use a different name for God. This is somewhat difficult to spot in some English translations of the Bible, but in most good translations, the name for God—"YHWH"—will be translated consistently as either "Lord" or "Lord God."

Meanwhile, another tradition used a more generic name for Israel's God—*Elohim*, which is usually translated simply to "God." Go back and look through those two Abraham stories that are repeated (Gn 12:10–20 and

Abraham and Isaac

Jacob

Gn 20:12ff; Gn 16:5–14 and Gn 21:8–21) and notice that the "Lord" is in one of the two, while "God" is always in the other version.

This famous clue involving the use of different words for God, combined with many of the other observations that we have pointed out, has led to a popular theory about the origins of the Bible. The basic idea is that there were originally *two* different "collections" of early stories and traditions. One version of these stories consistently used "YHWH" as the name for God. It is often suggested that this is the older of the two collections. This material was called the *J source* or *J document* because the letter "J" is used for "Jahweh," the German spelling of YHWH (German scholars first proposed the theory). The other collection of stories used "Elohim" as the name for God. The Elohim material was designated the *E source* or *E document*.

At some point in Israelite history these two sources were brought together (either as written sources, or as oral traditions that were remembered in different ways in different places) and when they were brought together, some of the stories were repeated.

It is interesting to ask why these ancient editors and writers decided to keep both versions of some of these stories in the collection. Why *two* versions of the Creation? Why *two* versions of Abraham telling Sarah, "Tell them you are my sister!"? There is no clear answer to this good question, but two possibilities strongly suggest themselves.

First, all of these stories in the Book of Genesis must have been treasured stories among the people who told them and knew them. It would be hard to give up a story that is traditional, and told in a way that people were used to. When stories were brought together to form a common tradition, different groups of people would probably be rather insistent that *their* version be included. Furthermore, sometimes the separate versions of the same story have slightly different messages—and perhaps both messages were considered to be significant and important.

However, a more popular theory is that the "E" source was actually added to the "J" source as a kind of commentary—perhaps working out some perceived difficulties of the "J" versions. Notice, for example, that Abraham is much nicer to Hagar in Genesis 21, the "E" version, than he is in Genesis 16, the older "J" version. Perhaps the editors added the second version so that we don't have such a negative, uncaring picture of Abraham, the great father of the Israelites.

But we also realize that the "final form" of the text—as we have it now—is important. So we must acknowledge that, because of their inclusion in the Bible, *all* of these stories were considered to be important and *all* of these stories are inspired. As the fathers of the Second Vatican Council taught:

> But, since holy Scripture must be read and interpreted according to the same Spirit by whom it was written, no less serious attention must be given to the content and unity of the whole of Scripture, if the meaning of the sacred texts is to be correctly brought to light. (*Dei Verbum*, 12)

The theories about sources or versions being combined is an attempt to understand how the present books of the Bible came about, or evolved.

The Importance of Ancestor Stories

Have you ever done any research into your family history? If not, would you like to someday? Why do you think research of this kind might be interesting? What is it about researching our "roots" that seems so fascinating for many people? Some people find that studying their family history helps them get a better idea of who they are. A follow-up point is this: If we understand more about ourselves, perhaps we can know a little more about how we should live, and the kind of people that we should try to be.

However, family history can include *both* positive and negative experiences. Sometimes we hear family stories and think, "That is a powerful story. My great grandparents worked hard so that their descendants would have a better life. I should work to improve my life too." But you might also discover some things you don't like: "My great-uncle made some of the same mistakes I am making. I want to learn from his mistakes and not repeat them." It seems clear to us that we should read the ancestor stories of Israel in both ways—to learn from the positive experiences, and sometimes the hard lessons from negative experiences!

Keeping in mind this information on why the ancestor stories were included in the Book of Genesis, it is time to move on to the principal figures of these stories, the patriarchs of the Jewish faith.

Section in Review

Quick View

- The stories about the patriarchs read like "cycles" of short stories.

- A series of clues in the Book of Genesis indicate that it was written at a much later date in Israel's history.

- Various clues in the Old Testament suggest that there are two different "collections" of stories and traditions, called the "J" source and the "E" source.

For Review

1. **Main Idea**: Which of the main characters in Genesis are most important? What evidence is there that the authors considered those characters most important?

2. **Main Idea**: How have Biblical scholars concluded that there were two sources for many of the stories that appear in Genesis?

3. **Critical Thinking**: Make a generalization based on the reoccurring stories in the Book of Genesis. Why would the readers and hearers of the stories accept them all?

For Reflection

- Choose a pair of stories from the Book of Genesis that are versions of each other. Identify which story is from the "J" source and which is from the "E" source. Consider the similarities and differences between them and explain why you think both versions of the story would have been included in the Bible.

- Ask your parents or grandparents to tell you stories about their lives that you have never heard. Ask probing questions about how they met, about having children, and similar questions about family life during those times.

God established a covenant with Abraham that was sustained despite some perceived threats.

Abraham: Father of Faith

Abraham is the first patriarch of the Jewish faith. With his wife, Sarah, his descendants make up a nation of people from whom God would bring Salvation. When he is first mentioned in the Bible, Abraham goes by the name Abram.

Abraham the Wanderer

Abraham is known as the "father of faith," not only for Judaism but also for Christianity and Islam. Interestingly, he is not a mighty general, a great king or ruler, or an influential leader of any kind. Rather, he is a herdsman and a wanderer.

Abraham was not native to the land of Palestine. The tradition states that Abraham was born in the ancient city of Ur in Mesopotamia and that God called him to go with his family from this familiar land "to a land that I will show you" (Gn 12:1).

Abraham's travel itinerary is anything but direct. He travels up the Tigris and Euphrates valleys to Haran, and then crosses over to the coast and travels to southern Palestine and the Negev desert, where Beer-Sheva is located. He and his family finally venture into Egypt and back again.

The Genesis account seems intent on showing that Abraham wandered throughout the entire known world. His journey foreshadows the one that the Hebrew people will later make in various stages of their history. For example, his return from Egypt is a preview of the Hebrews' journey out of Egypt, following the Exodus in the stories of Moses that will form the people of Israel.

Abraham's descendants also eventually journeyed far and wide in the Jewish Diaspora. And, St. Paul, another spiritual descendant of Abraham, traveled all over his known world—the Roman Empire—to share the good

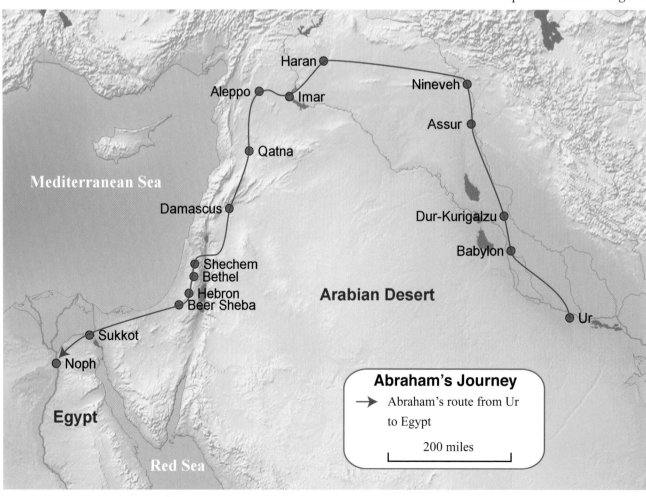

Abraham's Journey

→ Abraham's route from Ur to Egypt

200 miles

Abraham's Travels

Abraham and his family lived a nomadic lifestyle prevalent in the Ancient Near East. Research the following information on nomadic life during the time and place of Abraham:

- How large was a family group?
- Would more than one family group travel together?
- What distances were covered in one day on average?
- Did people walk? Ride animals? Use carts?
- What special arrangement for food and water would be needed for travel in arid regions?
- What common dangers did travelers face?

news of Jesus Christ, who was himself a traveling preacher teaching *all* people. God's message always "travels."

Covenant with Abraham

One of the most important elements of the Abraham traditions is the covenant God establishes with Abraham. Recall that a covenant is a solemn agreement between human beings or between God and people and that a number of such agreements are struck between important Biblical figures and God. The most important covenant in the Old Testament is God's covenant with Moses that includes the giving of the Law. There is also the covenant with Noah as mentioned on page 60. God also established a covenant with King David. The *terms* of God's covenant with Abraham are laid out in Genesis 12:1–3. First, God tells what he requires of Abraham:

> Go forth from the land of your kinsfolk and from your father's house to a land that I will show you. (Gn 12:1)

God's part of the agreement comes next:

> I will make of you a great nation, and I will bless you;
> I will make your name great,

> so that you will be a blessing.
> I will bless those who bless you and curse those who curse you.
> All the communities of the earth shall find blessing in you.
> (Gn 12:2–3)

Besides the terms, there is typically a *sign* or *symbol* of Biblical covenants. With Moses, for example, the sign is the giving of the laws themselves. With Abraham, there are two such signs. First, his name is changed from Abram to Abraham.[3] His wife's name is changed from Sarai to Sarah. More importantly, there is the sign of **circumcision**. The tradition of practicing circumcision on all males who are Hebrews is attributed to Abraham himself. Since Abraham's heirs were to come from Abraham's own natural child (and not an adopted child, as Abraham apparently thought at first [Gn 15]) then it seems obvious that this sign would somehow be connected to the idea of descendants or offspring. Thus, the sign was circumcision—a physical symbol on the male genital—since God's part of the covenant deals with offspring and descendants (Gn 17:1–10).

Understanding the promise made to Abraham is a crucial element for gaining a modern Christian understanding of the Bible. The Church teaches, for example, that God chose Abraham and

circumcision
The surgical removal of foreskin; it was the physical sign of the covenant between God and Abraham.

made a covenant with him and his descendants and that by the covenant God formed his people. Abraham's faith in God's promises is considered an act of righteousness; that is the "right" attitude a person should have toward God. As St. Paul pointed out, "For what does the scripture say? Abraham believed in God, and it was credited to him as righteousness" (Rom 4:3). The Church is an extension of the covenant with Abraham, part of God's people. As the *Catechism of the Catholic Church* explains:

> The people descended from Abraham would be the trustees of the promise made to the patriarchs, the chosen people, called to prepare for that day when God would gather all his children into the unity of the Church. They would be the root onto which the Gentiles would be grafted, once they came to believe. (*CCC*, 61)

Blessing and Threats

Another important theme in the early ancestor stories of Abraham is "blessings," which have been promised to him and his descendants by God. It is God who is the source of the blessings. But in conjunction to the blessings are related "threats" which are not of God's doing but attributed to human weakness and doubt.

In other words, in many of these stories, even though God has blessed and made a promise, there are also threats to that promise—possibilities that the promise will not be kept. For example, Abraham is promised heirs through his wife Sarah, but she doubts that she will be able to have children because of her age. Later, Abraham himself feels threatened. Will he have to sacrifice his child? These twists in the plot and drama also serve to make the lessons learned even more memorable. The sub-sections below look at a few more of these.

External Threats to Sarah: Genesis 12:10–20 and 20

Already in Genesis 12:10–20, the future of Abraham is threatened. Sarah is taken into the household of Pharaoh. The details of this brief story are so minimal that it does not answer many questions that we have, but the fact that Sarah experiences the "captivity" of Pharaoh—thus anticipating the later oppression of the Hebrews—is surely a central idea in this brief story. But the threat is also very clear. How can Sarah bear the promised descendants of

Abraham if she is in the harem of the Pharaoh? In 12:17 "the Lord struck Pharaoh and his household with severe plagues" (another reference to the later Exodus story?) so that he releases Sarah, and they are both asked to leave Egypt.

There is another example of this "external threat" in Genesis 20. There, the story is repeated with a ruler who is local in Palestine, and not from Egypt. Some of the other details are different. For example, the ruler in this version is warned by God (Gn 20:3) and therefore is able to avoid the sin of marrying a woman who is already married. Both versions of this story, however, represent "external" threats to God's promise.

Internal Threats to Sarah: Genesis 16 and 21:1–21

Unlike external threats from the Egyptian Pharaoh or a local ruler, Abimelech (in two stories in Genesis 16, and again in Genesis 21:1–21), Sarah has doubts that she is really going to be the bearer of the promised descendants of Israel. The internal threat is her lack of faith.

In Genesis 16, she is so doubtful that she will be able to become pregnant that she asks Abraham to have a son through Hagar, an Egyptian servant of Sarah. (Hagar's son Ishmael is honored as the father of another great people, the later "Ishmaelites," who are often thought to be the Arab peoples in popular tradition.) Then, in Genesis 21:1–21, Sarah does herself produce a son—Isaac—who is the answer to God's promise.

But the image of Sarah's character is called into question in both stories. First, because of her doubts of God's promise (see Gn 16), and secondly because of her jealousy of Hagar and her son, even though he is also an heir to Abraham. When Sarah notices Isaac playing with Ishmael, she demands that Abraham "drive out that slave and her son" (Gn 21:10). This seems very unfair. After all, Hagar had Ishmael only because Sarah suggested the plan.

What lessons could God have intended with these inspired writings? A key lesson involves Hagar herself. Hagar is a woman, a servant girl, and a foreigner, and yet the Bible shows how God's compassion extends beyond the central character of Abraham and his wife Sarah. In both Genesis 16 and Genesis 21, she is seriously mistreated, and yet God "hears her cries" and takes care of both her and Ishmael. The later Mosaic laws, and the

Hagar and Ismael expelled from the house of Abraham.

prophet Jeremiah, will teach that God demands care for "the widow, the orphan, and the foreigner" (e.g. Dt 27:19; Jer 7:6, 22:3). The story of Hagar clearly illustrates this "justice of God." She and Ishmael *are* a "widow, orphan, and foreigner" when they are sent away by Abraham.

Threat to the Heir: Genesis 22:1–19

Another incident that clearly follows the theme of promised blessing and threat is one of the most troubling in the entire Bible. It is the recounting of Abraham's near sacrifice of Isaac, Genesis 22:1–19. What a horrible threat this story seems to be. Could God actually have asked for a *human* sacrifice? Notably, there was human sacrifice in Canaanite religious practice, and in many other religious traditions surrounding the Israelites. That an ancient near eastern deity asks for human sacrifice would not have been unprecedented. It is possible that Abraham would have been sad, but not shocked, with this request so common in other religions all around him.

However, the author of Genesis represents this challenge as a "test" of human character (much in the same way Job's character is tested in the Book of Job). The climax of the incident is that God provides another sacrifice—the ram dies in place of Isaac—and thus saves the child. Child sacrifice is, in the story, finally not accepted. This is one of the lessons of the story: Hebrews do not sacrifice humans to their God. Some believe that the story is also about Abraham's trust that God would somehow provide a way through this test.

Christians can read the passage in yet another way. It is a profound anticipation of another "Father" who is anguished at the *human* demand that he "sacrifice a son" on the cross. God was faithful in affirming the promise—both at the mountain of Moriah in Genesis 22, and the mountain of Golgotha (see, for example, Mk 15:22). When God demanded sacrifice in Genesis 22, he provided an alternative to the loss of Abraham's son. When the crowds that had gathered before Jesus crying, "Crucify him!"—crowds that represent all human rejections of God's plan for our lives—we were not so generous.

There are several possible explanations for the contrast between blessings and threats in these incidents. Part of this interesting interplay is probably the inspired author's art. All good stories involve a twist to the plot—a danger that the hero must overcome—in order for the story to be dramatic. There is another more important message we must consider as we try to understand God's intentions. These stories of the patriarchs teach us to trust God as the giver of all blessings and to continue to trust him even when things seem difficult. A good story should surprise, upset, teach, and comfort. Genesis certainly does all of these and more.

Section in Review

Quick View

- Abraham's wanderings mirrored the travels of his Hebrew descendants.

- God established a covenant with Abraham and his descendants that extends to the Church today.

- God's promises to his people are never at risk.

For Review

1. **Main Idea**: Use the scale and map on page 68 to estimate the distances Abraham and his family traveled before they settled in Canaan.

2. **Main Idea**: What were the terms of the covenant God made with Abraham? What signs were given as evidence of the covenant?

3. **Main Idea**: How does the story of Hagar illustrate the "justice of God"?

4. **Critical Thinking**: What connections can be made between the stories about Abraham and Sarah and the stories of their Hebrew descendants?

5. **Critical Thinking**: What was the significance of the covenant for the Hebrew people? What does the covenant mean to the Church today?

For Reflection

Make a list of three blessings God has given you in your life. Then discuss the external and internal threats you have faced or are facing in connection with those blessings. What part of the stories of Abraham and Sarah helps to give you hope that God will overcome the threats you face?

God and Abraham

Write an essay on Abraham's relationship with God addressing each of these ideas: his call by God, his faith in God, and his friendship with God.

The life of the patriarch Jacob is characterized by trickery, reconciliation, and blessings.

The Blessing of Jacob

Isaac's role in the Book of Genesis is smaller than that of Abraham, Jacob, and Joseph. Isaac is a transitional character between the Abraham and Jacob stories.

Rebekah loves her younger son, Jacob, while Isaac seems to prefer his first-born, Esau. In order to secure Isaac's blessing on Jacob, Rebekah instructs him to deceive his father and take his older brother's place. Isaac is fooled, and Jacob gets his blessing, but then he must flee.

The familiar story of Genesis 27 begins the stories of Jacob, all of which involve one form of trickery or another. In a sense, then, the figure of Rebekah and the deception she introduces really set up the incidents involving Jacob.

Jacob and Laban: Trickery and Social Justice

Genesis 27–28 tells of Jacob's travels to the family of Laban, the brother of Rebekah. When Jacob meets Laban's daughter Rachel in Genesis 29, he promptly falls in love. Seeing an opportunity here (apparently living by clever strategy *was* common in Rebekah's family), Laban hires Jacob as a worker in order to help Jacob pay the bride price to marry Rachel. After seven years of labor as a Hebrew "slave" (remember the laws regarding the freeing of slaves in Exodus 21 and Deuteronomy 15), Laban allows Jacob to marry Rachel. But at the night-time wedding, his bride is covered with a wedding veil, and Jacob does not realize until the next morning the trick that Laban has played on him involving Rachel's older sister Leah:

> In the morning Jacob was amazed: it was Leah! So he cried out to Laban: "How could you do this to me! Was it not for Rachel that I served you? Why did you dupe me?" "It is not the custom in our country," Laban replied, "to marry off a younger daughter before an older one. Finish the bridal week for this one, and then I will give you

THE NAME "ISRAEL"

In the course of Jacob's struggle with a messenger of God in Genesis 32:22–32, Jacob is given a new name, as Abraham before him was given a new name.

When Jacob had subdued the messenger, the man asked him his name:

> He answered, "Jacob." Then the man said, "You shall no longer be spoken of as Jacob, but as Israel, because you have contended with divine and human beings and prevailed." (Gn 32:28–29)

The origins of *Israel* are related to the verb *sara* ("struggle") and the first syllable of *Elohim*, that is, "God."

the other too, in return for another seven years of service with me." (Gn 29:25–27)

But the trickery visited upon Jacob comes back to haunt Laban. After the second seven-year stint to earn again the price of marrying Rachel,[4] Jacob thought up a few tricks of his own. He agrees to yet another seven-year period of service to Laban, taking as his wages only the speckled, spotted, or streaked sheep and goats in Laban's flock at the end of that time (see Gn 30). Laban thinks that this is a terrific arrangement, and to further ensure his success in the deal, he immediately removes all but the solid-colored sheep and goats to prevent the imperfectly colored ones from breeding and reproducing more like themselves that would go to Jacob. But Jacob works some interesting "magic" in Genesis 30:37–40, showing striped sticks to the sheep as they mate and thus causing them to produce striped or speckled young. (Obviously modern readers aren't intended to press the science of this story too hard!)

At the end of the six years, Jacob's flock of "speckled" sheep and goats are huge, and he is a wealthy man. He has served Laban for fourteen years and is ready to return home, especially as Laban's sons are not pleased at the success Jacob has had in increasing his flocks from among their father's. Finally, when Jacob, Rachel, and Leah decide that it is time to make a quick getaway from the house of Laban, Rachel steals some valuables to add to the humiliation. When Laban confronts Jacob about his rapid departure and the theft, the speech that follows indicates that Jacob considered his own trickery to be justice for Laban's foul play (see Gn 31:38–42). Meanwhile, as readers, we are left to wonder whether or not we should admire or be embarrassed by the series of tricks and subtle plays in the stories of Rebekah, Jacob, Rachel, and Leah. Meanwhile, Jacob takes his large family of wives, children, and possessions and begins his return to Canaan.

Jacob's Return to Canaan

The next stories about Jacob concern his reconciliation with his own family. After leaving the land of Laban, Jacob must travel through the lands of Esau, and he is terribly afraid that his brother still harbors great anger at being betrayed when they were young men. He even has dreams of conflict in Genesis 32:22–32, an unusual story of Jacob's "wrestling with God" at Jabbok with a messenger of God who is in the form of a man.

To prepare for the meeting with Esau, Jacob sends gifts to his brother to appease his expected anger. In the end, however, Jacob's gifts are more than matched by Esau's forgiveness. Their reconciliation is one of the most striking examples of reconciliation and peacemaking in the Bible.

Read Genesis 33:4–9.

Jacob had stolen the blessing intended for the first-born, his brother Esau. When Jacob acknowledges his debt by sending gifts, Jacob finally says that he gives Esau a "blessing." Justice was done. Esau had cause to be angry, but Jacob repents and bows to his brother. Jacob's willingness to engage in the traditional forms of peacemaking leads to reconciliation with Esau, who lives in Seir. Jacob is able to remain in Canaan.

It could be argued that these stories represent the hope that Israel can at times live in peace with their neighbors, especially the Edomites, who are traditionally seen as descended from Esau. After all, Genesis 36:8 clearly states, "Esau is Edom." Edom was a nation across the Jordan River, and in the southern part of what is today the country of Jordan. The Edomites are often portrayed in the Bible as a people at war with Israel. In this case, Jacob is able to humble himself, ask for forgiveness, and even offer compensation for past injustices, all in the name of making peace. Part of the power of this story is to suggest that if Jacob and Esau can reconcile, even peace between nations is possible.

Section in Review

Quick View

- Much of Jacob's life is characterized by trickery.

- Despite the offense against his brother Esau, Jacob is able to reconcile with his brother, giving hope to future peace between the Israelites and their neighbors.

For Review

1. **Main Idea**: How did Rebekah and Isaac serve to introduce the more important figure of Jacob in Genesis 25:19ff. and Genesis 27?

2. **Critical Thinking**: What possible religious message is there in the stories of Rebekah's, Jacob's, and Laban's trickery?

For Reflection

- What are aspects of the relationships between the characters in these stories that remind you of your own family or families that you know? What lessons about family relationships can you draw from these stories?

- Put yourself in Esau's place. What is it that convinces you to be reconciled with your brother?

The Joseph narrative chronicles the story of the Hebrew people entering into eventual slavery in Egypt.

Joseph in Egypt: Foreshadowing the Exodus

Read Genesis 37–50.

The long narrative about Joseph introduces an entirely different kind of literature for the Book of Genesis. Instead of a series of short stories, Joseph is really an extended single story. It is impressive. Set in the great empire of Egypt, it rivals anything in the first five books of the Bible for sheer drama and character development.

Joseph is introduced as a dreamer and the preferred son of Jacob, being the oldest son of Jacob's beloved Rachel. Because Joseph is favored, his ten elder brothers (Leah's six sons and the four sons of Rachel's and Leah's handmaids) become resentful. Their resentment builds to such an extent that the brothers sell Joseph into slavery and deceive Jacob into believing him dead.

After he is taken to Egypt, Joseph sees his way through a series of serious challenges (again, the theme of threat) and becomes a trusted advisor to Pharaoh himself. In his capacity as advisor, the Old Testament narrative suggests that Joseph is himself responsible for Egypt's famous centralized economy dominated by the "god-king" that was Pharaoh. Eventually, Joseph is able to use his office to protect the lives of his family, who were in danger of starving in the famine conditions of Palestine.

There is a good deal of the Joseph narrative that is based on historical events and Egyptian culture.

Throughout most of ancient history—from about 3,000 BC through the Roman era at the time of Jesus—Egypt had a massive, centralized economy served by thousands of slaves and poor agricultural farmers. The massive architecture of Egypt, so impressive today to modern tourists, was built on the backs of massive amounts of human labor (often foreign slaves like the Canaanites and Hebrews) working to serve Pharaoh.

The administration of Egypt famously hoarded impressive amounts of wealth, collected on the basis of rich agricultural produce from the Nile River, and the widespread trade that Egypt engaged in with their agricultural surplus. Groups of people from the northern lands of Canaan would often take refuge in Egypt in times of severe famine, because the Nile River was considerably less susceptible to weather changes than the more fragile agricultural economy of Palestine.

Furthermore, there is little indication that there was much concern for the general wellbeing of the wider population, beyond the Pharaoh's religious responsibility to maintain good relations with the Egyptian gods, thereby "guaranteeing" the productivity of the land. It is hard to know whether the Joseph narrative is based on an ancient Hebrew admiration for the achievements of Egypt, or resentment of Egyptian dominance (and frequent interference) in the affairs of the Palestine economy. One question to consider is whether we are meant to admire Joseph's role in Egyptian dominance, or like Jacob's trickery, to question his judgment.

Finally, the Joseph stories set the stage for the main event of the Old Testament—the formation of the people of Israel by their Exodus experience and their efforts to carve out a life for themselves in Canaan. The Book of Genesis concludes with these words and a request made by Joseph to his brothers:

> "I am about to die. God will surely take care of you and lead you out of this land to the land that he promised on oath to Abraham, Isaac and Jacob." Then, putting the sons of Israel under oath, he continued, "When God thus takes care of you, you must bring my bones up with you from this place." (Gn 50:24–25)

These verses and words of Joseph lead the journey to the study of the Book of Exodus.

Parallels between JOSEPH and Other Biblical Stories

The stories of Joseph in Egypt—first at Potiphar's house, and eventually, working for Pharaoh himself—parallel a number of other stories in the Bible about Hebrew heroes who advise and work for world emperors.

For example, Daniel advises both Nebuchadnezzar and Darius the Persian; Nehemiah serves the Persian ruler Artaxerxes; Tobit once served the Assyrian monarch; and Mordecai and Esther also serve the Persian emperor. The parallel with Daniel is particularly strong, because Joseph, too, interprets dreams and is said to have impressive "wisdom and understanding." Both go through periods of trial (compare, for example, Daniel 2–3 with the story of false accusations made against Joseph and his imprisonment in Egypt in Genesis 39–40).

One of the lessons of all of these stories is that Hebrews not only can survive outside the land of Palestine but also can prosper. However, it's important not to forget the terrible tortures the Hebrews experienced: Joseph was unfairly imprisoned, Daniel was threatened by the mauling of lions, and Esther and Mordecai faced the mass murder of Jews in the Persian Empire. Life in the Diaspora had both dangers and rewards. It was often dangerous to maintain Faith in a "foreign land," but these heroes and heroines of Faith did precisely that.

Section in Review

Quick View

- The Joseph narrative is based on historical events connected with ancient Egypt.

- The Exodus is set in motion by the events in the Joseph stories.

For Review

1. **Main Idea**: How are the Genesis chapters about Joseph different from the preceding accounts of Abraham and Sarah, and of Jacob, Leah, and Rachel?

2. **Main Idea**: What historical evidence is there to support the Biblical story of Joseph?

3. **Critical Thinking**: Based on your reading of Genesis 37–50, is the Joseph narrative based on Hebrew admiration of Egypt or resentment of Egyptian dominance?

For Reflection

When Joseph reveals his identity to his brothers in Egypt, he attempts to reassure them that he does not intend to seek revenge on them. Read his explanation in Genesis 45:4–13. How is this moment of reconciliation different from Jacob's reconciliation with Esau?

GENESIS IN CONTEXT

The stories of the patriarchs Abraham, Isaac, and Jacob as well as the long narrative of Jacob's son, Joseph, are important because they were so relevant to the Jews who told and read them years later. For example, imagine how the Joseph stories (and also the Book of Daniel) provided hope and consolation to the Jews living as a minority in the Babylonian, Persian, Hellenistic, or Roman empires from 587 BC to the time of Christ.

Also, imagine how Jews living in exile would understand the famous tricks and deceitfulness of Jacob or the chicanery of the other characters in these stories— Rebekah and her daughters-in-law, Rachel and Leah. If the clever strategies of Jacob and the others were read in the context of being a Hebrew living in Babylon (Book of Daniel), Susa (Book of Esther), or Nineveh (Book of Tobit), then Jacob's behavior takes on a different meaning. In the context of oppressive political and social conditions of living as minorities in dominant empires, perhaps Jacob's strategies were taken as clever ploys of oppressed people who were trying to survive. Stories read in different settings sometimes sound very different indeed.

Further Reflections

In the beginning, God created the Heavens and the earth. God gave a beginning to all that exists. He alone is the Creator. All of creation depends on God who gives it being.

Creation reveals the common creative action of the Son and the Holy Spirit, inseparably one with the Father. The first creation story describes a "mighty wind" that swept over the created waters.

There is great mystery in God's creation, revealed in the creation stories of Genesis.

For example, he creates by wisdom and love. God did not need to create. Nor was the world created from blind chance or fate. Creation stems from God's free will—he wanted to share his wisdom, being, and goodness with his creation.

Also, God creates "out of nothing." God was able to make his light shine in the darkness (see Gn 1:3).

God creates an ordered and good world. Human beings are made in the "image of God" and called to enjoy a personal relationship with God.

> God created man in his image;
> in the divine image he created him;
> male and female he created them.

> (Gn 1:27)

God is infinitely greater than his works of creation. Yet, God is present to each part of his creation in the deepest and most intimate way. God never abandons his creation. Rather, he "at every moment, upholds and sustains them in being, enables them to act and brings them to their final end" (*CCC*, 301).

Though God created man in his image and friendship, man's freedom opened the door to the possibility of his turning from God and being mastered by sin. The eating of the forbidden fruit by Adam and Eve was the Original Sin of humanity.

Besides the stories of Creation, the Book of Genesis tells of the famous ancestors of the People of God, Israel, including Abraham and his wife Sarah. The Israelites will come together as a people based on their experience of the Exodus from Egypt. The story of Joseph in Egypt previews the Exodus experience.

Finally, God reveals himself in many ways. As all humans are ordered to God and destined to life in God, the Hebrews shared in the revelations of their God from their surrounding neighbors in the land of Canaan.

When the Hebrews return to Canaan after the Exodus from Egypt, a shared allegiance is maintained with Canaanites, though God's covenant with Israel will ultimately make them God's Chosen People.

Vocabulary Review

Directions: Fill in the blanks with one of the vocabulary words below. You will not use all the terms.

Ancestors Angel Circumcision Covenant Evolution Myths Paganism Patriarchs Story cycles

1. _____ was the sign of God's _____ with Abraham.

2. The most important _____ of the Hebrew people were Abraham, Isaac, Jacob, and Joseph who are known as the _____.

3. The creation accounts in the Book of Genesis are _____ (symbolic stories that express a spiritual truth), but the scientific theory of _____ does not prove these stories to be untrue.

4. Although Christians do believe in the spiritual and immortal creatures called _____, they do not worship them as idols or gods in any form of _____.

Directions: For each set of people explain how their stories illustrate God's promise to maintain a covenant with his people.

1. Adam and Eve
2. Abraham and Isaac
3. Jacob and Esau
4. Sarah and Hagar
5. Joseph and his brothers

Performance Assessment Project

The stories of the Book of Genesis were passed on through oral tradition for centuries. These stories helped the Hebrew people understand who God is and who they were as a people. Imagine that you are a storyteller passing on the stories of the Book of Genesis to a new generation of people. What message do each of the following stories express about God: the creation accounts, the flood story, the Tower of Babel, and the stories of Abraham, Jacob, and Joseph? What do these stories say about the identity of God's Chosen People? Provide a commentary on at least three stories with an explanation of how the story relates to your people's identity and the identity of God.

Called to Prayer

God created man in his image;

in the divine image he created him;

male and female he created them.

—Genesis 1:27

- **Reflection**: According to the New Testament, God is love. We, therefore, are both deserving of love and called to love. When are the times when you feel most in need of love? Who are the people in most need of your love today?

- **Meditation**: Imagine yourself meeting God face to face. He wants to tell you that as his creation, he loves you. How do you respond?

- **Resolution**: Consider how this truth about our creation affects the way we treat others. All people are created in God's image; therefore all people deserve our love and respect. Choose one person that you know needs to feel respected, and commit to doing something to help that person feel that way.

Notes

1. http://www.nationalgeographic.com/blacksea/ax/frame.html

2. Some modern Christians in parts of the Developing World still use "Babylon" to refer to powerful or oppressive governments (e.g. in Reggae music from Jamaica this is a common theme).

3. There is a great deal of speculation about the meaning of the actual words Abraham and Sarah. Does the extra syllable from "Abram" to "Abra-ham" derive from a word that refers to the sounds of many peoples, a multitude—thus the "sounds" of his many descendants? In any case, name changing was clearly a sign of submission to one who is more powerful (note how Nebuchadnezzar changes Mattaniah's name in 2 Kings 24:17).

4. Polygamy was still practiced in the time of the Patriarchs, though God's forming of an exclusive covenant with Israel prepared the Chosen People for the exclusiveness and indissolubility of married love (see *CCC*, 1609–1611).

CHAPTER OUTLINE

■ *The Book of Exodus tells the story of the Israelites' escape from slavery into a new covenant with God on Mount Sinai.*

■ *Despite Moses's weaknesses and failures, YHWH chooses him to lead his people out of slavery in Egypt.*

■ *The Israelites' escape from Egypt typifies God's saving work of the liberation of the oppressed.*

■ *The Israelites struggled to maintain faith in God after their liberation from Egypt.*

■ *The Ten Commandments are directives for how to live our lives.*

■ *The Biblical laws of the Old Testament focus on restorative justice and protection of the Israelite community.*

The Book of Exodus tells the story of the Israelites' escape from slavery into a new covenant with God on Mount Sinai.

Introduction

The Book of Exodus continues the story of Joseph and his brothers in Egypt where the Book of Genesis leaves off. As time passed, according to the introduction in Exodus, the positive accomplishments of Joseph were forgotten. When the Israelites "became so numerous and strong that the land was filled with them" (Ex 1:7) the Egyptian leaders were concerned about them siding with Egypt's enemies. This concern is given as the reason for the enslavement of the Hebrews.

As with the other books of the Torah, the stories of Exodus were collected and edited at the time of the Babylonian Exile, about seven hundred years after the events took place. The people exiled in Babylon would certainly have understood what it was like to be held in slavery and they would have been comforted and encouraged by stories that celebrated the liberation of slaves.

Exodus is just such a recounting of events, telling of the miraculous release of the Israelites from Egypt, their journey across the Red Sea to Mount Sinai where they entered into a special covenant with God. At Mount Sinai, through Moses, God gave the Israelites the Law—the moral, civil, and worship regulations that allowed them to become a holy people.

The Ten Commandments are at the heart of the Sinai Covenant. The *Catechism* teaches: "The 'ten words' sum up and proclaim God's law" (*CCC*, 2058). These are basic moral laws given by God to his people. The Book of Deuteronomy quotes Moses explaining the significance of the Ten Commandments:

> These words, and nothing more, the Lord spoke with a loud voice to your entire assembly on the mountain from the midst of the fire and the dense cloud. He wrote them upon two tablets of stone and gave them to me. (Dt 5:22)

The origins of the Ten Commandments and their meaning for people today will be covered in this chapter in the context of the Book of Exodus. The Book of

THE HYKSOS
FOREIGN RULERS IN EGYPT

The Joseph stories may have been situated in a brief period of foreign rule in Egypt that occurred between 1650 and 1500 BC. Egyptian records from that time do make reference to the rule of a people called the "Hyksos"—an Egyptian term for "foreigner." The **Hyksos** were probably not people of a distinct race, but most likely the rulers among the non-Egyptian population of the time. It would have been possible for a Hebrew like Joseph to rise to a high position among the Hyksos, and perhaps that explains the enslavement of the Hebrews. All those who served and benefited from the Hyksos rule may have been punished once the Egyptian rulers regained power.

Exodus follows a clear pattern. The major steps of the story are:

- The Call of Moses
- The Exodus: Confrontation Followed by Escape
- The Wandering of the People in the Wilderness
- The Reception of the Law at Mount Sinai
- The Approach to the Promised Land

Read Exodus 1.

The first chapter of Exodus is largely transitional material, bridging the gap from Joseph, the last major figure in the Book of Genesis to Moses, the central figure of the Book of Exodus.

Section in Review

Quick View

- Out of fear, the Egyptians enslaved the Hebrews and forgot the days of Joseph's assistance.
- Many connections can be made between the experience of slavery during the Babylonian Exile and the stories of Exodus.
- The Israelites made a special covenant with YHWH at Mount Sinai where he gave them the Ten Commandments and the Mosaic Law.

For Review

1. **Main Idea**: When were the stories of Exodus collected and edited into the form we have today? What connection was there between the stories of Exodus and the lives of the Jews at that time?

2. **Critical Thinking**: What connection might there have been between the imposition of slavery on the Hebrew people in Egypt and the period of "Hyksos" rule in Egypt between 1650 and 1500 BC?

3. **Critical Thinking**: Why are the Ten Commandments the centerpiece of the Sinai Covenant?

For Reflection

Ask your parents to tell you what they remember about your birth or your infant and toddler years. Try to find a story that seems indicative of the sort of person you are becoming, or that you want to be. Write the story, embellishing it a bit, if you like, until you think it tells something significant about you.

Despite Moses's weaknesses and failures, YHWH chooses him to lead his people out of slavery in Egypt.

The Call of Moses

Read Exodus 2:1–10.

Birth stories are rare in the Bible, but when they do occur they are usually a strong indication that the person born is going to be someone important. The Book of Genesis included stories about Isaac's birth, Jacob and Esau's, and Joseph's too. Their births were significant because of who they grew up to be.

Like people of other traditions, the Hebrews told birth stories of famous people—especially stories of previously barren women miraculously giving birth to great figures. Such storytelling was a way of honoring the memory of a famous person, much in the same way that traditions have arisen in the United States surrounding the youth of its founding fathers. For example, George Washington

Hyksos
A group of non-Egyptians who came to power in Egypt between 1650 and 1500 BC.

"never told a lie" and Abraham Lincoln "read book after book by firelight."

The Book of Exodus begins with the story of Moses's birth, the threat to his life from the edict of the Pharaoh, and his mother's attempts to protect him. The story of the infant Moses floating down the Nile River in a basket most likely had a long oral tradition. It is the only story that survives from his youth, but its existence in Scripture is enough to inform us that Moses's role will be an important one.

The Hebrew authors claim that Moses's name derived from the Hebrew verb *masha*—"to draw out" (Ex 2:10) though it is also strongly related to the names of Egyptian pharaohs "Thut<u>mosis</u>" or "Ah<u>mose</u>" meaning simply, "son of" or "progeny of." The special attention paid in Exodus 2:10 to the Hebrew root of the name Moses has great significance. This is the only point made in verse 10. It serves to establish Moses's Hebrew identity, despite his Egyptian upbringing, and refers both to his own being "drawn out" of the River Nile and to his efforts to draw the Hebrew People out of Egypt. At that point, the story abruptly ends, and an entirely different time in the life of Moses begins at Exodus 2:11.

Read Exodus 2:11–22.

With this next episode, Moses is an adult, confronting for the first time one of the main themes of the entire Mosaic tradition—the slavery of the Hebrew people. While there are doubts about the exact historical details of the Moses stories, the slave economy of Egypt is historically accurate, and is often referred to in Egyptian documents from that time. There are even ancient Egyptian writings that refer to the escape of slaves, although not in great numbers.

When Moses intervenes in two fights between Hebrew slaves and Egyptian slave masters, he immediately gets into trouble. In the first fight, Moses kills an Egyptian slave master to prevent him from beating a Hebrew slave. In the second, he is blamed by two Hebrews (who are fighting amongst themselves) for assuming that he has anything to teach them, and it becomes obvious that he has been recognized as the one who killed the Egyptian in the first fight. After these episodes, Moses

DOES GOD HAVE A NAME?

In Hebrew, after the tradition arose among the Jews that one should not speak YHWH, the holy name of God, the Jewish scribes came up with a little trick to remind readers not to pronounce it by accident—especially in *public* reading of the Scriptures.

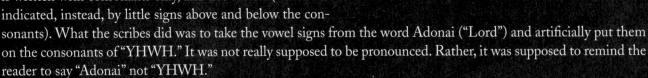

In order to understand this trick, remember that Hebrew is written with consonants only, and not vowels (which are indicated, instead, by little signs above and below the consonants). What the scribes did was to take the vowel signs from the word Adonai ("Lord") and artificially put them on the consonants of "YHWH." It was not really supposed to be pronounced. Rather, it was supposed to remind the reader to say "Adonai" not "YHWH."

At some point, the tradition was forgotten among Christians, and the word was misread, taking the consonants *and* the added vowels. This new word came out "Jehovah." This means that, contrary to what some Christians believe, "Jehovah" is not the "true" name of God. In fact, the opposite is true; it is a historically mistaken reading.

The traditional name for God is "YHWH" (usually pronounced "Yah-way," but even this is partly an assumed pronunciation). Parts of this name are heard in Hebrew personal names like "YAH-shua"=Joshua/Jesus, or "Jerem-e-YAH"=Jeremiah. Also Elohim is a name for God that was widely used, depending on the geographic region. Elohim was often thought to be more typical of northern Israel, and YHWH more common in southern Israel. Elohim appears in Hebrew names like "Mich-EL," "Dan-i-EL," and "Ari-EL."

lives for years among a desert-dwelling people called the Midianites, where he marries and learns to shepherd his father-in-law's flock. It is while he is living in the desert that he receives his amazing call to be the liberator of God's people.

This short introduction to Moses suggests that violence is not going to be the way of success for him. He will not defeat the Pharaoh in a great battle, nor free the slaves by force of arms. The inspired message of these early chapters of Exodus is that a power much greater than Moses's own human attempts is necessary to settle the issue of the Hebrews' slavery. God himself must liberate his people, though Moses will be the instrument he chooses to bring this about.

"I Am the One Who Is"

Read Exodus 2:23–3:23.

In Exodus 3, God calls Moses to his mission. Moses meets God in a fiery bush in the desert, a bush that at first attracts Moses's attention because it does not burn though it is engulfed in flames. In Exodus 3:14, God shares his name with Moses. It is a mysterious name, translated into English as "I am who I am"—but actually built on the basic Hebrew verb "is" from which the Biblical name "YHWH" derives. "It is a mysterious name because God is mysterious" (*CCC*, 206). Although Orthodox Jews do not pronounce this name (believing it to be so sacred that they must not speak it) Christians have never observed this practice, believing instead that what God has revealed is intended for our use and understanding. But that doesn't mean that there haven't been mistakes in what is to be understood (see "Does God Have A Name?" on page 84).

What is important in the Moses tradition is not necessarily the *name* of God, but rather *how* God is known and *what* God has done and will do: "God, who reveals himself as "I AM," reveals himself as the God who is always there, present to his people in order to save them" (*CCC*, 207).

Exodus 3:15–17 presents an interesting summary of who God is by mentioning the ancestors of Israel (Abraham, Isaac, and Jacob) as well as the events that will take place—liberation from Egypt and entry into the Promised Land. This is what is really important to the Hebrews. God is known by what he does, not by special names or words.

The Spanish film poster for The Ten Commandments. *The film starred Charlton Heston as Moses. The Spanish title is* Los Diez Mandamientos *and the poster shows Moses with the tablets in front of Pharaoh.*

Interestingly, even the name of Jesus communicates this fact. The name "Jesus" literally means "YHWH Saves." Even the name of the Messiah communicates that God is known by what he *does*, not primarily by what he is *called*.

Who Does God Call?

The movies love to portray great and mighty heroes. Consider the impressive figure of actor Charlton Heston playing Moses in the great film classic, *The Ten Commandments*. Even for children, Moses is portrayed as powerful and mighty, as in the animated film, *The Prince of Egypt*. How accurate are these portrayals of Moses?

In fact, Exodus 3 and 4 present a very reluctant hero. Moses has four objections to being chosen. First, he wonders, "who am I" to go about rescuing an enslaved people? (Ex 3:11). When God reassures him that it will be God, not Moses, doing the rescuing, Moses asks, essentially, "who are you?" (Ex 3:13). After hearing God's answer to this, Moses worries that the Israelites will not believe him, so God gives him a staff and shows him miracles that Moses can perform to convince the Israelites that God is with him (Ex 4:1–9). When Moses continues his objections, saying that he is not a good speaker, God promises to tell him everything he needs to say. At this point, Moses is running out of objections so he simply begs God to "send someone else!" (Ex 4:13). To this point, though it seems like we do not have a flattering portrait of Moses, actually we are learning much about the power of God and the value of prayer, that is, "the requesting of good things from God" (St. John Damascene as quoted in *CCC*, 2559). The *Catechism* points out:

> But in the dialogue in which God confides in him, Moses also learns how to pray: he balks, makes excuses, above all questions: and it is in response to his question that the Lord confides his ineffable name, which will be revealed through his mighty deeds. (*CCC*, 2575)

What else can we learn from this? Who does God call? The brave and the mighty? The great generals or the powerful leaders? No. God calls the simple and timid, the questioning and the doubtful, and often the weak and the few. God calling a man like Moses reminds us of Jesus calling men like Peter and Thomas despite their weakness and doubt. Moses is the classic "anti-hero" in the sense that he does not exhibit many qualities associated with human greatness. Yet, he is the hero of the Old Testament!

God, it seems, does not need the mighty—only the willing. Moses finally goes, clutching a staff in his hand as a reminder that he does not go alone. The story of God's people continues in a powerful and dramatic way.

Section in Review

Quick View

- Moses's name and the incidents surrounding his birth are significant clues to his importance in Scripture.

- God is known more by what he does than what he is called (i.e., YHWH, Adonai, Jehovah, Lord).

- Despite his weaknesses, God lifts up Moses as the hero of the Old Testament.

For Review

1. **Main Idea**: Why did the original editors of the Book of Exodus include the story about Moses's birth and adoption by one of Pharaoh's daughters?

2. **Main Idea**: Why do the Hebrew authors have Pharaoh's daughter give Moses a Hebrew name? What is the Hebrew meaning of the name "Moses?"

3. **Main Idea**: What four objections did Moses have to being sent to Egypt to free the Israelites from slavery?

4. **Critical Thinking**: Compare Moses, the reluctant hero of the Old Testament, to modern heroes today. How is God's hero different from the heroes you see in movies?

For Reflection

Have you ever been asked to do something that you weren't sure you could do, even though the person asking thought you could? How did you feel about being asked? How did you respond?

The Israelites' escape from Egypt typifies God's saving work of the liberation of the oppressed.

The Exodus: Confrontation Followed by Escape

Read Exodus 5–11.

There are many interesting elements to the great story of God's conflict with Pharaoh, and the horrific events that lead up to the final release of the Hebrews from Egyptian bondage. There are also a number of interesting understandings about how these stories (which include the ten plagues) are to be read.

One common understanding of the ten plagues is that each is directed against a specific Egyptian god. But trying to match up all the plagues with known deities and their images presents problems. Consider the following:

Plague	Egyptian God
1. Nile turned to blood	Khnum or Hapi (god of water or the River Nile)
2. Frogs	Heket (goddess of childbirth portrayed as frog)
3. Lice/gnats	?
4. Flies	?
5. Pestilence	Hathor (god portrayed as a bull)
6. Boils	?
7. Hail	Seth (god of wind and storms)
8. Locusts	Min (goddess of fertility and vegetation)
9. Darkness	Amon-Re (Sun god)
10. Death of Firstborn	Osiris (god of judgment or death)

Not only does this theory fail to account for the three plagues that *cannot* be associated with any known gods, but some of the gods are associated to the plague by their image (i.e., Heket and Hathor), others by the area over which they were understood to have influence (i.e., Seth, Min, Amon-Re, and Osiris), and some of these gods were never "worshipped" by the Egyptians at all (i.e., Khnum or Hapi). The idea that each plague was directed against a specific Egyptian deity is a clever argument, but ultimately must be set aside as contrary to what we know both of Biblical texts and Egyptian history and culture. In fact, the Biblical portrayal presents these plagues as directed against Pharaoh himself. He was, after all, considered a divine figure in Egypt whose responsibilities included the well being of Egypt itself.

Similar questions must be raised about another popular theory that these plagues were actually naturally occurring circumstances. Perhaps, for example, red algae of some kind turned the Nile red and made the water undrinkable (the first plague). Perhaps excessive flooding of the Nile River Valley left pools of standing water for mosquitoes (the third plague). Perhaps there was an outbreak of anthrax among the livestock of Egypt, infecting cattle and even making the people sick (the fifth and tenth plagues). Hail and storms and locusts are obviously both naturally occurring phenomenon (the seventh and eighth plagues). And so on.

Such an explanation starts out to prove that the story of the Israelite's escape from the Pharaoh is possible, that it can be believed because the plagues can be explained rationally. But others take that explanation one step further and argue that if the plagues are not miraculous at all, if they are merely "natural events," then Moses, Pharaoh, and all the people were entirely fooled into thinking that some "God" was behind these merely freakish events of nature. In truth no matter what way the story is examined, God was the initiator of these events. It was in the Exodus that "God formed Israel as his people by freeing them from slavery in Egypt" (*CCC*, 61).

The first nine plagues follow an arrangement of three sets of plagues, which are indicated by the special way that each set is introduced. Each set includes three different plagues:

Set A (plagues 1, 4, and 7)
- Introduced with a phrase instructing Moses to go to the pharaoh in the morning.

Set B (plagues 2, 5, and 8)
- Introduced with the phrase: "The Lord said to Moses, 'Go to Pharaoh. . . .'"

Set C (plagues 3, 6, and 9)
- Introduced by instruction from God to Moses or Aaron to perform an act.

Plague	Introductory Phrase	Set
Nile turned to blood	Exodus 7:15	A
Frogs	Exodus 8:1	B
Gnats	Exodus 8:12	C
Flies	Exodus 8:20	A
Pestilence (cattle dying)	Exodus 9:1	B
Boils	Exodus 9:8	C
Hail	Exodus 9:13	A
Locusts	Exodus 10:1	B
Darkness	Exodus 10:21	C

Pestilence, one of the seven plagues of Egypt.

The arrangement of the plagues into three sets by introductory phrases was an interesting literary technique. The purpose of the stories of the plagues is not to show God's power over Pharaoh or even that he can work miracles, but that God's will is for liberation of slaves and the creation of a people out of the enslaved and oppressed. What is important is that God revealed his will to the Israelites and they understood their history as a people in light of that revelation. These stories teach us about God and the formation of his people, the Israelites. They teach that God chooses slaves—that God liberates the oppressed. They teach that earthly powers, such as Pharaoh, cannot maintain oppression when God wills liberation. They also teach that with liberation comes responsibility.

The Release from Egypt

It appears most likely that, once again, two different oral traditions have been woven together in the Book of Exodus to tell the story of how the Israelites left Egypt. At the conclusion of the nine plagues in Exodus 10:28, Pharaoh and Moses have the following exchange:

> "Leave my presence," Pharaoh said to him, "and see to it that you do not appear before me again! The day you appear before me you shall die!" Moses replied, "Well said! I will never appear before you again."

But look at the words of the Lord to Moses that begin chapter 11:

> Then the Lord told Moses, "One more plague will I bring upon Pharaoh and upon Egypt. After that he will let you depart. In fact, he will not merely let you go; he will drive you away." (Ex 11:1)

Exodus 10 ended with Moses saying that the Israelites were leaving; yet Exodus 11 opens with God calling for another plague. A discriminating reader will wonder why.

The usual answer is that the end of Exodus 10 and the beginning of Exodus 11 is a rather awkward transition between *two originally different traditions about how the people of Israel left Egypt*. Chapters 7 to 10 of Exodus represent the "nine plagues" tradition and chapter 11 is the story of the Israelites leaving Egypt following the first

Passover. By weaving in the beginning of the Passover tradition at the end of Exodus 10, it becomes the "tenth" plague. But, perhaps it was once an entirely unique story about how the people left Egypt after one horrendous event—the death of the firstborn of Egypt.

Furthermore, by adding the Passover tradition to the tradition of the nine plagues, the text obscures a connection that would otherwise be more obvious—that the "Passover" event is directly related to the *beginning* of the story of Moses. Without the intervening chapters that relate the nine plagues, it is possible to connect the killing of the first-born Egyptian children (Ex 12:29–30) to the edict of the Egyptian pharaoh to kill the Hebrew boys at the time of Moses's birth (Ex 1:15–16). Rather than being merely horrendous or even cruel, the Passover event can be understood as punishment on the Egyptian people for the Pharaoh's original decree. Violence leads to violence.

The two traditions of the release of the Hebrews from Egypt may blur an exact understanding of how the Exodus actually took place in history.[1] But there was a distinct religious purpose to editing these materials together to form the story as it is now included in the Old Testament, mainly that God keeps his promises to his people and God is a God of liberation and not enslavement.

Another important teaching to keep in mind is that as Jews celebrate Passover today,[2] they commemorate the saving actions of God and give thanks for them. The "Exodus events are made present to the memory of believers so that they may conform their lives to them" (*CCC*, 1363). In the Church's liturgy, the memorial takes on a new, deeper meaning and the saving events actually become present: "When the Church celebrates the Eucharist, she commemorates Christ's Passover, and it is made present: the sacrifice Christ offered once for all on the cross remains ever present" (*CCC*, 1364).

Section in Review

Quick View

- The stories of the ten plagues in the Old Testament help us to understand God's intentions to bring liberation to the oppressed.

- Two different oral traditions seemed to have developed around the Israelites' escape from Egypt.

- While the Jewish Passover commemorates God's saving actions, the Eucharist actually makes present God's saving work on the Cross.

For Review

1. **Main Idea**: Why is the explanation of the plagues as evidence of God's superiority over the gods of the Egyptians insufficient?

2. **Main Idea**: What is the religious message that is conveyed through the story of Moses's confrontation with Pharaoh and the Israelites' release from Egypt?

3. **Main Idea**: Explain the origin of the celebration of Passover as it is described in Exodus 12.

For Reflection

- What does it mean that "God is a God of liberation and not enslavement?" How is sin a form of slavery? How can God help you to get free from sin?

 Passover Today

Write a script outlining the significant elements of a Passover celebration today. Include:

- Food and table preparation. Write a grocery list of foods for the meal and directions for food preparation and table setting.

- Write and answer the four questions asked of younger children at the Seder Meal.

- Retell the story of the Exodus in your own words.

The Israelites struggled to maintain faith in God after their liberation from Egypt.

The Wandering of the People in the Wilderness

Read Exodus 15–18.

After a canticle sung by Moses and the Israelites celebrating God's saving power (Ex 15:1–17), Exodus continues with another story cycle containing traditional stories about the life of the Israelites during the time they were wandering in the wilderness (Ex 15–18). Sometimes these episodes are referred to as **"murmurings,"** as they are primarily a series of complaints from the people against the leadership of Moses, and eventually, against God himself.

These chapters depict an unruly and restive people who have left Egypt, unsure of their future. They complain about food (Ex 16:1–4) and water (Ex 17:1–3), and they face serious dangers from desert peoples who are considerably less than hospitable (Ex 17:8–16). Finally, Moses's father-in-law Jethro suggests that Moses select some helpers from among the people to assist in organizing the group (Ex 18). This story provides a plausible explanation of the leadership of **elders** among the Hebrews, although this is not a particularly unusual social system for agrarian societies.

How many people wandered in the wilderness with Moses? The traditional number, 600,000 (Ex 12:37), seems unacceptably high. Not only is this number quite likely larger than the entire population of whole sections of Palestine, it

"murmurings"
The stories in the Book of Exodus of the complaints of the Israelites in the desert against Moses and against God.

elders
Mature, usually male, members of the Israelite community who met regularly to rule on specific disputes within the community.

Book of Numbers:
Organizing a People

The Book of Numbers also tells the story of the Israelites' journey, beginning with the Exodus, and continuing for thirty-eight years from their time at Mount Sinai to their arrival at the border of Canaan, the Promised Land.

Numbers gets its name from two censuses of the Hebrew people, one taken at the beginning of their desert journey (Nm 1) and the other near the end (Nm 26). The "numbers" of the Hebrews reported in each of the censuses may be exaggerated and interpreted in the same way as the numbers of people in the Exodus were. The book does explain the social organization of Israel into twelve tribes.

Two common themes from the Book of Exodus are also prevalent in the Book of Numbers. The first is YHWH's care for the Israelites. He leads them by day with a cloud and by night with fire. He provides food, water, and protection for their needs. The second theme involves Israel's "murmurings." As in Exodus, the people complain both about Moses and YHWH himself.

Relocation

Imagine you *have* to move immediately from your home and relocate to a land a great distance away. You are given only one wooden crate that you may fill with ten personal treasures: possessions, heirlooms, symbols of your life that will remind you of yours and your family's past. Write the ten things you will take with you.

How many of the ten items involved a memory of a time when you or your family reached out to others? Explain.

would represent a massive number of people trying to survive in the Sinai deserts. Pointing out that the Hebrew term usually translated "thousands," can also be translated "family group "or" village group typically solves the problem. So, if there were six hundred "family groups" that left Egypt, a more reasonable number would be no more than 6,000 (and perhaps much less)—certainly not over half a million people! We should also keep in mind that the Bible mentions that some Egyptians and possibly other

Greatness does not come on flowery beds of ease to any people. We must fight to win the prize. No people to whom liberty is given, can hold it as firmly and wear it as grandly as those who wrench liberty from the iron hand of the tyrant. The hardships and dangers involved in the struggle give strength and toughness to the character, and enable it to stand firm in storm as well as in sunshine.

—Frederick Douglass

Research and report on one or more of the following:

- ways in which former African American slaves identified with the Israelites in their quest for freedom;

- how Christianity was introduced to slaves and former slaves;

- how abolitionist texts relied on the Bible to support an end to slavery.

foreigners left with the Hebrews (Ex 12:38). So it was a group of mixed ancestry long before Israel was formed as a nation in the Promised Land.

Section in Review

Quick View

- Despite God's saving work, the Israelites often complained and doubted his ability to provide for them in the wilderness.

- Although a large number of Israelites escaped from Egypt, the estimated 600,000 people may be unacceptably high.

For Review

1. **Main Idea**: What are the two prominent themes of the stories of the Israelites' time spent in the wilderness?

2. **Main Idea**: How might the number of people who escaped Egypt actually be less than the 600,000 cited in the Book of Exodus?

3. **Critical Thinking**: Read Frederick Douglass's quote to the left. How does this point of view relate to the experience of the Israelites after their liberation?

For Reflection

Think about how the two themes of the wilderness stories are present in your relationship with God. What needs of yours has God met throughout your life? When have you "murmured," or doubted God's care, or the care of those whom God put in your life to care for you?

The Ten Commandments are directives for how to live our lives.

The Reception of the Law at Mount Sinai

The release of the Israelites from Egypt leads ultimately to their gathering at the foot of Mount Sinai and their reception of the "Law": the religious, civil, and ritual statute from God by which they were to become a holy people. In fact, it is only when the Israelites make an agreement with God at Mount Sinai that they fully become a people in whom the promise

Postcard with an image painted by Rubens showing Moses with the tablets containing the 10 Commandments, on the summit of Mount Sinai.

of a Savior for humankind would be fulfilled. Their liberation was only part of the agreement—learning and keeping their responsibilities as required by the Law was the other part. It is the Ten

Commandments that summarize the obligations of all who love God.

This agreement between God and the Chosen People is often referred to as the "Sinai Covenant." With the covenant comes the Law of Moses, often called "The Torah." The Law given to Moses is an expression of what man knows in his own soul to be right or wrong, the **natural law**. The basic principles of natural law extend to the entire human race. Natural law corresponds to three basic human drives and needs: (1) preserving life; (2) developing as individuals and communities; and (3) sharing life with others. The Ten Commandments provide the principal commandments of the natural law.

Hebrew Understanding of Covenant

Recall again that a covenant is an agreement between God and people. At Mount Sinai the most important covenant of the Old Testament is established. Essentially, it is a two-way agreement, with obligations for *both* parties involved. God agrees to be the God of this people—"I, the Lord, am your God" (Ex 20:2)—but this is immediately followed by the "stipulations" of the agreement for the people—the Ten Commandments. Note that these Commandments are made special in the Book of Exodus because *all* the people heard God speak these Commandments, whereas only Moses heard the remainder of the laws after Exodus 20:18, and then passed them on to the people.

In order to understand the central essence of Hebrew religion, we must understand that the basic covenant between God and the people obligates the people to obedience to the Law. Therefore, the very center of the relationship between God and the people in the Hebrew tradition is not focused on what the people *think about God*. Rather, it is concerned with *how they live their life*. Understanding that obedience to the Law is of primary importance to the Israelites helps us to understand the *entire* Old Testament, especially in the tradition of the Prophets (see Chapter 7, pages 147–166).

The Ten Commandments

If anyone knows anything about ancient Biblical law, it is usually that the Ten Commandments are the centerpiece. They are reproduced in two of the law collections, in Exodus 20 and again in Deuteronomy 5. A summary of the laws as listed in the Old Testament follows:

1. Israelites are to worship no other god but YHWH.
2. Israelites are to fashion no image (idol) to represent God.
3. Israelites are not to use the name of God in any oaths, or in magical rites or incantations, as if they can control the power of God. (Swearing is more than merely using "bad" language.)
4. Israelites are to observe and honor the Sabbath (Friday night, through Saturday until sundown) as a rest from work.
5. Israelites are to honor their parents.
6. Murder is forbidden.
7. Adultery is forbidden.
8. Stealing another person's property is forbidden.
9. Falsely accusing another Israelite of a crime is forbidden.
10. Acting on desires for a neighbors' position or possessions is forbidden.

Because these Ten Commandments were spoken directly to the Israelite people, the tradition arose late in Hebrew history, and into the period of Christianity, that these ten laws were central laws of the Old Testament. Jesus, himself, acknowledged them: "If you wish to enter into life, keep the commandments" (Mt 19:17). Since the time of St. Augustine in the fourth century, the Ten Commandments have been a source for teaching baptismal candidates. As such, "the tradition of the Church has acknowledged the primordial importance and significance" of the Ten Commandments (*CCC*, 2064).

The Ten Commandments state clearly what is required in the law of love of God and neighbor and Christians in every generation are obliged to keep them. The next subsections explain more about what that obligation entails for Christians for each Commandment.

I. I, the Lord am your God: you shall not have other gods besides me.

To *worship* God means we accept God as our Creator and ourselves as made in his image. To understand what it is to worship, think of some sins against the First Commandment: idolatry (false worship of many gods), atheism (denial of God's existence), and agnosticism (saying no one knows for sure whether God exists). Oppositely, the First Commandment asks us to practice the virtues of faith, hope, and love. Practicing our religion also helps us to keep the First Commandment.

II. You shall not take the name of the Lord, your God, in vain.

We must respect God's name and never use the name of God, Jesus, Mary, or the saints in an improper way. This means that when we take an oath or make a promise in God's name, we must be true to it. We should also respect our own name and strive for holiness. God made us and knew us from the beginning of time. Our name will be with us into eternity. This Commandment forbids *blasphemy*, a sin that involves hateful words against God, Jesus, or even the Church. Cursing is also a violation against this Commandment.

III. Remember to keep holy the Sabbath day.

The Sabbath was set aside by God, to remind us of the time at creation when God rested on the seventh day. It is a day intended for people to rest from their work and to praise God for his works of Salvation.

Sunday, the day of Christ's Resurrection, replaces the Sabbath for Christians. Sunday is linked with the Paschal Mystery, the Passion, Death, Resurrection, and Ascension of Jesus, commemorated in the Eucharist. Catholics are required by Church law to participate in Sunday Mass or its Saturday vigil. To deliberately miss Sunday Mass is mortally sinful. We also make Sunday holy by spending time with our families, visiting our other relatives, helping the poor, or doing other charitable acts.

IV. Honor your father and your mother.

The Fourth Commandment begins the second part of the Ten Commandments, which has to do with love for neighbor. This is appropriate, for love truly begins at home. How can you be loving to your friends and teachers at school, when you lambasted your mom or were rude to a sibling on the ride to school? You owe your parents (and other family members) respect and obedience for as long as you live at home. When you are older, you still must respect your parents and care for them when they are old, ill, or lonely. Teachers, civil authorities, religious leaders and other adults are also owed your respect according to this Commandment.

V. You shall not kill.

All human life is of immense value. This statement applies to human life from the first moment of conception until natural death. For this reason, this Commandment forbids abortion (the killing of an unborn baby) and euthanasia (mercy killing of the aged or sick).

There are times when killing is morally permissible, for example, in self-defense or when protecting the life of another. Killing in war may be morally permissible if a nation is defending itself against aggressors. Also, the traditional teaching of the Church does not exclude the use of the death penalty, if this is the only way to defend innocent lives against an unjust killer. However, the Church continues to teach that today there are very few, if any, situations in which execution of a person is necessary. Held in a secure prison, the offending person is kept away from society and has the chance to seek Redemption and conversion.

This Commandment also asks us not to "kill" our own bodies, and requires us to live healthy lives of exercise, wholesome eating, rest, and to avoid harmful addictions like alcohol and drugs.

VI. You shall not commit adultery.

The Sixth Commandment encompasses the whole of human sexuality. In the Old Testament, the offense of this Commandment primarily involved a husband having sexual intercourse with a married woman other than his wife. Jesus took the command further saying that "everyone who looks at a woman with lust" (Mt 5:28) has already committed adultery.

For people of any age or state in life, keeping this Commandment involves practicing the virtue of chastity. Chastity involves a self-mastery over one's sexuality, rejects lust (inordinate enjoyment of sexual pleasure), masturbation (deliberate stimulation of genital organs to derive sexual pleasure), fornication (sex between unmarried persons), pornography (displaying sexual acts for a third party to see), prostitution (selling of sexual acts), rape (forcing another into sexual intimacy), and homosexual acts (sexual activity between persons of the same gender).

Rather, this Commandment teaches us that sexual love must only be shared in the intimacy of a loving marriage, where sexual intercourse strengthens the unity of the marriage and is ordered to procreation, though not all conjugal acts result in procreation.

VII. You shall not steal.

The Seventh Commandment forbids *theft*, which is the taking of another's property against his or her will. This is a matter of justice, as we must respect the property rights of others.

Stealing, however, is more encompassing than just the unlawful taking of someone else's things. Stealing also includes cheating (e.g., on taxes or on a test), doing shoddy work on the job, and vandalism.

VIII. You shall not bear false witness against your neighbor.

We are to be truthful in our words and actions. Any misrepresentation of the truth is a violation of this Commandment. This would include deliberately withholding information in order to prevent someone from knowing the truth and also sins called *detraction* (telling a person's faults for no good reason) and *calumny* (making a false statement which harms the reputation of another).

IX. You shall not covet your neighbor's wife.

The word *covet* means to "desire something that is not one's own." In this case, like the Sixth Commandment, it is directly referring to the covenant of marriage.

Jesus restored God's original intent that marriage be indissoluble by forbidding divorce. Other sins against marriage are polygamy (having more than one spouse), incest (having sexual relations with relatives), sexual abuse of children, and living together before marriage.

X. You shall not covet your neighbor's goods.

Similar to the Seventh Commandment, the Tenth Commandment is opposed to greed, envy, and avarice (the seeking of riches and the power that comes with them).

The Tenth Commandment makes it clear that we desire things that give us pleasure. These desires are morally permissible as long as they do not lead us to crave things that belong to others.

Section in Review

Quick View

- There is an expression of natural law contained in the Law of Moses.

- The Old Covenant can be summarized as God promising to be Israel's God and the Israelites promising to follow the Ten Commandments.

- The Ten Commandments are the central laws of the Old Testament and essential to understanding the faith.

For Review

1. **Main Idea**: Why are the Ten Commandments made special in the Book of Exodus?

2. **Main Idea**: What did Jesus say to acknowledge the Ten Commandments?

3. **Critical Thinking**: Paraphrase each of the Ten Commandments in ways that express their meaning to you.

For Reflection

In your own words, explain what is required by each of the Ten Commandments.

The Biblical laws of the Old Testament focus on restorative justice and protection of the Israelite community.

Three Collections of the Law

In studying the Law in a Scripture course, it is also important to examine the Law from the perspective of those who first heard it, the people of Israel. For centuries, it has been noted that there are differences between the two "versions" of the Law of Moses that most resemble one another—namely the laws in the Book of Exodus and the laws in the Book of Deuteronomy. For example, although the Ten Commandments occur in both Exodus 20:1–17 and Deuteronomy 5:6–21, they are not identical in the two books. Although the laws themselves are almost the same, the reasons given for some of these laws differ. Finally, a third source of laws from the Book of Leviticus represents quite a different collection of laws altogether. So, it is generally held that there are *three different collections* of the Law in the "books of Moses." They are:

1. The Covenant Code (contained in Exodus 20–23)

2. The Deuteronomic Code (contained Deuteronomy 5–28)

3. The Levitical ("Priestly") Code (contained in the Book of Leviticus)

All three of these collections or codes contain **civil laws** (dealing with day to day issues of living in an agricultural society) and **religious laws** (especially Leviticus). A survey of these laws provides further insight into what was valued in the early life of Israel: family integrity, property, and animals.

Also note that the emphasis of Biblical laws is not on guilt and punishment, but on restoration of the community and the maintenance of social life. There is no mention of law enforcement (police) or prisons. In a small-scale agricultural society such as early Israel, laws and traditions were maintained by everybody together, but especially by the elders of the villages and towns. The elders met on a regular basis to determine specific cases based on traditional laws and values. When compensation was involved, it was not **punitive justice**, but rather **restorative justice** as much as possible. The idea was to

SACRAMENT OF RECONCILIATION

A Sacrament that brings a restoration of relationship between a sinner, God, and the Church is the Sacrament of Penance and Reconciliation.

The Sacrament is called "Reconciliation" because it offers to the sinner the love of God who reconciles. "Reconciliation with God is thus the purpose and effect of this sacrament" (*CCC*, 1468). The person who is reconciled to God is likewise ready to be reconciled with his or her neighbor. Jesus said:

> Therefore, if you bring your gift to the altar, and there recall that your brother has anything against you, leave your gift there at the altar, go first and be reconciled with your brother, and then come and offer your gift. (Mt 5:24)

restore the life of the community as much as possible, because these people had to continue to live together after each case was settled. It was partly the pressure of *personal honor* and the shame of violating themselves and their families that kept the Israelite society functioning.

The practice of laws in ancient agrarian Israel seems dramatically different from the way law functions in modern urban life. Today we hardly know our immediate neighbors much less the entire town or city. In our legal system, "restoring community" is not considered as important as punishing the guilty. The punishment is intended to be a deterrent for those who might break the law in the future. Also, the person who "wins" a case in a modern court will probably never see the other party again. Hardly a thought is given to what will happen to either party after a legal decision is rendered. In ancient Israel this was not the case, so law had to restore honor and society. Two parties facing off in a legal case would most likely continue to be involved with one another the rest of their lives. Hopefully you can begin to understand how it is different for ancient Hebrews and modern Christians to follow the Law of Moses.

Catholics today are not obliged to follow too many of the specific laws (e.g., laws regarding clean and unclean food) of the three collections in Exodus, Deuteronomy, or Leviticus. It is the Ten Commandments that contain a "privileged expression of the natural law" (*CCC*, 2070). We can and do capture the spirit of justice expressed in the Mosaic Law—especially as that spirit is strengthened with the coming of Jesus Christ and the preaching of the Gospel. For example, it is precisely the spirit of *justice* and *community* in the Mosaic Law that is embraced by Jesus in the Beatitudes preached in the Sermon on the Mount (see Mt 5:3–12). One way of speaking of the Sermon on the Mount is to see it as an expression of the "New Law" of the Gospel. It fulfills the Law of Moses, focusing on bettering relationships in the community, especially with the poor. The *Catechism of the Catholic Church* explains:

> The Lord's Sermon on the Mount, far from abolishing or devaluing the moral prescriptions of the Old Law, releases their hidden potential and has new demands arise from them: it reveals their entire divine and human truth. It does not add new external precepts, but proceeds to reform the heart, the root of human acts, where man chooses between the pure and the impure, where faith, hope, and charity are formed and with them the other virtues. (*CCC*, 1968)

Comparing the Collections of Laws

An interesting way to compare the Covenant Code, considered to be much older, with the Deuteronomic Code is to contrast the two versions of the same legal issue. Consider, for example, the issue of what the Hebrews most frequently called *slavery* but which was actually *indentured servitude*.[3]

The point is not to debate the issue of slavery per se. We know that the slaveholders of pre–Civil War America tried to justify slavery on the basis of the Bible. (Of course, they hoped that people would

civil laws
Laws dealing with the day-to-day issues that arise between people living, in the case of the Israelites, in an agrarian community such as the consequences when one person's animal injures another person, or when borders between properties are disputed.

religious laws
Laws that govern the actions of the priests, the regulations for sacrifice, and the building and maintenance of the Temple.

punitive justice
Laws that rely on punishment as a deterrent to criminal activity.

restorative justice
Laws that are concerned primarily with restoring community after an offense has occurred. The goal is to keep the community together, as the survival of the society depends on everyone fulfilling his or her role.

- In the Covenant Code, read Exodus 21:1–11. Compare this to passages from Deuteronomic Code (Dt 15:12–18; 23:16–17) on the same subject.
- Read and compare the Deuteronomy passages (10:11–18, 24:19–21, and 27:19) with those of the prophets (Is 1:17, Jer 7:6–7, Jer 22:3, Ez 22:7, Zec 7:10, and Mal 3:5) on the subject or widows and orphans. How are they alike? How are they different?

Jubilee

Every seventh sabbatical year (i.e., every forty-ninth year). In a year of Jubilee all debts were to be forgiven, and land that had been sold to pay a debt was to be returned to the original family. In this way, the wealth of the entire community was to be redistributed among the poor, preventing unrelieved poverty and large gaps between the rich and the poor.

not read too carefully, because what the Bible calls "slavery" is clearly not the same thing that African Americans sadly suffered in American history.) But there is more to be seen in these two laws, from different time periods, on the subject of indentured servitude. What do we notice in our comparison between the two? It is often suggested that Deuteronomy represents further moral development from the older Covenant Code, a humanizing of the laws of slavery.

Whether or not the Covenant Code is older than Deuteronomy, there is clearly a difference in the approach. Deuteronomy seems to reflect the time of the prophets (see Dt 24) during which interests in social justice were prevalent. Even the language of Deuteronomy seems similar to the language of the prophets. For example, Deuteronomy's famous interest in the poor and weak of society—especially the widow, the orphan, and often including the foreigner or stranger—illustrates this point.

The most unusual law code of the three, of course, is the Levitical Code. This code covers mainly priestly laws and traditions—for example, what the priests should wear, what the high priest is to do, how the tabernacle is to be built and maintained, and how sacrifices are to be classified and performed. The Book of Leviticus also includes laws dealing with concerns about purity and maintaining a sense of "being clean" that applied to the entire community. Purity laws are very interesting, although they may seem, again, a bit unusual for those outside the modern traditions that still practice forms of purity laws (Orthodox and Conservative Judaism and Islam practices forms of purity laws, but most forms of Christianity do not). Highlighted below are three areas of laws from the Levitical Code that are of most interest to modern Christians: laws of sacrifice, purity, and **Jubilee**.

Laws of Sacrifice: *Leviticus 1–6:7*

There were many different kinds of sacrifices made by ancient Hebrews, depending on the reasons for the sacrifice. For example, there were *whole offerings*, that is, "wholly burned" sacrifices in which an entire animal except its hide was consumed in fire on the altar. Its purpose was to give glory and praise to God. There were *cereal offerings*, consisting of grains like barley. Also, there were *peace offerings* in which the meat of the sacrificed animal was partially eaten by priests and those who offered the sacrifice. Also in some temples of other ancient people, and perhaps also in the Hebrew Temple, some of the leftover meat not consumed by the priests was actually sold. Thus ancient temples often doubled as the local butcher shop.

There is debate, however, about what the sacrifices mentioned in Leviticus were actually intended to accomplish. One explanation is that the person who brought a sacrifice offered the animal as a replacement for himself. He identified with the sacrificial victim and thus expressed his repentance. Another interpretation is that the sacrifice was intended to remove the sin from the holy Temple and its altar.

In other words, the Hebrews believed that *two* things happened when people sinned. First, they were guilty themselves and must be forgiven. This personal guilt was taken care of by the act of bringing the animals to the priests at the Temple. The gift represented repentance and sorrow, and served as the symbolic act of asking God for forgiveness. The acts of sacrificing the animals and sprinkling their blood on the altar took care of the *second issue*—the "pollution" of the Temple itself from the sins of the people. The actual killing of the animals and then the

The New MOSES

(*CCC*, 577–582, 1965–1974, 2574–2577, 2598)

Moses	Jesus
Pharaoh orders all male children to be slain (Ex 1:16, 22)	Herod orders all male children to be slain (Mt 2:16–18)
Moses survives (Ex 2:1–4)	Jesus survives (Mt 2:13–15)
Moses is raised in Egypt (Ex 2:5–10)	Jesus lived for a short time in Egypt (Mt 2:14–15, 19–21)
Moses encounters God on a mountain (Ex 3:1, 19:20–25)	Jesus speaks to his disciples on a mountain (Mt 5:1–2)
God presents the Ten Commandments through Moses on a mountain (Ex 3:1, 19:20–25, 24:12–18)	Jesus presents the eight Beatitudes during the Sermon on the Mount (Mt 5:3–12)
Moses is the Lawgiver (Dt 5:31)	Jesus is the New Lawgiver. He modifies and corrects words that God said through Moses (Mt 5:17–48)
Moses intercedes on behalf of the Israelites (Ex 33:11)	Jesus Christ is the "one mediator between God and the human race" (1 Tm 2:5)
God provides manna—the bread from Heaven—to the famished Israelites in the desert (Ex 16)	Jesus is the "bread of life" that came down from Heaven (Jn 6:32–58)
Moses lifts up a bronze serpent to heal Israelites bitten by serpents (Nm 21:4–9)	God lifted up Jesus so that "everyone who believes in him may have eternal life" (Jn 3:14)

The Gospel of Matthew treats Jesus as the New Moses. The Twelve Apostles are often thought of as the New Israel. The Gospel retells scriptural events to help explain and interpret events in the life of Jesus. The focus on the connections between Jesus and Moses came about because Matthew's Gospel was originally intended for a Jewish Christian audience.

The birth narrative in the Gospel of Matthew has a striking resemblance to the birth narrative of Moses in the Book of Exodus. In both stories a corrupt ruler (Pharaoh, Herod) orders the death of all the male children (of Egypt, of Bethlehem), though they are unable to kill the ones they truly desire to eliminate (Moses, Jesus).

Matthew also makes important connections between Moses and Jesus as "lawgivers." Matthew describes Jesus teaching extensively on a mountain in what is popularly known as the Sermon on the Mount (Mt 5:1–7:29). Just as Moses met God on a mountain (Ex 3:1; 19:20–25), the disciples came to learn from Jesus on a mountain. It is during the Sermon on the Mount that Jesus teaches the eight Beatitudes (Mt 5:3–12), similar to God's revelation of the Ten Commandments on a mountain (Ex 20; Dt 5). Jesus, then, goes on to critique some of the Mosaic Law, not to "abolish" but to "fulfill" and to challenge his disciples to a new way of living (Mt 5:17).

Reviewing the Connection

Review the comparison between Moses and Jesus at left. Look up the following passages and write down the implied comparisons between Jesus and Moses in your notebook:

- Exodus 2:1–10 and Matthew 2:13–15
- Exodus 20:1–17 and Matthew 5:1–12
- Exodus 14:21–22 and Matthew 14:25–33
- Exodus 16:4–15 and Matthew 14:13–21
- Exodus 1:2–5 and Matthew 1:1–5
- Exodus 12:1–27 and Matthew 26:26–29

handling of blood, therefore, seemed to be a kind of religious "cleansing agent" which was mainly for the *purification of the Temple*, and not for "forgiving" the person who offered the animal.

Clearly, coming to an understanding of what was intended in the sacrificial system has interesting implications for our Christian understanding of the death of Jesus—since it is often compared to the sacrifices made by the ancient Hebrews.

Purity Laws: *Leviticus 11*

One of the most interesting chapters of the "purity laws" in Leviticus is the section dealing with laws of clean and unclean animals. Consider Leviticus 11. The first section of the chapter is rather neatly divided into "classes" of animal—some of which are used for food:

1. Leviticus 11:2–8—land animals
2. Leviticus 11:9–12—sea animals (fish)
3. Leviticus 11:13–19—air animals (birds)
4. Leviticus 11:20–23—winged insects

It has often been suggested that these "food laws" are based on some primitive form of hygiene; that is, the laws were given to protect the people from foods that are frequently dangerous (especially in an era before bacterial infection was understood) such as shellfish, which are easily infected, or pork, which contains parasites if not properly cooked.

The explanation that these laws are based mainly on hygiene does not explain all of Leviticus 11, nor many other purity regulations in the rest of Leviticus. Another suggestion was that purity laws, and laws that reflect a fear of contamination from various things, represented the Israelites' social fears of contamination from the "outside."[4] The point is strengthened by the fact that many of the purity laws of Leviticus were particularly significant during the exilic period after the destruction of Jerusalem in 587 BC. In other words, the purity laws reflected a minority society that was concerned about the threats from assimilation with foreign cultures. This would parallel concerns about mixed marriages, for example, which one Biblical priest called "pollution" (Ezr 9).

"Clean" animals in this theory are animals that *stay in their categories*, rather than violate "borders" between certain traits (e.g., fish that do not have both scales and fins, like shellfish or amphibians) or animals that do not chew cud and have cloven hoofs (like camels and pigs).[5] Purity laws that reflected concerns of animals staying in their categories could be carried over to encourage people to stay in *their* categories in a multi-religious society like the Babylonian, Persian, and Hellenistic Empires which ruled over the Hebrew people. In short, "purity" can be one way of insuring that people maintain a unique identity.

Laws of Jubilee: *Leviticus 25*

The laws of Jubilee are the last of the Levitical laws highlighted here. The name "Jubilee" comes from the Hebrew name for "horn" as the beginning of each year was proclaimed by the blast of a horn. According to the laws of Jubilee, after forty-nine years each man was free to return to his own homeland.

How did this understanding of a Jubilee Year develop? The priests were obviously fascinated with the number seven. There are seven days to the week, and every seventh year was proclaimed a "sabbatical year." This is when all the slaves (i.e., indentured servants) were released from their debts, and various parcels of land were allowed to "rest," along with farm animals. But the most impressive of these cycles of seven was the seventh sabbatical year—a kind of "super sabbatical" that was called the "Jubilee Year."

During the Jubilee Year, all the tribal land that had been leased, lost to debt, or bought up by unscrupulous landlords (e.g., Is 5:8) was to be returned to the original tribal families. It was to be one massive redistribution of land! It was similar to the prophet Ezekiel's plan to equally redistribute land, which was probably a version of the Jubilee distribution (see Ez 45).

The laws of Jubilee show a radical concern for social justice. They also reflect a concern not only to deal with fair distribution of resources once, but also to revisit the issue of fair distribution on a regular basis. While we have little evidence that the laws of Jubilee were ever actually practiced on a regular basis, they at least offer a laudable ambition on the part of the Hebrew priests to reorient a society on the basis of a socially and economically just distribution.

The Approach to the Promised Land

The five books of Moses, the Torah or Pentateuch, end with the Israelite people still wandering in the wilderness. Most of these first five books consist of various collections of the Law of Moses, with some narrative description of the time spent wandering in the wilderness.

Chapters 27 to 34 of the Book of Deuteronomy detail the "final words of Moses" and cover the approach of the Israelites to Canaan. Moses retells much of the story of the Exodus and offers his interpretation of the Israelite's actions in the desert. He reminds the people to keep the covenant that God made with them at Sinai. Remember that the Torah was most likely recorded many years later when the Jewish people were themselves in Exile. Thus, the last words of Moses are in a sense truly directed at the Jews in Exile. The stories of the wandering Israelites making their way through the desert to the Promised Land likely brought them great hope, while the reminder to keep the covenant strengthened their resolve to resist assimilation into the various cultures that surrounded them.

According to Deuteronomy, Moses was allowed to view Canaan, but died and was buried before entering the Promised Land (see Dt 32:48–52; 34). The traditions of the Israelites in the Promised Land are not covered until the sequence of books known as the *historical books*.

Some Jewish scholars teach that the five books of Moses end while "we are still in the wilderness." So, they, in effect, are laws for wanderers, like all people are throughout their lives. Something else to think about!

Section in Review

Quick View

- The Law focused more on restoring community in an agrarian society than on punishing the guilty.

- Some differences between the *Covenant Code* and the *Deuteronomic Code* are present in the Old Testament.

- The *Levitical Code* focuses on priestly laws and traditions, including laws of sacrifice, purity laws, and laws of the Jubilee.

For Review

1. **Main Idea**: What three codes comprise the Law of Moses?

2. **Critical Thinking**: How was the purpose of law different in the society of early, agrarian Israel than it is in our modern, urban society?

3. **Main Idea**: What two things did the Hebrews believe happened when people sinned?

4. **Main Idea**: What was the purpose of the purity laws?

For Reflection

How might the spirit of the laws of the Jubilee be put into practice in your community, nation, or in the international community today? Decide whether you think making such an attempt would be beneficial or harmful. Write about what you imagine some of the consequences would be.

Further Reflections

Moses was the one chosen by God to lead the Israelites from their exile in Egypt.

To Moses, God revealed his divine name: YHWH, which means, "I am who I am."

The Exodus is the name for God's saving intervention that occurred in history, through which the Israelites were liberated from slavery. God made a covenant with them and they were brought to the Promised Land of Canaan:

> After the patriarchs, God formed Israel as his people by freeing them from slavery in Egypt. He established with them the covenant of Mount Sinai and, through Moses, gave them his law so that they would recognize him and serve him as the one living and true God, the provident Father and just judge, and so that they would look for the promised Savior. (*CCC*, 62)

A covenant is a solemn agreement between human beings or between God and human beings. The covenant with Moses is the primary covenant of the Old Testament. In this covenant, God revealed his Law through Moses in preparation for Salvation through the prophets, and ultimately the New Covenant established by Christ. The Ten Commandments are central to the Sinai Covenant.

For Jews, the events of the Exodus are not simply *recalled* in celebrations today. Rather, in every Passover, the Exodus events are made present and real so that Jews can conform their lives to these events. In the New Testament, the memorial takes on a new meaning. When the Church celebrates the Eucharist, Christ's Passover is made present. The sacrifice of Christ on the Cross is made present once and for all.

Vocabulary Review

Directions: Provide an example of each of the following:

1. Ten Commandments
2. natural law
3. civil laws
4. religious laws
5. punitive justice
6. restorative justice
7. Covenant Code
8. laws of sacrifice
9. purity laws
10. laws of Jubilee

Performance Assessment Project

Though life that is prescribed for the Israelites in the Torah is in many ways different from today, modern morality is rooted in Mosaic Law. Complete a detailed table comparing and contrasting the *Ten Commandments*, *Covenant Code*, *Deuteronomic Code*, and *Levitical Code*. Then, write a short essay explaining why you think the Old Testament Laws apply to our lives today.

Called to Prayer

I will sing to the Lord, for he is gloriously triumphant;

> *horse and chariot he has cast into the sea.*

My strength and my courage is the Lord,

> *and he has been my savior.*

He is my God, I praise him;

> *The God of my father, I extol him.*

The Lord is a warrior,

> *Lord is his name!*

—Exodus 15:1–3

- **Reflection**: The Israelites clearly admired God's power and his ability to fight for them when they were in danger. How can you use God's strength in your life today?
- **Meditation**: Which description of God (gloriously triumphant, my strength, my courage, my savior, God of my father, or warrior) resonates with you most deeply?
- **Resolution**: Write your own canticle of praise to God based on something he has done for you in your lifetime.

Notes

1. One other point of difference: At the end of the nine plagues (Ex 10:28–29), the people leave because Pharaoh tells them to go. In the Passover tradition, it is suggested that the Israelites have to leave Egypt quickly (Ex 12). The Israelites' *exodus*, or departure, from Egypt is described in Exodus 13:17–14:31. It includes the story of the miraculous crossing of Reed Sea or Sea of Reeds. The Israelites are able to cross, but the Egyptians drown.

2. If any of your Jewish friends invite you to a Passover celebration, don't miss it. It is a wonderful tradition to learn about and enjoy.

3. Indentured servitude describes an agreement in which a contract binds one person in service of another for a specific amount of time. At the end of the contract, the servant would be released from his or her duties. In the Mosaic Law, it was a way to pay debts, and the term was traditionally seven years.

4. This argument was made by anthropologist Mary Douglas in a 1966 book titled *Purity and Danger*.

5. Note that animals with one category, but not both, are excluded as "unclean" (e.g., the rock badger and hare of Lv 11:5–6).

The Journey Takes New Shape:

A People at Home

CHAPTER OUTLINE

■ *The Book of Deuteronomy completes the Mosaic Law. It has parallels with the Book of Exodus and some similarities to the six Biblical books that follow it.*

■ *The Israelites' settlement in Canaan is characterized by dependence on God for deliverance.*

■ *The Book of Judges provides the bridge between the settlement and establishment of a kingdom.*

■ *Archaeological evidence suggests that the formation of the nation of Israel probably took place over a long period of time as they settled in the hill country of Palestine.*

The Book of Deuteronomy completes the Mosaic Law. It has parallels with the Book of Exodus and some similarities to the six Biblical books that follow it.

Introduction

The Book of Deuteronomy closes just before the arrival of the Israelites in Canaan in about 1250 BC. This chapter will cover the history of the Israelites from the time they came to Palestine to the beginning of the monarchy around 1050 BC. This history was not recorded in the form we now have it until the Israelites were exiled in Babylon in 587 BC, several centuries later. The study will focus on two questions: How is it known that this portion of history was actually recorded during Babylonian captivity? And what are some similarities among the Book of Deuteronomy and the next six books of the Bible: Books of Joshua, Judges, 1 and 2 Samuel, and 1 and 2 Kings?

Deuteronomy means "second law." Actually, the material in Deuteronomy completes and offers explanation for the Mosaic Law founded at Mount Sinai. The historical events of the book are situated in the plains of Moab between the Chosen People's wanderings in the desert and the crossing of the Jordan River into the Promised Land, actually a period of no more than forty days.

The structure of the Book of Deuteronomy resembles that of the Book of Exodus. Note the similarities in this table:

The Book of Deuteronomy was written centuries after the Israelites had inhabited the Promised Land. At the time of the life of Christ, the Book of Deuteronomy and the Book of Psalms each had a significant religious influence for Jews. Jesus quoted the Book of Deuteronomy during the temptations he faced in the desert (see Mt 4) and in explaining to the lawyer which Commandment was the first and greatest (see Mt 22:35–39).

While grouped with the Torah, the Book of Deuteronomy also shares literary and religious themes with the six historical books that follow it in the Old Testament canon. (One theory suggests that these six books are actually six parts of one long work in the same way that the Gospel of Luke and the Acts of the Apostles from the New Testament were originally part of one written volume, though this remains only speculation.)

The connection between the Book of Deuteronomy and the other six historical books is not simply a question of literary style. There are several religious or theological themes that these books have in common—such as the central importance of the city of Jerusalem, especially the Jerusalem Temple.

In Deuteronomy, there are three regulations that are found only there:

1. the Temple is the *only* acceptable location for sacrifice on the face of the earth

2. astrology, the worship of stars, is forbidden

3. celebrating Passover is legally required among *all* the Israelites

These three regulations in Deuteronomy do not appear in the older collections of the law (in Exodus or

Exodus	Deuteronomy
From Egypt to Sinai (Ex 1–18)	From Sinai to Moab (Dt 1–4:43)
Covenant and Ten Commandments (Ex 19–20:21)	Covenant and Ten Commandments (Dt 4:44–5:22)
Concluding Ceremony (Ex 24)	Concluding Ceremony (Dt 27–28)
Apostasy of Aaron, Intercession of Moses, Renewal of Alliances (Ex 32–34)	Apostasy of Aaron, Intercession of Moses, Tablets Rewritten (Dt 9:7–10:5)

Common PHRASES

There are several phrases from the Book of Deuteronomy present in the other six historical books. Because of this, a connection is often made between Deuteronomy and these books. Check the following literary comparison by looking at the classic phrase from Deuteronomy about loving or following God with "all your heart and soul," which Jesus quotes as the greatest Commandment.

> Therefore, you shall love the Lord, your God, **with all your heart, and with all your soul**, and with all your strength. (Dt 6:5)

Though the phrase is never found in any other Book of the Torah, it is heavily used throughout the Book of Deuteronomy—for example, 4:29; 10:12; 11:13; 11:18; 13:4; 26:16; 30:2,6,10. The phrase turns up again in several places outside the Book of Deuteronomy, linking those books with Deuteronomy. For example, *in the Book of Joshua*:

> But be very careful to observe the precept and law which Moses, the servant of the Lord, enjoined upon you: love the Lord, your God; follow him faithfully; keep his commandments; remain loyal to him; and serve him **with your whole heart and soul**." (Jos 22:5)

In the first Book of Kings:

> . . . and the Lord may fulfill the promise he made on my behalf when he said, "If your sons so conduct themselves that they remain faithful to me **with their whole heart and with their whole soul**, you shall always have someone of your line on the throne of Israel." (1 Kgs 2:4)

The phrase is also used in 1 Kings 8:48 and in 2 Kings 23:3 and 23:25. From these examples it is clear that the history books borrowed language, style, and even moral themes from the Book of Deuteronomy.

in the older parts of Leviticus). Furthermore, they are not actually put into practice until the time of King Josiah (640–609 BC), a very late king of Judah (see 2 Kgs 22–24). It is King Josiah who actually legislates these regulations among the Israelite people. He allows sacrifice *only* in Jerusalem at the famous Temple. He forbids star worship and he states that the Passover celebration is to take place each year.

It is reported in 2 Kings 22:6 that the high priest in King Josiah's reign "found the Book of the law in the temple of the Lord." It is not until 2 Kings 22–24 that we actually have an Israelite king who enacts the unique laws of Deuteronomy (laws not found in the books of Exodus or Leviticus). It makes sense, then, that the book found in the Temple during Josiah's reign was the Book of Deuteronomy—the only part of the Law of Moses that specifically requires the same laws that Josiah passed. This also means that the Book of Deuteronomy was added to the Torah very late in history. After this book became influential, writers who were composing later materials were deeply influenced by its style as well as its important collection of laws.

In summary, there seems to be some relationship between the Book of Deuteronomy and the other historical books. Drawing from this information has helped to date the creation of these books. How so? Imagine that you are reading an American history book that claims to be comprehensive, and you do not know when that book was published. How might you decide roughly when the book was written? You would probably look at the *last* event described in the work. If the last event described in the book occurred when President George W. Bush was in office, you would likely conclude that the book was published shortly after the year 2008, when President Bush left office.

The last event described at the end of 2 Kings is the beginning of the Babylonian Exile. Thus we can conclude that this long historical sequence of books (which begins with Joshua and ends with 2 Kings) must have been written sometime after 587 BC. While there is some question as to whether *parts* of the six historical books were written before 587 BC, few Bible scholars, if any, dispute that the work was completed after 587 BC.

To summarize:

- The Book of Deuteronomy was discovered during the reign of King Josiah (2 Kgs 2:26).

- Josiah reigned 640–609 BC.
- The six historical books were written after 587 BC.

As we pick up the story in the Book of Exodus of the Israelites' foray into Palestine, it is important to keep two things in mind. First, all of the records of this experience were finally written during the same historical period. And second, they were written many years after the incidents they describe actually occurred.

Section in Review

Quick View

- There is a common literary and historical connection between the Book of Deuteronomy and other Biblical texts written in the same historical period.
- Biblical evidence suggests that the historical books that follow the Book of Deuteronomy were written after 587 BC, during the Babylonian Exile.

For Review

1. **Main Idea**: List the six books that follow the Book of Deuteronomy. What is a clue that has been used to determine when they were written?
2. **Main Idea**: What textual evidence links the six books? What elements of style and theological themes are consistent among the books?
3. **Critical Thinking**: What clues can you apply to the other books of the Old Testament in determining when they were written?

For Reflection

Look up and read carefully the seven passages listed on pg. 107 for the occurrence of the phrase "with your whole heart and your whole soul." Write about what it might mean for you to love God and follow his commandments with your "whole heart and whole soul."

> The Israelites' settlement in Canaan is characterized by dependence on God for deliverance.

Understanding the Events of Settlement

How did the early settlement of Palestine by the Israelites take place? The story of settlement is told in the books of Joshua and Judges and there are a couple of points on settlement that are interesting for study. But remember, the words of Joshua and Judges were inspired by God. They are intended to reflect a religious and economically just lesson that he wants to communicate to people of all ages. No matter how the land was settled, there is no doubt that the *religion* of the God named YHWH was quite different from the religions of Egypt and Canaan with all of their different gods and goddesses.

The common understanding from the Bible is that the settlement was, at least on some level, a "conquest." According to this traditional view, Joshua was put in charge of the people of Israel after Moses died. Joshua became a military leader and led a militia composed of the young men of the wilderness generation. This Israelite "army" (surely not a very well-equipped one!) attacked the "Promised Land" in military actions that began with the amazing conquest of Jericho. In fact, the Book of Joshua opens with a long section (chapters 2–6) about the conquest of Jericho.

Typically, the conquest of Jericho is dated between 1250 and 1200 BC. Certainly something called "Israel" existed in Palestine by the time Pharaoh Merneptah claimed to have defeated Israel in his inscription of 1207 BC. It is the earliest reference to Israel outside the Bible, and is an important source for dating the formation of

How We Love Others

Jesus equated love of others with love of God. He also said, "Love your enemies and do good to them" (Lk 6:35). Develop a concrete seven-day plan for "doing good" for those you have not got along with in the past. In this way you will be showing your love for them and for God. Write your plan for the week. Include the names of people you will try to reach out to and what you will try to do. At the end of each day, write a summary of what you were able to accomplish and how and why you adapted your plan.

Israel, because it tells us that there was a people in Canaan called Israel by around 1207 BC.

The description of the siege of Jericho (5:13–6:27) is well known, especially as a popular subject for children's books and songs. The very lengthy description of this battle at the beginning of the Book of Joshua alerts us to the fact that it was considered important as the opening battle for the land. (The entire record of the conquest battles is told in the first twelve chapters of Joshua, nearly half of which is devoted to the battle of Jericho alone.) According to Scripture, Jericho was conquered by means of a miracle of God, and the people only participated in the "cleanup" operation that followed the actual fall of the city. Chapters 12 to 21 of the Book of Joshua mainly explain how the land was divided among Israel's tribes, though "a very large part of the land still remains to be conquered" (12:1).

Rahab and the Fall of Jericho

Read Joshua 2–6.

The prostitute Rahab is a central character in the fall of Jericho. According to the Book of Joshua, she risked her life to help the Israelite spies. Certainly, Rahab had little reason to be loyal to Jericho. As a prostitute, she was likely abused by the men of the city and shunned by most of the women. For her assistance, the Israelites spared Rahab and her family when they destroyed the rest of the city.

Rahab is also a symbolic figure in the story of the conquest. The Law offered equality and social justice on a level to which the native Canaanites were not accustomed under their ancient elitist system of government and society. There were probably many poorly treated Canaanites like Rahab—especially lower-class workers and peasants—who abandoned their old society and joined with the new incoming group under Joshua.

Besides the role of Rahab, the other main issue to consider involving the fall of Jericho is the actual destruction of its famous walls. According to Joshua 6:1–20, God brought down the walls of Jericho following the shouts and marching of the Israelites. The miraculous nature of the story may reflect the religious tradition about warfare in early Israel (see "Israelite Warfare Traditions," pages 111–114).

The Taking of Jericho *by James Tissot*

The message, in this case, is that the miraculous fall of Jericho illustrates how the Israelites should depend on God over their own strength and abilities.

It is also possible that the story highlighted the miraculous nature of the battle in order to emphasize this point: when the Israelites have faith, God takes care of them. Since we know that the story was written at a much later time, perhaps the inspired author felt a particular need to emphasize the importance of trust in God. One of the major complaints of the prophets of the time of the Babylonian Exile, when these stories were recorded, was that the kings of Israel and Judah relied more on alliances with foreign nations than on God for protection against their enemies. This story was perhaps a reminder to the people to trust in God's power and his care for them.

Comparing Stories of Conquest

A different picture of the settlement of the Israelites in Canaan emerges from the stories in Judges. The Book of Judges includes an element of peaceful settlement of the land, in contrast with the more exclusive use of military

Joshua and Jesus

(*CCC*, 430, 667, 1544, 2581–2584)

In Greek, Jesus and Joshua have the same name, *Iesous*. This is the one indication of a connection between the mission and ministry of Jesus Christ and Joshua. Joshua led the people of Israel into the Promised Land, while Jesus leads his people into another Promised Land—eternal life. The Letter to the Hebrews is also a source connecting the two. Hebrews compares the "rest" that the Israelites shared with God in the Promised Land and the "rest" people share with God in Heaven. "Now if Joshua had given them rest, he would not have spoken afterwards of another day. Therefore, a Sabbath rest still remains for the people of God" (Heb 4:8–9).

Joshua	Jesus
In Hebrew, Joshua's name (*Iesous* in Greek) means "YHWH is salvation" or "YHWH saves"	Jesus' name in Greek is *Iesous*, which means "YHWH saves"
Joshua led the Israelites into the Promised Land (Jos 3)	Jesus leads God's people into the true Promised Land, Heaven (Heb 4:8–9)
Joshua is an intercessor between God and the Israelites (Jos 7:6–9)	Jesus Christ is the "one mediator between God and the human race" (1 Tm 2:5)

campaigns detailed in Joshua. The following differences can be found in the two accounts:

- The Book of Joshua finishes with the end of the conquest before settlement takes place (see Jos 23 ff.). But the Book of Judges suggests that some settlement preceded the battles of conquest!

- An encounter with Jabin, king of Hazor, is described in Joshua 11:1–11 where it is finally said that Hazor was "burned with fire." But in Judges 4:1–5:31, Jabin is mentioned again, Hazor is still in existence, and the city is being fought over once more. It is unclear why the battle is mentioned in both books. Judges may simply be a second, more detailed version of the same battle. Or it may be that the two books have two different accounts of what happened.

- Joshua describes a complete campaign of conquest: "And so the Lord gave Israel all the land he had sworn to their fathers he would give them. Once they had conquered and occupied it, the Lord gave them peace on every side, just as he had promised their fathers" (Jos 21:43). The Book of Judges suggests a much more mixed population of peoples throughout the land, with various pagan peoples existing alongside the Israelites "to this very day."

- There are even differences within the Book of Judges. In Judges 4, two tribes engage in the battle of Kishon. In Judges 5 the text says that six tribes were involved!

What is clear is that the books of Joshua and Judges both contain accounts of battles, biographies of soldiers, and details of the conquest of the land of Palestine (particularly the settlement of the twelve tribes). Both books describe God as being actively involved in the military campaigns, although often in highly unconventional battles. When the Israelites are faithful to God and to the covenant, he rewards them with victory. More information on this "literature and theology of warfare" is detailed in the next section.

Israelite Warfare Traditions

War was most certainly a major part of the experience of the Hebrew people. Recall that Palestine was in the middle of the main roads that linked Egypt with Mesopotamia. Israel was very familiar with the armies of each civilization, as they marched through Palestine on their way to engage each other. In short, given the location of

Archaeological EVICENCE

While recent archaeological study has not been able to corroborate all of the historical details of the Israelite's conquest of Palestine as recorded in the Bible, archaeologists have reached two main conclusions from that time and place:

1. The whole of the Middle East seems to have experienced social and political upheaval in approximately 1200 BC.

2. The upheaval was followed, during the opening centuries of the Iron Age, by what amounts to a "dark age" especially in Palestine—dark both in the sense that the ancient world underwent sociopolitical fragmentation and decline, and in that surviving written sources are scarce.[1]

 Dame Kathleen Kenyon

Write a short biography of Dame Kathleen Kenyon, a prominent archaeologist of the twentieth century. Include information about her major archaeological discoveries in the Holy Land.

Palestine, it seems hardly surprising that war is a major subject of the Old Testament.

But location alone does not account for all the warfare described in the Old Testament. The early Israelites were involved in many conflicts with ancient societies that had gods of war. These people believed that their gods went to war with their armies to help in the conflict. Consider the carving of the Assyrian monarch Assurbanipal. Flying over the head of the mighty Assyrian ruler is an image of the god, Assur, the national god of the empire, with his bow drawn. This carving illustrates the belief that the gods fought *with* the armies of the ancient world. The Israelites had a rather different notion about the connection of YHWH with warfare. Recall how Moses reassured the people as they prepared to cross the Red Sea:

> Fear not! Stand your ground, and you will see the victory the Lord will win for you today. These Egyptians whom you see today you will never see again. The Lord himself will fight for you; you have only to keep still. (Ex 14:13–14)

The unique idea in this passage is that the Lord will actually fight *for* Israel, not merely *with* Israel's warriors. The idea of warfare in earliest Israel was very unusual. It was fought miraculously by God alone, with minimal involvement of the people and sometimes, as with the case with the Egyptian defeat in the Red Sea, no involvement at all!

In Judges 7, this idea is illustrated again in a very powerful (and somewhat humorous) way. The judge Gideon thinks that he needs a huge army to defeat the Midianites. He starts with nearly 30,000 soldiers. But God tells him to *reduce* his armies. In the end, Gideon is told to go to war against the Midianites with an army composed of just three hundred men carrying horns in one hand and jars and torches in the other (see Jgs 7:20). They don't have a free hand to draw a sword or any other weapon! The point of this unusual story for the Israelites was that wars were won through the power of God, not men.

Also interesting to note are all the exemptions listed in Deuteronomy 20, allowing men to avoid fighting in a war. A man who had just planted a garden, built a house, or become engaged to marry was to refrain from fighting. Also, those who were afraid were supposed to go home (see Ex 20:8–9). The reason the exemptions are so liberal is again to show that it is only God's power that matters in war. As Moses told the soldiers:

> Hear, O Israel! Today you are going into battle against your enemies. Be not weak-hearted or afraid; be neither alarmed nor frightened by

Gideon Chooses the Three Hundred *by James Tissot*

them. For it is the Lord, your God, who goes with you to fight for you against your enemies and give you victory. (Dt 20:3–4)

This practice of God fighting miraculously alone for Israel did not continue. Why not? The reason is explained in the first Book of Samuel, when Israel chose a human king.

Read 1 Samuel 7–8.

In 1 Samuel 8, the people ask for a king, and Samuel the prophet is disappointed. God is also disappointed, so it seems, because he tells Samuel, "They are rejecting me as their king" (1 Sm 8:7). This passage infers that God is King! An ancient king was mainly a warrior. Rejecting God as their warrior and king meant the Israelites no longer trusted God to protect them by means of miracles. To make matters worse, the rejection of God as king and the request to "be like the other nations" (1 Sm 8:5) occur right after 1 Samuel 7, which tells of yet another miraculous deliverance of the Israelites from the Philistines by God. The request for a king in chapter 8 is doubly ungrateful, given what just happened.

Another intriguing point from 1 Samuel 8 is all the things that the people will have to face when they get a human king instead of honoring God as their king—mainly taxation and the military draft. The theological point is clear: in the past the Israelites trusted God for deliverance from enemies. Now they want to do it themselves. God tells the Israelites that they will suffer all the

It can never be claimed—though some have tried—that the Bible favors warfare over peacemaking. Those who hold to this false argument often cite examples of "Divine Warfare" found in the Old Testament. Their attempt to legitimize war from this argument ignores the teaching of 1 Samuel 8: traditional warfare in the Old Testament came only after the people rejected God as king. War was a result of Israel's unfaithfulness and lack of trust, not YHWH's desire to conquer other peoples in his name.

PEACE OVER WAR

The Church has long held to the position that war must be averted: "All citizens and all governments are obliged to work for the avoidance of war" (*CCC*, 2308). Yet, the Church also acknowledges that there are some situations where military force may be justified. The conditions for legitimate defense by military force are summarized in the "just war doctrine," which derives, in part, from the ideas elaborated by St. Augustine. Here are the main points of this doctrine:

- The war must have a "just cause" like self-defense and be called by a legitimate moral authority. Other elements of this doctrine are:
- The aggressor must have inflicted lasting, grave, and certain damage on the attacked nation(s).
- That all other means of settling the dispute must be shown too impractical or ineffective.
- There must be serious prospects for success of the war.
- Non-combatants are not to be targeted, and the use of weapons may not produce evils graver than the evil being perpetrated by the aggressor nation. The use of modern weapons of mass destruction weighs very heavily in this case (see also, *CCC*, 2307–2317).

Many Catholics throughout history have chosen to avoid war altogether through history and chose a completely non-violent solution (see American bishops' 1983 Pastoral Letter, *The Challenge of Peace: God's Promise and Our Response*). As the bishops' 1983 document states: "There is no notion of a warrior God who will lead the people in an historical victory over its enemies in the New Testament."

just war doctrine
Teachings of the Church that define the moral limits of warfare.

financial and social strains of maintaining a military just as the other nations do (1 Sm 8:10–18).

From this time on, the warfare of the Israelites becomes much more conventional in focus. There are only occasional reminders of the days of Miraculous Warfare—typically associated with prophets, especially Elijah and Elisha (see 2 Kgs 6).

In summary, there is a major change in the practice of warfare in Ancient Israel. There is an impression that some of the authors treated that earlier period as a kind of "golden age" when Israel trusted God more deeply and God responded with miraculous protection. Perhaps the story of the fall of Jericho reflects this same tendency to describe events as if they were "better then because of our greater trust in God." Whatever the case, the Old Testament authors associated conventional warfare with a time when the Israelites rejected God.

Section in Review

Quick View

- The conquest of Jericho in the Book of Joshua illustrates the need for dependence on God.

- Unlike the Book of Joshua, the Book of Judges depicts a more peaceful settlement of the land of Canaan.

- Other nations believed that their gods fought *with* them, the Israelites believed God fought *for* them.

For Review

1. **Critical Thinking**: Explain some of the differences in the accounts of the settlement of Canaan put forward in the books of Joshua and Judges. What conclusions have archaeologists reached about the time period of the settlement of Canaan by the Israelites?

2. **Main Idea**: Name an example of how God fought miraculously for his people.

3. **Main Idea**: Give an explanation of the just war doctrine first developed by St. Augustine.

For Reflection

Use the stories of Joshua and Judges to support your own argument for or against the use of warfare to resolve disputes among nations. Be as persuasive as you can.

The Book of Judges provides the bridge between the settlement and establishment of a kingdom.

Exploits of the Judges

The Hebrew word *shofet* was traditionally translated by the English word "judge," although the actual meaning of a *shofet* may be closer to "temporary military leader." The function of the judges as described in the Book of Judges included other responsibilities besides military leadership. For example, judges also settled political disputes within their own tribe and between tribes and continually reminded the people to turn to God.

The judges filled the gap in leadership between the time of Joshua (ca. 1200 BC) and the beginning of the monarchy (ca. 1030 BC). The judges were leaders who were spiritually selected by God to lead the tribal peoples—though they rarely led *all* of the tribes at the same time. Three of the most well-known judges are:

- **Deborah**, a woman who successfully called a war in which Israel was victorious, and is heralded in the famous "Song of Deborah" (Judges 5);

- **Gideon**, a man who had serious doubts about God's ability to lead his people; and

- **Samson**, who was considered wise, yet allowed his love for the wrong woman (a Philistine woman named Delilah) to lead him to foolish decisions.

While it is difficult to place dates on the exact time of the judges, a major theme of the judge stories seems to be that there *was* a time when God led the Israelites. Whenever God needed assistance, he would spiritually "deputize" a judge for a brief period. Also, when any of these judges was asked to be "king," he or she very dutifully reminded the people that *YHWH alone was their king*. The concluding chapters of the Book of Judges note some of the disintegration of the unity within and among the tribes of Israel, leading to the call for a new form of leadership. The final verse of Judges expresses this: "In those days there was no king in Israel; everyone did what he thought best" (Jgs 21:25).

The following sections briefly detail the stories of the three most famous judges:

Deborah

Read Judges 4–5.

Deborah is called both a prophet and a judge. Her story is a second version of the defeat of the king of Hazor.

After another incident of Israel offending YHWH, the Israelites found themselves under the reign of the Canaanite Jabin, who reigned in Hazor. The general of his army was Sisera. Deborah summoned the Israelite general Barak and asked him to march on the troops of Sisera. Barak responded to Deborah, "If you come with me I will go; if you do not come with me, I will not go" (Jgs 4:8). Deborah consented and also pointed out that God would eventually have Sisera fall under the power of a woman.

The fall occurred when Sisera was retreating from Barak's forces. When he sought to hide in the tent of a friend's wife, Jael, he expected her to help him avoid capture. Instead, she murdered him while he was asleep, driving a peg through his temple down into the ground. Sisera's cowardice in deserting his army and hiding behind a woman was seen as even worse than Jael's disregard for the customs of hospitality, which would ordinarily prohibit the murder of a guest.

The story is accompanied by a poem—the Canticle of Deborah—in which Sisera's fate is further ridiculed and Jael is redeemed:

> Blessed among women be Jael,
>> blessed among tent-dwelling women.
> He asked for water, she gave him milk;
>> in a princely bowl she offered curds.
> With her left hand she reached for a peg,
>> with her right, for the workman's mallet.

> She hammered Sisera, crushed his head;
>> she smashed, stove in his temple. (Jgs 5:24–26)

The poem itself is considered to be among the oldest passages in the entire Bible, perhaps written before the time of the Israelite monarchy.

Gideon

Read Judges 6–8:35.

Following the time of Deborah, the Israelites again offended the Lord and faced the rule of the Midianites. God raised a young man, Gideon, to lead the people as judge. Gideon protested to the Lord: "How can I save Israel? My family is the meanest (poorest) in Manasseh, and I am the most insignificant in my father's house" (Jgs 6:15). The Lord responded, "I shall be with you, and you will cut Midian down to the last man" (Jgs 6:16).

After Gideon led victory over the Midianites, the people wanted him to be king. He told them: "I will not rule over you, nor shall my son rule over you. The Lord must rule over you" (Jgs 8:23).

However, the story immediately reports that Gideon next asked the people for their gold taken as booty from the latest battle. From the gold, Gideon fashioned an *ephod*, which was likely a golden idol. The story shows how easily even a leader of Israel could be swayed away from God. Later, God brought a curse on Gideon's sons because of Gideon's idolatry.

Samson

Read Judges 13–16.

Samson's story begins with a legend of his birth, announced by an angel to his mother who was thought to be barren. (Remember, birth stories occur in the Bible when the person is to play a significant role in the history of Israel.) The

shofet
A Hebrew word traditionally translated in English as "judge" that more literally means "temporary military leader."

judge
In ancient Israel, one who acted as a temporary military leader, as well as arbiter of disputes within and between tribes. Judges were also expected to remind the people of their responsibility to God.

The prophet and judge Deborah

woman had her son take the Nazorite vow, described in Numbers 6:5, to set himself apart for the Lord and let his hair grow freely. The Lord said to her:

> As for the son you will conceive and bear, no razor shall touch his head, for this boy is to be consecrated to God from the womb. It is he who will begin the deliverance of Israel from the power of the Philistines. (Jgs 13:5)

The legend around Samson was that his strength came from his long hair. Actually, his reliance on God was the source of his strength. Among his legendary feats were these:

- He killed a lion with his bare hands, tearing it "in pieces as one tears a kid (goat)" (Jgs 14:6).

- He fixed torches on the tails of three hundred foxes and set them loose in the grain fields of the Philistines (Jgs 15:5).

- He killed a thousand men with the "jawbone of an ass" (Jgs 15:15).

- He pushed on two columns of the temple of Dagon, killing himself along with "more than those he had killed during his lifetime" (Jgs 16:30).

Earlier, Samson's fiancée betrayed him to the Philistines at their wedding feast and then married his best man. The men of Gaza laid an ambush for Samson while

THE BOOK OF RUTH

A glance at the table of contents of the Old Testament will show that the Book of Ruth comes immediately after the Book of Judges and just prior to 1 and 2 Samuel. This placement was made in later Greek and Latin canons of the Bible, probably because the book contains a genealogy that connects Ruth, a Moabite woman, with the family of King David. The book was most likely written sometime after the Babylonian Exile. But the book itself also claims to come from the time of the judges (see Ru 1:1).

The story of Ruth involves a foreign woman's fidelity to the Jewish family of her widowed husband. Ruth follows her mother-in-law, Naomi, back to the land of Judah after the death of her husband, despite Naomi's protests that she ought to return to her father's house and be married again. Once back in Judah, Ruth *is* married again, observing a law detailed in the Book of Leviticus that required her to marry her nearest male relative. This was a called a **levirate marriage**; it would allow her to bear a son who would be considered her first husband's heir. This law was intended to keep property within the same clan or family by ensuring that there was an heir even if a man died before he had a son. By eventually marrying Boaz, her relative by marriage, Ruth was sealed by covenant to the Israelite family, becoming an ancestor of King David (and of Jesus). Although Ruth was a foreigner, she accepted the God of her Jewish husband and today is honored for her choice.

♥ Loyalty

Among her many positive traits, Ruth was loyal to her first husband, his family, and his religion. Write a poem, short essay, or design a piece of artwork that expresses the story and character of Ruth.

he was with a harlot in their city. Samson's weakness was his foolish love for Delilah. His infidelities caused the loss of his personal strength in the same way Israel's infidelities to the Lord caused a loss of their independence and power as a nation.

The Book of Judges provides more evidence of the need for Israel's reliance on YHWH. When the Israelites are faithful to the covenant, the Lord supports them. When they are not, they fall under the rule of oppressors. What the Book of Judges does not do, however, is provide much additional detail on the formation of Israel as a people and the development of their religious codes.

Section in Review

Quick View

- The judges were military leaders, spiritually selected by God to lead the tribes of Israel.

- Deborah was both a prophet and judge.

- Gideon was victorious, but his faith faltered.

- Samson's strength was unmatched, but his weakness—love for Delilah—caused the Israelites to lose their independence.

For Review

1. **Main Idea**: What was the function of the judges in Israel following the settlement of Palestine?

2. **Main Idea**: What was the traditional response of the judges if the people of Israel asked them to be king?

3. **Critical Thinking**: Name the main religious point throughout the Book of Judges about the relationship between Israel and God.

For Reflection

Read the full account in the Book of Judges of one of the three judges: Deborah (Jgs 4–5), Gideon (Jgs 6–8), or Samson (Jgs 13–16). Write a short "profile of courage" of the judge you have chosen.

Archaeological evidence suggests that the formation of the nation of Israel probably took place over a long period of time as they settled in the hill country of Palestine.

Israel at Home in Palestine

Returning to the larger question of how Palestine was settled by the Israelites, the answers to two related questions can help shed more light on the issue:

1. Did most of the people who formed the twelve tribes of Israel come to Palestine from Egypt with Moses?

2. Or, were most of these people native to the land, simply changing their religious and political identities upon the arrival of some returning slaves from Egypt?

From archaeological evidence it can be determined that the central hill country of Palestine suddenly grew in population in the early Iron Age, between 1200 and 1000 BC. In previously uninhabited land, where only about twenty-three villages once existed, archaeologists have identified some 114 new villages from that period.[2] Furthermore, judging from the material remains of many of these villages,

levirate marriage
The marriage of a widow to a near relative of her deceased husband. The first male child of a levirate marriage would be considered the legal son of the widow's first husband.

their pottery styles are virtually the same as Canaanite cities on the coastal plains.

Everyone agrees that new villages suddenly appeared in the hill country. But where did the people who formed these villages originate? Were they all former slaves from Egypt? Consider for a moment if they were not all former slaves from Egypt.

The Book of Judges, which describes slow settlement among other peoples, supports this position rather than the organized military campaign as described in the Book of Joshua. The stories of a slow settlement and the similar pottery and architecture suggest that some of the new villages in the hill country were established by people who had never left Canaan and who had never been slaves in Egypt. Instead, they simply left the larger coastal towns and the Transjordan (land across the Jordan River from Palestine) and settled in the new villages in the hills.

There are a number of reasons why people from the lowlands of Canaan might have relocated to the hillsides. There was general unrest throughout the Ancient Near East in this time. Egyptian authority was weakened, and there were small warring city-states in the area that is now Syria and Lebanon. Perhaps the people wanted to escape the upheaval in the cities caused by invaders. Also, the groups of "sea peoples" (some of whom were the famous Philistines) arrived from what are today Greek territories, and their arrival may have pushed some of the peasants further into the hills to escape these new warriors.

There is some evidence to indicate that the Philistines and other sea peoples may have come to Canaan because of climatic changes that made their own homelands uninhabitable. Perhaps the radical climate changes and political pressures in these centuries forced major population shifts, which might have caused many peoples to abandon the Canaanite cities on the coast for an independent existence in the hills. After all, the Bible not only records conflict with the Philistines, but it also points out that they were fearsome warriors. Perhaps the many battles of the Book of Joshua and Judges were generally correct memories of conflict, retold much later in simplified and well-ordered terms.

It is also possible that people left the Canaanite city-states because life there was oppressive—especially for the poor. Their movement may have been a revolutionary response to their poverty, a deliberate escape to a place where land did not end up in the hands of the few wealthy landowners and kings of the Canaanite cities. The Law of Moses contrast dramatically with what we know about the older Canaanite religious views. Certainly the stories of the prophets emphasize a great contrast between the injustice and violence of the Canaanites, and the more just and equal sharing of the Mosaic Law. This new society would have been appealing to people who were poor and oppressed.

According to the stories that fit more typically under the Book of Judges than the Book of Joshua, the settlement process was much slower than Joshua's "lightning campaign" and likely took between two and three hundred years or longer. Certainly there may have been some violence in the lives of the Israelites (raiding parties, trouble with Canaanite cities, conflict with the Philistines) as described in both Joshua and Judges, but these battles may not have been part of a large organized conquest of one people by another. Instead, the formation of a people in the hillsides of Palestine may have been the result of a combination of the common interests of the arriving former slaves from Egypt and the rural peoples caught between the competing interests of major empires (Egypt and Mesopotamia) and affected by the lesser political ambitions of smaller states and cities. Although almost all scholarship rejects the idea of a huge migration of former slaves from Egypt—certainly not 600,000 as the traditional Biblical number would have it—there is also little doubt that some Hebrew slaves came from Egypt and that Moses was most certainly a historical figure who led and taught them during their wilderness sojourn between Egypt and Palestine. With some people already living

Israel Climate Changes

Produce a chart that details month-to-month climate changes (including rainfall totals) for at least three different regions (e.g., coastal, mountain, desert) of modern Israel. Further explore the question of how radical differences in the climate might cause people to prefer to live in other regions of the nation other than the coast. Cite other evidence gleaned from news articles and real estate statistics on the subject.

Modern-day Palestine

in Canaan (e.g., Rahab), these groups organized into a coherent identity—the Tribes of Israel.

The entire process resulting in the formation of a people of Israel settled in Palestine may not have been complete until the start of the monarchy (ca. 1000 BC). Under this view, it was only when the Israelites looked back while in exile in Babylon that they were able to write and edit the version of the experience that appears in the books of Joshua and Judges. But why do the books of Joshua and Judges represent the foundation of Israel as a military conquest by people exclusively outside of Canaanite society? Why is this the case when evidence suggests that in reality people from Canaan joined in the formation of the Israelite people during the course of a slow settlement of the region?

The books of Joshua and Judges were written after the fall and destruction of Jerusalem in 587 BC. One of the central questions the authors faced was why God allowed this to happen. Was it because the people lacked faith? Remembering the settlement stories as part of an organized conquest may well have been motivated by the religious lessons the authors wished to teach a later generation. Perhaps the laying out of the events in Joshua and Judges was meant to exaggerate the contrast between the loss of faith in the present time (the time of exile), which resulted in catastrophe, and the trust of the people in the earlier era, which resulted in great feats of conquest and glory. It is as if God inspired the authors to say, "Look what we accomplished when we truly trusted YHWH, rather than our own resources."

The Israelites: People of the Hills

However the Israelites actually settled Palestine, it is clear that

- the hill country of Palestine was the area that became the homeland for the people of Israel.

- Israelite social formation began to emerge at the Iron Age (1200–1000 BC) and continued to evolve to a monarchy system after 1000 BC.

Other elements of an Israelite government and social structure can be gleaned from both the Bible and other historical and archaeological sources.

The basic social unit of a village in Israel was the *Bet Av* ("House of the Father"). This was a patriarchal household of extended family members. There is even strong evidence that the famous "four pillar house" that archaeologists have identified in many early Israelite villages was the basic physical unit of residence for these "Bet Av" units.

Bet Av
The basic social unit of the Israelite society, a patriarchal household of immediate and extended family members.

Mishpachah
The Hebrew word for the "clans" that were associations of related Bet Av, gathered together to help with planting and harvesting, and with defense against aggressive neighbors.

The *Bet Avs* were themselves gathered into associations that became known as "clans" (a *Mishpachah* in Hebrew). These clans probably arose from two natural needs—agricultural needs for families to help each other with planting and harvest, and military needs for families to help defend each other.

Finally, as the Israelites emerged as a people, so did the traditional twelve "tribes," which the Hebrew tradition traces back to one of the sons of Jacob. The geographical regions they occupied may have also originally identified these tribes.

The village-based tribes were governed by councils of elders—the heads of the various "Houses of the Father." Many Biblical texts explain that day-to-day judgments and general order were maintained by appealing to these elders. The elders made decisions based on traditional laws that were supplemented by the formal religious traditions associated with Moses (whose laws may well have included much of these traditional village laws in the first place). Some anthropologists compare early Israel to villages in developing societies today, some of which have elders who preside over village life.

Early Israelite Religious Practices

The Biblical texts tell us that the early Israelites were influenced by the Canaanites, even in religion. They turned to Baal to help insure abundant crops and livestock in defiance of the covenant, though they did not entirely abandon YHWH. While there are clear signs of Canaanite influence throughout the Bible, the Israelites' religion eventually became a distinct tradition, radically different from all the surrounding religious options.

The Israelite religion was revolutionary in its expectations of the people. The life of the people in the hills of Palestine was to be a place to model this new social existence. But more temptations followed, and the worshippers of YHWH eventually had their strength and moral convictions tested. The time of the kings was one of even greater betrayal of the covenant, until eventually the people were removed from the land and sent into exile.

Section in Review

Quick View

- It may be that the Israelites who settled in the hill country of Canaan were a combination of former slaves from Egypt and native Canaanites who moved from the lowlands.

- The social structure of was centered on twelve tribes, which the Israelites traced to the sons of Jacob.

For Review

1. **Main Idea**: List some of the indications that the settlement of Canaan occurred at a slower pace than the conquest stories of the Book of Joshua describe.

2. **Main Idea**: What was the religious lesson that the authors of Joshua and Judges meant to convey with their conquest stories?

3. **Main Idea**: Describe the social organization of the villages of ancient Israel.

4. **Critical Thinking**: Is it more likely that the people who formed Israel were all former Egyptian slaves or partially natives to the land of Canaan? Why?

For Reflection

How is the social organization of modern America similar to and/or different from that of ancient Israel? What do you think you would have liked or disliked about the *Bet Av* and *Mishpachah* system?

Further Reflections

The stories of the judges are of charismatic leaders who courageously cared for the well being of the tribes of Israel in the times of crisis.

The Book of Judges includes the Deuteronomic cycle of judgment on Israel in these stories. For example, note the pattern of (1) apostasy (abandoning God), (2) oppression by Gentiles, (3) penitence by Israel, and (4) deliverance to freedom in the following passage:

> Because they had thus abandoned him and served Baal and the Ashtaroth, the anger of the Lord flared up against Israel, and he delivered them over to plunderers who despoiled them. He allowed them to fall into the power of their enemies round about whom they were no longer able to withstand. Whatever they undertook, the Lord turned into disaster for them, as in his warning he had sworn he would do, till they were in great distress. . . . Whenever the Lord raised up judges for them, he would be with the judge and save them from the power of their enemies as long as the judge lived; it was thus the Lord took pity on their distressful cries of affliction under their oppressors. But when the judge died, they would relapse and do worse than their fathers, following other gods in service and worship, relinquishing none of their evil practices or stubborn conduct. (Jgs 2:13–15, 18–19)

As this passage shows, the problems of the tribe can be traced to disloyalty to YHWH. Only when the people are oppressed by enemies do they seek repentance. YHWH responds to their change of heart and sends a judge to deliver them from the evil they face. When peace is restored, however, they return to ignoring God and worshipping idols. Then the cycle repeats itself.

The religious theme found in Joshua and Judges is also found in the New Testament. *Conversion*—a radical reorientation of one's life—is a central element of Christ's preaching. Catholics seek this type of repentance and renewal in the Sacrament of Penance. As the *Catechism of the Catholic Church* teaches:

> Conversion is first of all a work of the grace of God who makes our hearts return to him. . . . God gives us the strength to begin anew. It is in discovering the greatness of God's love that our heart is shaken by the horror and weight of sin and begins to fear offending God by sin and being separated from him. (*CCC*, 1432)

Like the Israelites before, people today often return to their sinfulness and remain in need of conversion over and over.

Vocabulary Review

Directions: Match the person or term with the description below.

Bet Av   **Deborah**   **Deuteronomy**   **Gideon**   **Joshua**   **Judges**   **Just war doctrine**
Levirate marriage   **miraculously**   *Mishpachah*   **Ruth**   **Samson**

1. _____ had legendary strength that came from his reliance on God.

2. _____, a Moabite woman who was an ancestor of David, married the nearest relative of her deceased husband, a practice known as _____.

3. The Canticle of _____ praises Jael for killing Sisera and may be among the earliest written material of the entire Bible.

4. The _____ ("House of the Father") was composed of immediate and extended family members that were a part of larger clans known as _____.

5. _____ is the name of the Church teachings that define the limits of warfare.

6. Literally, _____ means "second law."

7. The _____ were temporary military leaders and arbiters of disputes, who reminded Israel of their responsibility to depend on God.

8. The Israelites thought that God fought _____ *for* them, not merely *with* them.

9. The Book of _____ depicts a violent conquest of Canaan, while the Book of _____ reveals a more peaceful settlement of the land.

10. The judge _____ had serious doubts about his ability to lead the people of Israel and eventually gave in to idolatry.

Performance Assessment Project

Poetry and music were popular tools in ancient storytelling. Many of these poems and songs found their way into the Bible. Biblical authors used these devices to highlight the key events of stories, to honor the heroes, and to illustrate the most important message behind the stories. Write a song or a poem retelling the story of the settlement of Canaan for the Israelites in Babylonian Exile. What messages would be particularly important for them to hear? What people or events would be particularly memorable and important in their situation?

Called to Prayer

Then the angel of the LORD came and sat under the terebinth in Ophrah that belonged to Joash the Abiezrite. While his son Gideon was beating out wheat in the wine press to save it from the Midianites, the angel of the LORD appeared to him and said, "The LORD is with you, O champion!" "My LORD," Gideon said to him, "if the LORD is with us, why has all this happened to us? Where are his wondrous deeds of which our fathers told us when they said, 'Did not the LORD bring us up from Egypt?' For now the LORD has abandoned us and has delivered us into the power of Midian." The LORD turned to him and said, "Go with the strength you have and save Israel from the power of Midian. It is I who send you." But he answered him, "Please, my lord, how can I save Israel? My family is the meanest in Manasseh, and I am the most insignificant in my father's house." "I shall be with you," the LORD said to him, "and you will cut down Midian to the last man."

—Judges 6:11–16

- **Reflection**: Have you ever blamed God for things that have gone wrong in your life? How did you communicate this with him? How did he respond?

- **Meditation**: As the most insignificant member of his *Bet Av*, Gideon doubts his ability to free the Israelites from the Midianites, yet God chooses him. Imagine that God is calling you to overcome some great problem today. What will your objections be? How will God reassure you that he will be with you?

- **Resolution**: Everyone goes through difficult times, but the Old Testament reassures us that we must trust in God. Offer a prayer to take away any doubts you have about the future. The future is in God's hands.

Notes

1. Joseph Calloway Archeological Museum.

2. See the excellent summary in chapter 1, "New Understandings of the Israelite Settlement Process," in Robert Gnuse, *No Other Gods*, Sheffield Academic Press: Sheffield, 1997, 23–61.

3. Polygamy was still practiced in the time of the Patriarchs, though God's forming of an exclusive covenant with Israel prepared the Chosen People for the exclusiveness and indissolubility of married love (see *CCC*, 1609-1611).

The Monarchy:
The Journey Takes a New Direction

CHAPTER OUTLINE

■ *Israel's request for a human king has many consequences.*

■ *Israel constantly struggled with the idolatry that surrounded them in Canaan.*

■ *The first kings of Israel united and strengthened the tribes of Israel, leading to the establishment of a capital and Temple in Jerusalem.*

■ *Political and religious division plagued Israel for centuries after the death of Solomon.*

■ *In time both Israel and Judah would be conquered by foreign powers.*

Chapter Six

Israel's request for a human king has many consequences.

Introduction

As mentioned in Chapter 5, Israel's request for a human king had immediate, negative consequences—the most important of which was that YHWH considered the request a rejection of his kingship over the people. At the same time, the prophet Samuel warned Israel about the eventual, long-term consequences of having a king. Among the things a king would require of the people, Samuel told them:

- Their sons would be assigned to run before his chariot.

- They would be required to be his soldiers.

- They would do his farming and plowing.

- They would make his military and farming equipment.

- Their daughters would be his ointment-makers and cooks.

- Their best produce would be used to feed his officials and profits will be given to the king's servants.

- Their own servants and work animals would be taken to give service to the king as well.

Samuel concluded, "He will tithe your flocks and you yourselves will become his slaves. When this takes place, you will complain against the king whom you have chosen, but on that day the Lord will not answer" (see 1 Sm 8:17–18).

Still, for all this, the people did not give in. "Not so! There must be a king over us. We too must be like other nations, with a king to rule us and to lead us in warfare and fight our battles" (1 Sm 8:19–20).

Chapter 8 of the first Book of Samuel hardly presents a ringing endorsement for an Israelite monarchy. Because King **David**, his predecessor **Saul**, and his son and successor, **Solomon**, are among the most remembered and revered heroes of the Old Testament, it may be surprising to learn that the monarchy was not an overall positive experience for Israel. That is why it is important to begin a chapter on the Israelite monarchy by remembering the

Samuel annoints David

negative consequences that resulted from the people's request for a king and the ways these results were recorded in the Old Testament.

Many Biblical scholars believe that 1 Samuel 8 was not written *before* there were kings, but rather, long *after* the fall of monarchy, as a commentary on what happened. The monarchy was placed in this context in order to send a message to the Jews reading the text many years later: "We should have known better than to do this," and perhaps even, "We are not meant to have any king but YHWH. We are better off with no king." Perhaps this was meant to comfort and even guide them during the time of exile.

Also, in reading 1 Samuel 8, note the incident that precedes Israel's request for a king: the routing of the Philistines in 1 Samuel 7. For twenty years, the Israelites had "turned to the Lord," giving up their foreign gods and worshipping God alone. Once again, God had miraculously delivered the Israelites from the powerful Philistine army. The request for a king was probably precipitated by Israel's fear of the Philistine armies, yet there is irony in the timing: just after a twenty-year period of faithfulness and a mighty display of God's power to defeat their enemies, the Israelites suddenly didn't trust God's power to protect them. They wanted a king, such as other nations had, to fight their battles. This incident serves only to highlight the religious significance of the stories that Israel prospers when the people honor the covenant, yet time and again, they turn their backs on YHWH.

The Monarchy: Positives and Negatives

It is important to read the story of Israel's kings with balance. There were also many positive aspects of the monarchy in Israel's history. For example, Israel became a nation with a strong central leadership, as opposed to a fragmented cluster of clans as during the time of the judges. A holy city was built in Jerusalem. And from the family of King David, a dynasty was formed with an ancestral line that eventually led to the birth of the Messiah, or one anointed by God. Jesus Christ is connected in Scripture to the Davidic line (see Mt 1:6 and Lk 23:31).

While many positive aspects of the monarchy are explicitly tied to King David, it is equally true that the Scriptures also detail his failings—including his ill-fated affair with a married woman, Bathsheba, when he abused his powers and killed her husband to cover his sin (see 2 Sm 11–12). David's son, Solomon, too, ended his life having compromised his faith in God for the sake of political alliances with nations all around him.

The Old Testament (especially 1 and 2 Kings) is critical of Israel's other kings as well. For example, the kings are criticized for an economic system that favored the rich while hurting the poor. In fact, only two of Israel's forty-two kings, Hezekiah and Josiah, received unmitigated praise:

[Hezekiah] pleased the Lord, just as his forefather David had done. It was he who removed the high places, shattered the pillars, and cut down the sacred poles. He smashed the bronze serpent called Nehushtan which Moses had made, because up to that time the Israelites were burning incense to it. He put his trust in the Lord, the God of Israel; and neither before him nor after him was there anyone like him among all the kings of Judah. (2 Kgs 18:3–5)

Before [Josiah] there had been no king who turned to the Lord as he did, with his whole heart, his whole soul, and his whole strength, in accord with the entire law of Moses; nor could any after him compare with him. (2 Kgs 23:25)

When these Scripture references of praise for Hezekiah and Josiah are measured with failings of Israel's kings (including at its very origin in 1 Samuel 8), the influence of the prophets who called the people (including the kings) back to a proper observance of the Law stands out in a prominent way.

Section in Review

Quick View

- When the Israelites called for a king like their neighboring nations, the prophet Samuel warned them of some negative consequences.

- Israel's monarchy was ultimately one of both success and failure.

For Review

1. **Main Idea**: What were the consequences Samuel warned the Israelites about should they choose a king?

2. **Main Idea**: What is the religious significance of 1 Samuel 7–8?

David
The king of the united kingdom of Israel from 1009 to 969 BC. He conquered the Trans-Jordanian states, gaining control of the major trade routes linking Egypt and Mesopotamia. Jesus was a descendant of David.

Saul
The first king of Israel, anointed by the prophet Samuel. He was never able to fully unite the twelve tribes and organize them into a recognizable nation.

Solomon
David and Bathsheba's son, the last king of the united monarchy. He was renowned for his wisdom as well as for his wealth and his many large building projects. In addition to the king's palace and numerous walled fortresses throughout Palestine, he also built the Temple of Jerusalem to house the Ark of the Covenant.

3. **Critical Thinking**: Why might accounts about Israelite's monarchy written during the Babylonian Exile include some of its negative aspects?

For Reflection

What do you perceive to be the advantages and disadvantages of living under a monarchy as opposed to a democratic government?

Israel constantly struggled with the idolatry that surrounded them in Canaan.

Religious Developments during the Monarchy

Pagan and polytheistic practices, which appeared throughout the time of the judges, continued to crop up among the Israelites during the time of the kings. The Old Testament offers testimony to this. The investigation into how and when this occurred is best begun at the end of the monarchy, during the reign of King **Josiah** in 640-609 BC.

According to 2 Kings 22:2, Josiah "pleased the Lord and conducted himself unswervingly just as his ancestor David had done." Josiah was considered a righteous king because of his determination to purify the religion of the state and return it to a faith more devoted to YHWH. The previous kings had encouraged polytheistic practices and worship. The author of the Book of Zephaniah makes this clear in his sweeping criticism of the extensive idolatry of Judah at the beginning of Josiah's reign. Consider, for example, what Josiah had to do in order to purify the Jerusalem Temple.

Read 2 Kings 23:1–15.

This passage reveals much about the state of Israelite religious practice under the monarchy. Canaanite gods and goddesses, like **Baal** and Asherah, are mentioned. The First Commandment condemns such idolatry, the worship of false gods. YHWH is the living God who gives life and intervenes in history (see *CCC*, 2112). There have never been, nor are there now, "other" gods or goddesses.

The passage also alludes to some of the pagan Canaanite practices: offerings made in Temple, images of the gods, and astrological practices (e.g., burning incense to Baal, to the sun, moon, and signs of the Zodiac). It mentions sexual rites associated with pagan religions (e.g., cult prostitutes) and even human sacrifice. Remember, Josiah's reign came at the end of Israel's monarchy. The pagan practices mentioned in this passage developed during the reigns of the preceding kings of Israel. This passage in 2 Kings provides a clear indication of how far the kings of Israel before Josiah had taken Israelite worship into a mix of pagan religions. Josiah had to clean up Solomon's famous Temple. Recall that the First Commandment states that "you shall worship the Lord your god and him only shall you serve." Worship of false gods was the greatest offense against YHWH for those living at the time of the kings. Superstition is also a violation of the First Commandment.

Who Was Tempted to Paganism?

What was the nature of the pagan religion of the Canaanites that is so often condemned in the Bible? Who were the false gods Baal and Asherah so often mentioned? In the past century a great deal more about Canaanite religion has been learned, largely because of one magnificent archaeological discovery—the ruins of **Ugarit**.

Ugarit was an ancient capital city at the center of a small territorial expanse that flourished in the second millennium (2000–1180 BC). Evidence suggests that the site was finally abandoned following a major destructive act in 1180 BC. What makes this archaeological

Baal

site so significant is the amount of texts found in it. Most of the texts were written in a local language now known as "Ugaritic." This language closely resembled Hebrew. In fact, it is often suggested that Hebrew is a dialect of the same language family as Ugaritic.

Among the many different kinds of texts discovered at Ugarit were a number of religious texts that told stories of some of the Canaanite gods and characters known to us from the Bible—most prominently the god Baal. Baal was considered the god of fertility and was often associated with images of storms and rain. A rain god would have been very important to a largely agricultural society, particularly in the relatively arid climate of Palestine.

Many of the texts in Ugarit portrayed Baal in battle. The two most interesting of these battles are the one between Baal and Yam ("Yammu") the god of the sea, and the battle between Baal and Mot, the god of death.

The battle between Baal and Yam echoes the better-known story of the Babylonian god Marduk against the Babylonian god of the sea, Tiamat. The Babylonian story contains an account of the creation of human beings. Thus, a large number of people of ancient Mesopotamia and the coastal regions were familiar with a creation epic that included the idea of a great battle between gods—especially the god of the storm versus the god of the sea. The sea often represented chaos to the ancient peoples, so it is possible that the conceptual idea behind this myth was that Baal defeated chaos and disorder, and this defeat allowed organized civilization to emerge. Order came from chaos.

The other great battle was the struggle between Baal and Mot. In this battle, Baal is initially defeated and sinks down into the underworld—the world of the dead where Mot is ruler. Baal is there assisted by his wife-sister Anat, and is able to re-engage the battle and rise up out of the underworld in victory over Mot. Some scholars of Ugaritic literature have suggested that the Baal-Mot conflict may actually be tied to regular celebrations of the changing of the seasons. Autumn, when everything is "dying," must be the time of Baal's defeat by Mot. In Ezekiel 8:14, there is a reference to "weeping for Tammuz (Baal)." This may be a "mourning" rite associated with an autumn observance of Baal's descent into the underworld.

When it is spring, and everything is rising into new life again, this is the time when Baal is victorious over Mot and rises into the world of the living. It is possible that the Canaanite/coastal peoples like those at Ugarit actually had certain rituals and rites surrounding this myth and connected to the changing of the seasons. Spring has invited festivals of fertility in many different societies.

THE BOOKS OF CHRONICLES

The two books of Chronicles form a unified historical work that represents a fascinating "rethinking" of Israelite history that was written a few hundred years later than the books of Samuel and Kings. The books of Chronicles cover the time span between the reign of Saul and the Exile, roughly the same period as covered in the books of Samuel and the books of Kings. However, the Chronicles omit certain themes from other historical sources and write a report that stresses two religious themes: true worship of YHWH and the importance of the priests to God's People. This history emphasizes issues of interest to the community well into the period of Persian Rule (539–333 BC).

Josiah
The last independent king of Judah, and one of only two kings to receive unmitigated praise in the Old Testament. He initiated religious reforms attempting to purify the worship of YHWH in the Temple. He was killed in a battle with the Egyptians who then established a puppet government in Jerusalem.

Baal
The Canaanite god of fertility, associated with storms and rain. He was the most prominent of the Canaanite gods and the one most often worshipped by the Israelites.

Ugarit
An ancient city of the Canaanites that was discovered in 1928. Many texts were found there, from which scholars have learned a great deal about the Canaanite religion.

Archeological site of Ugarit

Jezebel

A Canaanite princess, married to Ahab, one of the kings of the northern kingdom. She orchestrated the murder of Naboth in order to gain his property for her husband.

The Ugaritic texts provide insight into why pagan worship was tempting for the Israelites. First, it was the common religion of the area. Many of the people who lived near or even among the Israelites practiced some form of it. Second, it was associated with fertility, and agriculture was obviously the main basis of all ancient economies. What was good for the economy probably seemed absolute and true. Third, and perhaps most importantly, it was a religion that served the establishment. Kings and priests ruled the people according to these religious ideas, which provided stability and an explanation for why things were the way they were. But it was a stability that was often oppressive, since these traditional fertility religions bolstered the authority of the kings and told the common people that their state in life was determined by the gods.

Estimates are that pagan religion supported a social structure in which five percent of the population (kings, priests, and landowners) ruled over the remainder of the population—mostly landless agricultural peasant workers. These peasant workers were all kept locked in the belief that these "gods" must be kept happy and that the kings must be obeyed.

Consider the famous story of **Jezebel** (1 Kings 21). She was a Canaanite princess who married the Northern Israelite king, Ahab. Hebrew law limited the power of the king so that even he could not seize whatever land he wanted, but Jezebel the Canaanite thought this was ridiculous and took matters into her own hands. Ahab wanted property that by right belonged to an Israelite peasant named Naboth. Jezebel had Naboth executed and took his land. She was acting as a Canaanite ruler might have. This story illustrates what pagan religion would mean in terms of its social consequences. It contrasts sharply with the stories of the prophet Elijah, living with and saving the lives of a widow and her only son in the name of the one, true, God, YHWH (see 1 Kgs 17).

It is easy to see why Israel clashed so strongly with the societies who honored the ancient pagan and polytheistic religions. The central event of Israelite religion was the liberation of slaves away from the greatest known "king" of the ancient world—the Pharaoh of Egypt. Furthermore, the basis of the religion of Israel was a collection of "laws" that guaranteed that all people shared with one another, took care of one another, and made sure that nobody ruled oppressively over another. Israelites offered care for the "widow, the orphan, and the foreigner"—the weakest members of society. The Israelite religion was a revolutionary religion of changing circumstances (it started by ending slavery in Egypt) while maintaining community ties that were not oppressive.

So why were the kings of ancient Israel so deeply tempted to encourage pagan religion in their kingdom? A polytheistic religion with many gods supported the rule of the kings more than

Judaism, which placed even the highest king under judgment for his behavior. (Interestingly, it was for this reason that American slaveholders never wanted their African slaves to learn to read. Although they wanted their slaves to be "Christian," they feared the slaves might read the Bible and learn about Moses and the release of the Hebrews from slavery.)

Section in Review

Quick View

- Josiah's efforts to purify the Temple indicate the extent to which the Israelites broke the First Commandment.

- The archaeological discovery at Ugarit shed light on the stories of ancient Canaanite gods.

- The religion of Israel clashed with that of the Canaanites in its focus on justice and care for others, especially the weak.

For Review

1. **Main Idea**: List some of the pagan practices that made their way into the Israelite communities during the period of the monarchy.

2. **Main Idea**: What were the most common complaints made against the kings of Israel and Judah? Which two kings were praised and why?

3. **Main Idea**: What are two religious themes stressed in 1 and 2 Chronicles?

4. **Critical Thinking**: What made the religion of Israel distinct from their Canaanite neighbors?

For Reflection

What Bible stories seem radical or dangerous to you, or might seem so if people began to take them seriously? Why are they risky? Who or what could they change?

The first kings of Israel united and strengthened the tribes of Israel, leading to the establishment of a capital and Temple in Jerusalem.

The "United" Monarchy: Saul, David, and Solomon

The monarchy began under the conditions of both internal and external crisis. At the same time that the tribes of Israel were consolidating, or at least loosely bringing themselves into a sometimes stormy union. The legendary Philistines were coming together to take their share of Palestine.

The social dynamics of 1200–1000 BC Palestine included interesting and complex interactions between traditional Canaanite settlements, newly emerging Israelite settlements, and Philistine settlements. The conflicts between the Israelite and Philistines became most severe at times. In the midst of these conflicts, the Israelite tribes determined to organize themselves more effectively against the Philistine threat.

The Philistines threatened in two significant ways. First, they had the ability to fashion weapons with iron, which tribal Israel was not yet capable of doing. Iron was a decided advantage over bronze, not only in weaponry but in agriculture as well. Iron plows, for examples, were much sturdier and more effective for farming. Agricultural advantage meant economic advantage. Second, the Philistines' military strength was partly based on their effective self-organization. Tribal Israel, on the other hand, was rather poorly organized. There were clearly times when the Philistines dominated over tribal Israel.

Saul and the Philistines

Read 1 Samuel 9–10.

Saul, from the family of Benjamin, was selected the first king of Israel. When the prophet Samuel first caught sight of Saul, the Lord told him: "This is the man of whom I told you; he is to govern my people" (1 Sm 9:17). However, Saul was a deeply troubled leader with a fragile mental state. He failed to establish a centralized government.

During Saul's rule, Israel was probably not an organized entity at all, much less an actual state. He was as much the last of the judges as he was the first king. He "reigned" over a loose-knit organization of tribes and people who were mostly farmers. It has been estimated that the largest settlement in his "kingdom" probably amounted to no more than 100 people. There was no capital city or administrative center.

Saul was essentially a warrior with limited success against the Philistines—especially in the southern Israel hill country where his heartland was located and where the emerging state of Judah would be located. The following description of a battle led by Saul and his son Jonathan provides a clue to the difficulties the Israelites faced in battling the Philistines during the time of Saul:

> Not a single smith was to be found in the whole land of Israel, for the Philistines had said, "Otherwise the Hebrews will make swords or spears." All Israel, therefore, had to go down to the Philistines to sharpen their plowshares, mattocks, axes, and sickles. . . . And so on the day of battle neither sword nor spear could be found in the possession of any of the soldiers with Saul or Jonathan. Only Saul and his son Jonathan had them. (1 Sm 13:19–20, 22)

Eventually, Saul's unfaithfulness to YHWH and the charismatic rise of one of Saul's assistants, David, led to the anointing of Israel's greatest and most well-known king.

David's Rise to Power

Read 1 Samuel 16–17.

David was king approximately 1009–969 BC. His rise to power is described in differing Biblical accounts.

David is first introduced when the prophet Samuel is impressed with one of the older sons of Jesse, though he does not have a clear sense from God that this young man is really the future king. As the story continues, God scolds Samuel for trusting in only outward appearances of the older sons, all of whom God rejects. When Samuel asks Jesse if he has any other sons, Jesse replies,

> "There is still the youngest, who is tending the sheep." Samuel said to Jesse, "Send for him; we will not begin the sacrificial banquet until he arrives here." Jesse sent and had the young man brought to them. He was ruddy, a youth handsome to behold and making a splendid appearance. The Lord said, "There—anoint him, for this is he!" Then Samuel, with the horn of oil in hand, anointed him in the midst of his brothers; and from that day on, the spirit of the Lord rushed upon David. (1 Sm 16:11–13)

David goes on to succeed Saul eventually as the chosen king of Israel, though the story of how it happens varies. Part of the difficulty is that David's reign has to be clearly justified, since he is not of the family of Saul. The first Book of Samuel represents Saul as having been rejected for his sin (see 1 Sm 15:1–35), but there are two different traditions about how David came into Saul's employ: in the first, David becomes Saul's "armor-bearer" (1 Sm 16:14–23); in the second version, David comes to Saul after the famous incident when he kills the Philistine warrior, Goliath, in a single battle (1 Sm 17). David is then presented to Saul as a conquering hero.

After a series of wars between the relatives of Saul and David and his associates, David finally consolidates his reign. But the path to the throne for David is clearly paved in blood. He systematically eliminates rivals to the throne from the family of Saul, he also engages in military conquests that include not only successful raids against the Philistines, but also successful military campaigns against the political communities across the Jordan River—the peoples of Ammon, Moab, and Edom.

The significance of conquering these Trans-Jordanian states cannot be overemphasized, since this was the path of most of the major trade routes through Palestine, linking Egypt, Phoenicia, and the Mesopotamian Empires. Controlling these trade routes meant David's regime would also control taxes and payment of passage fees.

Standard of Living

Research the division of wealth in the nation and the world. What percent of the people control the total income? What is the gross national product? What is the average income for families? What is the poverty level? How many people live at the poverty level. Compare the division of wealth to the division the prophets found unacceptable in Israel and Judah.

THE DAVIDIC LINE

The second Book of Samuel records a central promise made to David by the Lord:

> It was I who took you from the pasture and from the care of the flock to be commander of my people Israel. I have been with you wherever you went, and I have destroyed all your enemies before you. And I will make you famous like the great ones of the earth. I will fix a place for my people Israel; I will plant them so that they may dwell in their place without further disturbance. Neither shall the wicked continue to afflict them as they did of old, since the time I first appointed judges over my people Israel. I will give you rest from all your enemies. The Lord also reveals to you that he will establish a house for you. And when your time comes and you rest with your ancestors, I will raise up your heir after you, sprung from your loins, and I will make his kingdom firm. . . . Your house and your kingdom shall endure forever before me; your throne shall stand firm forever. (2 Sm 7:8–12, 16)

The prophecy is the basis for the Jewish expectation of a Messiah, a son of David, which Jesus would eventually fulfill. The Gospels of Matthew and Luke provide genealogies of Jesus that trace his ancestry through David.

Genealogies of Jesus

Read the two genealogies of Jesus in the Gospels: Matthew 1:1-17 and Luke 3:37-38. Research: Why does Jesus' genealogy in Matthew trace to Abraham and the one in Luke trace to Adam? Why do you think Jesus' genealogy in Luke's Gospel is not placed until the third chapter?

David's regime seems to have become wealthy on precisely these terms.

There is only brief archaeological evidence of David's kingdom or mention of its existence outside the Bible. An inscription from a later time period, from the kingdom of Moab, does refer to the royalty in Israel as the "House of David." This is the oldest non-Biblical reference to the time of David. It may be more accurate to think of David's role as king as one of military leadership, for there is no doubt about his place in this history of Israel.

God blessed David, and despite his many sins, David remained loyal to God. Later generations saw in David someone God used to establish the nation as part of his divine plan. In praising David, their greatest king, the Israelites acknowledged the God who favored his Chosen People.

Solomon: A Mixed Portrait

More than with his father, David, there is considerable archaeological evidence of King Solomon's role as an administrator of a united kingdom. This makes sense, because Solomon was reputed to be the great builder in the Bible. Solomon not only built up Jerusalem, including an actual palace and the Temple itself, but he also built many other walled cities as military fortresses. Many of these walled fortresses—dated to nearly the exact period of Solomon's rule—have been excavated by archaeologists to lend non-Biblical evidence to his rule.

The Biblical portrait of Solomon is a mixture of positive and negative impressions. Among the positive impressions is the famous story of a king who wisely settles a dispute between two women who both claim an infant as her own (see 1 Kgs 3:16–28). Another is the story of Solomon's response when God tells him to ask for anything he wants and God will grant it to him. Solomon asks God only for the gifts of "an understanding heart to judge your people and to distinguish right from wrong" (1 Kgs 3:9).

God is so impressed with this request that he promises Solomon both wisdom and the wealth that comes with human success. But it is clear that the bright portrait of Solomon dims as he grows older. He engages in a number of political marriages, and the Biblical historians portray this as the source of his downfall—not because civil law did not permit many wives (ancient treaties were often sealed by exchanging royal children in marriage),

Judgment of the King Solomon by Louis de Boullogne the Younger

Ark of the Covenant
The portable shrine built to hold the tablets on which Moses wrote the Law. It was a sign of God's presence to the Israelites. Solomon built the Temple in Jerusalem to house the ark.

Showbread
The twelve loaves of bread presented on the altar every Sabbath as an offering to YHWH. The priests consumed the bread at the end of every week. (This is also sometimes spelled "shewbread" but the pronunciation does not change.)

but because many of these were pagan women whom Solomon allowed to foster polytheistic religious practices among the Israelites.

But there is an even more serious issue blotting Solomon's record—namely how he treated his own people. Even his great building accomplishments are called into question: How could Solomon afford such extravagant projects? An older section from 1 Kings claims that Solomon enslaved foreigners and maintains that he would never enslave or overburden his own people with the tasks of his great building campaigns:

> All the non-Israelite people who remained in the land, descendants of the Amorites, Hittites, Perizzites, Hivites, and Jebusites whose doom the Israelites had been unable to accomplish, Solomon conscripted as forced laborers, as they are to this day. But Solomon enslaved none of the Israelites, for they were his fighting force, his ministers, commanders, adjutants, chariot officers, and charioteers. (1 Kgs 9:20–22)

But in another part of the record of Solomon, it states clearly that he certainly *did* force his own people into labor: "King Solomon conscripted thirty thousand workmen from all Israel" (1 Kgs 5:27). From this passage it is not completely clear if the workers were all actual Israelites. However, the proof that they were is most evident in the events that overtake Solomon's son and successor, Rehoboam.

When Rehoboam hears that the Northern Israelite peoples are upset and angry over their years under Solomon, he goes to meet with the elders of the Northern Tribes and find out why they are so upset:

> They said to Rehoboam: "Your father put on us a heavy yoke. If you now lighten the harsh service and the heavy yoke your father imposed on us, we will serve you." "Come back to me in three days," he answered them. (1 Kgs 12:3–5)

When the people returned, Rehoboam showed little of his father's reputed wisdom. His answer to the people led directly to the split of the kingdom, into a northern kingdom and southern kingdom. Rehoboam told them:

> "Whereas my father put a heavy yoke on you, I will make it heavier. My father beat you with whips, but I will beat you with scorpions." (1 Kgs 12:11)

These words of Rehoboam make the case against Solomon fairly tight. Solomon enslaved his own people and a large percentage of them resented it. Eventually, a group broke away from the Southern Kingdom and formed a separate state under a new king, Jeroboam. Usually the final split between the two kingdoms is dated at the death of Solomon, approximately 922 BC.

THE TEMPLE OF SOLOMON

King David had great concern for the **Ark of the Covenant**, which had been housed in a tent through Israel's wanderings in the wilderness. His desire was to build a Temple for the ark. However, the Lord, through the prophet Nathan, said that such a place was unnecessary. "In all my wanderings everywhere among the Israelites, did I ever utter a word to any one of the judges whom I charged to tend my people Israel to ask: Why have you not built me a house of cedar?" (2 Sm 7:7). Nevertheless, David's son, Solomon, proceeded with the plans for a Temple. Chapters 6 to 8 of the first Book of Kings describe in detail the building, furnishing, and dedication of the Temple.

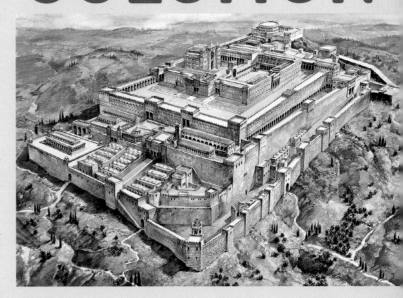

Many details of the Temple reflected Canaanite-Phoenician patterns. Its basic floor plan consisted of three parts. Approaching from the east, one walked between two freestanding, bronze-covered pillars into a small vestibule. This opened into the largest of the three rooms, the Holy Place. It was about sixty feet long and contained an incense altar, a table of **Showbread**, and ten candlesticks. Canaanite art of pomegranates, lilies, and palms decorated the walls. The third room, the Holy of Holies, was thirty square feet in measurement. There were no windows. This room housed the Ark of the Covenant. On both sides of the Ark were cherubims. This was the place where YHWH was believed to be present, enthroned over the ark. Other rooms along the back and side walls were used for storage. The Temple's small size was due in great part to the fact that only priests could enter the building. Worshippers stood in the courtyard *near* the Temple.

Throughout the years of the monarchy, a close connection was maintained between the Temple and the kings. The Temple was destroyed in the Babylonian capture of Jerusalem in 587 BC. It was rebuilt after the exile (520–515 BC). The Romans destroyed this "second Temple" in 70 AD.

Building Solomon's Temple

Build or draw a model of Solomon's Temple to scale. Read 1 Kings 6; 7:13–51 (note that a cubit equals 1 1/2 feet). Make sure to include the following features: winged creatures, Ark of the Covenant, Holy of Holies, store rooms, the Holy Place, porch, free-standing pillars, and bronze tank. Write a report mentioning at least ten other facts about Solomon's Temple gleaned from the Bible and other resources. Finally, spend some time before the Blessed Sacrament at a Catholic church or chapel. Compare the tabernacle design to the Ark of the Covenant. Pray for the gift of wisdom in the presence of the Lord.

Section in Review

Quick View

- The Philistines, the major military threat to Israel, had significant military advantages.

- David was able to lead Israel to military victories that his predecessor Saul was unable to accomplish.

- King Solomon is known for his great building projects, though the burden of the construction fell on the people of Israel.

For Review

1. **Vocabulary**: How is the Ark of the Covenant related to Solomon's Temple?

2. **Main Idea**: What advantages did the Philistines have over the Israelites during Saul's reign?

3. **Main Idea**: What were the accomplishments of King David? What were his failings?

4. **Main Idea**: What was the chief complaint of the people against King Solomon?

5. **Critical Thinking**: Critique the prophet Samuel's predictions about the long-term consequences of having a king?

For Reflection

Why do you think King Solomon built the Temple? Read 1 Kings 8 for clues about what the Temple meant to the Israelites. What does the church building mean to Catholics today?

Political and religious division plagued Israel for centuries after the death of Solomon.

The Divided Monarchy

When Solomon died, Israel divided into two separate kingdoms. The Southern Kingdom was called **Judah**. It consisted of the traditional territory of only two tribes: Benjamin and Judah. The Northern Kingdom was called "Israel" and was made up of the other ten tribes. The two kingdoms existed side by side for several centuries, ruled by a succession of kings. Both Judah and Israel engaged in several internal struggles during those years as well as fighting battles with outside nations, including the Arameans.

Judah's kings considered themselves the legitimate rulers because their ancestors could be traced to King David. However, the unequal division of the tribes hints that the majority of the people from the former united Israel rejected the kings of Judah because of the abuse of Solomon and the threats of Rehoboam.

The books of 1 and 2 Kings tell details of the divided monarchy. Some kings have several details provided about their reign. Others are mentioned very briefly indeed. The next sections report on some of the highlights of this historical period leading to the sieges of the Northern Kingdom by the Assyrians in 722–720 BC and of the Southern Kingdom by the Babylonians over a century later.

The Insurrection of Jeroboam

Jeroboam, son of Nebat, led the insurrection against King Rehoboam and founded the Northern Kingdom of Israel (see 1 Kgs 12:12–33; 2 Chr 11:1–4). There are a number of interesting elements to Jeroboam's story. As King Solomon's officer, he was in charge of forced labor (1 Kgs 11:28). Did he, like Moses, observe the suffering of "his people" and come to be a voice for liberation from the enslavement of Solomon's regime? It is certain that Jeroboam fled Solomon's anger after speaking out against the people's mistreatment. He sought sanctuary in an unlikely place—in the land of Pharaoh Shishak of Egypt (see 1 Kgs 11:40).

Jesus and the Temple

(CCC, 583–586)

From his birth to death, Jesus participated in the life of the Temple in Jerusalem. He had deep respect for the Temple and considered it a privileged place to encounter God (CCC, 583–584). Yet, the Gospels also report that Jesus predicted that the Temple would be destroyed. Actually, Jesus made this claim in reference to himself and his own body. He explained to his disciples, "I say to you, something greater than the temple is here" (Mt 12:6). While on trial before the Sanhedrin his accusers exclaimed, "This fellow said, 'I am able to destroy the temple of God and rebuild it in three days'" (Mt 26:61).

The Temple was a place of sacrifice and atonement, though some Old Testament prophets criticized the practice: "For it is love that I desire, not sacrifice, and knowledge of God rather than holocausts" (Hos 6:6). Jesus is the last sacrifice that eliminates the need to continue to take burnt offerings to the Temple.

More Temple imagery is found in the letters of St. Paul. Paul makes a connection between the Body of Christ, the Church, and the Temple. "Do you not know that you are the temple of God, and that the Spirit of God dwells in you" (1 Cor 3:16)? The Church is the Body of Christ and Christ's Body is the new Temple on earth. This fulfills Ezekiel's prophecy of the new covenant when God will "place [his] sanctuary among [his people] forever" (Ez 37:26).

Temple	Jesus
God's dwelling place among his people (2 Sm 7:5–6; 1 Kgs 6:10, 8:25; Ps 11:4)	Jesus is God's "definitive dwelling place among men" (CCC, 586) (Jn 2:21, Mt 12:6)
Daily sacrifices were made in the Temple (Lv 1–5) God desires love, not just sacrifice (Hos 6:6)	Christ's one sacrifice takes away sin (Heb 10:12)

Judah
The name of the southern kingdom after the splitting of the monarchy. It included the territory originally belonging to just two of the twelve tribes, Judah and Benjamin.

Establishment religion
A religion that tends to support the power of the ruling class over the common people. In the case of the Israelite monarchy, it joined YHWH worship with the worship of other Canaanite gods.

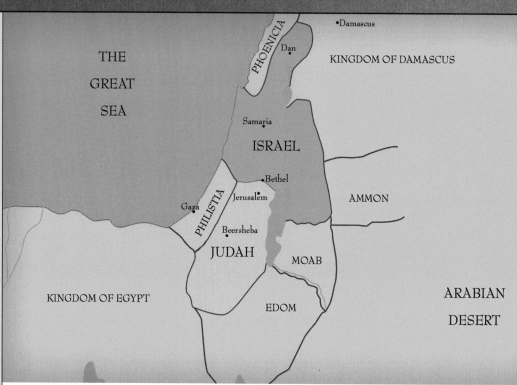

When Solomon died, Israel divided into two separate kingdoms. The northern kingdom was called "Israel." The southern kingdom was known as "Judah."

Shishak may have accepted Jeroboam as a protected guest because Shishak entertained the thought of reasserting Egyptian dominance in the lands of Canaan lost during the rules of Saul, David, and Solomon. Egyptian records carved on the walls of the Temple of Karnak on the banks of the Nile River (still visible today) verify that Shishak most certainly did engage in military campaigns in Judah and Israel. Egypt probably did re-take control of the region during Shishak's rule. As 1 Kings reports:

> In the fifth year of King Rehoboam, Shishak, the king of Egypt, attacked Jerusalem. He took everything, including the treasures of the temple of the Lord and those of the royal palace, as well as all the gold shields made under Solomon. (1 Kgs 14:25–26)

What the relationship of Jeroboam was to this campaign is not clear.

According to 1 Kings 15:1, Jeroboam continued to rule in the north after the reign of Rehoboam in Judah ended.

Rivalry and Religion in the Northern Kingdom

Read 1 Kings 12:26–33.

Jeroboam feared the reunification of Judah and Israel that might possibly arise through continued worship at a single Temple in Jerusalem. In the northern cities of Dan and Bethel, Jeroboam brought gold calves and built temples there. He also appointed priests from among the people living in those areas who were not Levites, the traditional tribe of priests.

Most people living in the north were already disillusioned by the burdens placed on them by Solomon and Rehoboam so that their loyalties to Jerusalem and the Temple had waned before the establishment of temples in Dan and Bethel. The sacrificing of golden calves in these temples led to the sin of idolatry (1 Kgs 12:30).

The continued social, political, and religious relationship between Judah and Israel was one of constant conflict—conquest and counter-conquest. These battles with one another were complicated by the involvement of other local regimes and larger empires.

By 900–800 BC the rise of the Neo-Assyrian Empire, based in the northern Mesopotamian city of Nineveh, caused difficulties for all the regimes in the area of Palestine, Syria, and the coastal port cities of what is today Lebanon. The Assyrian Empire used brute force to dominate the entire region. By 722 BC, the Assyrian Empire finally conquered all of the Northern Kingdom.

1 and 2 Kings (and 2 Chronicles) describe the period between 922 and 722 BC as a time of corruption of the kings of both Judah and Israel. Though there were many notable achievements of these various kings, the Bible focuses more on the survival and perpetuation of the form of YHWH worship that was consistent with the messages of the prophets, and opposed to the official versions of the religious establishments supported by Israel's and Judah's rulers.

The rivalry between and often within Judah and Israel can be described as a conflict between a form of YHWH worship that also allowed the worship of other lesser deities in addition to YHWH, and a more prophetically inspired form of worship that was *exclusively* devoted to YHWH.

Each of these religious views had strong links to particular socioeconomic ideas about how society ought to be organized. Those who believed YHWH alone should be worshipped (represented strongly by the prophets) seem to have had a more radical orientation on the Law. They supported a community where the rich shared with the poor, where social balance was maintained, where justice was practiced, and where land was distributed fairly to all. The other perspective, identified in the Bible as a form of paganism, was more closely identified with the ancient polytheism of the Canaanites and with the kings and landowning classes. In short, this view might be called an **Establishment religion**. Perhaps the most powerful expression of this difference is given in the famous story of Elijah and the prophets of Baal recorded in 1 Kings 18.

Section in Review

Quick View

- After the death of Solomon, Israel was divided into two kingdoms, Judah and Israel.

- The rivalry between the Northern Kingdom of Israel and the Southern Kingdom of Judah lasted for centuries.

- A conflict arose during this time between two forms of YHWH worship.

For Review

1. **Main Idea**: What was the root cause of the division of Israel into the Northern and Southern Kingdoms?

2. **Main Idea**: Why did Jeroboam build alternative temples in Dan and Bethel?

3. **Critical Thinking**: What were the differences between the two forms of YHWH worship that were prevalent during the period of the divided monarchy? What relationship was there between these religious viewpoints and people's socioeconomic views?

For Reflection

In thinking about today's society, how can you make generalized connections between people's religious viewpoints and their socioeconomic opinions? Ask your parents or another adult whose opinion you value what connections they make between their religious beliefs and their political or economic behavior.

Jewish People Dancing around Golden Calf *by Nicolas Poussin*

Naboth's VINEYARD

Read 1 Kings 21.

In this story, Jezebel and Ahab abuse their royal powers by expropriating the land of an Israelite peasant by the name of Naboth. There is a miscarriage of justice, and Jezebel is portrayed as the central player in the entire episode. In short, Jezebel—a royal figure with Canaanite roots—is blamed for an open violation of the Mosaic covenant notion of justice and land distribution. Jezebel refused to acknowledge these limitations on royal power and privilege. The Jezreel Valley where Naboth's vineyard was located became a flash point of conflict for the anti-Canaanite forces of the Northern Kingdom. For example, 2 Kings 9–10 details Jehu's massacre of the line of Ahab precisely in the same valley.

What this tradition suggests is that these cited battles were not strictly between two groups who merely worshipped differently. The battles reflected a struggle between two rival ways of life with two radically different social, political, and economic policies. The Canaanite religion was the establishment religion. The YHWH religion of the prophets had a profound sense of social justice and care of the poor and disenfranchised. This is a critically important difference if we are to understand why there was so much animosity between the two rival religious perspectives in the Bible.

In time both Israel and Judah would be conquered by foreign powers.

The Last Days of the Independent Monarchy

The first great outside threat to the Northern Kingdom of Israel was the **Neo-Assyrian Empire** in Mesopotamia. The preface *neo* means "new" and indicates that there were some older empires in this same location. This empire was located in what today is the northern portion of Iraq.

Another threat to Israel came from a rising local power, based in the ancient city of Damascus in Syria. Damascus organized a group of "coalition states" that recognized Damascus as their head. The Assyrians directed a great deal of their fury at keeping the Damascus coalition subservient, though they were not always successful. When Damascus was powerful, the coalition frequently engaged in conflict with the Northern Kingdom of Israel.

The ongoing tensions between Damascus and Assyria weakened each state and distracted them from attacking Judah and Israel. The years between 785 and 730 BC were fairly prosperous for both Hebrew states, especially the Northern Kingdom of Israel. During this time, prophets condemned the fact that this prosperity benefited mainly elite landowners. It was during this period that the prophet Amos decried the lifestyles of the rich:

> They trample the heads of the weak
> into the dust of the earth,
> and force the lowly out of the way. (Am 2:7)

Assyrians Assert Power

The wealth and success of the Northern Kingdom leadership began to unravel with the accession of Tiglath-Pileser III (745–727 BC) as ruler of Assyria. He revived the military power of Assyria, and began to reassert that power in the west, including the Northern Kingdom of Israel. His successors, Shalmaneser and Sargon II crushed a revolt that broke out in that region.

Finally, in 722 BC, the Assyrians completely crushed the Northern Kingdom of Israel. As part of their dominance, the Assyrians practiced a military strategy of

deportation. The Assyrian conquerors would remove the upper class and elite of the captured society and exile them elsewhere in their vast territories in order to crush any revolt before it even got started.

At the conquest of Israel, the Assyrians carried away a substantial number of the northern elite (most likely the royal family members, military leaders, landowners, and any others who might threaten a revolt) and dispersed them. These exiles are often referred to as the "Ten Lost Tribes of Israel." Although this group is never heard from again in history, the Assyrians certainly did not exile the entire population of the Northern Kingdom. After all, the Assyrians were interested in resources and taxes. They would certainly have left the majority of the population in place to work the land and provide wealth to the new Assyrian overlords.

The Assyrians and Judah

The Old Testament suggests that Hezekiah, the king of the Southern Kingdom of Judah, escaped Assyrian wrath and was allowed to stay on the throne by actually aligning with the Assyrians. In fact, Hezekiah maintained relations to Assyria as a vassal until a conflict broke out between 705 and 700 BC at the rise of Sargon II. Sargon attacked Jerusalem. In order to survive the long siege, Hezekiah dug the famous tunnel that still exists in Jerusalem. This tunnel allowed water from the Gihon Spring to flow within the walls of Jerusalem, so that the people in the walled city could have fresh water and a chance for survival.

The Assyrian siege of Jerusalem is worth mentioning because it is one of the rare occasions when an event is covered by more than once source that we can read even today. In this case Sargon's own Assyrian archives *and* the description in 2 Kings 18–20 each have an account of the siege. Both sources agree that the siege was unsuccessful. In 2 Kings 19:35–36, an "angel" miraculously strikes down the Assyrian soldiers. Assyrian records say that Sargon simply determined that his point of strength had been made, and he broke the siege. In the end, Hezekiah's tribute to Sargon's successor, Sennacherib, the Assyrian king, guaranteed he would remain on the throne in Judah though the Northern Kingdom had been decimated.

Archaeologists have determined that there was some movement of population to the southern state of Judah from the north after Israel collapsed. The eighth century BC brought even more changes to the region. Egypt reasserted its independence and the tribes south of Assyria (centered near the ancient city of Babylon) unified to rise and conquer Assyria itself, leaving only Egypt and Babylon with power in the region.

Babylonian Destruction of the Southern Kingdom

Read 2 Kings 23:36–25:26 and 2 Chronicles 2–23.

After 722–720 BC the Northern Kingdom of Israel no longer existed as an independent political state. The Southern Kingdom of Judah continued for another 135 years, although for part of this time, it was under the imperial control of Egypt or Babylon. Babylon had asserted independence in one form or another from Assyria from the middle of this turbulent century onwards. When the Chaldean tribes of Babylon unified the southern peoples into an imperial power, their ambitions were finally realized. Their young prince Nebuchadnezzar, who finally defeated the last of the Assyrian forces, also conquered the Egyptian forces in two great battles north of Palestine (609 BC and 605 BC). The way

Neo-Assyrian Empire
A new empire in the Mesopotamian region that eventually conquered the Northern Kingdom, sending its ruling class into exile in 722 BC.

The pool of Shiloh, Hezekiah's tunnel in Jerusalem

was clear for Nebuchadnezzar to control the land route to Egypt.

The final days of Judah were largely determined by the rivalry between the Egyptian and Babylonian Empires. From 609 to 597 BC, following the death of King Josiah in a battle with the Egyptians, the royal house in Judah (King Jehoiakim and his son, King Jehoachin) consisted of Egyptian puppet rulers. Pharaoh Necho established their government in Jerusalem in order to create a buffer between Egypt and Babylon.

When Nebuchadnezzar defeated Jerusalem in 597 (young King Jehoiachin surrendered), he chose one of the descendants of Josiah to be the figurehead of Babylonian rule in Jerusalem. King Josiah (640–609 BC) seems to have been predisposed to an alliance with Babylon. Perhaps that alliance explains Nebuchadnezzar's choice of Mattaniah, whom he renamed "Zedekiah," to rule Jerusalem.

Zedekiah was initially loyal to Babylon. He was eventually persuaded by Egyptian agents (including a false prophet Hananiah [see Jer 26–29]) to attempt a revolt against Babylonian power and join a coalition with Egypt. The results were catastrophic. Nebuchadnezzar's forces returned to Jerusalem in 587 or 586 BC and devastated it. The catastrophe of the fall of Judah in 587 BC was a major event in the history of God's People. The years that followed the Exile were marked by a reorientation in the way the Jews kept their part of the covenant with God. The implications of the end of the monarchy will be explored further in Chapter 7.

To summarize the events of this chapter: It is clear that Hebrew fate was largely determined by the ambitions of regional powers in Egypt and Mesopotamia. The reigns of the various kings of the northern and southern kingdoms take place under the shadow of these larger conflicts. From a religious point of view, the stories chronicled in the time of the kings also pointed a finger at the Chosen People themselves for choosing kings for themselves other than YHWH and for breaking the covenant by worshipping foreign gods.

Section in Review

Quick View

- The Neo-Assyrian Empire rose to power and conquered the Northern Kingdom of Israel in 722 BC.

- Judah resisted military defeat and maintained its independence from the Assyrian Empire by paying tribute to their king.

- Caught between the two powers of Egypt and Babylon, Judah eventually fell at the hands of the Babylonian King Nebuchadnezzar.

For Review

1. **Main Idea**: When and to whom did the Northern Kingdom fall? What happened to the people who were there?

2. **Main Idea**: When and to whom did the Southern Kingdom fall? What happened to the people of Judah?

3. **Main Idea**: What reason did the prophets give for the fall of Israel and Judah?

For Reflection

What parallels are there in modern history to the exile of the Jews from Israel and Judah following their conquest by the Assyrians and the Babylonians? How do you think it would feel to be an exile?

Further Reflection

The prophet Samuel was displeased when the people asked for a king. Samuel felt they did not need a human king because YHWH was their king. He prayed and the Lord answered,

> Grant the people's every request. It is not you they reject; they are rejecting me as their king. As they have treated me constantly from the day I brought them up from Egypt to this day, deserting me and worshiping strange gods, so do they treat you too. (1 Sm 8:7–8)

The monarchy was founded with the naming of Israel's first king, Saul. David, Israel's greatest king, and his son Solomon followed. From the family of David, Jesus was born. Jesus' ancestry to David is traced through his foster father, Joseph (see Mt 1:1–17).

Jesus constantly reminded his disciples of the differences between himself and David, saying his kingdom was "not of this world." Furthermore, Jesus noted the violence so often used to settled differences between nations and said: "Offer no resistance to one who is evil. When someone strikes you on your right cheek, turn the other one to him as well" (Mt 5:39).

The Kingdom of God initiated by Jesus is one of servanthood and compassion, not power and domination. Remembering this helps to put the relation of Jesus to David in context: Jesus is a New David, but he is not David. Jesus is a different kind of King for a different kind of Kingdom. The earliest Christians, who were all Jews, would have understood this irony.

Jesus Christ (in Greek, "anointed one") is the one whom God the Father anointed with the Holy Spirit and established as priest, prophet, and king. Christians share in the royal office of Christ, drawn in by his Death and Resurrection. Christ's kingship is different than that of earthly kings. Christ does not serve from a base of force. Rather, he is the humble servant who "did not come to be served but to serve and to give his life as a ransom for many" (Mk 10:45). Christians who reign with Christ the King do so in service, particularly in the service of the poor and suffering. This reign of service is much different than the one the Israelites envisioned. As St. Leo the Great wrote:

> What, indeed, is as royal for a soul as to govern the body in obedience to God? (*Sermo* 4, 1:PL 54, 149)

Vocabulary Review

Directions: Explain the relationship between the two people or terms.

1. David, Saul

2. Samuel, David

3. Rehoboam, Jeroboam

4. Judah, Neo-Assyrian Empire

5. Ark of the Covenant, Temple

6. Jezebel, Naboth's Vineyard

7. Josiah, Solomon

8. Ugarit, Baal

9. Zedekiah, Nebuchadnezzar

10. Establishment religion, prophets

Performance Assessment Project

Create a job description of an ideal king of Israel based on the successes and failures of the kings of Israel and Judah that you studied in this chapter.

Called to Prayer

Can it indeed be that God dwells among men on earth? If the heavens and the highest heavens cannot contain you, how much less this temple which I have built! Look kindly on the prayer and petition of your servant, O LORD, my God, and listen to the cry of supplication which I, your servant, utter before you this day. May your eyes watch night and day over this temple, the place where you have decreed you shall be honored; may you heed the prayer which I, your servant, offer in this place. Listen to the petitions of your servant and of your people Israel which they offer in this place. Listen from your heavenly dwelling and grant pardon.

—1 Kings 8:27-30

- *Reflection*: Where do you go to offer your prayer to God? What special places make it easiest for you to connect with the Lord?

- *Meditation*: Think deeply about the meaning of the phrase "the heavens and the highest heavens cannot contain you." Try to imagine who God is, based on this Scripture passage.

- *Resolution*: Find a special place to spend some time with God. It could be in a church, chapel, home, or out in nature. Offer your prayers in that place and spend some time in silence focusing on God's presence in your life.

God's Prophets:

At the Heart of the Journey

CHAPTER OUTLINE

■ *The prophets in the Old Testament are categorized into certain groups.*

■ *The prophets took on many important roles within the community of Israel on behalf of God.*

■ *The prophets Elijah, Elisha, Amos, and Hosea called the people of the Northern Kingdom back to exclusive worship of God and just treatment of others.*

■ *Despite the prophets' call for repentance, the Northern Kingdom fell in 722 BC.*

Chapter Seven

The prophets in the Old Testament are categorized into certain groups.

Introduction

The prophet is a special kind of messenger from God. Prophets were present through the early and late stages of the Old Testament. In fact, the Hebrew word associated with prophet, *nabi*, is connected first with Moses. Moses was the prophet who heard God's message of liberation and shared it with the people while they were still enslaved in Egypt. Moses's brother, Aaron, was also called a prophet because he spoke for Moses before the Pharaoh.

The prophets are mentioned throughout the historical books. Samuel, the last of Israel's judges, was also called a prophet. Deborah, another judge, was a "prophetess" (Jgs 4:4). The second Book of Samuel mentions the prophet Nathan confronting David about his sinful behavior involving Bathsheba and Uriah, though no other information is told of him. Also included among these "former prophets" are the prominent figures of Elijah and Elisha.

Prophecy became a literary movement, too. The sayings of selected prophets were gathered up and kept, just as the earliest Christians kept the sayings of Jesus. Amos (approximately 740 BC) was the earliest prophet whose gathered sayings were written in book form. After Amos, other books were formed from the sayings of different prophets. And then, somewhat mysteriously, the books of prophetic messages ceased in the Old Testament, although the early Christians also had prophets.

The group of "latter prophets" (as opposed to the former prophets who appear in the earlier historical books) was made up of three **major prophets** (Isaiah, Jeremiah, and Ezekiel) along with a larger group of **minor prophets** (Hosea, Joel, Amos, Obadiah, Jonah, Micah, Nahum, Habbakuk, Zephaniah, Haggai, Zechariah, and Malachi). "Major" and "minor," incidentally, are terms that refer to the size of the book, not to the importance of the prophet or his message.

A main objective of this chapter is to introduce the origins of the prophets. Several ideas will be explored, each one contributing to how the prophets took on a central role with God's People of the Old Testament. Biographical sketches of four prophets (Elijah, Elisha, Amos, and Hosea) who preached God's justice prior to the fall of the Northern Kingdom will be offered in this chapter.

Chapter 8 will cover more of the prophets' messages specifically related to the fall of the Northern and Southern Kingdoms and the exile of Israel to Assyria and Judah to Babylon. First, let's return to the question of the origins of the prophets.

Section in Review

Quick View

- The many prophets of the Old Testament are categorized as "former," "latter," "major," and "minor" prophets.

For Review

1. **Vocabulary**: Explain the difference between "former" and "latter" prophets and between "major" and "minor" prophets. List examples of each.

2. **Main Idea**: Which prophet was the first to have his sayings collected in a written work? Where does this book appear in the Bible?

For Reflection

Read from the books of the minor prophets until you find a few verses that seem to you to apply to a current event or situation. Copy the passage and then explain how it applies and what you think the prophet would have to say about that event or situation today.

The prophets took on many important roles within the community of Israel on behalf of God.

Marks of the Prophets

Several common marks or roles of the prophets provide clues to their origins.

First, prophets received a call from God and felt compelled to leave their former way of life to follow it. Amos, for example, was a shepherd: "The Lord took me from following the flock, and said to me 'Go, prophesy to my people Israel'" (Am 7:15). This call from God came in different ways. Prophets heard voices, had dreams, saw visions, or received inspiration to share God's message. In some ways, they were like the oracles of other (ancient Greek) religious traditions to which people went to ask questions about God. However, false prophets are also mentioned in many places throughout the Old Testament, sometimes making it difficult to determine who were the true prophets.

Second, the prophet often spoke messages that were unpopular with the ruling establishment. In response, the king sometimes tried to rid himself of the prophet in the belief that doing so would keep the prophet's dire message from coming true. Needless to say, "killing the messenger" did not, in any way, make the message less true. In general, the message of the prophets was to warn the people to repent for their sins under the penalty of punishment if they failed to do so. More characteristics of the prophets follow.

Cross with snake in memory of Moses's death at Mt. Nebo, Jordan

The Prophets Inherited the Role of Moses

The concept of a person being called by God or his angel to perform a particular task or to play a certain role in the life of the community of Israel is central to the understanding of prophets. The **call narratives** of Isaiah and Jeremiah each follow a similar pattern:

1. The setting is one of mystery or holiness.
2. God initiates the call.
3. The person resists.
4. God reassures the person.
5. God sends the person on a mission.

Read Jeremiah 1:4-10 and Isaiah 6:1-9.
This pattern is the same as Moses's call to be God's deliverer of the people of Israel in Egyptian slavery:

> Moses, however, said to the Lord, "If you please, Lord, I have never

nabi
The Hebrew word translated as "prophet."

major prophets
Three of the latter prophets, Isaiah, Jeremiah, and Ezekiel, whose books in the Old Testament are quite lengthy.

minor prophets
The twelve prophets of the Old Testament whose recorded sayings are much briefer than those of the major prophets: Hosea, Joel, Amos, Obadiah, Jonah, Micah, Nahum, Habbakuk, Zephaniah, Haggai, Zechariah, and Malachi.

call narrative
A story that describes a person's initial awareness that God wanted him or her to do something specific. The calls of the prophet have five common elements: there is something mysterious and holy about the encounter; God acts first; the prophet resists; God reassures; God sends the prophet on his or her mission.

been eloquent, neither in the past, nor recently, nor now that you have spoken to your servant; but I am slow of speech and tongue." The Lord said to him, "Who gives one man speech and makes another deaf and dumb? Or who gives sight to the one and makes another blind? Is it not I, the Lord? Go, then! It is I who will assist you in speaking and will teach you what you are to say." (Ex 4:10–12)

Like Moses, the prophets Isaiah and Jeremiah protested that they were not good enough to speak for God. It seems that the similarity is intentional. The latter prophets were carrying on the work of Moses. Was Moses the first prophet? Consider this passage from the time of Moses's death:

> Since then no prophet has arisen in Israel like Moses, whom the Lord knew face to face. (Dt 34:10)

The prophets usually based their criticism of Israel on the statutes and commandments of Moses; these ethical guidelines were the basis for their denouncing Israelite behavior. All of this suggests a strong connection between Moses the "lawgiver" and the prophets as "law protectors" (insisting that the Law of Moses be obeyed). So, in determining the origins and development of the prophets, the connection with Moses is important. But it is still not the complete picture of the prophets.

The Prophets Were "Spiritual Warriors"

There is textual evidence throughout the Old Testament to support the identification of the judges as prophets also. As mentioned, the judge Deborah, who was a military leader, was directly called a prophet (see Jgs 4:4). Other judges shared the experience of being called by God, or by an angel of God, to their position of leadership. Recall the story of the call of Gideon as he was selected for leadership:

> . . . the *angel of the Lord appeared to him* and said, "The Lord is with you, O champion!" (Jgs 6:12)

Or consider the call of Samson before his birth,

An angel of the Lord appeared to the woman and said to her, "Though you are barren and have had no children, yet you will conceive and bear a son." (Jgs 13:3)

Compare these calls with the call of Moses at the burning bush:

> There *an angel of the Lord appeared to him* in fire flaming out of a bush. As he looked on, he was surprised to see that the bush, though on fire, was not consumed. (Ex 3:2)

The appearance of "an angel of the Lord" at the moment of the call of these judges indicates that, like Moses, the judges were also considered prophets. They combined the vocations of prophet (a person summoned by God or his messenger and selected by God to guide his people) and king (someone chosen to be a warrior and to lead the people to military victory). A judge was a "warrior-prophet" in a sense, combining both roles in one vocation.

When the Israelites decided to choose kings of their own, they wanted warriors to fight their battles and lead them to victory over adversaries (recall 1 Sm 8). The kings of Israel were more one-dimensional than the judges. They were warriors without the spiritual dimension that came from being called directly by God.

Did this mean that God stopped "calling on" men and women to speak to the people during the time of the kings? Indeed not. It was during the time of the kings that the prophetic movement became particularly influential and important. Remember, it was the prophet Samuel who identified the king the people had asked for. Although God chose Saul and then David to rule as King of Israel, he did not call them directly, nor did his angel appear to them. Instead, God communicated his choice to his prophet Samuel. Samuel anointed Saul and later David as a sign to the community of God's choice. One way to describe the prophets during the time of the kings is "demilitarized judges," since warfare became the business of the kings. The prophets then became the "spiritually selected messengers of God."

This idea suggests that prophecy was rooted in the early military leaders of Israel, before the rise of the monarchy under Saul, and later, the House of David. The Old Testament supports the idea that prophets once had a military role in early Israelite society. For example, when

a servant of Elisha doubted the prophet's strength, Elisha prayed for the appearance of a "heavenly army":

> "O Lord, open his eyes, that he may see." And the Lord opened the eyes of the servant, so that he saw the mountainside filled with horses and fiery chariots around Elisha. (2 Kgs 6:17)

Passages like this strongly associate prophets with miraculous acts of warfare. This could be because of the prophets' earlier association with warfare from the time of the judges. In the time of the kings, the prophets retained their connection to the military activities of Israel since they were often consulted about the likelihood of victory prior to battles. Still, there is more to the prophets than this.

The Prophets Were Social Revolutionaries

The Old Testament prophets showed passionate concern for the poor whenever they suffered oppression by the rich. It is hardly accidental, then, that the strongest prophets (e.g., Amos, Jeremiah, Isaiah, and Ezekiel) appeared precisely during the time when there was the worst oppression and mistreatment of the poor. Their testimony on behalf of the poor was forthright, unflinching, and forceful. God would revoke his word from the Israelites:

> Because they sell the just man for silver,
>   and the poor man for a pair of sandals.
> They trample the heads of the weak
>   into the dust of the earth,
>   and force the lowly out of the way.
> Son and father go to the same prostitute,
>   profaning my holy name.
> Upon garments taken in pledge
>   they recline beside any altar;
> And the wine of those who have been fined
>   they drink in the house of their god. (Am 2:6–8)

Many of the prophets announced that God would judge Israel by a single "measuring stick" of their righteousness. In other words, God would judge Israel how they treated the weakest members of their society: the widow, the orphan, and the foreigner. The Law demanded that the people most "at risk" in society be cared for so that they could survive, and live reasonably stable lives, rather than being neglected or taken advantage of by the rich. Isaiah and Jeremiah made very clear what they considered the faults of Israel:

> Woe to those who enact unjust statues
>   and who write oppressive decrees,
> Depriving the needy of judgment
>   and robbing my people's poor of their rights,
> Making widows their plunder,
>   and orphans their prey!

What will you do on the day of punishment,

>   when ruin comes from afar?
>   (Is 10:1–3)

Thus says the Lord: Do what is right and just. Rescue the victim from the hand of his oppressor. Do not wrong or oppress the resident alien, the orphan, or the widow, and do not shed innocent blood in this place. (Jer 22:3)

Also read Isaiah 1:17; Ezekiel 22:3, 7; Zechariah 7:10; and Malachi 3:5.

These passages make it clear that the prophets were concerned about the social and economic practices of their times, especially the oppressive behavior of the rich in both the kingdoms of Judah and Israel. The religious concern of the prophets—to serve YHWH and no other gods—was always accompanied by their social and political concerns.

When Jesus taught about compassion for the poor (e.g., Mt 25:31–46) he was clearly standing in the prophetic tradition of ancient Israel. Thus, the element of justice is crucial to understanding the prophets. But it is still not the whole picture of the role of the prophets.

The Prophets Were Messengers of God

The common understanding that prophets were "messengers of God" gains credence from consistent textual evidence.

First, the prophets almost always spoke in the first person, as if God were speaking. They often began their speeches with the famous words: "Thus says the Lord," which means quite literally, "Here is the message from God." This short little bit at the beginning of the speeches is often referred to as the "**messenger formula**." It may have been borrowed from other correspondences in the ancient world, particularly messages sent between kings. For example:

>   [Ben-hadad] sent couriers to Ahab, king of Israel, within the city, and said to him, "This is Ben-hadad's message. . . ." (1 Kgs 20:2–3)

When the prophet says "Thus says God" (in one form or another), it certainly resembles the language of other messengers in the Old Testament. Though prophets began speeches using other formulas as well, the prevalence of the "messenger formula" makes a clear connection between the prophets and other messengers, thus enabling us to identify the prophets as "messengers of God."

In addition, the prophets are often classified as God's servants:

>   And though the Lord warned Israel and Judah by every prophet and seer, "Give up your evil ways and keep my commandments and statutes, in accordance with the entire law which I enjoined on your fathers and which I sent

messenger formula
The opening words of a prophetic speech, attributing what follows to God, as in "Thus says the Lord . . ." or "The Lord said . . ."

oracle
A brief, poetic declaration preceded by the messenger formula, "Thus says the Lord," which establishes it reliably as a message from God. Pagan religions also use the word sometimes for the person who delivers the message, as was the case with the famous "oracle of Delphi."

Modern Prophets

Prophets of the Old Testament were messengers, law-protectors, advocates for the poor, and servants. Find news articles on modern prophets who fit in each of the same categories. Cut out the articles and attach to a poster. Write a brief explanation for each on why the person fits the particular category.

LITERARY STYLES OF HEBREW PROPHECY

The basic literary style of the written prophecies in the Old Testament is an **oracle**. An oracle, in its basic form, is a brief, poetic declaration following the formula establishing it as a message from God: "Thus says the Lord." Most of the books of the latter prophets are collections of oracles that resemble the poetic texts of the books of Psalms and Proverbs. However, only the prophetic books of Obadiah, Micah, Nahum, Habakkuk, and Zephaniah are entirely written in poetic form. The oracles in the Book of Ezekiel are contained within autobiographical narratives of the prophet. Biographical information was not crucial in these works. However, there is usually a superscription that indicates the prophet's family connections and the kings who ruled during the time the oracles were given.

While the prophets themselves may have recorded some of the autobiographical material of the prophets, the oracles were likely collected over long period of time by the prophet's disciples. It is important to remember that the prophecy of the writing prophets began as oral speech first delivered in meetings between the prophets and those who heard them. The settings varied between places such as the court of the Temple (see Jer 7:1–2), a lesser shrine (see Am 7:13), or a city gate (see Jer 17:19). These speeches were only written down years later.

you by my servants the prophets," they did not listen. (2 Kgs 17:13–14)

From the day that your fathers left the land of Egypt even to this day, I have sent you untiringly all my servants the prophets. (Jer 7:25)

By now we have seen that there are reasons to identify the prophets with many different roles. How are we to know which is correct? Are the prophets messengers, law-protectors, advocates for the poor, or servants? The answer is: all of the above!

All of these points tell something of the origins and development of the Old Testament prophets. They also make it clear that prophecy was a complex and multifaceted phenomenon in ancient Israel. The central role of the prophets in the Old Testament is undeniable. While the historical books often condemned the kings of ancient Israel, the prophets were revered, at least by the time their stories were recorded.

Section in Review

Quick View

- Called out of their former lives, prophets often spoke messages that were unpopular with their kings.

- The prophets had a special connection with Moses.

- The prophets were deeply concerned with social and economic justice.

- The prophets presented God's words using the "messenger formula" followed by poetic oracles.

For Review

1. **Main Idea**: What are the five marks or roles of the prophets? Briefly explain each.

2. **Main Idea**: Who was the first prophet? What do all the later prophets have in common with him?

3. **Main Idea**: What were the main social concerns of the prophets? What religious issues troubled them?

For Reflection

Do you think that there are "prophets" in the world today? How would these marks help you recognize a modern prophet or identify a false prophet?

The prophets Elijah, Elisha, Amos, and Hosea called the people of the Northern Kingdom back to exclusive worship of God and just treatment of others.

The Servants, the Prophets

The prophets of the ninth and eighth centuries BC fulfilled their roles as God's servants by continually calling the people back to make right the relationship with YHWH. During this time many Israelites had begun to worship the god Baal (and perhaps other Canaanite gods as well) along with YHWH.

There were four prophets of this time in the Northern Kingdom—Elijah, Elisha, Amos, and Hosea—who called the people back to YHWH. They reminded the people that YHWH was a jealous God who demanded their loyalty and required justice for others. They continued to teach that:

- *There is only one true God and that God is YHWH.* The prophets reminded people that God is the creator of Heaven and earth. He is the Lord of all nations. They taught that all other gods are without power; in fact, they do not even exist.

- *The people must renounce sin.* The prophets reminded people of the Law and the covenant demands that they worship God with a commitment to truth and justice.

The servant prophets modeled and announced these messages. They called on the people to take to heart and to follow.

More information on four prophets of the ninth and eighth centuries BC follows.

Elijah

Though there are many stories of Elijah, there is no "Book of Elijah." The name *Elijah* means "The Lord is my God." This was the central message of Elijah's mission. Elijah is considered the father of the prophets. He lived in the Northern Kingdom in the ninth century BC, under the rule of King Ahab who married the Phoenician princess, Jezebel. The key to understanding Elijah is understanding the tension in Israel between the worship

Elijah denouncing Ahab

of YHWH and the influences of the ancient Canaanite religion. Elijah, in many ways, was a spiritual warrior in a struggle that sometimes became violent.

Read 1 Kings 17–18.

Elijah is introduced somewhat suddenly in 1 Kings 17. He is identified as a "Tishbite," but that is all. There is no "call narrative," and there is very little biographical information about his background. He is suddenly thrust into history by his confrontation with Ahab:

> As the Lord, the God of Israel, lives, whom I serve, during these years there shall be no dew or rain except at my word. (1 Kgs 17:1)

The announcement was short and shocking: God decreed that there would be no rain. Elijah then fled east across the Jordan River, where he was fed miraculously by ravens. (This story reminds us of the miraculous feeding of the Hebrews in the wilderness after their liberation from Egypt.)

Eventually Elijah was sent to a widow woman in Zarephath near Sidon. Zarephath was north of the kingdom of Israel and was territory where Canaanite worship of Baal was particularly strong. Here, Elijah met a humble woman and her son, who were starving to death and apparently preparing to die even as Elijah arrived. Elijah was able to reassure the widow of God's promise to feed her family for as long as the drought lasted, and, later, to raise her son back to life after he died of an illness. This striking series of events powerfully reminds Christian readers of some of the ministry of Jesus—a comparison, of course, that is not missed by the writers of the Gospels (see Lk 4:25-26).

In 1 Kings 18, at Mount Carmel (near present day Haifa on the northern coast of Israel), there is a dramatic contest between Jezebel's hired priests and priestesses of Baal and Elijah, the sole defender of worship to YHWH. Recall from Chapter 5 that the Canaanites believed Baal to be the god of rain, produce, and fertility. But Elijah's own life demonstrates that it was YHWH who was in control. By stopping the rain, YHWH proved that he alone was the provider of the rain. By feeding the woman and child (and Elijah himself), YHWH demonstrated that the God of Israel was, in fact, the provider of the produce of the fields. Finally, by healing the child, YHWH demonstrated that it was the God of Israel who provided human life, not Baal. In the great demonstration described in 1 Kings 18:21–46, Elijah proves that YHWH is the true God.

Unfortunately for Elijah, Jezebel was angry about the defeat. She threatened his life. So Elijah took refuge at Mount Horeb (Sinai)—the same place where Moses received the laws and encountered YHWH. This location was fitting, for it was Elijah's mission to restore God's covenant and the pure faith among the people. Elijah met the Lord at Horeb—not in a strong and heavy wind, not in an earthquake, and not in a fire. Rather, "after the fire there was a tiny whispering sound. When he heard this, Elijah hid his face in his cloak and went and stood at the entrance of the cave" (1 Kgs 19:12–13).

Elijah rightly holds a place among the great prophets of the Old Testament. Elijah, through it all, was a prophet who symbolized the struggle between the religion of YHWH and the religion of the Canaanites. At the transfiguration of Jesus, Elijah appeared along with Moses. Future generations of Jews thought Elijah was the one who would announce the coming of peace to the world at the end of time. He was also believed to be the precursor to the Messiah. In fact, when Jesus came to the earth, many thought him to be Elijah, while the New Testament cast John the Baptist in the role of Elijah announcing Jesus as Messiah.

The Biblical authors understood the importance of Elijah. Though there is no miraculous birth story to introduce him, there is a uniquely miraculous story to mark his passing: He is described as being transported to Heaven in a whirlwind. Conversing with his successor, Elisha, "a flaming chariot and flaming horses came between them, and Elijah went up to heaven in a whirlwind" (2 Kgs 2:11).

Elisha

The fact that some events in the life of Elisha parallel the life of Elijah demonstrates that Elisha "carries on" the work of Elijah. It also further communicates the idea that

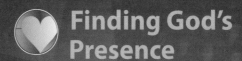

Finding God's Presence

God came to Elijah, not in the form of fire or earthquake or strong wind, but in a tiny whispering sound: a still, small voice (1 Kgs 19). The prayer form called *meditation* is a way to find God in such a manner. Meditation involves a search or quest to help you understand what God wants you to do, why he wants you to do it, and how you can accomplish what he wants.

Use the following process to help you discover God's presence in your life.

- Select a quiet, peaceful place to meditate. Assume a comfortable position.

- Focus on your own needs, what is going on in your life right now, and how you are currently relating to God.

- Use the Scriptures, particularly the Gospels, holy icons, liturgical texts of the day or season, writings of the spiritual fathers, or other great works of spirituality to help you to hear what the Lord is asking.

- After you have spent time listening to God, write a short prayer to the Father or a resolution that will help you to grow in Christ Jesus.

Elijah and John the Baptist

(*CCC*, 554–555, 718–719, 2581–2584)

Elijah was a prophet of special significance for the Jewish people at the time of Jesus. When Jesus asked his disciples, "Who do people say that I am?" (Mk 8:27), they replied that some were saying that he was not Elijah or John the Baptist.

Elijah also had important eschatological significance. Unlike the other prophets of the Old Testament, Elijah did not die. His successor, Elisha, watched as Elijah was lifted up to Heaven on a chariot of fire (2 Kgs 2:8). Many rabbis in the first century taught that Elijah would return before the coming of the Messiah, based on an interpretation of Malachi 3:23, "Lo, I will send you Elijah, a prophet, before the day of the Lord comes."

Elijah made an important appearance in the Gospels during the Transfiguration, when Jesus was seen glorified alongside both Elijah and Moses (Mt 17:1–13). This event harkens back to Moses's encounter with God in the burning bush on Mount Horeb (Ex 3). In Elijah's case, we should recall Elijah's encounter with God on the same mountain in a "tiny whispering sound" (1 Kgs 19:12). At the Transfiguration Jesus is revealed as God's beloved Son, not as another Elijah (Mk 9:7).

There are also significant connections between Elijah and John the Baptist. Upon their return from the mountain, Jesus explains that he is not Elijah, but

Elijah	John the Baptist
Elijah was to come before day of the Lord (Mal 3:23–24)	John the Baptist comes to prepare the way for Jesus (Mk 1:2)
Elijah frequently preached in the wilderness near the Jordan River (1 Kgs 17:3–6)	John the Baptist lived and preached in the wilderness near the Jordan River (Mk 1:5)
Elijah wore a "hairy garment" with a "leather girdle about his loins" (2 Kgs 1:8)	John the Baptist was clothed in camel hair, with a leather belt around his waist (Mk 1:6)

Elijah's return has been fulfilled in the person of John the Baptist (Mt 17:11–13). This is corroborated in Luke during the annunciation of John the Baptist's birth when the angel proclaims that John will go forth "in the spirit and power of Elijah" (Lk 1:17). John also has similar styles of preaching, living in the wilderness and dressing in hairy clothing.

the God of Israel continues his powerful work among the people of God through his servants, the prophets. In 2 Kings 2, Elijah literally "throws his mantle" on the back of Elisha; he transfers his cape-like shawl to the shoulders of Elisha to symbolize Elisha's "promotion." Elisha is honored as the successor:

> The guild prophets in Jericho, who were on the other side, saw him and said, "The spirit of Elijah rests on Elisha." They went to meet him, bowing before him. (2 Kgs 2:15)

The stories of 2 Kings 4 involving Elisha also resemble the famous miracles of Elijah. Like Elijah, Elisha sides with the suffering of the poor (2 Kgs 4:1–2). Again, the parallels with the Gospels are clear. These early prophets are shown breaking all kinds of social norms and conventions—honoring the poor, women, and people who need help and healing.

The stories of Elijah and Elisha set the stage for the prophetic books that make up a large section of the Old Testament. One can summarize the main concerns of Elijah and Elisha as: social justice and religious devotion to YHWH. These two issues are always connected. Devotion to YHWH as taught in the Law requires a commitment to social justice. These two themes will carry through all of the prophets of the Old Testament.

Amos

Amos is described as a shepherd and tree farmer from Tekoa, near Bethlehem, in the Southern Kingdom. His prophetic ministry takes place during the rule of Jeroboam II (786–746 BC). Amos is the first prophet for whom there is a separate, recorded collection of sayings. As with the other books of the prophets, the Book of Amos was probably collected and recorded by the prophet's disciples. Like Elisha's relationship to Elijah, it seems clear that prophets almost always had disciples with whom they were close and who participated in their itinerate travels and ministry.

Because of his background as a shepherd, Amos is often depicted as one from working-class origins. However, that assumption depends on the interpretation of Amos 7:14-15, where Amos says to the priest of Bethel:

> I was no prophet, nor have I belonged to a company of prophets; I was a shepherd and dresser of sycamores. The Lord took me from the following

The prophet Amos

flock, and said to me, "Go, prophesy to my people Israel." (Am 7:14–15)

From the passage it is not clear whether Amos was a hired shepherd or the owner of the land and flocks. One idea is that the first two chapters of the Book of Amos indicate that Amos knew too much about international events to be a poor farm laborer. However, Amos could have been well-informed and still have been a hired shepherd!

The prophet Amos was perhaps strongest on the issues of social justice. He spoke out against many of the sins of those living in the Northern Kingdom: genocide, cruelty, anger, dishonesty, greed, lawlessness, sexual excess, desecration of the dead, rejection of the prophets, robbery, violence, selfishness, deceit, injustice, and pride. He also condemned the abuses of the wealthy. He was particularly angry at an abusive lifestyle that extorted work from the poor for very low wages. At times this concern of Amos reaches a spectacular literary flourish. Speaking to the people of Samaria who had been living in luxury, oblivious to their sins and the threat of the Assyrians, Amos said:

Lying upon beds of ivory,[1]
    stretched comfortably on their couches,
They eat lambs taken from the flock
    and calves from the stall!
Improvising to the music of the harp,
    like David, they devise their own
    accompaniment.
They drink wine from bowls
    and anoint themselves with the best oils;
    yet they are not made ill by the collapse of
    Joseph!
Therefore, now they shall be the first to go into
exile,
    and their wanton revelry shall be done away
    with. (Am 6:4–7)

It is easy to imagine the indulgent parties described in this passage—people wealthy enough to have furniture with inlaid ivory (not native to Palestine, so it must have been imported), to feast on young animals (a luxury that would appall most of the poor), and to drink wine (according to Amos 2:8, this wine was bought with the taxes and fines they imposed on the poor) not from cups, but from *bowls*—abandoning any moderation at all.

Amos was particularly angry at the wealthy for pouring excess money into shows of Temple worship. The rich seemed to justify their oppressive lifestyles by purchasing many animals for Temple sacrifice, and thus made great public shows of their "piety." Amos spoke strongly against this practice:

I hate, I spurn your feasts,
    I take no pleasure in your solemnities;
Your cereal offerings I will not accept,
    nor consider your stall-fed peace offerings.
Away with your noisy songs!
    I will not listen to the melodies of your harps.
But if you would offer me holocausts,
    then let justice surge like water,
    and goodness like an unfailing stream. (Am
    5:21–24)

As with other Old Testament prophets, Amos's message was often one of judgment. However, most of the time when prophets preached a warning, the warning itself was intended to keep the dire event from happening. There is some debate about whether or not the prophet Amos had any hope that the people of the Northern Kingdom would be able to adhere to his words and thus avoid the judgment he predicted. Some scholars are of the opinion that Amos did not believe Israel could possibly comply, hence making him a "prophet of doom":

Then the Lord said to me:
The time is ripe to have done with my people
Israel;
    I will forgive them no longer.
The temple songs shall become wailings on that
day,
    says the Lord God.
Many shall be the corpses,
    strewn everywhere.—Silence! (Am 8:2b–3)

Amos and Society's Moral Decline

Amos viewed a society whose moral backbone was in decline. Not only were the rich land grabbing from the poor, but also other serious issues abounded. Read the following passages and write what issue Amos is speaking out against in each:

- Amos 5:12
- Amos 8:5
- Amos 2:6–7; 5:11–12; 8:4–6

Amos did know that the destruction of the people by God was intended to be instructive, not destructive. Though people persisted in their sinfulness, Amos believed that such behavior could never completely frustrate the plan of God for the Salvation of humankind. The closing words of the Book of Amos reveal his hope in a future that would bring God's blessings again:

> But I will not destroy the house of
>   Jacob completely . . .
> I will bring about restoration of my
>   my people Israel;
>   they shall rebuild and inhabit
>   their
>   ruined cities,
> Plant vineyards and drink the
> wine,
>   set out gardens and eat the
>   fruits. (Am 9:8b, 14)

Hosea

The Book of Hosea offers some brief biographical information on the prophet. Hosea was born and prophesied in the Northern Kingdom. His ministry overlapped that of Amos and probably began in the last years of Jeroboam II. Both prophets seemed to anticipate the fall of Israel to the Assyrian Empire in 722 BC.

Hosea, however, had quite a different character from Amos. Where Amos was the unrelenting prophet of despair and destruction, Hosea seemed to hold out some hope for Israel. There were other differences between Hosea and Amos as well.

To begin with, Hosea lived a very interesting life! In the opening verses, it is explained that God called Hosea to marry a known prostitute, Gomer. The Lord said to Hosea:

The prophet Hosea

> Go, take a harlot wife and harlot's children,
>   for the land gives itself to
>   **harlotry**,
>   turning away from the Lord.
> (Hos 1:2)

This action was no doubt shocking to the people who knew and listened to Hosea. Yet it makes very clear the fact that Hosea was a prophet who must be both *watched* and *listened to*. In other words, Hosea acted out part of his message in his own life. His first audience—and readers of the Book of Hosea—must pay attention to what his strange actions may mean.

harlotry
In the Old Testament, this term refers not only to a woman's illicit sexual behavior, but perhaps even more commonly to the practice of worshipping Canaanite gods along with YHWH. Jezebel is referred to as a "harlot" in this sense, not because she was ever unfaithful to Ahab.

Hosea did marry Gomer, and then proceeded to have three children with her—each child named for one of Hosea's controversial ideas. The name of the first child, Jezreel, implied a criticism of the house of King Jehu for the murder of the entire house of Ahab in the valley of Jezreel. Even though Jehu thought he was doing God's will when he murdered all the members of the family of Ahab, Hosea hinted strongly that he went too far, and his bloodshed was an unnecessary brutality. The name would have been understood as a criticism of the royal house of Jehu. Hosea was obviously unafraid of political comment.

Hosea then named his second child Lo-ruhamah. This translates literally as "she is not pitied." Hosea's message connected with Lo-ruhamah was a dire warning:

> The Lord said to him:
> Give her the name Lo-ruhamah;
> I no longer feel pity for the house
> of Israel:
> rather, I abhor them utterly.
> (Hos 1:6)

Finally, Hosea's third child has the most ominous name of the three: Lo-ammi, which means "not my people." The warning attached to this name was most deeply threatening:

> Then the Lord said:
> Give him the name Lo-ammi,
> for you are not my people,
> and I will not be your God.
> (Hos 1:9)

This was the ultimate threat because it was a reversal of God's promise to Israel in the covenant promise made to Moses:

> I will take you as my own people, and you shall have me as your God. You will know that I, the Lord, am your God when I free you from the labor of the Egyptians and bring you into the land which I swore to give to Abraham, Isaac and Jacob. (Ex 6:7–8)

In the following sections of the Book of Hosea, it is clear that the prophet is "acting out" the role of God, and that his controversial marriage symbolizes God's relationship with Israel. Gomer's unfaithfulness mirrors Israel's desertion of YHWH in favor of worshipping Baal. *Read Hosea 2*.

In chapter 2 of Hosea, it appears as if the prophet is angry with his wife, Gomer, and makes many kinds of threats against her (presumably for adultery on her part). But as the chapter proceeds, the reader learns that it is *really* God's relationship with Israel that is threatened:

> I will punish her for the days of
> the Baals,
> for whom she burnt incense
> While she decked herself out
> with her rings and her jewels,
> and, in going after her lovers,
> forgot me, says the Lord.
> (Hos 2:15)

After these words one would expect the prophet to bring final condemnation and judgment. But here the Book of Hosea takes a fascinating turn. Just at the moment when one would most expect to hear a word of condemnation and judgment from the prophet, suddenly he assures the reader of God's forgiving compassion:

> So I will allure her;
> I will lead her into the desert
> and speak to her heart. (Hos
> 2:16)

Not only does God speak words of forgiving compassion, the rest of the section reads like a wedding vow as God

Asherah
The Canaanite goddess sometimes called the "Queen of Heaven." She was the consort of Baal and the goddess of fertility. The practice of sacred prostitution was connected with the worship of Asherah.

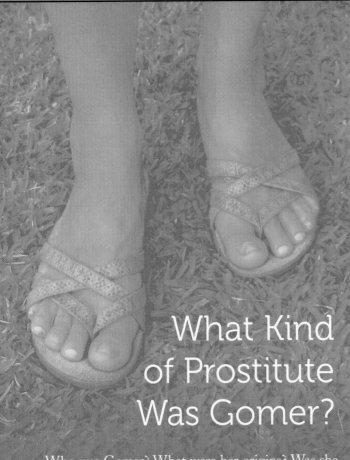

What Kind of Prostitute Was Gomer?

Who was Gomer? What were her origins? Was she Hebrew or a foreigner? These are interesting questions that the Book of Hosea does not explicitly answer. However, clues are offered. Note the instructions given by God to Hosea at the beginning of chapter 3:

> Give your love to a woman
>   beloved of a paramour, an adulteress;
> Even as the Lord loves the people of Israel,
>   though they turn to other gods
>   and are fond of raisin cakes. (Hos 3:1)

These "raisin cakes" were a specific offering for the Canaanite goddess Asherah, sometimes called "the Queen of Heaven" by the Canaanites and some heretical Hebrews (see Jer 7:18).

Gomer may have been a Hebrew woman who had become a Canaanite temple prostitute, involved in the sexual rites of Canaanite worship. This would complete the message of Hosea: like Gomer, Israel "prostituted herself" to Canaanite gods. This was surely a startling way of communicating, but then prophets were never known for quiet, unassuming behavior.

proposes marriage to his adulterous partner, Israel, as a way to reestablish their relationship:

> I will make a covenant for them on that day,
>   with the beasts of the field,
> With the birds of the air,
>   and with the things that crawl on the ground. . . .
> I will espouse you to me forever:
>   I will espouse you in right and in justice,
>   in love and in mercy;
> I will espouse you in fidelity
>   and you shall know the Lord. (Hos 2:20a, 21–22)

In Hosea 3, God tells the prophet to take Gomer back as his wife. This is symbolic of God's everlasting love for his people: after a period of trial (the dissolution of the kingdom), the people will fully return to their relationship with the Lord. Human passion is compared favorably to God's love for humanity, and this is an important message. The prophet compared the love of God with the two most powerful passions in human existence: the love between a husband and a wife and the love between a parent and a child (see Hos 11:1–4). This faithfulness and love of YHWH for his people is the lasting message of the Book of Hosea.

Section in Review

Quick View

- The prophets called people back to God and committed themselves to truth and justice.

- Elijah is one of the greatest prophets of the Old Testament and has important connections to the New Testament.

- Elisha resembled his predecessor Elijah in both word and deed.

- Amos spoke out against the rich of the Northern Kingdom.

- The prophet Hosea's marriage with the harlot Gomer symbolizes God's relationship with Israel.

For Review

1. **Main Idea**: What were the two main concerns of the prophets Elijah and Elisha?

2. **Main Idea**: What were Amos's biggest complaints about the behavior of the people?

3. **Main Idea**: There was more to Hosea's prophecy than what he *said*. What was unique about the way that Hosea revealed God's word to the people?

For Reflection

Skim through the books of Amos and Hosea to find four or five passages that you believe still apply today. Copy them and write a brief explanation of how you think they are relevant to today's society.

Despite the prophets' call for repentance, the Northern Kingdom fell in 722 BC.

The Contrasting Styles of the Prophets

God sent prophets to the Northern Kingdom in the centuries prior to the Assyrian takeover and relocation. If a common theme can be named between the ninth-century-BC prophets (Elijah and Elisha) and the eighth-century-BC prophets (Amos and Hosea) it would be: "Repent of your sins and God will save you. Fail to repent and you and your nation will be doomed." A secondary theme—gleaned especially from Hosea—is that God can bring good even from destruction. Even the people's sinfulness will not cause YHWH to abandon his covenant with the people.

The contrast between these two "writing prophets"—Amos and Hosea—is quite clear. Amos was a nearly unrelenting prophet of judgment and doom while Hosea portrayed God as a loving, compassionate, and deeply forgiving God for whom sin was equivalent to the deeply painful betrayal of a loved one.

All the prophets of this time were at once "conservative" and "radical." They were conservative in the sense that they sought to preserve the devotion to YHWH that required obedience to the Law; they "conserved" the covenant obligations. At the same time, they often introduced radical new ideas along the way. For example:

- Elijah and Elisha both asserted the basic incompatibility between Canaanite paganism (with its enslavement of the people under a false religion that justified the elite privilege of a few against the economic rights of the many), and true YHWH worship (which insisted upon a more just division of wealth within the community and the responsibility of all community members to care for one another).

- Amos questioned a luxurious, materialistic lifestyle that depended on the poverty of others despite the great displays of "piety" at the Temple that were possible because of it.

- Hosea taught about God's compassion and forgiveness using human love as a metaphor and example.

The Fall of the Northern Kingdom

From the ninth century to the seventh century (ca. 800–609 BC), the Assyrian Empire was a brutal military power in the Ancient Near East. By 738 BC, the Assyrian ruler Tiglath-pileser (known by his Babylonian name Pul; see 2 Kgs 15:19) was receiving taxes from the Syrian states Hamath, Tyre, Byblos, and Damascus—and Israel.

Tiglath-pileser went even further. He oversaw the strengthening of Assyria's central government so that the local Syrian states had little authority in managing their own affairs, even on a local level. Tiglath-pileser also streamlined the process by which new lands could be incorporated under Assyrian rule. This was the beginning of the end for the Northern Kingdom of Israel.

King Pekah of Israel invaded the Southern Kingdom in 734 BC to try to force King Ahaz of Judah to join a coalition with Damascus against Assyria. Ahaz had other ideas. Instead, he sent tribute to Tiglath-pileser and asked for Assyrian help against Israel. The Assyrians easily destroyed the coalition and made Israel a vassal state. When Shalmaneser V succeeded Tiglath-pileser in 726 BC, Israel's king, Hoshea, saw a window of opportunity. He sought out Egypt's help. The plan again backfired. Assyria invaded Israel and captured the city of Samaria in 722 BC. Many of its upper class residents and landowners were deported to upper Mesopotamia (see 2 Kgs 17:6).

Though the mass population of Israel was left in the north to continue to work the land for the Assyrians, the kingdom of Israel itself ended in 722 BC.

Elijah denouncing Ahab

Chapter 8 will explore the warnings of the prophets of the Southern Kingdom, one of whom was a near contemporary to Amos and Hosea—namely, Isaiah. These southern prophets warned about Judah's impending punishment from God: its fall to Babylon, again a consequence of disobedience and betrayal of the covenant with YHWH.

Section in Review

Quick View

- The prophets of the Northern Kingdom preached many types of messages, including some with a radical bent.

- The northern kingdom fell at the hands of the Assyrian Empire in 722 BC.

For Review

1. **Main Idea**: What is the common theme that unites the four prophets of the Northern Kingdom?

2. **Critical Thinking**: What is the main difference between Amos's and Hosea's prophetic messages?

3. **Main Idea**: What new ideas did each of the four prophets introduce to the religion of YHWH?

For Reflection

Think about the love relationships you have in your life with your parents, grandparents, siblings, cousins, or best friends. What have you learned about God through those relationships?

Further Reflection

The prophets were central figures in the Old Testament. Their insistence on exclusive YHWH worship and real justice for the poor makes them even more truly heroic than the kings. But there is one more dimension to the prophets we have not yet touched upon. In addition to their roles as protectors of the law, military leaders, social reformers, servants, and messengers, the Old Testament prophets prepared the people for the coming of Jesus Christ, the Messiah. Read chapter 2 of Matthew's Gospel (verses 5–6; 15; 17–18; 23) to see how the stories of Jesus' birth fulfill the prophecies of the Old Testament prophets.

The prophetic words of Hosea, Isaiah, and others about the coming Messiah served more than one purpose. In the immediate context of the prophet's own lifetime, they were hopeful messages that looked forward to the end of the difficult times the people of Israel were facing. The Messiah to come was yet another proof that God would not abandon his people. But more than that, in the long run, the prophets' writings and actions prepare us for the kind of Messiah Jesus Christ would be.

Jesus's social concerns place him squarely in the tradition of the Old Testament prophets, a role he willingly adopts. Consider the evidence of the following passage from the Gospel of Luke, which Jesus reads from the Book of Isaiah:

> The Spirit of the Lord is upon me,
>   because he has anointed me
>   to bring glad tidings to the poor.
> He has sent me to proclaim liberty to captives
>   and recovery of sight to the blind
>   to let the oppressed go free,
> and to proclaim a year acceptable to the Lord.
>
> (Lk 4:18–19)

Jesus read these words from the scroll of Isaiah in the synagogue in Nazareth and immediately applied them to himself: "Today this scripture passage is fulfilled in your hearing" (Lk 4:21). He continued by making comparisons between himself and the prophets Elijah and Elisha, making clear his own understanding that he, too, was working in the tradition of the Old Testament prophets.

Like the Old Testament prophets, Jesus affirmed his compassion for the poor and suffering. Comparisons between Jesus, Elijah, and Elisha reveal how closely connected Jesus is to the Old Testament prophets. Remember the three miracles of Elijah that confirmed God's supremacy over Baal: the three-year drought God announced through Elijah; the miraculous feeding of the widow, her son, and Elijah himself; and the healing of the widow's son. The Gospels record miracles that parallel, yet go beyond each of these.

Read the following passages to see how Jesus continued the prophet's work: Luke 8:22-25, Luke 9:10-17, and Luke 7:11-17.

The Holy Spirit is also associated with both the prophets of the Old Testament and Jesus in the New Testament. Elisha's succession to Elijah is announced in these words: "The spirit of Elijah rests on Elisha" (2 Kgs 2:15)—that is, the same Spirit that inspired and sustained Elijah, the Holy Spirit, is now with Elisha. Prior to Jesus' speech in the synagogue, the Gospel reports "Jesus returned to Galilee in the power of the Spirit" (Lk 4:14). The *Catechism of the Catholic Church* teaches that

> Jesus Christ is the one whom the Father anointed with the Holy Spirit and established as priest, prophet, and king. (*CCC*, 783)

Like Jesus, the whole People of God share in these offices of Christ and are called to live and preach prayer and compassion to all.

Vocabulary Review

Directions: Identify the prophet or prophets that correspond to each of the following descriptions.

Amos   **Elijah**   **Elisha**   **Ezekiel**   **Hosea**   **Isaiah**   **Jeremiah**

1. Major prophets
2. Minor prophets
3. Their call narratives follow a similar pattern of God's call, their resistance, God's reassurance, and God's sending them forth.
4. "former prophets"
5. "latter prophets"
6. Had a strong message of social justice pointing out how the poor suffered despite the luxuries of the rich and "pious"
7. His marriage to Gomer symbolized God's relationship with Israel.
8. Encountered God in a tiny whispering sound
9. Succeeded Elijah and shared his message of social justice and religious devotion
10. Portrayed God as a loving, compassionate, and forgiving God

Performance Assessment Project

King Jehoash's reign (789–782 BC) is briefly described in 2 Kings 13:10–11; 14:1–15. He is known for condoning idolatry and robbing the Temple of its gold and silver after defeating the kingdom of Judah in battle. His reign fell between the lives of the prophets Elisha and Amos. If you were the prophet during King Jehoash's reign, what message would you have for the king and his people? In what format would you present God's message to them? Write a series of messages that relate to the messages of the prophets of the Northern Kingdom but are directed specifically at King Jehoash and the people of Israel.

Called to Prayer

> *I will make a covenant for them on that day,*
> > *with the beasts of the field,*
> *With the birds of the air,*
> > *and with the things that crawl on the ground.*
> *Bow and sword and war*
> > *I will destroy from the land,*
> > *and I will let them take their rest in security.*
> *I will espouse you to me forever:*
> > *I will espouse you in right and in justice,*
> > *in love and in mercy;*

I will espouse you in fidelity,

and you shall know the Lord.

—Hosea 2:20–22

- **Reflection**: Recall that Hosea is presenting this message to a sinful people. God forgives his people for their sins. When have you sinned and received the forgiveness from God for your faults? How did this make you feel?

- **Meditation**: Read this message from the prophet Hosea thoroughly. Imagine that God is speaking this directly to you. How would you respond to him? How would these words make you feel?

- **Resolution**: The Lord's Prayer includes the words "forgive us our trespasses as we forgive those who trespass against us." Make a commitment to forgive someone who needs your forgiveness today.

Notes

1. It is interesting that Amos mentions "bed of ivory" enjoyed by the very rich. Archaeologists have discovered a large hoard of ivory items dated to this time period. Since ivory is a valuable commodity which is not native to Palestine, the discovery would seem to indicate that trade was active during this period and the Israelites were successfully amassing wealth for themselves through that trade.

Turning Point in the Journey:
The Destruction of Judah, Exile, and Return

CHAPTER OUTLINE

■ *In the Southern Kingdom of Judah, Isaiah and Micah called the people back to God.*

■ *The Babylonian Exile was a trying time for both the deported people of Judah and those who remained in the conquered land.*

■ *The prophets Ezekiel, Jeremiah, and Isaiah continued to be God's voice in a time of great desperation.*

■ *The Jews were blessed with a return to Judah, but they were unable to regain their freedom.*

■ *Restoring the Temple and deepening one's spiritual life were key themes during the times of Exile.*

In the Southern Kingdom of Judah, Isaiah and Micah called the people back to God.

Introduction

King Ahaz's decision to align with Assyria may have saved Judah from the same fate as Israel, but it only delayed the end that was to come. This chapter describes some of the events leading to the destruction of Jerusalem, the exile of the kingdom of Judah to Babylon, and the eventual return of many exiles to the land of Palestine with the help of the Persian king, **Cyrus**.

The end of the independent Hebrew states—first Israel, then Judah—presented the most significant change in the life of the Chosen People since the time of their formation during the Exodus. Just how serious was the change that ultimately brought the destruction of Jerusalem and the exile of many of its residents? Old Testament historian, John Bright, offers this perspective:

> When one considers the magnitude of the calamity that overtook her, one marvels that Israel was not sucked down into the vortex of history along with the other little nations of western Asia.[1]

During the time of exile, God's People finally took the warnings of the prophets to heart and began to recommit themselves to the covenant with YHWH and the Law.

Isaiah

Judah before the Exile

As mentioned before, Judah was a much smaller kingdom than Israel in both land and population. It included the hills around Jerusalem as well as some land in the Negev desert. The people subsisted on farming and sheep herding. They also traded with Egypt and Arabia. Though the kings of Judah were descendants in the Davidic line, the kings of Israel were more charismatic during this time of division.

Solomon's son Rehoboam, who had provoked the wrath of Israel and the division of the kingdom, was succeeded in Judah by his son, Abijah, who ruled from 915 to 913 BC. Abijah recaptured part of the northern land, including Bethel, but the territory was hard to hold. The next two kings—Asa and Jehoshaphat—continued the skirmishes with Israel, but also attempted some reforms designed to reestablish the covenant with their people. Asa had to quell an Egyptian incursion from the south. While this was happening, Israel was able to move troops within five miles of Jerusalem. Only after Asa aligned with Damascus was he able to secure Jerusalem again (see 1 Kgs 15:16–22). Jehoshaphat (873–849 BC) instituted a series of judicial reforms, including a court of appeals. He attempted an alliance with the Northern Kingdom during the reign of King Ahab of Israel.

Jehoshaphat's successors, however, married into the family of the northern king Ahab and Jezebel and from that point the same problems faced in the Northern Kingdom—including idolatry [introduced previously] and injustice—infected Judah. It was during this time, the ninth and eighth centuries BC, that two prophets—Isaiah and Micah—emerged.

Isaiah

The New Testament quotes Isaiah more than any other prophetic book. However, the Book of Isaiah presents some interesting dilemmas for analysis.

Isaiah of Jerusalem, the prophet for whom the book is named, is said to have started his ministry in the reign of King Uzziah (see Is 1:1). Uzziah died about 740 BC. The problem with accurate dating occurs with the mention of the Persian emperor Cyrus in Isaiah 45:1. Cyrus defeated Babylon in 539 BC. It is virtually certain that the same prophet did not begin his career before 740 and then live to see the rise of Cyrus the Persian two centuries later.

This issue along with others has led to the understanding that the Book of Isaiah actually contains the work of more than one writer, from more than one time. The Book of Isaiah is usually divided as follows:

- *Isaiah 1–39.* These chapters are mostly stories about, and sayings of, the actual prophet Isaiah of Jerusalem for whom the book is named.

- *Isaiah 40–55.* A second, unnamed poet or prophet is generally credited with this portion of the book. Examination of the texts and message of this portion of the Book of Isaiah will accompany our study of Judah in exile in Babylon.

- *Isaiah 56–66.* Disciples of the prophet, writing from Jerusalem and the Diaspora after the exile, were thought to have collected these final chapters. These chapters emphasize the importance of the Temple and invite all nations to join Israel as God's Chosen People.

The first thirty-nine chapters of the Book of Isaiah detail the ministry of the prophet in Jerusalem. At the Temple, Isaiah had a vision of the Lord in glory. Isaiah was humbled and proclaimed his unworthiness to be God's messenger. The story tells of one of the seraphim (an angel) touching Isaiah's mouth with an ember from the altar and thus removing his sinfulness.

> Then I heard the voice of the Lord saying, "Whom shall I send? Who will go for us?" "Here I am," I said; "send me!" (Is 6:8)

The prophet then foretold to the people their stubbornness, which would eventually lead to the fall of Judah. Isaiah asked the Lord how long this period would be:

> Until the cities are desolate,
>   without inhabitants,
> Houses, without a man,
>   and the earth is a desolate waste.
> Until the Lord removes men far away,
>   and the land is abandoned more and more. (Is 6:11–12)

The first thirty-nine chapters of the Book of Isaiah include several other notable passages, including the **Vineyard Song** (Is 5) that depicts the Chosen People as the vine of God. This image recurs in the New Testament in the words of Jesus (Mt 21:33–44) and the letters of Paul (Rom 11:23–24).

Micah

Micah was another prophet from the late eighth century BC. He was a contemporary of Isaiah and also preached in Judah. His warning was traditional: If the people did not return to the Lord and observe the Law, they would be destroyed.

Micah witnessed the fall of Samaria and the advance of the Assyrians on Jerusalem in 701 BC. He was the first prophet who preached the eventual fall of Jerusalem:

Cyrus
The Persian king who allowed some of the Jews to return to Jerusalem after he conquered the Babylonians in 539 BC. This event is typically understood to mark the end of the Exile. However, many Jews remained in the Diaspora, never returning to Palestine, which remained controlled by the Persians.

Vineyard Song
An important passage of the Book of Isaiah depicting the Chosen People as the vine of God. This image recurs in the New Testament in the words of Jesus and the writings of the Apostle, Paul.

The Prophets and the Advent Liturgy

During Advent (and Christmas) many of the readings are taken from the Old Testament prophets, especially Isaiah. Read the following passages from the Sundays in Advent. Write how they refer to the coming of the Messiah and God's kingdom.

- Jeremiah 33:14–16
- Isaiah 40:1-5, 9–11
- Isaiah 35:1-6a, 10
- Isaiah 7:10–14

Therefore, because of you,
> Zion shall be plowed like a field,
> and Jerusalem reduced to rubble,
And the mount of the temple
> to a forest ridge. (Mi 3:12)

Micah's prophesy concerning the birth of the Messiah in Bethlehem (Mi 5:1) is cited in the Gospels (Mt 2:6; Jn 7:42).

Section in Review

Quick View

- In the ninth century BC, Judah began to experience the same problems of idolatry and injustice that Israel experienced.

- The Book of Isaiah has many important connections with the New Testament.

- The Prophet Micah was a contemporary of Isaiah and shared a traditional message.

For Review

1. **Main Idea**: Who were the major prophets of the Southern Kingdom before the fall of Jerusalem to Babylon?

2. **Main Idea**: How can we tell that more than one prophet wrote the Book of Isaiah? How is the Book of Isaiah divided?

3. **Main Idea**: What was the message of the prophet Micah? What was special about his prophecy?

4. **Critical Thinking**: According to the prophets, what caused the fall of Judah? What do you know from previous books of the Old Testament that leads you to believe that God will restore the people?

For Reflection

Read the Vineyard Song in Isaiah 5, and the parable Jesus told in Matthew 21:33–44 that seems to be based on it. List the parallels between the two. Does the vineyard make a good image for the Catholic Church today? Why or why not?

The Babylonian Exile was a trying time for both the deported people of Judah and those who remained in the conquered land.

The Exile of Judah

The Assyrians threatened God's People (and many other nations) for nearly two hundred years; then their power began to wane. In 612 BC the Babylonians and Medes overtook the Assyrian capital city of Nineveh. The prophet Nahum spoke of the fall of Nineveh (see Na 2:2–14). Shortly after Nahum, the prophet Habakkuk warned that the Babylonian King Nebuchadnezzar II would not stop with Nineveh and Egypt (captured in 605 BC). Babylon would set its sights on Judah, he warned:

> Look over the nations and see,
> > and be utterly amazed!
> For a work is being done in your days
> > that you would not have believed, were it told.
> For see, I am raising Chaldea,
> > that bitter and unruly people,
> That marches the breadth of the land
> > to take dwellings not his own. (Hb 1:5–6)

The prophet was correct. Nebuchadnezzar's siege of Jerusalem began in 597 BC. From Nebuchadnezzar's own inscriptions, he appointed in Jerusalem "a king of his liking, took heavy booty from it, and brought it into Babylon."[2] The Judean king Jehoiachin, only on the throne for three months, surrendered and was deposed and deported to Babylon.

He wasn't the only one. With him went many other leaders and craftsmen of Jerusalem. According to 2 Kings 24:14, the number of exiles taken at that time was 10,000. Adding 7,000 artisans and 1,000 "smiths" (2 Kgs 24:16), the total reached 18,000. The Book of Jeremiah, on the other hand, lists 3,023 persons carried into captivity on this first excursion (Jer 52:28). Even if the smaller number of Jeremiah (3,023) is accepted, it must be multiplied by an average family size, since Nebuchadnezzar's regime was known to carry away whole families.

Nebuchadnezzar did place a king of his own choosing in Jerusalem—Mattaniah, third son of King Josiah, who was renamed "Zedekiah." He was a weak ruler who was

Nineveh ruins

never accepted by the Jews. Zedekiah ruled for ten years until he attempted to revolt against the Babylonians.

Among the more striking archaeological confirmations of Biblical history was the discovery of a "ration list" in the ruins of Babylon—a text that mentions Jehoiachin.[3] The text also provides a postscript on Zedekiah: He eventually fell prey to the promises of Hophra, son of Psammetichus II of Egypt, and withheld tribute to Babylon. In other words, Zedekiah foolishly attempted to assert his independence from Babylonian rule.

In August 587 BC Nebuchadnezzar returned to Jerusalem, and the city finally fell. Zedekiah's resistance was crushed, and he was captured. His sons were killed before his eyes, and then his eyes were put out before he was taken "in fetters" to Babylon (see 2 Kgs 25:7).

Evidence of the Destruction

It seems beyond dispute that Jerusalem was treated severely. Archaeological finds show a total cessation of occupation of the towns near Jerusalem. These sites also indicate that vicious battles were fought there. Modern archaeologists confirm much of what Kathleen Kenyon

discovered in her early twentieth-century digs in certain Jerusalem locations.

> [Kenyon's excavations] yielded a picture of ruin and desolation that confronted the first returnees of 539–538. While some people had no doubt continued to live in Jerusalem, the archaeological picture is one of their squatting among the rubble, which increased as the terrace walls . . . collapsed through lack of care and the debris accumulated in impassable piles on the lower slopes. No great change in the condition of the city occurred until the time of Nehemiah's arrival in 445.[4]

It is difficult to estimate the human extent of the crisis. For example, if around 20,000 Jews were previously exiled, how many more residents of Jerusalem and the surrounding area were taken? Higher estimates reach as much as 50,000–60,000. Some estimate those numbers as being almost the entire population of the region. It is important to note, however, that the Bible does not even attempt to determine the numbers of those who fled or were killed.

Lamentations
The Book of Hebrew poetry written in response to the devastation in Jerusalem by those who remained behind after the conquest of 587.

Marduk
The main state god of the Babylonians during the reign of Nebuchadnezzar. It was to his temple in the city of Babylon that the Temple furnishings and vessels from the Temple of Solomon were carried following the destruction of the Temple and Jerusalem in 587 BC.

By combining the archaeological evidence of destruction and difficult times in exile with Scripture references that indicate the emotional response of the Jewish people, the horrific picture of what happened is very clear. The following psalm is just one of many passages that reveal the depth of the Jews' sense of loss and despair over the loss of their homeland:

> By the rivers of Babylon
>   we sat mourning and weeping
>   when we remembered Zion.
> On the poplars of that land
>   we hung up our harps.
> There our captors asked us
>   for the words of a song;
>   Our tormentors, for a joyful
>   song:
>   "Sing for us a song of Zion!"
> But how could we sing a song of
> the Lord
>   in a foreign land?
>
> If I forget you, Jerusalem,
>   may my right hand wither.
> May my tongue stick to my palate
>   if I do not remember you,
> If I do not exalt Jerusalem
>   beyond all my delights. (Ps 137:1–6)

The entire Book of **Lamentations** is a collection of sorrowful poetry that gives us an even better sense of the devastation of the exilic events:

> How lonely she is now,
>   the once crowded city!
> Widowed is she
>   who was mistress over nations;
> The princess among the provinces
>   has been made a toiling slave.
>   (Lam 1:1–2)

The Babylonians destroyed the Temple of Solomon. They carried many of the religious implements of worship into exile with the people. The policy of Nebuchadnezzar was to place captured religious implements or statues in the temple of **Marduk**, the main state god, in the city of Babylon in order to symbolize the capture of the people and the defeat of their gods. In the case of the Jews, a capture of Temple vessels served the same purpose. (This practice may underlie the stories of Belshazzar's feast in Daniel 5 and the return of the Temple furnishings in Ezra 1–6.)

There would have been a succession of crises for those Jews who remained in Jerusalem during the exile. The famous ancient Jewish historian, Josephus, suggested that Nebuchadnezzar was back in Palestine again in 582, probably in reprisal for the murder of Gedaliah, the Jewish governor he left in charge after the siege of 587. The historical evidence suggests a series of traumatic events experienced by the Jews—whether in exile or back in the land.

Status and Treatment of the Exiles

The Book of Lamentations includes poetry of the devastation in Jerusalem by those who apparently remained behind after the conquest of 587. But what about the people who were taken as exiles? We possess very little written information from the Babylonians themselves about how they treated the Jews or any other exiled communities. But one inscription of Nebuchadnezzar II reads, in part, as follows, indicating forced labor:

> . . . the whole of the races, people from far places, whom Marduk my Lord delivered to me—I forced them to work on the building of Etemenanki—I imposed on them the brick-basket.[5]

Archaeological surveys of the central flood plain of the Euphrates River—the source of water for the entire agricultural life of the surrounding region—show that there were increases in settlements during the time of Babylonian rule. This increase may have been due in part to the influx of deported people from Judah and other conquered peoples.

The Old Testament describes the conditions of exile in very dark terms. Several places mention the exiles being held with chains and bonds (e.g., Na 1:13, 3:10; Is 52:2; and Ps 107:14). The second Book of Chronicles reports of the imprisonment of Jehoiakim: "Nebuchadnezzar, king of Babylon, came up against him and bound him with chains to take him to Babylon" (2 Chr 36:6). The Book of Lamentations also speaks of sieges and chains after the conquest of Jerusalem:

> He has hemmed me in with no escape
>   and weighed me down with chains;
> Even when I cry out for help,
>   he stops my prayer;
> He has blocked my ways with fitted stones,
>   and turned my paths aside. (Lam 3:7–9)

There are frequent descriptions of the exiles as prisoners. The "release of prisoners" is mentioned often, indicating the kind of treatment they received (see Ps 146:7–8; Zec 9:12; Is 42:7, 61:1).

Section in Review

Quick View

- Judah was unable to resist the onslaught of the Babylonian empire in 587 BC.

- Historical evidence suggests that the city of Jerusalem and the exiled people of Judah suffered greatly at the hands of the Babylonians.

For Review

1. **Main Idea**: What archaeological evidence is there to support the Biblical story of the conquest and exile of Jerusalem?

2. **Main Idea**: What happened to King Johiachin? Why did Nebuchadnezzar return to Jerusalem ten years after the original conquest? What became of King Zedekiah?

3. **Critical Thinking**: Describe the probable conditions the Jews faced in exile.

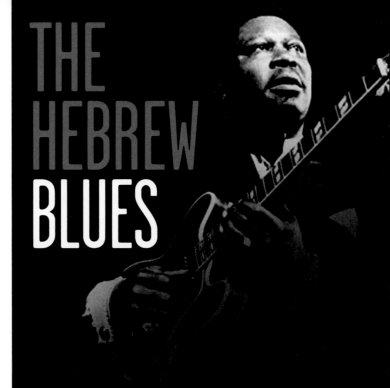

THE HEBREW BLUES

There is a famous African American musical style known as "the blues." This is a music that comes from the suffering of the African American people in American history, especially around the Mississippi Delta region. The songs often talk about family suffering, imprisonment, and even starvation. Though themes in the Book of Lamentations involves themes with a deeper significance than hurt and sadness, the musical style "Hebrew blues" does allow for a hint as to why poetry was written and re-read in times of trouble. Why would you want to read sad poetry more than once? Why write it in the Bible so that it is read over and over again?

Perhaps a famous blues musician can help us understand this. The well-known bluesman B.B. King once said with a smile: "Sometimes life gives you the blues—but singing the blues can always give you life!" What he meant is that sometimes expressing your feelings, even hurt or sadness, can begin to make you feel better because you have said it, especially if you "sing" your sadness to God. The Prophet Jeremiah often prayed his sadness to God in passages that have come to be known as "The Confessions of Jeremiah." Some of the most famous are Jeremiah 15:10–21, 17:14–18, 18:18–23, and 20:7–18. They are well worth reading. It seems the Prophet Jeremiah knew about "the blues," too!

For Reflection

Imagine that you are among the people conquered by Nebuchadnezzar and taken to Babylon as forced labor. Write a prayer to God, describing a typical day and expressing your feelings.

The prophets Ezekiel, Jeremiah, and Isaiah continued to be God's voice in a time of great desperation.

Prophets of the Exile

Ezekiel and Jeremiah were two prophets whose lives overlapped with the events of the Babylonian Exile, but from two very different perspectives. Ezekiel was deported to the Babylonian heartland where he lived with other exiles from Judea. Jeremiah remained behind in Jerusalem until he was taken by force to Egypt by a group of Jews who were sympathetic to assistance offered by the Egyptians in their attempt to break free from Babylonian rule.

A third important prophet of the Exile will also be covered in this section. The anonymous prophet whose message is recorded in Isaiah 40–55 consoled the exiles and wrote of a promised time of peace beyond suffering. He described this time as a new Exodus. The prophet also may have considered Cyrus, the Persian king who liberated the Jews, as God's Messiah.

Ezekiel

Of the sparse information known about Ezekiel, his writings reveal that he was a priest. Although some of the other prophets may have been from priestly families, Ezekiel seems to have been the only prophet who served actively as a priest. Priests were in charge of maintaining the purity of individuals and all of Israel. Part of this task was accomplished by conducting Temple sacrifices. Another part of the priest's ministry was to advise the people on issues of conduct and day to day living.

Ezekiel was deported with the first group of exiles in 597 and began his role as a prophet five years later in Babylon. He was the first prophet called to prophesy outside the Holy Land. Ezekiel's "call narrative" describes a vision of cherubim who gave him a scroll containing the Word of God, which he was to proclaim to the people. The words "Lamentation and wailing and woe!" were written on the scroll that he was instructed to eat. This event was the first in a series of bizarre visions and actions Ezekiel experienced through the course of his prophesying (Ez 3:1–4). For example, he shaved, burned, and divided his hair as a sign of the fate of the people of Jerusalem when Nebuchadnezzar defeated them for the second time (Ez 6:1–4), and he pantomimed the actions of the exiles (Ez 12:1–20).

The Book of Ezekiel is laid out with a clear division of parts:

- *Ezekiel 1–24.* This section—known as "Oracles of Judgment"—warns of Jerusalem's impending doom, sometimes reaching a rather severe level of rhetoric and anger.

- *Ezekiel 33–48.* These "Oracles of Hope" speak of the restoration of Jerusalem after the Exile and culminate in a grand vision (Ez 40–48) in which Ezekiel "sees" a hopeful reestablishment of the Israelite state under equitable and just circumstances.

This division leaves a somewhat enigmatic section in Ezekiel 25–32. An editor may have added these chapters at a later time, because the subjects of chapters 24 and 33 are precisely the same: the fall of Jerusalem. It seems that these originally connected chapters were split by the insertion of the passages that now make up chapters 25–32.

Ezekiel 25–32 is sometimes called the "Oracles against the Nations," because it contains speeches of judgment directed against foreign nations. Why were these chapters inserted in this part of the Book of Ezekiel? It is easy to figure out at least part of the answer. Look at the timing and placement of these speeches: they were placed in the text at the very moment of Jerusalem's destruction by a foreign nation (Babylon). Perhaps they were meant to assure the reader that the evil done to Jerusalem would have its consequences for the perpetrators.

The unique character of the Book of Ezekiel is best understood by the series of visions and actions of the prophet.

The Visions of Ezekiel

1. The Call (Ez 1–2)

The first vision is really the "call narrative" of Ezekiel; he receives his "commission" as a prophet in the first two chapters. In this vision, Ezekiel sees the throne of God in Heaven, accompanied by a series of strange creatures and equipped with wheels and wings. The theme appears to be movement: the creatures are moving and the setting for the throne of God is moving. Before his vision is complete, however, Ezekiel is called to be a prophet, even though he is told that the people may well reject his message:

> But speak my words to them, whether they heed or resist, for they are rebellious. (Ez 2:7)

It was at this point of his commissioning that Ezekiel was handed a scroll covered with writing on front and back. The Lord then makes an unusual request:

> Son of man, eat what is before you; eat this scroll, then go, speak to the house of Israel. (Ez 3:1)

Ezekiel ate the scroll "and it was as sweet as honey" (Ez 3:3). Then, God said:

> Son of man, go now to the house of Israel, and speak my words to them. (Ez 3:4)

Ezekiel was so overcome with this experience that he sat stunned for seven days.

2. The Transport to Jerusalem (Ez 8–11)

In his second great vision, Ezekiel is transported to Jerusalem with other exiles from Babylon. They are stopped on four occasions, each time moving closer and closer to the Temple. At each stop, Ezekiel is appalled by what he sees—pagan worship and rituals being performed—right up to the steps of the Temple itself.

Keeping in mind that Ezekiel was a priest, this vision of the severity of pagan mixing with the religion of YHWH must have been particularly distasteful. At the end of his "tour of sin" around the Temple complex, Ezekiel is placed on a hillside overlooking Jerusalem, and he sees something that he wouldn't imagine in his worst nightmare. The Spirit of God actually leaves Jerusalem:

Ezekiel

> And the glory of the Lord rose from the city and took a stand on the mountain which is to the east of the city. (Ez 11:23)

Ezekiel was shown two important things in this vision: (1) the extent of the pagan corruption in Jerusalem, and (2) the fact that God was not permanently "locked" to the Temple; his spirit could be found anywhere and everywhere. This second point was very important to exiles that might have believed that when they left Jerusalem, God had been left behind.

3. The Valley of the Dry Bones (Ez 37)

In the most widely known vision from the Book of Ezekiel, the prophet is set among a valley of bones, a horrific sight. One theory is that this valley was in the midst of a battlefield, and the dry bones represented the fallen of Israel who had died in the battles and destruction of the

Ezekiel's vision of the Valley of the Dry Bones

The princes of Israel will no longer oppress my people, but will leave the land to the house of Israel according to their tribes. Thus says the Lord God: Enough, you princes of Israel! Put away violence and oppression, and do what is right and just! Stop evicting my people says the Lord God. (Ez 45:8–9)

This vision let the people know that the restored Israel would not go back to its old ways. A new and just Israel was on the horizon.

The Acts of Ezekiel

Some of the actions of Ezekiel give the impression that he was mentally unstable, because of the extreme variations of his personality. For example, examine these seven acts of Ezekiel:

1. After his call from the Lord, Ezekiel sits in his own house. Unlike many of the prophets who seek out the people to whom God wishes to speak, Ezekiel waits until people come to him. Even then, he speaks only when the Lord opens his mouth (see Ez 3:24–27).

2. Ezekiel builds a model of Jerusalem, complete with battering rams, siege walls, and other weapons of war. He then lies—first on his left side and then on his right side—facing the model. He eats impure food cooked in an impure manner—probably representing the sickness, death, and starvation of the people living under siege conditions (Ez 4).

3. Ezekiel cuts off his hair, and then divides it into thirds: cutting one part, burning one part, and throwing one part to the wind. This likely represents the fate of the people of Jerusalem in the coming destruction. One third will die by the sword of the invaders, another third will burn in the fire of siege and conquest, and yet another third will flee as refugees or be taken as prisoners of war to the "far corners of the earth" (see Ez 5).

4. Ezekiel packs an exile's bag and is seen leaving the city again and again, re-enacting the events of being conquered and exiled by Babylon (Ez 12).

5. Ezekiel returns to his model of the city of Jerusalem, adding a road approaching it from Babylon. This is likely meant to show that Nebuchadnezzar would return to Jerusalem to destroy it (see Ez 21).

exilic events themselves. Before his eyes, Ezekiel sees the bones drawn together, filled out with flesh and skin, and restored to life.

Remember, this vision is recorded in the "Oracles of Hope" section. Ezekiel is seeing a vision of the restored Israel. The message from this vision is that restoration is possible. Even the devastation of the destruction brought down on Israel as a result of the conquests of Assyria and Babylon can be overcome in the plan of God.

4. The Restored Israel (Ez 40–48)

The entire final section of the book contains a dramatic vision about the restoration of Israel. There are many details about the reconstructed Temple and some elements of the city. But what is particularly interesting is the fact that Ezekiel envisions a redistribution of land in this vision. Each of the tribes is to get equal shares of land in the restored Israel. The royal leader will only be given a set amount of land and will no longer oppress the people. This vision describes Ezekiel in the tradition of the earlier prophets, speaking for the rights of the people against the greed of the royal and aristocratic leaders:

6. When Ezekiel's wife dies suddenly, he does not mourn for her in the customary ways; instead, he puts on his sandals and turban and goes about as usual. When the people question him about it, he tells them that this will be their response, too; when Jerusalem falls—there will be no time for mourning (see Ez 24:15–26).

7. After the vision of dry bones, Ezekiel joins together two sticks marked "Israel" and "Judah" to represent the reunification of the old rival states of the Hebrews (see Ez 37:15–22).

What do these symbolic acts mean? Were these just theatrics meant to impress the importance of his message on the people? Was he, in fact, mentally unstable? A comparison with the poems of the Book of Lamentations suggests another idea:

- *Compare Ezekiel 3:22–27 and Lamentations 3:7–9.*

  Ezekiel sits confined in his home with hands tied by cords. Lamentations speaks of a prophet hemmed in and bound by chains.

- *Compare Ezekiel 4:1–3 and Lamentations 1:11; 2:12; 4:4; 9–10.*

  The siege of Jerusalem forces some people to eat impure foods, or foods prepared in an impure manner. Lamentations echoes the concern with the ability to feed oneself and family properly. (Also see Jer 52:6 and 2 Kgs 25:3).

- *Compare Ezekiel 5:1–17 and Lamentations 1:1; 2:21.*

  Ezekiel acts out the tri-fold punishment of Jerusalem: a third of the people burnt in the city, a third dying by the sword, and a third exiled ("strewn to the wind"). Lamentations bemoans the lonely, once crowded city.

- *Compare Ezekiel 12 and Lamentations 1:3, 18.*

  Ezekiel prepares "an exile's baggage" and is led through a hole in a wall to exemplify being taken as a prisoner of war. He is reliving the events of the exile—first, his own exile to Babylon, and second, his image of events to come when Jerusalem will fall and be utterly destroyed. Lamentations mourns the

A truckload of Afghans leaving Iran under United Nations supervision

fate of Judah, finding no place to rest as her people are led into exile.

- *Compare Ezekiel 21 and Lamentations 2:21; 5:9.*

    In Ezekiel, the image of the sword is used to refer to Babylonian forces. In Lamentations the image of the sword is a symbol for foreign rule.

The Book of Lamentations expresses in powerful, emotional terms the devastation of the city of Jerusalem, and the profound grief of the people of Judah and Israel. When the Book of Ezekiel is read with Lamentations, we realize how deeply Ezekiel suffered from the devastation of the siege he went through in 597 BC, and the destruction that he and others heard about while in Babylon in 587. His actions, therefore, must be understood, not as the ravings of one afflicted with mental illness, but as the outpouring of an overwhelming sense of grief, loss, and pain.

Today we know much more about the psychological impact of warfare and disaster. Ezekiel is as much a prophet for modern times as he was for the exiles in Babylon. He suffered the same fate as the millions of homeless and refugees fleeing warfare and hunger today who also must deal with the psychological and spiritual impact of a horrific situation. God chose a broken refugee to be a prophet of hope to all who find themselves in a similar situation.

Jeremiah

Jeremiah

Jeremiah began his ministry as a prophet during the reign of King Josiah in approximately 626 BC. He finally disappeared from the pages of history in 587 BC. Unlike Ezekiel, Jeremiah remained in Jerusalem through all the events of the siege and the exile of the people.

According to Jeremiah, Judah was paying a price for its sins and the best course of action would be to submit to Babylon so that Jerusalem could escape destruction. Jeremiah walked through the streets of Jerusalem with a wooden yoke on his shoulders preaching this message. This course of action was not popular among God's People, especially among those who wanted to forcibly resist Nebuchadnezzar.

But Jeremiah hoped to avoid the destruction of the Temple. He also understood the current political subjugation to Babylonian rule to be God's response to the people's sinfulness. As such, they should not resist it, but should submit to it and repent of their idolatry and their

abuse of the poor in their midst, in the hope that God would relent and return them to their previous position. It is possible that if Jerusalem had not tried to revolt against Babylon in 587, the first Temple would have remained standing. As it was, however, the Temple was destroyed along with the whole city of Jerusalem in response to Zedekiah's revolt.

In the Temple Sermon of Jeremiah 7, the prophet's full message is clear as he warns that those who oppress refugees, orphans, or widows will not be spared just because they come to the Temple. They must first reform their evil ways.

Read Jeremiah 7.

Jeremiah stood in the very Temple area itself, and proclaimed his message. Here are the main points:

- The sacrificial system does not automatically take away the consequences of sin. The sacrifice is invalid if the person intends to sin again.

- Jerusalem is not immune to punishment just because the Temple stands there. God destroyed Shiloh, another famous Temple, and he can destroy Solomon's great Temple as well.

- The sins of pagan worship and oppression of the "alien, orphan and widow" are severely condemned (v. 6).

Perhaps most famous point is Jeremiah's bitter attack on the Temple itself as a "den of thieves" in Jeremiah 7:11. These are the very words used by Jesus to condemn the corrupt Temple practices of his day (see Mt 21:13). Anyone who heard Jesus' warnings would have instantly recognized the reference. Jesus was quoting one of the most radical accusations made by *any* of the prophets, and in Jeremiah, the prophet went on to suggest that the Temple would in fact be destroyed for the sins of the people. Was Jesus implying this too? (The Temple Jesus knew was destroyed in 70 AD, not long after his Ascension to Heaven around 33–34.)

The Confessions of Jeremiah

Jeremiah, like Ezekiel, had to struggle with the personal trauma of being a prophet with an unpopular message. A series of "confessions" in the Book of Jeremiah describe much of his personal agony:

Read Jeremiah 8:18–23; 15:10–21; 17:14–18; 18:18–23; 20:7–18.

In the final confession, Jeremiah reveals an intimate connection with God and his commitment to preaching his word in spite of derision he receives from those who oppose him:

> Yes, I hear the whisperings of many:
>   "Terror on every side!
> Denounce! let us denounce him."
> All those who were my friends
>   are on the watch for any misstep of mine.
> "Perhaps he will be trapped; then we can prevail
>   and take our vengeance on him."
> But the Lord is with me, like a mighty champion:
>   my persecutors will stumble, they will not
>   triumph." (Jer 20:10-11)

Eventually, Jeremiah's enemies did manage to silence him. He was smuggled to Egypt by some Jews who supported Egyptian hopes to bring Judah into an alliance of nations opposed to Babylon. After Jeremiah was taken to Egypt, no further mention of him occurs in the Bible. Presumably he died there, a lonely and unpopular prisoner of Jews who did not agree with his theology or politics.

Prophet of the Book of Isaiah

The messages of both Ezekiel and Jeremiah, though dire, hint at new beginnings for Israel. Recall (see page 171) that chapters 40–55 of the Book of Isaiah are generally credited to a second, unnamed prophet or poet who prophesied at the end of the Babylonian Exile.

The prophet understood that Persia was soon to be the new power of the region and that its more tolerant ruler, Cyrus, would be God's instrument to return the Jews to their homeland. Cyrus, indeed, was a key factor in the end of Babylonian captivity for the Jewish exiles even though the Persians maintained rule over the lands of Palestine and the Jewish people.

Chapters 40–55 include four Servant Songs. A messianic figure, known as the "Servant of God" is described as having the mission to bring righteousness to the world. He is opposed, suffers, and is put to death.

Read Isaiah 42:1–4; 49:1–6; 50:4–9; 52:13–53:12.

The Servant Songs are clearly connected with the mission of Jesus. The fourth song describes the redeeming nature of Jesus' Death:

> But he was pierced for our offenses,
>   crushed for our sins;
> Upon him was the chastisement that makes us whole,
>   by his stripes we were healed. (Is 53:5)

It is important to remember that the prophet's words had comfort for the people at the time they were written as well as 500 years later with the coming of Jesus Christ. So, whom might the prophet have been referring to as the Suffering Servant at the time these words were written?

The prophet clearly believes that at least one identity of the "Suffering Servant" is the Jewish people themselves, due to their experience in exile. They are collectively the "Servant of God." And if this is the case, then what is their new mission to be? Is it to forget what they have learned in their suffering and to punish the nations that hurt them so badly? Some passages seem to indicate this (see Ps 137:1, 8–9), but these sacred words represent another tradition, one that recognizes that suffering has given the people a more peaceful and loving way to view and respond to the rest of the world:

Jesus
the Suffering Servant
(*CCC*, 440, 572, 601, 608, 713)

St. Paul proclaimed, "Christ died for our sins in accordance with the scriptures" (1 Cor 15:3). Paul could have been referring to many Old Testament passages, but he likely had Isaiah's Suffering Servant songs in mind when he wrote those words. The Book of Isaiah (Is 42–53) contains a series of Suffering Servant songs that early Church interpreted in reference to Jesus. These songs are some of the most quoted Old Testament passages in the New Testament. Isaiah wrote that Redemption comes through suffering, which Jesus echoed when he revealed his identity to his disciples.

At the turning point of Mark's Gospel (Mk 8:27–34), three titles for Jesus are revealed, including Messiah (Christ), Son of Man, and the Suffering Servant. Jesus taught his disciples that "the Son of Man must suffer greatly and be rejected" (Mk 8:31). Jesus willingly suffered Death on the Cross in order to bring about Salvation for humanity just as the Suffering Servant in Isaiah sacrificed his life for his people.

The Suffering Servant in Isaiah was innocently killed but made no complaint. He bore the guilt of his people and was led to slaughter like a lamb for sacrifice. Similarly, Jesus bore the sin of the world and sacrificed his life in order to bring justification for the world. The passion narratives bear striking resemblance to the Suffering Servant songs. Jesus, the Lamb of God, was killed despite his innocence and offered no objection to the ridicule of those who killed him. He bore the sin of the world and won justification for sinners.

Isaiah's Suffering Servant	Jesus
He had done no wrong nor spoken any falsehood (Is 53:9)	Neither Pilate nor Herod could find fault in Jesus, but he was crucified by the will of the crowds (Mt 27:23–24; Mk 15:14; Lk 23:4, 14–15)
Like a lamb, he was led to slaughter (Is 53:7)	Jesus is the Paschal Lamb of God (Jn 19:36, 1 Cor 5:7)
	Jesus was mocked by the soldiers, chief priests, elders, scribes, and even Herod, but Jesus never spoke a word in response (Mt 27:27–31, 41–42; Mk 15:16–20, 31-32; Lk 23:11, 36)
He was treated harshly but without complaint (Is 53:7)	"When he was insulted, he returned no insult" (1 Pt 2:23)
He bore the guilt of his people and won forgiveness for their sins (Is 53:5–6, 8, 11–12)	Appearing to his disciples, the Risen Jesus refers to himself as the suffering Messiah who rose from the dead for the forgiveness of sins (Lk 24:26, 46–47) "He himself bore our sins . . . so that, free from sin, we might live for righteousness" (1 Pt 2:24)

It is too little, he says, for you to be my servant,
to raise up the tribes of Jacob,
and restore the survivors of Israel;
I will make you a light to the nations,
that my salvation may reach to the ends of
the earth. (Is 49:6)

In this passage, the prophet goes far beyond simply preaching the restoration of Israel. Now, the people of God will be a missionary people, with a "light" to take to all the nations.

While many other identifications of the Suffering Servant have been proposed (e.g., the prophet himself, or another prophet living at that time), the Church is clear in its pronouncement that the Suffering Servant prophecies are fulfilled in Jesus Christ. The *Catechism* teaches:

> The Scriptures had foretold this divine plan of salvation through the putting to death of "the righteous one, my Servant" as a mystery of universal redemption, that is, as the ransom that would free men from the slavery of sin. Citing a confession of faith that he himself had "received," St. Paul professes that "Christ died for our sins in accordance with the scriptures." In particular, Jesus' redemptive death fulfills Isaiah's prophecy of the suffering Servant. (*CCC*, 601)

Section in Review

Quick View

- The prophet Ezekiel was deported with the exiles in 597 BC and proclaimed a message of both judgment and hope in times of great despair.

- The prophet Jeremiah called for reform of Temple worship and fair treatment of others to avoid the destruction of the Temple.

- The Suffering Servant of God was an important message in the Book of Isaiah.

For Review

1. **Critical Thinking**: Compare and contrast the two major prophets of the exile, Jeremiah and Ezekiel.

2. **Critical Thinking**: What was unique about Ezekiel and his call to be one of God's prophets? How were his messages unusual, or unusually delivered? What

are some possible explanations for the intensity of his prophetic speech and actions?

3. **Main Idea**: What was the contribution of Deutero-Isaiah to the messages of the prophets in exile? What new understanding of the exile did this prophet share with the people?

For Reflection

Read the Book of Lamentations. Think about current events around the world. What people would be very likely to understand the message of Lamentations today? Why?

The Jews were blessed with a return to Judah, but they were unable to regain their freedom.

The Exiles Return to Judah

The end of the Neo-Babylonian regime came in 539 BC with legendary swiftness. Cyrus the Persian king, after unifying the Persian tribes and defeating the Medes, conquered the city of Babylon. According to classical sources (e.g., the Greek historian, Herodotus), Cyrus was able to conquer the city without violence because the Persians surprised the Babylonians during the celebrations of the New Year—an historical event also reflected in the story of Belshazzar's Feast (see Dn 5). According to the Book of Isaiah, God used Cyrus as an instrument of change.

Thus says the Lord to his anointed, Cyrus,
whose right hand I grasp,
Subduing nations before him,
and making kings run in his service,
Opening doors before him
and leaving the gates unbarred:
I will go before you
and level the mountains;
Bronze doors I will shatter,
and iron bars I will snap.
I will give you treasures out of the darkness,
and riches that have been hidden away,
That you may know that I am the Lord,

the God of Israel, who calls you by your name. (Is 45:1–3)

The Biblical sources about the early Persian period (e.g., Ezra 1–6) indicate that the Persians were relatively generous in their return of exiles of all nations and races to their homelands, including the Jews. But this generosity can be exaggerated. It was not entirely altruistic. The missions led by the Jewish leaders Ezra and Nehemiah back to Palestine, accompanied by former exiles, were probably a calculated Persian imperial policy. An increased military presence was needed on the western flank facing the Greek enemies—particularly after an Egyptian revolt in 460 (sometimes called the **Inarus Revolt**) in which the Greeks were involved. (The Persian ruler Artaxerxes I in 454—a time very close to the period of Ezra and Nehemiah—eventually crushed this revolt.)

Part of the exaggeration of Persian benevolence is the idea that the Exile actually ended in 539. Really all that ended was Neo-Babylonian dominance of the Jews and it was quickly replaced by Persian dominance. Although some of the Jews were allowed to return to Jerusalem, not by any means did all of them do so. And their return was not an altruistic policy of returning people to their homeland and restoring their sovereign status. Persian policies were just as powerfully oriented toward gaining material wealth and control of territory as were those of any of the regimes before it. The Persian Empire was particularly famous for levying all kinds of taxes throughout its Empire and pressing peoples into forced labor for massive building projects. There was no interest in helping citizens acquire business success or economic independence on their own. In fact, the Persian government referred to all the citizens of the Persian Empire as "slaves." One famous historian of the Persian Empire wrote:

Labor and production in Persia were organized on a huge scale by the central administration in a way that would seem to leave relatively little scope for what we should call modest private enterprise . . . [even] sheep raising was also organized on a large scale.[6]

Likewise, we read in the Book of *Nehemiah* that the Jews were slaves in their own land under the Persians:

But, see, we today are slaves; and as for the land which you gave our fathers that they might eat its fruits and good things—see, we have become slaves upon it! Its rich produce goes to the kings whom you set over us because of our sins, who rule over our bodies and our cattle as they please. We are in great distress! (Neh 9:36–37)

Long-Term Exile

The prophet Jeremiah foretold of seventy years of exile for the Jews:

Seventy years these nations shall be enslaved to the king of Babylon; but when the seventy years have elapsed, I will punish the king of Babylon and the nation and the land of the Chaldeans for their guilt, says the Lord. (Jer 25:11–12)

However, **post-Exilic** Biblical writings, such as Daniel, imply that the people were still in exile in the Persian period and beyond—to the time of Hellenistic rule beginning under Alexander the Great, who conquered Palestine in 333 BC. The regimes that followed in Alexander's wake—Hellenistic rulers who were descendants of Alexander's

---

Inarus Revolt

An Egyptian revolt against the Persians in 460 that had Greek support. It may have influenced Cyrus's decision to allow the Jews to return to Palestine and rebuild Jerusalem, as it would have allowed for increased military presence on the western flank of the Persian Empire facing Greece.

post-Exilic

Referring to the time after the return of the exiles to Jerusalem in 539 BC.

remnant

The exiles and former exiles who remained faithful to YHWH during the time of captivity and who were expected to restore Jerusalem.

generals—practiced the same kind of economics and politics of material gain. Historian Peter Green describes the Hellenistic rulers who ruled Palestine from 323 (after Alexander died) through 64 (when the Roman Empire ruled Palestine directly) in the following way:

> The main, indeed the overwhelming, motivation that confronts us in these Greek or Macedonian torchbearers of Western culture, throughout the Hellenistic era, is the irresistible twin lure of power and wealth. . . ."[7]

The point is simply this: the Hebrews from 587 BC through the early Christian period lived under Imperial designs who controlled power, wealth, territory, and human resources. In short, the Hebrew people lived under foreign rule for nearly 600 years before the time of Jesus and continued to live under Roman domination in Palestine for centuries after Jesus as well. These political, economic, and social realities provided the context for the time that the Old Testament was brought together as a collection of writings. It is also the context for the entire New Testament.

In summary, what is known about the end of the Babylonian Exile is that the Persians eventually invaded Babylon and allowed at least some of the exiled Jews to return to their homeland. The Persians even sponsored some of the caravans that returned to Judah, complete with some of the holy items from the Temple that were originally captured by the Babylonians. The condition of the land and community found in Judah upon the exiles' return is difficult to assess. It is often presumed that some form of religious life continued in the ruins of the Temple, but there is no direct evidence of it.

Some conflict broke out between those who returned from exile and those who had been left behind in Judah. The prophet Ezekiel rejected the claim that the survivors in Judah had any claim to the land; he says that the new Israel should be formed by the exiles (see Ez 33:23–29). Likewise, Jeremiah saw that no good could come from the people left in Judah under Zedekiah or those who had fled to Egypt. Jeremiah compared the returning exiles and those who remained to good and bad figs:

> The good ones are very good, but the bad ones are very bad, so bad they cannot be eaten. (Jer 24:3)

The exiles and former exiles that had remained faithful to YHWH during the time of captivity are known as God's **remnant**, the remnant spoken of by the prophets, including Isaiah:

> A remnant will return, a remnant of Jacob,
>   to the mighty God. (Is 10:21)

Section in Review

Quick View

- Although the Persian king Cyrus returned some of the Jews to Judah, they did not regain their freedom.

- For the centuries after the Exile, the Jews continued to live under imperial leaders—even up to the time of Christ.

- The remnant remained faithful to YHWH during the exile and rejected those that remained in Judah or fled during the Exile.

For Review

1. **Main Idea**: When did the Babylonian regime come to an end? Who assumed power in the area with the end of the Babylonian empire?

2. **Critical Thinking**: What improvements were there in the condition and treatment of the exiles under the new regime? What aspects remained unchanged?

3. **Main Idea**: Who were the leaders of the Jerusalem community after the return from exile? What did they think was important to the community?

For Reflection

Think of a time when you looked forward to returning to a place or an activity you had really enjoyed before. Were you able to return? Was it as good as you remembered? Why, or why not? Compare your experience to the experience of the people returning to Jerusalem from exile?

Rebuilding Judah

Research and report from archaeological resources on the building campaign in Judah when the Jews returned from captivity in Babylon. Include in the report information on the rebuilding of Solomon's Temple, including differences in dimensions between the first and second Temples.

Restoring the Temple and deepening one's spiritual life were key themes during the times of Exile.

Major Themes of Writing before, during, and after the Exile

The times of the divided kingdom, the Exile, and its aftermath are arguably the most important for anyone who studies, reads, and prays with these sacred texts. This period of time produced the greatest amount of the material that makes up the Old Testament. Understanding the cultural, political, and religious practices of the time helps to put these texts into context. Chapter 9 will cover more of the largest section of post-Exilic writings—the wisdom literature. For now, we will explore some of the major themes of writing during the years surrounding the Exile, including what it was like for the Jews to live under Persian rule.

A Temple-Centered People

Chapters 40–55 of the Book of Isaiah address a new hopefulness based on the idea that the Persians would institute a new regime, perhaps less oppressive than the Babylonian empire. But with the reality of life in Babylonian Exile ending and life under Persian rule just beginning, the Jews had a chance to reflect on what directions their life would take as the People of God.

Several questions persisted: Were they meant to return to Palestine and rebuild the Temple in Jerusalem? Or, given that there were still Jews living outside of Palestine even after the end of the Exile, was there any reason the Jews should focus on reclaiming political rule? Should they be more concerned with rededicating themselves to interior spiritual life?

Prophets Haggai and Zechariah sought to encourage the Jews to complete the rebuilding of the Temple. The returning exiles laid the foundation for the Temple in 538 BC, but enthusiasm quickly waned. In the years that followed, the people worked on rebuilding their own homes and businesses, and the Temple project remained incomplete. Haggai began a campaign in 520 BC to encourage the people to re-start the work. Within months, the project began.

Zechariah's ministry began two months after Haggai's. He, too, encouraged the completion of the Temple. The Book of Zechariah records a series of visions he received about work on the Temple and about the future glory of Jerusalem. In Zechariah 9:9–17, the prophet's oracle calls for restoration of Jerusalem led by a Messiah who comes not as a conquering warrior, but in lowliness and peace:

> See, your king shall come to you; a just savior is he, meek, and riding on an ass, on a colt, the foal of an ass. (Zec 9:9)

The Temple was, in fact, rebuilt about 520–515 BC. Neither Haggai nor Zechariah recorded its completion. But many of the older people, who had seen the former Temple, were disappointed that the new structure was not as impressive. Upon the laying of its foundation:

> Many of the priests, Levites, and family heads, the old men who had seen the former house, cried out in sorrow as they watched the foundation of the present house being laid. Many others, however, lifted up their voices in shouts of joy, and no one could distinguish the sound of the joyful shouting from the sound of those who were weeping; for the people raised a mighty clamor which was heard afar off. (Ezr 3:12–13)

For some Jews—both young and old—the rebuilding of the Temple was the absolute key to their receiving God's blessing (see Hg 2:15–19). For many, their existence under Persian rule required that their religious identity be complete, even if they were not allowed to be a politically independent entity. The completion of the Temple was key to this.

In the Persian Period (539–333 BC), another historical Biblical text was written for the Bible, the two books called first and second Chronicles. A great deal of the material in Chronicles was based on the older historical books of the Bible, namely Joshua, Judges, 1 and 2 Samuel, and 1 and 2 Kings. However, the historical perspective in Chronicles is much different than these other works.

In the Chronicles version, the kings of the Davidic line are praised or condemned not so much for their

Model of the Second Temple at the Israel Museum in Jerusalem

loyalty to YHWH, but rather for their dedication to building projects—especially the building of the Temple and the city of Jerusalem. Chronicles presents a Temple-centered version of prior Hebrew history probably because, for Jews living under Persian (and later, Hellenistic) rule, the Temple was the center of Jewish identity.

Compare the two descriptions of King Asa from the older first Book of Kings and the second Book of Chronicles from the Persian period. Notice the different emphasis:

> Asa pleased the Lord like his forefather David, banishing the temple prostitutes from the land and removing all idols his father had made. He also deposed his grandmother Maacah from her position as queen mother, because she had made an outrageous object for Asherah. . . . Asa's heart was entirely with the Lord as long as he lived. He brought into the temple of the Lord his father's and his own votive offerings of silver, gold, and various utensils. (1 Kgs 15:11–13, 15)

> Asa did what was good and pleasing to the Lord, his God, removing the heathen altars and the high places, breaking to pieces the sacred pillars, and cutting down the sacred poles. . . . He removed the high places and incense stands from all the cities of Judah, and under him the kingdom had peace. He built fortified cities in Judah, for the land had peace and no war was waged against him during these years because the Lord had given him peace. He said to Judah: "Let us build these cities and surround them with walls, towers, gates and bars. The land is still ours, for we have sought the Lord, our God; we sought him, and he has given us rest on every side." So they built and prospered. (2 Chr 14:1–2, 4–6)

For many Jews living under Persian rule, the building of the Temple and cities was remembered as the most important part of pre-Exilic history. The Temple's centrality to religious identity could also be maintained even for Jews living in the Diaspora. This is one reason why the High Priest, the leader of the Temple administration, rose to become the most important leader of the Jewish people from about 400 BC until the time of Jesus. The Temple was indeed the central institution in the life of many Jews after the Exile.

JONAH: THE RELUCTANT MISSIONARY OF PEACE

It is unfortunate that the Book of Jonah has often been written off as a mere child's story. This inspired story actually contains an important theological message. A fuller appreciation of this requires that we place the book in its most likely historical context.

The Book of Jonah likely comes from a late historical period, after the destruction of Jerusalem in 587 BC. Thus, the book derives from the long period of occupation of the land of the Hebrews, but also a time when thousands of Hebrews lived as minorities throughout the Diaspora.

The city of Nineveh was, for a time, the capital of the Neo-Assyrian Empire. The Assyrians conquered the Northern Kingdom of Israel in 722 BC and deported a group of the upper class from that region. In this story, Jonah is called to deliver his prophetic message to the center of one of the most feared and hated regimes the Hebrews ever faced. (Also, Nineveh is a symbol of the non-Jewish population.)

Any sane Jew feeling himself "called" to the center of the Assyrian Empire would probably hop a boat heading in the opposite direction. And that is exactly what Jonah does. But Jonah soon realizes that there is no escape from the God of the Hebrews. Even the sea monsters are subservient to God.

The heart of the Book of Jonah is the psalm of thanksgiving that appears in Jonah 2:3–10. Biblical scholarship has suggested that the psalm is much older than the Book of Jonah and that the story of Jonah was modeled to fit around the psalm, illustrating the meaning (a teaching method that Jewish rabbis came to call a *midrash*).

The references in the psalm to missing the Temple (Jon 2:4), being away from the land, and the allusions to prison (Jon 2:6) all suggest that it dates from the Exile when the people in the Diaspora lamented their fate (cf. Ps 107:10–16; 137; Is 42:7; Lam 3:34). So it seems clear that the Book of Jonah derives much of its power and meaning by being read in the Diaspora. This is a major clue to the meaning of the text.

Jonah's news to the king and people of Nineveh has a most interesting result: The king descends from the throne, removes his robe, and all the people fast and mourn. The king also decreed:

Jonah telling of Nineveh's coming vanquishment

Every man shall turn from his evil way and
from the violence he has in hand. (Jon 3:8)

In other words, the Assyrians repent their ways and change their behavior. God recognizes the Assyrian's repentance, and Jonah is furious at God's compassion. It is, of course, the same compassion that earlier saved his own sea-soaked skin. But now that God is showing compassion to an *enemy*, it is too much.

There is no escaping the power of this story: The Book of Jonah is about God's compassion for *all* people, even those who are not Jews. God cares for the well-being and transformation of all. But there is more.

The Book of Jonah is often described as a parable with a double meaning. Jonah, we must remember:

- is called by God
- rejects the call
- is sent into darkness
- is released to a mission

Does this sound familiar? This pattern is the general historical theme of the Bible, preeminently represented in the books of Joshua, Judges, 1 and 2 Samuel, and 1 and 2 Kings. In fact, some believe that the prophet Jeremiah's famous comments may have originally inspired the Book of Jonah:

> He has consumed me, routed me,
>   [Nebuchadnezzar, king of Babylon,]
> he has left me as an empty vessel;
> He has swallowed me like a dragon:
>   filled his belly with my delights,
>   and cast me out. (Jer 51:34)

In this tale, *Jonah is Israel*. The people of Israel were called by God, but sinfully rejected the call and listened to their own voices. As punishment, they were sent into exile. If Jonah does represent Israel, what have the people learned from the experience of the exile? The author of Jonah teaches that there is now a radical redefinition of what it means to be the People of God. If this is true, then Jonah is a symbol of Israel herself, missionary to the world and agent of God's Salvation. But Jonah is reluctant; sin and rejection of God's laws sent Israel into exile as Jonah was sent into the belly of the big fish.

With Jonah (and Isaiah 49:6), the point is made that *during* the Exile some of the Jews finally came to understand the profound nature of their call from YHWH. It was the same call that was repeated and taken up so powerfully in the teaching and example of Jesus. Jesus, too, renewed God's call and initiated his kingdom. Jesus told the people: "You are the light of the world" (Mt 5:14).

Prayer Traditions of the Diaspora

For people living in the Diaspora, history had other lessons to teach. From post-Exilic literature, a tradition of prayers emerged that repeated several of the same themes, including:

- shame associated with the sins of ancestors (Ezr 9:6–7; Neh 9:16–17; Dn 9:8; Bar 1:15b–17)

- exile or slavery as conditions that were warned about (Ezr 9: 7–9; Neh 9:36–37; Dn 9:12; Bar 2:1)

- the importance of the Law (Ezr 9:10-11; Neh 9:13; Dn 9:5; Bar 1:18)

These samples serve to illustrate the continuity of these themes over a period exceeding hundreds of years of tradition (these books were written over a 400-year period of history), but they also raise questions about why such ideas would be continuous. The answer is simple. The prayers were also reminders not to repeat the sins of the

Our Participation in the Prophetic Mission

The *Catechism of the Catholic Church* teaches that lay people contribute to Christ's prophetic office and fulfill their own prophetic mission by evangelization, "that is, the proclamation of Christ by word and the testimony of life" (*CCC*, 904 quoting *Lumen Gentium*, 35). Good evangelization goes hand in hand with good listening skills. Really getting to know a person is an excellent first step in being a witness to the Gospel. Look for ways to practice the following good listening skills:

- Give your full attention to the speaker. Make eye contact. Eliminate other distractions while you are listening.

- Focus on what the person is saying. Usually this does not involve remembering facts and details. Rather, it involves focusing on a central theme or feelings behind what the person is saying.

- Show your interest. For example, ask clarifying questions. Also, nod or say things like "I see" or "I understand" as the person is speaking.

- Summarize what the person has said. Recap the highlights of the conversation. For example, say, "As I understand it, you were saying . . ."

past—from the time of the monarchy. The prophet's call for Israel to be the "Servant of God" (see pages 181–183) pointed the way to a new future.

Section in Review

Quick View

- Rebuilding the Temple is a common theme throughout the Exile and in post-Exilic Old Testament writings.
- Remaining prayerful was a reminder of God's covenant to the people living in the Diaspora.
- The Book of Jonah reveals a radical redefinition of the meaning of the People of God.

For Review

1. **Main Idea**: When was the Temple rebuilt? What made rebuilding the Temple so important to the people returning to Jerusalem from exile?

2. **Critical Thinking**: What is the biggest thematic difference between the history presented in 1 and 2 Kings and that in 1 and 2 Chronicles?

3. **Main Idea**: What three themes emerge in the prayers of post-Exilic literature?

For Reflection

Write your own prayer expressing sorrow or shame for a wrong you have done, awareness of the consequences of that wrong act, and understanding of God's desire for you not to repeat it. (Note: You do not have to mention the wrongdoing by name.)

Further Reflection

The returning Jews from Babylonian Exile longed for the restoration of the monarchy. There was also considerable feeling that the enemies who perpetrated the horrendous series of events on the Jews should be punished. Consider Psalm 137, written from the time of the Exile. The psalm begins by expressing the sadness of the people, but concludes with a call for vengeance:

> Remember Lord, against Edom
> that day at Jerusalem.
> They said: "Level it, level it
> down to its foundations!"
> Fair Babylon, you destroyer,
> happy those who pay you back
> the evil you have done us!
> Happy those who seize your children
> and smash them against a rock! (Ps 137:7–9)

In short, the Jews looked for the restoration of Davidic power and were also seeking vengeance for their defeat.

On the other hand, while some Jews supported a violent restoration of the monarchy and punishment of enemies, the Exile also inspired another type of thinking among the authors of Scripture. In this view, the Jews were to be a People of God who would reach out to and inspire other nations. Chapter 2 of Isaiah explains how the people will be delivered from war and violence by the coming of a restored world under God, when all nations will stream to the mountain of God:

> In days to come,
> the mountain of the Lord's house
> shall be established as the highest mountain,
> and raised above the hills.
> All nations shall stream toward it;
> many peoples shall come and say:
> "Come, let us climb the Lord's mountain,
> to the house of the God of Jacob,
> That he may instruct us in his ways,
> and we may walk in his paths." (Is 2:2–3)

For these Jews, the Exile created a new sense of mission. Israel was not merely going back to its old and violent ways. It was going to become a nation recommitted to the covenant and to becoming the People of God, which would eventually be embodied in Jesus Christ.

Vocabulary Review

Directions: Explain the relationship between each set of terms, people, or places.

1. Jeremiah, Jesus
2. Cyrus, Isaiah
3. Micah, Samaria, Jerusalem
4. Marduk, Nebuchadnezzar
5. Babylonian Exile, Lamentations
6. Ezekiel, Jeremiah

7. remnant, Isaiah

8. Haggai, Zechariah

9. 1 and 2 Kings, 1 and 2 Chronicles

Performance Assessment Project

The Babylonian Exile was a true turning point in the history of the people of Judah. During the Exile, the Jewish people longed for the days when they maintained their sovereignty and ability to worship God in the Temple in Jerusalem. After their return, things were never the same. Compare and contrast the life of the Jews before the destruction in 587 BC, during the Babylonian Exile, and during the post-Exilic period.

Called to Prayer

Out of my distress I called to the LORD,
 and he answered me;
From the midst of the nether world I cried for help,
 and you heard my voice.
For you cast me into the deep, into the heart of the sea,
 and the flood enveloped me;
All your breakers and your billows passed over me.
Then I said, "I am banished from your sight!
 yet would I again look upon your holy temple."
The waters swirled about me, threatening my life;
 the abyss enveloped me;
 seaweed clung about my head.
Down I went to the roots of the mountains;
 the bars of the nether world
 were closing behind me forever,
But you brought my life up from the pit,
 O Lord, my God.
When my soul fainted within me,
 I remembered the Lord;
My prayer reached you
 in your holy temple.

—*Jonah 2:3–8*

- **Reflection**: Jonah offers this prayer of thanksgiving from the belly of a large fish. Despite his sorrow, he remembers the Lord. When have you remembered God during a time of hardship? When have you failed to remember him? Write about one or both of these times.

- **Meditation**: Imagine that you are Jonah. You have just rejected God's call and been sent into the sea with little hope of survival. Imagine yourself praying this prayer to God. How do you feel? What do you expect God will do?

- **Resolution**: What is God calling you to do today? Are you listening? Take some time to listen to God in prayer. Set aside some time to clear your mind and listen or have a conversation in prayer with him about what you should be doing with your life today, tomorrow, this year, and beyond.

Notes

1. John Bright, *History of Israel* (Westminster: Philadelphia, 1981) pp. 345, 347 respectively.

2. ANET, 564 - thus March 15/16, 597.

3. 80, "Post-Exilic Palestine: An Archaeological Report," S. S. Weinberg, *Proceedings of the Israel Academy of Sciences and Humanities* 1971(4) 78–97.

4. Ibid.

5. F.H. Weissbach, *Das Hauptheiligtum des Marduk in Babylon* (Leipzig, 1938) 46-47. The translation from Weissbach's German is my own.

6. J.M. Cook, *The Persian Empire* (Shocken: New York, 1983) 89–90.

7. Peter Green (Alexander to Actium) 187.

A Spiritual Journey:
A Look at Wisdom and Apocalyptic Literature

CHAPTER OUTLINE

■ *Post-Exilic Old Testament texts are primarily focused on wisdom literature and apocalyptic literature.*

■ *The short, wise sayings of the Old Testament wisdom literature are universally applicable.*

■ *Wisdom literature became popular during the post-Exilic Diaspora despite its differences from other Old Testament texts.*

■ *The apocalyptic literature of the post-Exilic Jews used symbolic language to express both a sense of unrest and a reassurance that God was in control.*

■ *The Book of Daniel is the prime example of the apocalyptic literature that Jews (and later Christians) found important during times of persecution.*

Post-Exilic Old Testament texts are primarily focused on wisdom literature and apocalyptic literature.

Introduction

After the Exile, the Persians and later the Greeks ruled over the Israelites. Then came Roman domination, which lasted through the life of Christ. At this time, two unique literary responses to Faith emerged and became refined in the Jewish communities living in the Diaspora—wisdom literature and apocalyptic literature. Both forms of literature focused on four main themes: God's creation, the natural laws, the future, and the meaning of life itself.

Wisdom literature was a part of many different cultures in the Middle East. These various cultures all had collections of wise sayings, proverbs, and short stories to help people deepen their faith and understand how to live. The Jewish wisdom authors borrowed from the collections of nations such as Egypt and Greece, and those peoples likely borrowed from Jewish writings, as well, for additions to their own collections. In the Old Testament, wisdom literature includes the books of Job, Psalms, Proverbs, Ecclesiastes, Sirach, and Song of Songs.

While Hebrew tradition borrowed and adapted a great deal from the writings of other cultures, it remained clear and unique about one thing:

> The beginning of wisdom is the fear of the Lord,
>   and knowledge of the Holy One is understanding. (Prv 9:10)

According to Hebrew wisdom literature, people are to revere God and respect his power. Humans should know that God is the Creator, and we are only the created. The first nine chapters of the Book of Wisdom express "fear of the Lord" as the moving force behind a wise person's way of life.

The second form of literature to be examined in this chapter is known as **apocalyptic literature**. The Greek word *apokalypsis* means "revelation" or "unveiling." Apocalyptic literature claims to reveal or uncover the truth. The Book of Daniel is the only example of purely

apocalyptic literature in the Old Testament. Portions of Isaiah (24–27), Ezekiel (38–39), Zechariah (1:7–6:8), and Joel (2:1–11; 4:1–21) are other examples. Between the second century BC and the first century AD, other apocalyptic books—both Jewish and Christian—were written. The Revelation to John in the New Testament is the best known of these.

Section in Review

Quick View

- The wisdom literature of the Old Testament offers advice on how to live.

- Apocalyptic literature unveils hidden truths about God using symbolic images.

For Review

1. **Main Idea**: What is wisdom literature? Give examples of wisdom literature from the Old Testament.

2. **Main Idea**: Describe apocalyptic literature and give an example of it from the Old Testament.

3. **Critical Thinking**: What is unique about the wisdom literature of the Bible when compared to the wisdom literature of Persia, Egypt, or the other cultures that influenced the Hebrew community?

For Reflection

Wisdom is a gift of the Holy Spirit. Reflect on how you have grown in wisdom since you were a young child. Write a letter to a younger person explaining what you have learned about life or relationships.

The short, wise sayings of the Old Testament wisdom literature are universally applicable.

Wisdom Literature: Themes and Styles

The purpose of wisdom literature is fairly clear. Wisdom literature has to do with gaining what is called in Hebrew *hokma*, or "wisdom." The wisdom described is basically moral in character, and involving lessons in truth, moderation, prudence, and kindness.

Many people seek guidelines, proverbs, or general principles to help them determine the best way to live their lives. Some may ask an older or more experienced person for his or her opinion of a decision or an idea. Sometimes a favored teacher or coach will impart lasting

Your Life and Wisdom Literature

Consider this exercise. Ask yourself what you think about when you are on your own time—when your mind is free from thoughts about work, school, or activities. Where does your mind go in its wandering? Probably to things like money, your goals in life, relationships—and also the meaning of life. These are precisely the things that the wisdom books of the Old Testament—Job, Psalms, Proverbs, Ecclesiastes, Song of Songs, Sirach (Ecclesiasticus), and Wisdom—address. The subject of wisdom literature is life itself! Read the following passages from the Book of Sirach. For each passage, write one way you will apply it to your life or how you will make a greater effort to follow it in your life:

- Sirach 2 (duties to God)
- Sirach 3:1–16 (duties to parents)
- Sirach 4:20–21 (sincerity and justice)
- Sirach 5:11–6:1 (sincerity in speech)
- Sirach 6:5–17 (true friendship)
- Sirach 17:19–27 (return to God)
- Sirach 19:5–16 (proper use of speech)
- Sirach 23:7–15 (proper use of tongue)

Benjamin Franklin

wisdom through short sentences that are often repeated frequently enough that they are committed to memory.

The Book of Proverbs is precisely that—a collection of short, wise sayings—so it is a good place to begin looking at wisdom literature. One characteristic of proverbs specifically, and wisdom literature in general, is how universal they are. The message of any wise saying is usually applicable between cultures and across different eras as well. Consider the following two "proverbs":

> The journey of folly must be traveled a second time.

> Don't be proud of your knowledge, but consult the ignorant and the wise. The limits of art are not reached; no artist's skills are perfect.

Both of these sayings strike us as quite true and wise even though the first saying is taken from a modern, twenty-first-century African culture, while the second comes from Ancient Egypt and is more than 4,000 years old. Both sayings communicate their message perfectly well for today's audience. This is the fascinating thing about wisdom—it seems to apply to anyone, anywhere. Perhaps this is because human nature does not change much from culture to culture or over the centuries. People

everywhere seek answers to the meaning of life and want to live in the best way possible. People are still made happy or unhappy in the same ways. They want to know why they are here, what the point of life is, what will bring them the most happiness, how best to get along with other people, and what will be the most meaningful work for them to do. Wisdom offers insights into just these sorts of perennial questions.

It should hardly come as a surprise then that some of the same wisdom sayings from the Book of Proverbs appear in ancient Egyptian writings. Although the Hebrew authors needed to resist any encroachment of foreign religion in their worship of YHWH, they were more willing to exchange insights into less explicitly theological questions with their foreign neighbors. The early American statesman, Benjamin Franklin, followed similar principles. Franklin was fascinated with short, wise sayings and collected a number of them to pass on to his friends. Many of them are still familiar today, for example:

> Early to bed, early to rise, makes a man healthy, wealthy and wise.

> A penny saved is a penny earned.

These sayings, too, could apply to anyone, anywhere, at any time.

The wisdom books (listed above) share styles as well as the themes we have been discussing. One popular writing style contrasts the behaviors of a wise person with those of a foolish person. Here are some examples from the Book of Proverbs:

> A wise son makes his father glad,
>   but a foolish son is a grief to his mother. (Prv 10:1)

> Wisdom builds her house,
>   but Folly tears hers down with her own hands. (Prv 14:1)

> A wise son makes his father glad,
>   but a fool of a man despises his mother. (Prv 15:20)

Jesus taught using this same formula:

> Everyone who listens to these words of mine and acts on them will be like a wise man who built his house on rock. . . . And everyone who listens

to these words of mine but does not act on them will be like a fool who built his house on sand. (Mt 7:24, 26)

Wisdom in the Bible

The wisdom movement originated outside Israel in neighboring nations. It revolved around a sage who operated within the organized government and was supported by its leaders. A sage is defined as a person venerated for his or her experience, judgment, and wisdom. The second Book of Samuel describes a "gifted woman of Tekoa" who was sought out for her advice (2 Sm 14:2). However, most sages identified in the Old Testament seem to have been the "wise counselors" of other nations, and they are generally not well thought of by the Old Testament authors. For example:

> Utter fools are the princes of Zoan!
> > the wisest of Pharaoh's advisers give stupid counsel. (Is 19:11)

> I will make [Babylon's] princes and her wise men drunk, her governors, her prefects, and her warriors, so that they sleep an eternal sleep, never to awaken, says the King whose name is the Lord of hosts. (Jer 51:57)

Sages are rarely mentioned in Israel itself, so it's uncertain whom the authors of the Biblical wisdom sayings might have been. It may be that the authors of wisdom literature in the Bible were men with experience and wealth in ancient Israel. Consider this example from Proverbs:

> He is in a bad way who becomes surety [takes on a loan] for another,
> > but he who hates giving pledges is safe. (Prv 11:15)

Obviously, poor people would not have to worry about whether or not they should accept another person's debt. No one making such a loan would consider their pledge to be worth much in the first place.

Also, note this passage from the Book of Sirach:

> Seek not from the LORD authority,
> > nor from the king a place of honor. (Sir 7:4)

This passage advises people to remain humble before a powerful person who might be easily offended. Only the wealthy would be in a position to meet royalty on any regular basis. Passages such as these are the basis for the supposition that the upper class authored much of wisdom literature.

However, some wisdom sayings deal with issues and use images that come from the simpler life of the majority of the people: family concerns, reputation, and images taken from the experience of agriculture, farming, and herding. This makes it more likely that the wisdom sayings in the Bible were collected from all levels of society.

Section in Review

Quick View

- Wisdom literature is composed of short, wise sayings that are universally applicable.

- The authors of the wisdom sayings may have been from the upper class, but some sayings suggest a simpler life.

For Review

1. **Main Idea**: What is the purpose of wisdom literature? What questions does it try to answer?

2. **Critical Thinking**: Describe a common style of wisdom writing found in Proverbs. Where else in the Bible can you find this style?

For Reflection

- Spend a few minutes thinking about your friends and about friendship in general. Write two or three short sentences (your own proverbs), using the contrasting style described in the text, which express your views on friendship. Perhaps describe how a friend should be chosen or what you must do to be a good friend.

- Look through the Book of Proverbs for a few minutes. Are there any proverbs there that you are familiar with? Write them down. Then find a few more that you think would help you live better. Write them down, too.

Wisdom literature became popular during the post-Exilic Diaspora despite its differences from other Old Testament texts.

Wisdom Books: A Unique Form of Spirituality

Wisdom literature in the Old Testament is a unique form of spirituality. Except in the later Book of Sirach, the central themes and characters of the Old Testament (the Exodus, the Patriarchs, YHWH's presence in history, and the Law) scarcely appear in Biblical wisdom literature.

This is surprising. These teachings and people were essential to the religious identity of the Jews. It would seem logical, then, that these central teachings and characters—especially the Law of Moses—would find a prominent place in wisdom literature with its teachings about the meaning of life and how to live. But for the most part, they do not. Instead, Hebrew wisdom literature focuses more on God as Creator and on creation itself. Readers discover who God is by studying what he has made. The tough questions presented by God to Job are an example of this:

> Where were you when I founded the earth?
>> Tell me, if you have understanding.
> Who determined its size; do you know?
>> Who stretched out the measuring line for it?
> Into what were its pedestals sunk,
>> and who laid the cornerstone,
> While the morning stars sang in chorus
>> and all the sons of God shouted for joy? (Jb 38:4–7)

Everything about God's identity in this passage centers on God as Creator rather than as YHWH, the God of the Patriarchs, the Chosen People, and the Mosaic covenant. Wisdom literature describes God by what he has made; it is descriptive, rational, and objective. This is a different form of spirituality than that found in the writings of the prophets, which tend to be more emotive and charismatic.

The spirituality of wisdom—knowing God by what he has made—is actually very similar to the faith of those today who seek God through their discoveries as physicists, astronomers, biologists, or mathematicians. Their studies give them a more profound sense of the work and accomplishments of God. Modern science is very similar to Hebrew wisdom literature in that it, too, is rational and based on observation. The very presence of wisdom literature in the Bible suggests that faith can come from rationality and careful study as well as through Revelation.

Is all Hebrew wisdom literature from the post-Exilic era of Biblical history? This is likely so, although some part of the Proverbs may be from as early as the time of the kings. It is traditional to assign much of wisdom literature to King Solomon, but this is mainly because Solomon was known as a wise king (see 1 Kgs 3). Solomon certainly did not write all of the wisdom literature, or even all of the Book of Wisdom, which is sometimes called the "Wisdom of Solomon."

Many suggestions have been made to explain why wisdom literature became popular in the post-Exilic Diaspora. They include:

- The Jews were impressed with the wisdom teachings in other cultures and were inspired to collect their own texts of wise sayings and stories.

- Based in human realities, wisdom literature could be shared with people of other cultures. It was an area of common ground between Jews and foreigners.

- Wisdom sayings were comforting to a minority people living under foreign rule. They reminded the Jews of how to live a good and prosperous life and of their status as God's Chosen People.

- The Diaspora was seen as a threat to the Jewish community. Parents were concerned about their children remaining grounded in their faith and staying out of trouble. It has been suggested that as urban areas formed after the time of Alexander the Great (323 BC), a delinquent element of teens was also present (see, for example, Prv 1:10–15). Wisdom literature was intended to train young people.

Wisdom literature was another response of the Jews to the challenges of living as a minority people in the ancient world. The next sections briefly examine the wisdom books of the Old Testament. The Book of Psalms is covered in more depth on pages 203–206.

Christian Views of Suffering

Read the following quotations on suffering of famous saints and answer each related question in your journal.

God measures out affliction to our need.

—St. John Chrysostom

Do you believe that God only gives you the amount of suffering that you can reasonably handle? Explain.

There is no such thing as bad weather. All weather is good because it is God's.

—St. Teresa of Avila

How do you find good in suffering?

Whenever anything disagreeable or displeasing happens to you, remember Christ crucified and be silent.

—St. John of the Cross

What is the lesson that Christ teaches you about the meaning of suffering?

Job

The author of Job is unknown, but the book itself was probably written between 500 and 400 BC. Though there are some similarities to the text of Job and Egyptian and Babylonian literature of the time, the work is highly unique.

The standard belief of the time was that a good person would be rewarded with good health, material wealth, and general good fortune (see, for example, Psalm 37). But human experience then, as now, was sometimes contrary to this. Bad things did happen to good people. The Book of Job rejects the simplistic belief that good is rewarded and evil is punished. Job does not so much solve the problem of the suffering of the innocents as it ponders it, lives with it, and explores it.

The faithful Job, a wealthy man with a large, loving family and many possessions loses everything: first his possessions, then his family, and finally his own health. He does not understand why any of this has happened, but rejects the conventional wisdom of his friends that he must have sinned in some way. He rejects as well the idea that God sends trials to those he loves, and he finally cries out to God for an explanation. Although God does not explain himself to Job, he does remind Job of

his prerogative as the Creator of all. This face-to-face encounter is enough to console Job and restore his trust in God. His faith has been strengthened and deepened by his suffering and his experience of God. The story has a happy ending with Job being restored to health and prosperity and having more children, however the main lesson of Job is the revelation about the perplexing question of why God permits physical and moral evil.

Proverbs

The Book of Proverbs was collected as the best of the Israelite wisdom tradition, probably in the fifth century BC. Some of the proverbs may well date back to the time of Solomon. Other proverbs come from unknown times and places.

The proverbs teach three types of wisdom: knowledge of God's created world, the skill of making right choices, and the art of living before God. Some proverbs are also secular, with little or no religious implications. As introduced on page 196, most of the proverbs teach by comparison. "The fear of the Lord is the beginning of wisdom" (Prv 1:7) is the main teaching of the text. Wisdom is also known as the "firstborn" of God:

The Lord begot me, the firstborn of his ways,

> the forerunner of his prodigies of long ago. (Prv 8:22)

Ecclesiastes

The title of the book is the Greek translation of the Hebrew word *qohelet*, meaning "someone who calls an assembly." The title refers to someone like a preacher or teacher who presides over a meeting, but not to an actual historical person. Ecclesiastes is a loose collection of proverbs, laments, poems, and rhetorical questions. *Qohelet* may simply refer to "a gatherer," that is a person who gathered or assembled all these sayings. It was written about the third century BC.

The book is concerned with the value of human life. Hard work does not guarantee happiness, for it is often marred by suffering. Riches and pleasures will not bring happiness nor guarantee a long life. Talents and skills generally result in the stress of competition with others for praise and honor, which even if won is fleeting. A major theme of the book is the vanity of all things. People cannot find happiness and answers to the mysteries of life without God. The author eventually recognizes that

> there is nothing better than to be glad and to do well during life. For every man, moreover, to eat and drink and enjoy the fruit of all his labor is a gift of God. I recognized that whatever God does will endure forever; there is no adding to it, or taking from it. Thus has God done that he may be revered. (Eccl 3:12–14)

Song of Songs

Though the Song of Songs has been attributed to Solomon, its language and style reveal that it was written after the Babylonian Exile. It is a collection of love poems. The title itself is a Hebrew way of saying "the greatest of songs."

The love poems express the alternating views of two lovers describing each other in very erotic language. From a Jewish point of view, the poems refer to the love between YHWH and Israel. Catholics have interpreted the Song of Songs as an allegory describing Christ's love for the Church. Song of Songs is also a joyful celebration of the love between a husband and wife in a marriage blessed by God, and as such is read during the Liturgy of the Word at wedding Masses.

Wisdom

The complete title of this book is "Wisdom of Solomon," although the author actually was a Jew living in Alexandria in Egypt. The book was written in Greek and reveals an **Hellenistic** influence, though the author was also deeply versed in the Hebrew Scriptures.

The Book of Wisdom was the last Book of Old Testament to be written, sometime in the middle of the first century BC. It has been divided into three main sections:

- The Book of Eschatology (1:1–6:21). This section speaks of the reward of justice. While human destiny is in God's hands, the choices made by a person can make a difference.

- Praise of Wisdom (6:22–11:1). Wisdom is personified as the spirit of God. The author reviews Israel's history to show how God's wisdom was present through all times.

- God's Special Providence during the Exodus (11:2–19:22). This section focuses on two main ideas related to the Exodus: (1) the sufferings of the Egyptians were due to their own sins and (2) the evils that effected all

---

Hellenistic
Relating to the culture, history, or language of Greece after the death of Alexander the Great in 323 BC.

parallelism
A characteristic common to Hebrew poetry in which two lines express the same or opposite thoughts, one right after the other.

An Inward Journey:
The Book of Psalms

More than any other part of the Old Testament, the psalms present an inward journey of worship and prayer that prepares Christians for the coming of Jesus and his proclamation of God's kingdom.

The term *Psalms* is derived from a Greek word that comes from the name of a stringed instrument called a "psalter," a kind of harp. The Book of Psalms actually refers to "songs to be sung with a psalter." The Hebrew word for the Book of Psalms is *Tehillim*, which means, "praises."

Literary Styles of the Psalms

The overall literary style of the psalms is poetry. Understanding Hebrew poetry requires understanding the poetic style called "**parallelism**" in the verses of the psalms. There are two types of parallelism. The first type refers to the practice of restating the same thought. The second kind of parallelism alternates between opposing thoughts (e.g., light and dark, night and day).

Psalm 2 offers an example of a parallel verse form that simply repeats the same thought in different words:

> Why do the nations protest
>> and the peoples grumble in vain? (Ps 2:1)

The parallel thoughts are easy to read. *Nations* equates with *people* and *rage* is parallel to *grumble in vain*.

An example of parallelism that contrasts opposing thoughts is Psalm 1:

> For the Lord watches over the way of the just
>> but the way of the wicked leads to ruin.
>> (Ps 1:6)

Note the difference. In the Bible, "the way" is a common term for "manner of living" or moral conduct. The Lord approves the "way of the just," while the "way of the wicked" is not permitted to continue.

Finally, another literary style of the psalms has the lines of a verse building up or advancing a thought, almost like a stair-step:

> They are like a tree
>> planted near streams of water,
> that yields its fruit in season;
>> Its leaves never wither;
>> whatever they do prospers. (Ps 1:3)

It is important in reading Biblical poetry—including prophetic poetry, but especially the poetry of the Psalms—to pay attention to the relationship between the lines in different verses. Noting the different types of parallelism or the building of lines within a verse can assist a reader in determining the meaning of the verse and the entire psalm.

Origins of the Psalms

The evolution of the psalms over a long period of time is clear to anyone who reads the references to David in the first few dozen psalms, but then reads the references to the Babylonian Exile—hundreds of years after the time of David—in Psalm 137. In fact, many who have studied the Psalms suggest that originally there were five "books" of the Psalms (that perhaps coincided with the five books of the Pentateuch). The five original books were:

> Book 1: Chapters 1–41
> Book 2: Chapters 42–72
> Book 3: Chapters 73–89
> Book 4: Chapters 90–106
> Book 5: Chapters 107–150

The evidence that these books were originally separate is twofold:

1. The final chapters of each book (i.e., 41, 72, 89, 106, and 150) include a doxology that ends with "Amen. Amen." This would have been a conclusion that appeared at the end of each separate book.

2. There is one "doublet" or repeated passage in the Book of Psalms. Psalm 14 and Psalm 53 are the same. In other Biblical research, doublets are evidence that two different text versions have been brought together, creating some duplication of material.

As to actually dating the psalms, the evidence above provides several clues. Traditionally, it was thought that King David was the author of the Psalms, at least through Psalm 72 that states: "end of the psalms of David, son of Jesse" (Ps 72:20). The historical books of the Old Testament mentioned that David, as a young boy, played a stringed instrument in the court of King Saul. The idea of David writing psalms comes from the early report that David actually played a psalter, though the Greek name of the instrument is evidence enough that the period of the psalms was much later than the time of David.

In fact, almost two-thirds of the Book of Psalms comes from the period of the Second Temple, that is, after 520 BC but before 333 BC. The correct dates for most psalms are hard to determine exactly. Those that mention historical events are easier. Again, Psalm 137 is the easiest example because it mentions a historical event—the Babylonian Exile. It is certain that Psalm 137 can be no *older* than 587 BC. The historical Psalms 105 and 106 must have been written after the last events mentioned in their poetic lines. The historical survey of Psalms 105–106 includes references to the destruction of Jerusalem and the Babylonian Exile. For example:

> So the Lord grew angry with his people,
>   abhorred his own heritage;

> He handed them over to the nations,
>   and their adversaries ruled them.
> Their enemies oppressed them,
>   kept them under subjection. (Ps 106:40–42)

Psalm 29 may be the oldest psalm in the Bible because its poetry is considered very similar in style to Canaanite poetry of an earlier era. In Psalm 29, YHWH is depicted as a storm God with thunder and lightning as his weapons. For example:

> The voice of the Lord strikes with fiery flame;
>   the voice of the Lord rocks the desert,
>   the Lord rocks the desert of Kadesh. (Ps 29:7–9)

Psalms about the Temple (e.g., Ps 65:5; 68:30), obviously, cannot come from David, because his son, Solomon, built the first Temple. Furthermore, it is not always clear which Temple is being talked about—Solomon's Temple or the Second Temple built around 520–515 BC).

Different Kinds of Psalms

However the Book of Psalms came together, there is agreement that many different kinds of psalms make up the overall collection. Not all the psalms seem to have been written for the same occasion or purpose. There are four main categories of Psalms as follows:

1. Psalms of Lament (sorrow over tragedies)

The psalms of lament come in two types, individual and communal. That is, the speaker in the psalm is either a single person or the entire Hebrew community. They are psalms requesting God's help and protection in dealing with a variety of needs. Many of these psalms conclude with a few lines of thanksgiving and praise for God's response to the appeal for help.

- Psalm 3 (military threat)
- Psalm 10 (legal problems or grievances from fellow Israelites)
- Psalm 38 (personal illness)
- Psalm 44 (communal laments for groups to sing)

2. Psalms of Praise and Thanksgiving

Psalms in this category focus on praising God. They often begin with an invitation to join in the praise and continue with a list of reasons for praise and thanksgiving to God.

- Psalm 19
- Psalm 33

3. Psalms of Instruction

These psalms can be divided into two types. The wisdom psalms share the same themes as the wisdom literature that has been discussed throughout this chapter (see page 197–199). The **historical psalms** retell portions of the history of the Chosen People.

- Psalm 1 (wisdom psalm)
- Psalm 104 (wisdom psalms)
- Psalms 105–106 (historical psalms)

4. Liturgical Psalms

Some psalms were intended for use during Temple celebrations. They often reveal a dialogue structure and may have been written to be sung by two choirs or by a cantor with the congregation responding.

- Psalm 24 (perhaps to be sung while traveling to the Temple)

How were the psalms used? Some, such as the liturgical psalms, were used for worship in the Temple. Other psalms were used for religious festivals outside of the Temple. There is no description in the Bible of exactly how the psalms were used in Temple services, but it is presumed that choirs sang some of them (see Ps 68:27). All but thirty-four of the psalms have titles or musical directions. These addendums were added much later than the text of the psalms themselves.

Obviously not all the psalms were intended for Temple singing. It would be hard to imagine an occasion for singing the historical psalms, such as Psalms 105–106, unless students sang them as a way to recall the history of Israel. That would be especially valuable for Hebrew children growing up in the Diaspora where songs would be an effective way to maintain identity and to provide a connection with their religious and spiritual traditions.

Other psalms seem to have been used for entirely different occasions. *Read Psalm 35, a lament psalm.* The psalm is an appeal to God for help. But help against whom? Verses 1–3 describe the threat of an enemy. However, verses 11–14 refer to "unjust witnesses" that have risen up and spoken against the psalmist, repaying "evil for good." It may be that the help requested from God in Psalm 35 is to settle an argument between two groups of Israelites. In cases like this, where the argument is with fellow Israelites, the dispute would have been brought to the Temple where the two parties would have appealed to the priests. The priests in turn would instruct them to seek God's vindication to settle the dispute, which may have been over money, debts, business, or marriage contracts. It is not certain how the psalm might have fit into the process of seeking a judgment from the priests, but it does seem to be connected to that process.

Part of the continuing appeal of the Book of Psalms is that these songs to the Lord help modern readers "hear the hearts" of the Israelites despite the great differences of time and culture that separate them. The psalms help to engage readers and pray-ers of all generations in the most intimate moments of pain, praise, joy, and sorrow of the ancient Hebrews. Jesus himself turned to the comfort of one of the lament psalms at the moment of his Death:

> My God, my God, why have you abandoned me,
>> Why so far from my call for help,
>>> from my cries of anguish? (Ps 22:2)

historical psalm
A psalm recounting events from the history of Israel such as the covenant with the Patriarchs, the Exodus, or the settling of the Promised Land.

It is important to note here that the psalm Jesus chose ends in triumph just as Jesus' pain was ultimately vindicated in his Resurrection—the triumph over the Cross and over death. The psalms are expressions of the deepest human pain and highest human joys. When we are feeling such joy that we are speechless or such deep pain that we don't know what to say, the words of the psalms can become our words, too.

Feature In Review

Quick View

- The Book of Psalms has a distinct poetic style.

- The five "books" that make up the Book of Psalms were probably derived from many different time periods.

- The four types of psalms were used in Temple worship but also in personal prayer as they are often used today.

For Review

1. **Vocabulary**: What are the two forms of "parallelism" that can be found in the poetry of the Psalms? Find two examples of each.

2. **Main Idea**: What is the evidence that the Book of Psalms was originally five separate books?

3. **Critical Thinking**: List and describe the four different types of psalms. Find an example of each.

For Reflection

Many of the psalms have been rewritten into songs that we sing at Mass today. Skim through the Book of Psalms looking for words and phrases that you recognize from songs you have heard at Mass. Make a list of at least four songs you know that are based on the psalms and identify the psalm from which the song is taken. Indicate whether the words have been largely rewritten or taken nearly word for word from the psalm.

the enemies of Israel were a part of God's Salvation offered to his Chosen People.

Sirach (Ecclesiasticus)

The Book of Sirach is unique among wisdom books because the author is identified: Jesus, son of Eleazar, son of Sirach. He was likely a sage who lived in Jerusalem and who had great love for the law, priesthood, Temple, and worship. The book, which contains numerous sayings, laments, psalms of praise, and moral maxims was written in Hebrew in the second century BC. The book has also been called *Liber Ecclesiasticus*, meaning "Church Book," because it was used extensively by the early Church in the formation of catechumens and in the instruction to the faithful. It is the longest, and most widely cited, of the writings included in the Latin Christian Bible not found in Hebrew Scriptures.

Sirach is similar to the Book of Proverbs in style but it is better organized, with proverbs addressing similar topics grouped together. In fact, it has been considered an updated Proverbs for the later challenges facing Israel.

Section in Review

Quick View

- The spirituality of Biblical wisdom literature focuses on God as Creator rather than as YHWH.

- The Book of Job focuses on why bad things happen to good people.

- Proverbs, Ecclesiastes, and Sirach are composed of series of short sayings about wisdom and right living.

- Although Song of Songs and the Book of Wisdom were traditionally attributed to Solomon, these books were written after the Babylonian Exile.

For Review

1. **Main Idea**: What is the most striking difference between the spirituality of the wisdom books and that of the rest of the Old Testament?

2. **Main Idea**: When were the wisdom books written? List some of the reasons why wisdom literature was popular at that time.

3. **Critical Thinking**: List the six books (other than Psalms) that comprise the wisdom literature of the Old Testament, and briefly state what makes each one unique.

For Reflection

How would you comfort a friend who was suffering? Why do you think bad things happen to good people? What good can come from suffering?

The apocalyptic literature of the post-Exilic Jews used symbolic language to express both a sense of unrest and a reassurance that God was in control.

The Rise of Apocalyptic Literature

Apocalyptic literature has some things in common with the wisdom literature, including the time period in which some of these books were written. Two different answers to the same question—how can God's People live under foreign rule?—were provided by these styles of literature. Wisdom literature primarily looked back to the teachings

of creation and the experience of God to determine the proper course of action. Apocalyptic literature looked forward to what God was *about to do* in history.

For some Jews, comfort came in teaching that the world was rational, that a God who planned everything to the smallest detail had created it. This cool, sober, and rational approach to life was well represented by wisdom literature. For others, however, life under Persian, Greek and Roman rule seemed out of control. The apocalyptic visionaries reassured their readers that God was still in control—even of events that seemed entirely irrational.

Defining Apocalyptic Literature

Read the following passages:

A Spirit took me and brought me up into the fifth heaven. And I saw angels who are called "lords," and the diadem was set upon them in the Holy Spirit, and the throne of each of them was sevenfold more brilliant than the light of the rising sun . . . and they were dwelling in the temples of salvation and singing hymns to the ineffable most high God. . . . Truly, I, Zephaniah, saw these things in my vision. . . .

Wall with graffiti, Palestinian side, between Bethlehem, West Bank and Jerusalem, Israel

And Enoch, the blessed and righteous man of the Lord took up his parable while his eyes were open and he saw, and said, This is a holy vision from the heavens which the angels showed me: and I heard from them everything and I understood. I look not for this generation, but for the distant one that is coming . . . and I took up with a parable saying, The God of the universe, the Holy Great One, will come forth from his dwelling, and from there he will march upon Mount Sinai and appear in his camp emerging from heaven. . . .

In the first year of King Belshazzar of Babylon, Daniel had a dream as he lay in bed, and was terrified by the visions of his mind. Then he wrote down the dream; the account began: In the vision I saw during the night, suddenly the four winds of heaven stirred up the great sea, from which emerged four immense beasts, each different from the others. The first was like a lion, but with eagle's wings. While I watched, the wings were plucked; it was raised from the ground to stand on two feet like a man, and given a human mind. The second was like a bear; it was raised up on one side, and among the teeth in its mouth were three tusks. It was given the order, "Up, devour much flesh." After this I looked up and saw another beast, like a leopard; on its back were four wings like those of a bird, and it had four heads. . . .

The first passage above is from the Apocalypse of Zephaniah. The second passage is from the Book of Enoch. Neither book is in the Bible. However, the third passage is from the Book of Daniel (7: 1–6). All three are examples of apocalyptic literature.

Although there are not very many examples of apocalyptic literature in the Bible—only Daniel 7–12 and the Revelation to John in the New Testament are fully developed examples—it was clearly a very popular form of literature for many nations and cultures of the day. Many of these books have survived to help us study and compare with those apocalyptic writings that *are* in the Bible.

Recall that *apocalypse* means "revelation." Apocalyptic literature is a "literature of revelation." In more detail,

- Apocalypse is a literature of revelation within a narrative framework. It tells a story.

- The revelation is given by an otherworldly being to a human recipient.

- The revelation discloses an ultimate reality that exists at the current time, but which also involves another supernatural world.[1]

There are two main models of apocalyptic writing from among the dozens of examples known. The first involves otherworldly journeys. The second is known as "historic symbolic," that is, it uses symbols to represent people, places, and historical events. This second type of apocalyptic literature is used in the Bible. However, it is worth noting that the apocalyptic journey (where the author "visits" levels of Heaven or Hell) is a style that was also well-known by Biblical authors (see 2 Cor 12:2).

Specific characteristics of the historic symbolic style of apocalyptic literature are:

- The writings are written in a style emphasizing spiritual and social turmoil. Things are not right in the world, and the writer expresses a great sense of unrest.

- There is often a sense of urgency in the writing. The changes that are coming in the world (or the entire cosmos!) are coming very soon.

- History as understood by humans is coming to an end.

- Beyond the coming catastrophes is a new paradise (The Book of Revelation speaks of a "new Heaven and a new earth").

- In most cases, the apocalyptic writing features a mediator—some heavenly being (e.g., the angel Gabriel in the Book of Daniel) who explains the bizarre visions and images that the "seer" is reporting in the book.

- Typically, the apocalyptic literature describes visions populated by strange and alarming beasts—multi-headed dragons and animals that combine features from different species (e.g., winged leopards, etc.).

- Many images are consistent across different apocalyptic works (which is why a reader of Daniel 7–12 will recognize some of the images that turn up in the Book of Revelation, as well as in apocalyptic books outside the Bible).

Jesus *as the* Son of Man

(*CCC*, 440, 663–664, 697)

Jesus identified himself by the title the "Son of Man." This title had important eschatological significance based on the visions in the Book of Daniel. The prophet Daniel saw the Son of Man "seated at the right hand of the Power and coming with the clouds of heaven" (Dn 7:13). According to the vision, the Son of Man would descend from Heaven and rule an everlasting kingdom on earth. Similarly, Jesus stressed the eschatological nature of his ministry through preaching the Kingdom of God. This Kingdom which Jesus initiated would be a kingdom "that shall not be destroyed" (Dn 7:14) or as the Nicene Creed puts it, the "kingdom will have no end."

When Jesus spoke about the end of the world and his return, he used imagery from Daniel to show that his words were being fulfilled. Jesus said to his disciples, "When the Son of Man comes in his glory, and all the angels with him, he will sit upon his glorious throne" (Mt 25:31 referencing Dn 7:13-14). Likewise, the Kingdom of God, which is already present in Jesus, will come to fulfillment on the last day.

Son of Man	Jesus
Came on the clouds of Heaven (Dn 7:13)	Jesus describes the coming of the Son of Man on clouds (Mt 24:30)
Seated at the right hand of the Power, he received dominion, glory, and kingship (Dn 7:13–14)	Jesus describes the return of the Son of Man in glory, and the angels with him, when he will sit upon his throne (Mt 25:31; 26:64)
Nations and peoples of every language serve him (Dn 7:14)	Jesus ordered the Apostles to make disciples of all nations (Mt 28:19) and at Pentecost people from many nations speaking many languages could understand the Gospel which the Apostles proclaimed (Acts 2:7–11)
"His dominion is an everlasting dominion that shall not be taken away, his kingship shall not be destroyed" (Dn 7:14)	God's Kingdom is eternal (2 Pt 1:11)

- The literature is typically written under a pseudonym or pen name, probably because it is usually controversial political writing that is critical of present regimes and governments. It would be dangerous for the author to be identified. Also, symbols are used in the subject of the writing as well. For example, the Book of Revelation refers to the Roman Empire as "the Beast."

Most of these characteristics are typical of the apocalyptic writings both within and outside of the Bible. It is important to be aware that apocalyptic is a literary style with *many* examples.

Section in Review

Quick View

- Apocalyptic literature reassured the Jews that God was still in control despite their Imperial rulers.

- Two models of apocalyptic literature include otherworldly journeys and "historic symbolic" people, places, and historical events.

For Review

1. **Main Idea**: Where does apocalyptic literature appear in the Bible?

2. **Main Idea**: List three characteristics of apocalyptic literature and describe the two most common models of apocalyptic writing. Which one of the two appears in the Old Testament?

3. **Critical Thinking**: Identify all the characteristics of the historic symbolic style you can find in the passages from the Apocalypse of Zephaniah, the Book of Enoch, and the Book of Daniel on pages 207–208.

For Reflection

Read the descriptions of the wisdom books again (beginning on page 200) and skim through them in your Bible before choosing one to explore in more depth. What drew you to the book you chose? Identify two or three favorite passages and explain their meaning and the significance they have for you.

The Book of Daniel is the prime example of the apocalyptic literature that Jews (and later Christians) found important during times of persecution.

Apocalyptic Writing in the Old Testament

The Book of Daniel is the only pure source of apocalyptic writing of the Old Testament. However, the prophets Isaiah, Ezekiel, Joel, and Zechariah do employ the apocalyptic style in certain places.

For example, the Book of Joel employs apocalyptic imagery in a number of places. Joel sees in a terrible plague of locusts that ravages the land a sign of God's impending judgment on the people. He also describes a vision of the future when all the nations will gather in the Valley of Jehoshaphat to face God's judgment. The Book of Joel has a very eschatological tone that is common to apocalyptic literature. **Eschatology** refers to a study of the "last things" such as death, judgment, immortality, Heaven and Hell, and the like.

The first part of the Book of Zechariah (1:1–6:8) contains apocalyptic visions of such varied things as four horsemen, a lamp stand, a flying scroll, a flying bushel basket, and four chariots. All of these visions were intended to promote the rebuilding of the Temple and to encourage

eschatology
A study of the "last things," such as death, judgment, immortality, Heaven and Hell, and the like.

HIDDEN BOOKS OF THE BIBLE?

What about the other apocalyptic writings of the period? Why are they not included in the Bible? This is an easy question to answer. These "other" apocalyptic writings are not in the Bible because they were not accepted by the Church Fathers as having been inspired by the Holy Spirit. Thus, they have no place in Sacred Scripture.

Usually, the particulars of the decision were easy—many of these books were clearly forgeries or just plain strange, and were rejected by the earliest Christians. Other books were read and enjoyed, but not considered central to the purpose of the Old Testament, to reveal the coming of the Savior, Jesus Christ. (The Book of Enoch is cited in Jude 1:14, for example. It was read but still not considered central.)

Even though these books are not part of Sacred Scripture, they are very useful to historians. These books[2] are helpful indicators of what was important and what some Jews and Christians were thinking about in various times of Hebrew and Christian history.

the people after the disruption and devastation of the Exile.

It is the Book of Daniel that is the main example of apocalyptic literature in the Old Testament. Chapters 7 to 12 contain apocalyptic visions of the future. When Jesus is called before the Sanhedrin (the Jewish court), he evokes the words of Daniel in speaking of the coming of the Son of Man on the clouds of Heaven:

> Then Jesus answered, "I am;
>   and 'you will see the Son of Man
>   seated at the right hand of the Power
>   and coming with the clouds of heaven.'"
>   (Mk 14:62; see also Dn 7:13)

More information about the narrative and apocalyptic nature of Daniel follows.

Daniel

In the Hebrew Scriptures, the Book of Daniel is classified with the Writings. These books include wisdom literature and the psalms. The Catholic canon includes Daniel with the prophetic books. While it does contain prophecy, the Book of Daniel also contains history.

The Book of Daniel has three main divisions:

- Daniel 1–6. This part includes six stories about a young Jewish boy, Daniel. Along with his friends, Daniel remains faithful to YHWH under the reigns of King Nebuchadnezzar II and the Persian kings. These stories probably originated in the Persian era, but were retold during the persecution of the Jews by Antiochus IV (see Chapter 10).

- Daniel 7–12. This section contains four symbolic visions that center on the heavenly destruction of Israel's enemies, especially Antiochus IV (see below).

Daniel's Visions

The first of Daniel's visions in Daniel 7 repeats a good deal of the dream of Nebuchadnezzar in Daniel 2. Do the following: (1) Identify the four empires symbolized in both Daniel 2 and Daniel 7. (2) Name the images used to symbolize the empires in Daniel 2. (3) Name the beasts used to symbolize the empires in Daniel 7.

- Daniel 13–14. Three other stories found only in the Septuagint (not considered inspired by Jews and Protestants) end the book. In one of the stories, Daniel saves a young maiden named Susanna.

The Book of Daniel brought comfort to the Jewish people during the time of persecution carried on by Antiochus IV Epiphanes in 167–164. This was also roughly the time it was composed. Consider that during the period from 200 BC to 100 AD apocalyptic literature was very popular. By using symbols and giving the story a supposedly historical context, the author could speak more freely than the oppressive government would normally allow.

The visions of Daniel 7–12 repeat the dream of Nebuchadnezzar in Daniel 2. In Daniel 7:1–28, the prophet sees four beasts coming from the sea. The beasts signify the Babylonian empire, the kingdom of the Medes, the Persian Empire, and the empire of Alexander. The message of these visions is that pagan kingdoms grow progressively worse; reaching their climax in the "little horn" that represents Antiochus (Dn 7:8). The people are destined to suffer under him for a period of three and a half years. Relief will come only when God himself intervenes.

Why did apocalyptic writing appeal so much to Jews in the centuries prior to, during, and immediately after Jesus' life on earth? Most likely, the apocalyptic books arose in circumstances of oppression, when the social and political policies of the Persian, Greek, or Roman rulers became especially brutal. In such circumstances, the Jews literally cried out to God and had visions from God of hopeful reassurance that he was with them. The highly symbolic nature of the writing protected the authors—as well as the readers—from persecution, since the language would be difficult to decipher by those outside the cultural context of the author and his intended audience.

Consider the mood and thinking surrounding apocalyptic literature. The times were bad and the Jews held on to the belief that God was going to bring about immediate change. This is one of the central messages of apocalyptic visions: God is in control. What seems awful and unpredictable is *not* outside of God's control.

Section in Review

Quick View

- Although the Book of Daniel is the only apocalyptic book in the Old Testament, more apocalyptic themes appear in other prophetic books.
- The Book of Daniel and its symbolic language about Imperial oppressors would have been appealing to the Jews leading up to and during the time of Christ.

For Review

1. **Main Idea**: In what Old Testament books do examples of apocalyptic writing occur?
2. **Critical Thinking**: Why did the author of the Book of Daniel, who lived in the second century BC, write as if the character Daniel had lived during the reign of Nebuchadnezzar?
3. **Main Idea**: Explain the appeal of apocalyptic writing during the time that Israel was ruled by the Babylonian, Persian, and Roman empires.

For Reflection

Search through the apocalyptic material in the Bible and try to visualize one of the "beasts" described. Write how this beast might symbolize someone or something in the modern world.

Further Reflection

Hebrew wisdom literature was part of a larger cultural phenomenon of the ancient Near East. Great "pearls of wisdom" were collected as short maxims and shared among cultures. Hebrew wisdom was influenced by the wisdom sayings of Egypt and Mesopotamia in particular.

Wisdom writings were based on tradition. Their subject matter was taken from looking back at the gleaned experience of the Hebrews and other peoples to answer current questions and problems of the day. The value of wisdom is best summarized at the opening of the Book of Proverbs:

> That men may appreciate wisdom and discipline,
>   may understand words of intelligence;
> May receive training in wise conduct
>   in what is right, just and honest;
> That resourcefulness may be imparted to the simple,
>   to the young man knowledge and discretion.
> A wise man by hearing them will advance in learning,
>   an intelligent man will gain sound guidance,
> That he may comprehend proverb and parable,
>   the words of the wise and their riddles.
> The fear of the Lord is the beginning of knowledge;
>   wisdom and instruction fools despise. (Prv 1:2–7)

Apocalyptic writing was another popular style of the time. One modern understanding of apocalyptic literature is that it is intended to predict the future through the use of secret codes and hidden messages. This is not accurate. By the very fact that God revealed himself so perfectly and clearly in Jesus Christ, it is obvious that hiding messages in secret codes is not God's style.

Jesus himself warned against trying to predict future events:

> Asked by the Pharisees when the kingdom of God would come, he said in reply, "The coming of the kingdom of God cannot be observed, and no one will announce, 'Look, here it is,' or, 'There it is.' For behold, the kingdom of God is among you." (Lk 17:20–21)

Both wisdom literature and apocalyptic literature teach people to live in the present and to behave as members of God's People. Whether looking backward or forward, these Scripture styles are instructions for living in God's world—now and for all time to come.

Vocabulary Review

Directions: Identify each of the following as wisdom literature or apocalyptic literature and describe one defining characteristic of the book.

1. Job

2. Daniel

3. Wisdom

4. Psalms

5. Ecclesiastes

Directions: Describe the literary style of each of the following books.

1. Proverbs

2. Psalms
3. Daniel
4. Job
5. Song of Songs

Performance Assessment Project

The Jewish people living in post-Exilic Diaspora expressed themselves through wisdom literature and apocalyptic literature. Why were these forms so popular during this time period? Imagine if you were professionally publishing some of these Old Testament books during the post-Exilic time period in the form that printed books are published today. Design the book's front and back cover including any information that you would use to attract people to read the book. Write the text that will go on the back of the book and on the inside cover to describe the book and its author. Keep in mind that your objective is to get people interested in reading the book, based on what you know about why the book was popular during the post-Exilic time period.

Called to Prayer

> The law of the LORD is perfect,
> refreshing the soul.
> The decree of the LORD is trustworthy,
> giving wisdom to the simple.
> The precepts of the LORD are right,
> rejoicing the heart.
> The command of the LORD is clear,
> enlightening the eye.
> The fear of the LORD is pure,
> enduring forever.
> The statutes of the LORD are true,
> all of them just;
> More desirable than gold,
> than a hoard of purest gold,
> Sweeter also than honey
> or drippings from the comb.
> By them your servant is instructed;
> obeying them brings much reward.

> —Psalm 19:8–12

- **Reflection**: Which of God's laws have been most instructive to you? Which laws are most rewarding to you?

- **Meditation**: Choose one description of God's law from this psalm (the law of the Lord . . . ; the decree of the Lord . . . ; etc.) and spend some time thinking about it deeply. Record every image or thought that pops into your head as you meditate upon this phrase.

- **Resolution**: Read your list of thoughts from the meditation. What is God calling you to do through this passage? Is there a person or an action that needs your attention? Make a commitment to make the change.

Notes

1. Professor John Collins has written many works on Apocalyptic literature. Some of this material is drawn from his masterful commentary on Daniel published from the *Hermeneia Commentary Series* (Fortress Press).

2. One excellent translation of these apocalyptic texts not found in the Bible is *The Old Testament Pseudepigrapha: Apocalyptic Literature and Testaments* (Old Testament Pseudepigraphia, Vol 1) edited by James H. Charlesworth, New York: Doubleday, 1983.

The Journey Leads to the Time of Jesus and Beyond

CHAPTER OUTLINE

- *The Jews reacted in different ways to living under foreign rule.*

- *The process of Hellenization became a dividing factor between the Jews and their foreign rulers and among the Jews themselves.*

- *Although the Hasmoneans won Jewish independence, they were not well received as leaders by the Jewish community in Palestine.*

- *The Jews reacted to foreign rule through cooperation, military resistance, and spiritual resistance.*

- *After the destruction of the Temple, the Jews became more focused on rabbinic teachings and synagogue worship.*

Chapter Ten

The Jews reacted in different ways to living under foreign rule.

Introduction

From about six centuries before the time of Christ and extending to his life and beyond, the Jews lived under a succession of foreign rulers. Not until the establishment of the state of Israel following World War II did the Jews ever regain control of their own governance in their own land. Living dispersed from the land (the Diaspora) and under foreign control in the Holy Land was the reality of Jewish experience from the time of the Babylonian Empire (587 BC) onward. After the Babylonians, the Jews lived in Palestine under a succession of rulers to the early Christian era. These included:

- The Persian Empire (539–333 BC)

- Alexander the Great and the Hellenistic (Greek) Rulers (see below) that followed his death (323–64 BC)

- The Ptolemies who ruled Palestine from Egypt (323–200 BC)

- The Seleucids who ruled Palestine from Babylon and the East (200–64 BC)

- The Roman Empire (64 BC to the early Christian centuries)

Very few Biblical books actually claim to have been written, or give evidence of having been written, during the Persian Period. It seems that the Persian Period was given over more to the organization of the writings that make up a great deal of the Old Testament, rather than to writing much new material. When Ezra visited Jerusalem around 450 BC he referred to "scrolls of the Law" (see Neh 8:1–4). These scrolls were the beginning of the Bible that was already taking shape. But there would be an important change in the life of the Hebrews with the coming the Macedonians under Alexander the Great. Stories from the books of Daniel (chapters 1–6), Tobit, Esther, and Judith reveal what life was like in the Diaspora and in Palestine during this period.

This chapter presents an overview of the years prior to the birth of Christ and the last books of the Old Testament authored during this period.

How God's People Lived under Foreign Rule

The Old Testament reflects different ways the Jews chose to survive while ruled by foreigners. There were some occasions when Jews served as advisers to foreign rulers and were able to function peacefully under foreign kings or regional governors. Stories from the books of Daniel (1–6), Tobit, and Esther suggest there were dangers in being a minority people. If the people remained faithful to YHWH, however, survival was possible.

Some Jews held a much more nationalistic perspective of the situation. These Jews wanted to throw off foreign rule completely in order to return to their own monarchy or some other form of self-rule and government. Biblical books such as 1 Maccabees and Judith reflect a more "proactive" stance for reclaiming Jewish independence.

The differing views on how the Jews ought to approach foreign rule during this time are important because this same issue surfaces among Jews living at the time of Jesus—even among his own disciples. In tracing the issue, it is helpful to consider what

Alexander the Great

the Biblical stories in the books of Daniel (1–6), Tobit, Esther, and Judith reveal about the conditions faced by the Jews while living under foreign rule.

Daniel 1–6

Recall that the Book of Daniel is divided into three sections (see pages 211–212) and was finished between the years of 167 and 164 BC, though it is set in the royal household during the Babylonian Exile four hundred years earlier. The stories in chapters 1 to 6 are built around Daniel, a young Hebrew taken into the Babylonian king's service where he distinguishes himself by his interpretation of dreams and prophecy. Daniel and his companions very carefully observe Jewish laws in spite of opposition from others in the royal court. For example, in chapter 1, rather than eating the king's food and wine (which has not been prepared according to the Law), Daniel and his friends eat only vegetables and water for ten days to prove that by obeying God's laws they will be even healthier than the others in the court.

In chapter 6, Daniel refuses to worship pagan idols and disobeys the petition of the king not to address petitions to God for thirty days. He continues to pray in his room three times a day until the men who have promoted the petition of the king (expressly to be able to punish Daniel) catch him in the act. Though the king hates to punish his faithful servant, the law he has signed binds him. Before casting Daniel into the lions' den, the king says to him: "May your God, whom you serve so constantly, save you" (Dn 6:17).

God sends an angel to keep the lions' mouths closed so that Daniel will not be hurt. The message of this story, as with the others in chapters 1 to 6, is that cooperation with civil authorities combined with faithful prayer and obedience to God's law will protect the Jews and allow them to survive and even thrive under foreign rule.

Tobit

The Book of Tobit is written as a religious novel. It is a deuterocanonical book from the second or third century BC. In 1955, fragments of the book in its original language (Aramaic) were found near the Dead Sea. As with the stories in Daniel 1–6, Tobit emphasizes the benefits of traditional forms of Jewish piety—prayer, fasting, and almsgiving. Its message is that God will never abandon his people as long as they remain faithful to him.

Tobit is set at the time of the fall of the Northern Kingdom to the Assyrians. It is actually two stories. The characters—Tobit, his wife Anna, and their son Tobiah—are deported to Nineveh. Their story takes place there. Tobit suffers several trials, including blindness from cataracts.

In another city some miles away, a young woman, Sarah, also experiences misfortune. All seven of the men she has married have died on her wedding night at the hands of a jealous demon. The stories come together when Tobiah marries Sarah, survives the wedding night under the protection of the angel Gabriel, defeats the demon, and returns home with Sarah to help his father

regain his sight. These tales contain some striking insights about living as a faithful minority in a foreign land.

In chapter 13, Tobit praises God in a joyful prayer. It, too, reminds the Jews of the need to remain faithful in spite of hardships:

> He scourged you for your iniquities,
>> but will again have mercy on you all.
>
> He will gather you from all the Gentiles
>> among whom you have been scattered.
>
> When you turn back to him with all your heart,
>> to do what is right before him,
> Then he will turn back to you,
>> and no longer hide his face from you. (Tb 13:5–6)

The religious message is that the virtue of God's people will triumph over the sinfulness of their oppressors and their own sinfulness.

Esther

The Book of Esther is another example of a story whose message says it is better for the Jews to negotiate with foreign kings and function religiously under foreign rule than to oppose them with military force or other forms of extreme nationalism. The story is set in Persia during the reign of Ahasuerus (or Xerxes I). Esther, a beautiful Jewish maiden, is chosen to replace the former queen of Persia. Meanwhile, Ahasuerus, because of the influence of a power-hungry assistant named Haman has decreed that all Jews should be obliterated. Haman targets the Jews for destruction because Mordecai, Esther's uncle, refuses to kneel in worship to him.

Esther persuades the king to reverse the decision (see Est 6–8). The king—because of his love for Esther—spares the Jews, and Haman is hanged instead. The Jews celebrate this triumph with a great feast (see Est 9). The feast is the origin of the Jewish spring festival *Purim*, which means "lots" (referring to the lot that Haman drew to determine the day to slaughter the Jews).

The message of Esther is much the same as the one in the Book of Daniel: cooperation with the civil rulers and refusal to compromise in religious matters, combined with the traditional elements of Jewish faith—prayer, fasting, and almsgiving—will ensure God's protection. There is another similarity between the two stories. In both stories, it is not the king whom the Jews have to fear; it is the

Esther and Ahasuerus

unscrupulous, jealous, or power-hungry men who surround the king that threaten the Jews' survival.

Esther is also unique because it exists in two forms—a Hebrew edition and a longer Greek edition. The Greek text is not simply added to the end of the Hebrew text; it is interspersed within it. In the *New American Bible*, the added text appears in chapters A through F, which interrupt the numbered chapters of the Hebrew story.

Judith

The Book of Judith tells another story with a message about what the Jews must do to survive life in the Diaspora under foreign rule. The story introduces a fictional woman named Judith ("Jewish woman") in chapter 8, after King Nebuchadnezzar's general Holofernes has besieged the Jews for thirty-four days and cuts off their water supply rather than attack them directly and risk the loss of his soldiers. As the people perish, the Jews are considering surrender. Judith chides the Jews for their inaction and promises that YHWH will save his people through her.

Faithfulness to YHWH, as in the other stories described above, was paramount in the protection of the Jews living in the Diaspora. But Judith does more than resist passively. After praying, she actively stands up for her Faith on behalf of God's People. She disguises herself, enters the enemy camp, and beheads Holofernes (see Jdt 13:4–10). This type of proactive response is interspersed in the historical events related to the Jews living under foreign rule in the centuries prior to the birth of Christ.

Section in Review

Quick View

- Little Biblical material was written after the Babylonian Exile until the coming of the Greeks in the fourth century BC.

- Under foreign rule, some Jews cooperated with the foreign rulers while others supported resistance.

- The books of Daniel, Tobit, Esther, and Judith reflect the Greek influence on the Jews and the different ways of living under foreign rule.

For Review

1. **Main Idea**: Explain the two options of the Jewish people in their relationship with the foreign powers that rule over them. Which option is endorsed by Jesus?

2. **Critical Thinking**: What do the books of Esther and Daniel have in common?

3. **Critical Thinking**: In what ways is the message of Judith different from that of Esther? In what ways is it similar?

For Reflection

Have you ever faced a time when you had to choose between what your Faith required and what a coach, teacher or other authority wanted you to do? Perhaps you had a game that would make it difficult for you to attend Mass on Sunday. Or a pizza party on a Friday night during Lent—and all the pizzas had pepperoni! How did you resolve the conflict? Would you make the same choice today? What would you do?

The process of Hellenization became a dividing factor between the Jews and their foreign rulers and among the Jews themselves.

Tracing Jewish History Prior to the Maccabean Revolt

The history that led up to the Maccabean Revolt and the events that occurred right up to the time of direct Roman rule in 63 BC are complex. It is important to understand some of the historic events of this time period. They provide an important backdrop to events immediately preceding the time of Jesus.

Under Persian Rule

The Persian Period lasted more than 200 years, from the time of Cyrus' conquest of Babylon in 539 until the arrival of Alexander the Great in 333 BC. Little is known about what daily life was like under the Persians. The most significant sources are the Biblical books of Ezra and Nehemiah, and these short works do not report the general conditions of living under the Persian Empire. At least part of the oral tradition that formed the stories of Daniel 1–6 may reflect conditions in the Persian Period, but it is difficult to be certain.

The Persians controlled vast amounts of land extending from Egypt in the West to the Indus River in the East. Palestine was part of a large Persian province known as "Beyond the River." The Jews did have a fair amount of religious and personal freedom, although they were without political rights. The official Persian religion was **Zoroastrianism**, a religion that held that the universe was caught in a constant struggle between light and darkness. The influence of this religion on the Jews can be seen in their growing belief in angels and in the larger role assigned to Satan, the fallen angel. By the second century BC, the books of Daniel and 2 Maccabees clearly stated these beliefs.

The Beginning of Hellenization

The famous general Alexander the Great brought sweeping changes to the region. His time of campaigns was a

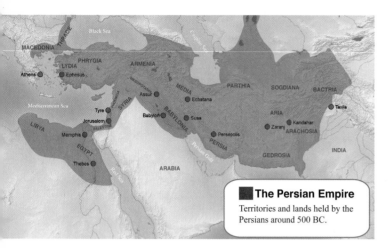

The Persian Empire
Territories and lands held by the Persians around 500 BC.

short nine years (334–323 BC) but he conquered massive amounts of territory: Asia Minor in 334 BC; Phoenicia, Palestine, and Egypt by 333–332 BC; the crushing defeat of the Persian army and the ensuing capture of Babylon, Susa, and Persepolis by 331 BC. One legend of Alexander tells that when he reached northern India and realized there were no more lands to conquer, he wept.

Alexander introduced Greek ideals, language, learning, dress, and customs to the people whose lands he controlled. Greek athletic contests became popular, and the common Greek language, *koine*, became the official language of the Near East. (The process of imposing Greek culture on conquered civilizations is called Hellenization.) Greek remained the common language of the Middle East until AD 500 when Latin replaced it. The *Septuagint* translation of the Hebrew Scriptures and the entire New Testament were written in Greek. As a result of the extent of Alexander's Empire and the success of his policy of Hellenization, all of Western culture retains the influence of Greek thought, learning, values, and ideals to this day.

The principle Biblical sources describing Hellenistic influence on the Jews are the first and second books of Maccabees. The first Book of Maccabees was written to describe events from the Jewish revolt in 167 down to the period of John Hyrcanus (134–104 BC), the first ruler of the brief Jewish dynasty known as the Hasmoneans. The second Book of Maccabees focuses mostly on the events of the revolt itself, but has a more pious tone than 1 Maccabees. The Jewish historian Josephus, who lived during the time of Christ, provides more information about this period. However, his sources are sometimes called into question.

Upon his death at the young age of thirty-three, Alexander's vast empire was divided among his generals. Although there were periods of cooperation between them, there were many incidents in which one general would dispute with another to try to reestablish control of a larger territory.

The two generals that had the most effect on the Jews were Ptolemy, who ruled in Egypt, and Seleucus of the Seleucid family, who ruled from Syria and controlled large parts of Alexander's eastern empire (Mesopotamia and the Northern Palestine/Lebanon territories). Once again, geography became destiny. The struggles between these two ruling dynasties over the little strip of land that was Palestine determined the fate of the Jews for the next few centuries.

The Rule of the Ptolemies

The **Ptolemies**, rulers in the dynasty that descended from Alexander's general, Ptolemy, controlled Palestine from about 320–200 BC. The Ptolemies were known for retaining strong, centralized economic control of their territories and laying heavy taxes on the occupied people. However, the Ptolemies also allowed religious autonomy and apparently made no outright efforts to impose Hellenization on the Jews. Whether forced or not, the Jews themselves divided into two factions over the issue of Greek influence. One group began to adopt Greek customs—games, plays, athletics, and philosophy. The other group was staunchly opposed to Greek assimilation and remained strictly loyal to Jewish practices and customs. Of course Greek culture inevitably had some influence even on the traditional factions.

The Egyptian city of Alexandria also came under the

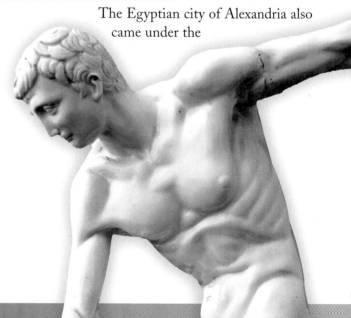

rule of the Ptolemies. Alexandria was a great seaboard city—the "Jewel of the Mediterranean"—and an important cultural and economic center. One of the most important developments under the Ptolemies was the construction and maintenance of the great Library of Alexandria.

The Jews in Palestine were free to immigrate to Alexandria. A Jewish community began to grow there as many Jews settled in Alexandria to take advantage of its cultural and economic opportunities. The Alexandrian Jewish community would remain an important center of Jewish culture in the Diaspora for centuries after this. It is likely that the Book of Wisdom originated in Alexandria around 100 BC. Most likely, the great task of translating the Hebrew Scriptures into Greek was also undertaken in Alexandria. (See "The Septuagint," page 224.)

Seleucid Rule

The Seleucid rulers, who based their part of the old Alexandrian Empire in Babylon and the Eastern cities, also ruled over much of Syria. In approximately 200 BC, these rulers drove out the Egyptian-based Ptolemies and came into power in Palestine under the leadership of Antiochus III. While the Jews hailed the Seleucids as liberators at first, Jewish life under Seleucid rule deteriorated rapidly. The Roman Empire was also increasingly becoming a strong and forbidding presence in the region. It was during this time that historical events began to get complicated.

There was considerable internal turmoil among the Jewish community in Palestine early in the reign of the Seleucids over the issue of control of large sums of Temple funds. The Temple acted as the most secure "bank" for the Jews in this region, and thus considerable sums of money were accumulated in Temple treasuries. This made the Temple and its administrators prime targets of the Seleucid rulers. (Temples of most religions throughout the region served as the local "bank" so they were nearly always prime targets for outside conquerors who often went to the temple, first, when they invaded a city.)

Inevitably, a struggle broke out among Jewish factions over who would be the High Priest and thus earn the right to negotiate financial and trade deals with the Seleucids. There were other key administrative positions for Jews to seek as well—such as the right to collect taxes. A tax collector's reward was to keep whatever he collected beyond the obligations to the government. Obviously, the potential for abuse under such a system was very great.

These internal debates were made worse by the fact that a growing faction of Jews continued to be more Hellenized in attitude, practice, and outlook. Accompanying this, these Jews became less and less scrupulous about the observation of traditional Jewish practice and rites. Such Hellenistic attitudes inevitably drew a reaction from more traditional Jews. After all, the Jewish people had lived under pagan imperial control since 587 BC. They had no real ruler, and did not control their land, so their traditions and faith were the centerpieces of their existence. This placed the Temple at the center of the political and religious controversies of both groups of Jews.

Antiochus IV and the Impending Revolt

The Temple debates led to two opposing Jewish factions confronting each other: the Hellenized Jews and the more traditional group. The confrontation came to

Zoroastrianism
The official religion of the Persian Empire, which understood the universe to be caught in a constant struggle between light and darkness. Jewish belief in angels and in Satan's influence can be traced to the influence of this foreign religion.

koine
The common Greek language introduced in Palestine by Alexander the Great in 333 BC. It is the language of the Septuagint and remained the common language of Palestine until Latin replaced it in AD 500.

Septuagint
The oldest complete edition of the Old Testament. It is a Greek translation of earlier Hebrew texts, probably written in Alexandria during the time of Ptolemaic rule over Palestine. The word itself, *Septuagint*, is Latin for "seventy" which refers to the traditional story that seventy scholars from the Holy Land were brought to Alexandria to accomplish the translation.

Ptolemies
The dynasty descending from Ptolemy I, a general under Alexander the Great, who ruled Egypt and Palestine from 320 to 200 BC when they lost control of the land to the Syrian empire.

the forefront when a wealthy Jewish family (the house of Tobiah) who had created their financial dynasty from their business dealings with the Hellenistic administration attempted to remove Onias III as High Priest. The more traditionalist Jewish families considered Onias to be the legitimate head of the Temple.

Both Jewish factions appealed to the Seleucids for support. But the Seleucid family at the time was also unstable. Antiochus III died and was followed by Seleucus IV. But Seleucus IV was soon killed, probably by the one who then assumed the throne, the infamous Antiochus IV who called himself "Epiphanes" ("God is with us").

In order to consolidate his power, Antiochus IV acted quickly in dealing with the Jews. When Onias came to Antioch to appeal for his rightful role as the High Priest, Antiochus IV imprisoned him, and appointed his brother Jason as the High Priest, most likely because Jason and his supporters had bribed him. Jason was sympathetic to the Hellenized Jews. Three years later a powerful family called the Tobiads outbid Jason, and the disastrous Menelaus was made High Priest. Menelaus further enraged the more traditional Jews by his support of Greek traditions. He even cooperated with Antiochus IV in the construction of Greek shrines in Jerusalem and the looting in the Temple.

Antiochus IV was as zealous about Hellenization as Alexander the Great had been. Believing that the Jews were the cause of many of his problems (including his unsuccessful efforts to take control of Egypt), he virtually banned the practice of traditional Jewish religion. He forbade study of the Law, observance of the Sabbath, circumcision of male children, and Temple sacrifice (unless it was pagan sacrifice).

THE SEPTUAGINT

The *Septuagint* (Latin for "seventy") is the term used to refer to the Greek translation of the Hebrew Scriptures. Simply using the Roman numeral LXX often indicates this. Until the discovery of the **Dead Sea Scrolls**, the Greek versions of the Old Testament were the oldest actual manuscripts available for doing textual analysis of the Bible in ancient languages. They are still the oldest complete editions of the Bible.

The legend of the Septuagint appears in a book known as the "Letter to Aristeas." This work says that the Ptolemies were deeply disturbed to find that the Library of Alexandria did not include the great writings of the Jews. So they brought seventy-two Hebrew elders (six from each tribe) to Egypt and commissioned them to translate the Bible into Greek. (These seventy-two translators are where the Septuagint gets its name.) The translators divided into teams, and when they were finished, a miracle had occurred. Each of their translations was exactly the same! Though a delightful story, the only verifiable truth to the tale was that the Septuagint was produced in Egypt in the time of the Ptolemaic rule over Palestine.

In actuality, the writing of the Septuagint does not appear to have been a well-organized effort. There are indications of many different translators at work on the various books. There were clearly multiple attempts to translate similar passages. The resulting earliest work—known as the "Old Greek"—was itself often criticized and re-translated by others.

There are some interesting curiosities about the Greek versions of the Scriptures. For example, material that was written at a later period—closer to the time of the Septuagint translation—was added to a number of older books. The Book of Esther, for example, grew to almost twice the size of the Hebrew version. Daniel picked up a number of new chapters. Whole books, such as Sirach, Tobit, Judith, and the Maccabean literature, were all eventually made a part of this collection. This expanded collection of books became for Christians the "Old Testament."

These additional books and passages are what make the "Catholic Bible" different from the "Protestant Bible." It is not that Catholics "added" these additional books; rather, Martin Luther and the Protestants removed them in the sixteenth century. Today these books that are unique to the Greek versions of the Old Testament are known as the "deuterocanonical" books.

It is likely that Antiochus IV was acting under the advice of some of his Hellenized Jewish supporters, who wanted to gain a permanent advantage over the traditionalist Jews. In fact, among the Jews who were attracted to Greek culture, Antiochus IV's policies met with little or no resistance. Among these "modernist" Jews, Greek dress and participation in the gymnasium were popular. Some of these Jewish males even had surgery to reverse their circumcisions in order to avoid embarrassment when participating in athletics in the nude! Those who participated in athletics at the gymnasium had to recognize the Greek gods who were the gymnasium's patrons. Worship of false gods was the greatest abomination to traditional Jews.

The policies instituted by Antiochus IV were certainly brutal in their own right. But it is important to understand that some of Anitochus IV's mandates were instituted in response to the internal conflict among the Jews that Antiochus was determined to use to his own advantage.

Section in Review

Quick View

- Not much is known about Jewish life under Persian rule, but it is likely they were allowed some religious and personal freedoms.

- Alexander the Great initiated the Hellenization of Jewish culture and writing.

- After Alexander the Great's death, Palestine was once again in the middle of a struggle between two great political powers.

- Hellenization came to a new level during the reign of the Seleucid Antiochus IV.

For Review

1. **Main Idea**: What influence did the time spent under the control of the Persians have on Jewish faith?

2. **Critical Thinking**: Describe the process of Hellenization. Why do you think Alexander the Great would have insisted on Hellenization in the lands he conquered?

3. **Critical Thinking**: Explain the importance of the Jewish community in Alexandria. What brought them there? What were they able to achieve?

4. **Main Idea**: Who were the Seleucids and when and how did they come to power in Palestine?

5. **Critical Thinking**: What was the source of internal division within the Jewish community in Jerusalem? How did this affect the relationship between the Jewish community and the Seleucid ruler, Antiochus IV?

For Reflection

How did the division between Hellenistic Jews and traditional Jews like today's arguments between today's opposing political parties and viewpoints? Give examples.

Dead Sea Scrolls
Ancient scrolls containing the oldest known manuscripts of the books of the Old Testament in Hebrew. They were discovered in caves near Qumran on the Dead Sea between 1947 and 1953.

Investigating the Dead Sea Scrolls

Research and report on the relationship of the Dead Sea Scrolls to the Old Testament. Include controversies surrounding the scrolls, especially over their translation and publication. Also add information on the Church's response to the finding of the Dead Sea Scrolls. Finally, make a list of the five websites you found most valuable in your researching this topic.

Although the Hasmoneans won Jewish independence, they were not well received as leaders by the Jewish community in Palestine.

From the Maccabees to Roman Control

The conditions of internal conflict and resentment over the barbarous mandates of Antiochus IV were soon to reach their boiling points. Antiochus certainly did not understand the uncompromising nature of Jewish monotheism, the belief in YHWH alone. As Jewish resistance to his policies mounted, Antiochus enacted sterner measures. When Antichous suffered the humiliating forced withdrawal of his troops from Egypt at the order of the Romans near 167 BC, he blamed the Jews. He then unleashed his army on the Jews in Jerusalem and issued an edict forbidding the practice of Judaism in all traditional forms. Jews were even forced to eat foods forbidden by the Law.

Read 2 Maccabees 6:18–7:1–42.

The final offense came when an altar to Zeus was erected in the Temple in Jerusalem and unclean swine's flesh was sacrificed on it. Jews considered this act to be an "abomination of desolation" that defiled the entire Temple. The first Book of Maccabees describes some of the desperation of the traditional Jews' situation:

> . . . the king erected the horrible abomination upon the altar of holocausts, and in the surrounding cities of Judah they built pagan altars. They also burnt incense at the doors of houses and in the streets. Any scrolls of the law which they found they tore up and burnt. Whoever was found with a scroll of the covenant, and whoever observed the law, was condemned to death by royal decree. So they used their power against Israel, against those who were caught, each month, in the cities. . . . But many in Israel were determined and resolved in their hearts not to eat anything unclean; they preferred to die rather than to be defiled with unclean food or to profane the holy covenant; and they did die. Terrible affliction was upon Israel. (1 Mc 1:54–58; 62–63)

Judas Maccabeus

In the village of Modin, north of Jerusalem, a revolt against the Seleucid powers broke out, led by Mattathias and his sons. Mattathias, a local priest of the family later known as the Hasmoneans, refused the order to sacrifice to Greek gods and killed the king's officer who came to his village to enforce it. Mattathias called all Jews who were loyal to their faith to resist and fight against Antiochus. Support came from a group known as the **Hasidim** ("loyal ones"). This group was probably the forerunner of both the **Pharisees** and **Essenes**, later Jewish sects with similarly resistant positions against Hellenistic influences.

When Mattathias died shortly after the revolt began, leadership passed to one of his five sons, Judas, who turned out to be a brilliant military strategist. Judas was called "Maccabeus," which may be translated as "the Hammer." A series of victories by Maccabeus against local military forces led to revolutionary control of the Temple in Jerusalem in December 164 BC, three years to the month from the time that the Temple was profaned.

Judas Maccabeus pursuing Timotheus

After the Temple's purification and rededication, the Jews offered sacrifices there again. This event is still commemorated by Jews in the celebration of *Hanukkah*, the "Festival of Lights." According to Jewish tradition, a miracle occurred at the rededication of the Temple. The lamp, which was supposed to burn in the Holy of Holies, was fueled with special oil. But when the Maccabees had purified the Temple and were ready to rededicate it, they found only enough oil to fuel the lamp for one day. Despite this, the lamp remained lit throughout the days of celebration, until more could be made. Today's menorah has nine candles. One is used for lighting the other eight, the number of days the oil miraculously lasted during the Maccabees' celebration of the rededication of the Temple.

Read 1 Maccabees 4:36–59.

Even though the Temple was liberated and some elements of traditional Jewish practice were restored, the conflict between the Maccabees and the central Seleucid administration continued to rage on. Judas eventually sent a delegation to Rome in order to secure a treaty (see 1 Mc 8:17–32). This may be an indication that Judas had more than religious motivations in mind; he was now acting like an independent statesman and may have had nationalist aspirations. When Judas was killed in battle in 160 BC, the open military element of the revolt ended. But the leadership that the revolt had created in the Maccabean family—the descendants of Mattathias known as the "Hasmoneans"—remained a permanent element in the political life of Palestine from 160 until the Romans determined to rule Palestine directly in 63 BC.

The Maccabees

After Judas died, his brother Jonathan led the Jews for seventeen years. He was the first of several rulers who oversaw a return of a certain level of Jewish independence to Palestine after the centuries of subjection to Persian and Greek rule.

Jewish independence was not yet complete. The Seleucid government still influenced Jewish leaders. Two pretenders to the Seleucid throne—Alexander Balas and Demetrius—sought Jonathan's support. Jonathan chose to support Demetrius. He was rewarded with the title of High Priest and allowed to assemble an army. When

Jonathan was killed, Simon, the last surviving son of Mattathias, took over as High Priest. In 141 BC Simon's forces overthrew the remaining Syrian fortifications and proclaimed the long awaited Jewish independence, winning decrees of independence from both the Syrians and Rome (see 1 Mc 13–16):

> Thus in the year one hundred and seventy, the yoke of the Gentiles was removed from Israel, and the people began to write in their records and contracts, "In the first year of Simon, high priest, governor, and leader of the Jews." (1 Mc 13:41–42)

Though the Maccabees were not of the Davidic line, some officials and Jews decreed that Simon would be their permanent leader and high priest "until a true prophet arises" (1 Mc 14:42). This may have angered some more traditional Jews and seems to have led to the development of the Essene movement, a sect that lived in the desert and survived until the second century AD.

Simon did establish a period of peaceful rule until he was assassinated by his son-in-law in 134 BC. His son, John Hyrcanus, who is considered the first ruler of an independent Judea in the **Hasmonean Dynasty**, succeeded him.

Hasmonean Dynasty

John Hyrcanus ruled until 128 BC. Although Judea had official declarations of independence from both Syria and Rome, for all practical purposes, John Hyrcanus was a puppet king to these larger empires, much as Zedekiah was in 587 BC. John Hyrcanus began a campaign to expand Jewish territories, eventually nearly replicating the land Israel held at the time of King David. His forces subdued the Edomites, causing the males to be circumcised and forcing all to obey the Law. (This forced conversion of the Edomites, or Idumeans, would come back to haunt the Jews in the person of Herod, who was an Idumean and a hated ruler over the Jews a century later.) John Hyrcanus led the destruction of the Samaritan temple at Mount Gerizim. He also renewed the treaty that Judas Maccabeus had made with the Roman senate.

The Hasmonean kings following John Hyrcanus were equally involved in political gains and nationalism. His successors sanctioned even more moral decay within Judaism, acting like the political and economic modernists they initially defeated. The Hasmoneans cooperated with Greek leaders, and they often assisted the Seleucid dynasty in battle as a loyal ally. Nationalism once again created circumstances of compromise.

Internally, the Jewish population was reacting to these political and religious measures in different ways. The reactions led to the development of Jewish sects that remained active through Jesus' time. The **Sadducees** were originally an aristocratic group of wealthy Jerusalem Jews who viewed the strict letter of the Torah and the Temple sacrifices to be the most important institutions in Jewish life. They denied the doctrine of an afterlife or resurrection of the dead because these teachings were not found in the Torah. The Sadducees were supporters of the Hasmonean king Alexander Janneus, and Alexander responded by favoring their status.

The Pharisees (from the term *parash* for "separate") rivaled the Sadducees. They openly opposed the religious and political policies of Alexander Janneus, for which they paid a severe price. Alexander had several hundred Pharisees executed by crucifixion because of their opposition. Alexander's wife, Salome, however, reconciled with the Pharisees during her reign as queen and allowed them to have the dominant hand in determining local policy.

The Pharisees established much of their identity during this time, an identity that would be prevalent in New Testament times. The particular emphasis of the Pharisees was on study and interpretation of the Law. The Pharisees exhibited a great respect for their learned teachers and preserved the written commentaries of these teachers with a reverence almost equal to that which they accorded the older Scriptures themselves. The Pharisees also placed a strong emphasis on pious religious rites in the home—for example, washings and prayers before meals. The Pharisees eventually introduced two new institutions into Jewish religious practice: a local meeting place designed for prayer and study known as the **synagogue** and a local leader who was revered for his piety and learning, eventually called a **rabbi**. Jesus himself was most likely raised within the Pharisaic tradition of Jewish faith and practice. St. Paul and other early Christians certainly came from that background, as well.

As mentioned on page 228, a group known as the Essenes reacted to the internal bickering and secularism within Jerusalem by withdrawing from Jerusalem completely. The Essenes went to the desert around the Dead Sea, bringing copies of most of the books that would later be made into the Old Testament. They also wrote and studied bizarre apocalyptic books about the coming devastation they believed would place them back in authority in Palestine—a great battle between "The Sons of Darkness" and "The Sons of Light." This desert community is usually considered responsible for hiding the Scriptures, in the caves by the Dead Sea, which were only discovered again between 1947 and 1953.

Roman Rule

The Hasmoneans continued to bicker internally. Salome (76–67 BC) appointed her elder son, Hyrcanus II, as high priest. After Salome's death, Hyrcanus and his younger brother Aristobulus II fought over power. Aristobulus became king and high priest, although Hyrcanus continued to plot for those positions. All of this chaos opened the door for the Romans, the major military power of the region, to intervene in Palestine in 63 BC.

The Roman general Pompey stripped the Hasmoneans of their power. Palestine was made part of the Roman province of Syria. Pompey separated the civil

Resurrection of the Dead

The second Book of Maccabees is among the first places in the Scripture with explicit references to the resurrection of the dead. Read the following passages from 2 Maccabees with references to the resurrection of the dead:

- 2 Maccabees 7:9–11
- 2 Maccabees 7:23–24
- 2 Maccabees 12:41–46

Trace the idea of resurrection of the dead in the Old Testament using the notes and cross-references in your Bible. Also use a Bible concordance to seek out more information on the topic.

As followers of Christ, we believe that we too will rise from the dead and will be united in body and soul on the last day. St. Paul described the difference in the body before and after death:

> It is sown corruptible; it is raised incorruptible. It is sown dishonorable; it is raised glorious. It is sown weak; it is raised powerful. It is sown a natural body; it is raised a spiritual body. If there is a natural body, there is also a spiritual one. (1 Cor 15:42–44)

As baptized Catholics, "it is also true that, in a certain way, we have already risen with Christ" (CCC, 1002). Nourished in this life by the Eucharist, how we rise on the last day exceeds imagination and understanding. Though "how" we will rise can only be accessed by Faith, participating in Eucharist does give us a foretaste of how our bodies will be transfigured in Christ.

Write a short essay detailing your own belief in the Resurrection and how your belief in the Resurrection centers on Jesus Christ. Also, touch on some specifics of how you view life after you die and rise.

THE DEAD SEA SCROLLS

In the spring of 1947, two teenage Bedouin boys chased a young goat into one of the many caves by the shore of the Dead Sea in Palestine. When one of the boys threw a rock into the cave to try to scare the young goat back out, he heard the sound of shattering pottery. When they checked to see what made the noise, the boys found eight earthenware jars containing parchment scrolls. Eventually scrolls and fragments of scrolls containing writings in Hebrew and Aramaic of the Hebrew Scriptures, Biblical commentaries, and other writings were found in eleven caves in the area. The scrolls were sold several times to antique dealers before four of the scrolls eventually came into the hands of the Patriarch of Jerusalem. It was at that point that the scrolls began to make international news.

These scrolls are known as the *Dead Sea Scrolls* or *Qumran Scrolls* because they were found near the ruins of a settlement at Qumran on the shore of the Dead Sea. The Dead Sea Scrolls were the single most important archaeological discovery of the twentieth century (although *many* other important discoveries occurred during that period). They are important because the scrolls contain at least part of every single Book of the Hebrew Bible (except Esther). Some of the books were almost entirely complete (e.g., Isaiah), while others are only partially intact. The Dead Sea Scrolls provide Hebrew manuscripts of the Old Testament more than one thousand years older than any Hebrew manuscript previously possessed. Biblical scholars are now able to check the previously known Hebrew versions against pieces and manuscripts so much older. The readability of the Hebrew texts has been improved dramatically.

Almost equally important for modern historical research are the dozens of previously undiscovered Scripture commentaries that were found. These commentaries were written by the Essenes, who left Jerusalem during the Hasmonean period—probably in protest against the corruption they experienced there—and who probably stored scrolls in the caves in the first place. Their bitter writings directed against the corrupt Hebrews and their leaders back in Jerusalem were often violent, although there is no evidence that the Essenes took violent action against the Hasmoneans. They considered themselves to be the "Sons of Light" who would soon engage in spiritual (and perhaps actual) battle against the "Sons of Darkness." These Essene documents help to explain the different ways that Jews thought about their faith in this period and how influential apocalyptic thinking was on some of these groups.

Almost all the Dead Sea material has now been translated into English in excellent editions with good notes. Only small pieces remain to be translated—a difficult task as some pieces have only a few letters on them.[1]

and religious powers in Judea, appointing his own high priest in Jerusalem and setting up a puppet king who had to answer to Rome. The Jews remained under Roman control until the seventh century AD, when the Moslem invasions began.

Rome originally ruled Jerusalem, Palestine, and Syria through a governor, Scaurus, leaving religious authority to the high priest, who was influenced by Antipater of Idumaea, a region south of Palestine. Antipater and Hyrcanus II played politics, and Rome gave Antipater the title of procurator of Judea while Hyrcanus was named *ethnarch* ("ruler of the people") in addition to being high priest.

In 37 BC one of Antipater's sons, Herod, became king of Judea. He was aided by the Roman Octavius, who became the Emperor Augustus of Rome. One of Herod's ten wives was a Hasmonean, but Herod himself had no blood ties to King David. He was a brutal ruler both within and outside of his own family, but he was noted for his building projects in and around Jerusalem. To gain some support from his subjects, he ordered the restoration of the Second Temple (originally built in 515 BC). The project was not finished until 63 AD, seven years before the Romans destroyed the Temple once again.

It was during the last days of Herod while Augustus was emperor (see Lk 2:1) that Jesus, a descendant of King David, was born. Jesus' birth occurred in Bethlehem, where his foster father Joseph had gone to enroll in a government census.

Section in Review

Quick View

- The religious intolerance of Antiochus IV led to the revolt of the Maccabees.

- By leading the Jews to independence, the Maccabees (later known as the Hasmoneans) took both political and religious power as ruler and high priest.

- The Hasmonean kings took up military campaigns that made enemies with their neighbors.

- In reaction to the Hasmonean rule, some Jews formed groups that became known as the Sadducees, Pharisees, and Essenes.

For Review

1. **Main Idea**: What were the offenses of Antiochus IV that led to the Maccabean revolt?

2. **Critical Thinking**: What unfortunate characteristic did the kings of the Hasmonean dynasty have in common with the kings of the Judean and Israelite monarchies?

3. **Main Idea**: Why are the Dead Sea Scrolls so valuable?

For Reflection

Explain your opinion on the division between church and state. What do you think would be the ideal relationship between the two?

The Jews reacted to foreign rule through cooperation, military resistance, and spiritual resistance.

Cooperation or Resistance: What Was the Best Course for the Jews?

Into the time of Jesus and beyond, the Jews lived under foreign rule. After surveying the centuries before Christ from the time of the Exile to the first century BC, it is interesting to consider which was the better response of the Jews to foreign rulers. Was it better for them to cooperate with the rulers in the hope of maintaining some semblance of religious and cultural life? Or was it better to resist to the point of military action in the hope of regaining independence? Or was there even another way? As the New Testament teaches, these questions were also important to Jesus' disciples.

This section examines some of the pros and cons surrounding possible responses to this issue.

Cooperation with Foreign Rule

Cooperating with the foreign empire, to the point of adopting the conqueror's values, lifestyle, and even religious views, was the choice of the modernists or Hellenists. Defiance of the occupying powers and refusal to accept any political or cultural, let alone religious, influence was the choice of other groups. Many of these latter groups, such as the Essenes, eventually found it necessary

Hellenistic religion and culture. It is likely that such apologetics were written, but were not kept by those who tended to support one of the resisting factions.

Political and Military Resistance

Political and military resistance to foreign rule was clearly the view advocated by the Maccabean revolt and the Hasmonean rulers who benefited from the Maccabees' success. Also included in this view were those who sought to establish the Temple as a recognized authority among the Jewish people and those who struggled with the ruling powers over the question of who would be the high priest.

Revenge for centuries of exile and foreign rule was of high priority to writers and supporters of the Maccabean movement. For example, Mattathias, the instigator of the revolt, said:

> Judas Maccabeus, a warrior from his youth, shall be the leader of your army and direct the war against the nations. You shall also gather about you all who observe the law, and you shall avenge the wrongs of your people. Pay back the Gentiles what they deserve, and observe the precepts of the law. (1 Mc 2:66–68)

In battle, Judas referred in prayer to the original monarchy and traditions of warfare in ancient Israel:

> Blessed are you, O Savior of Israel, who broke the rush of the mighty one by the hand of your servant David and delivered the camp of the Philistines into the hand of Jonathan, the son of Saul, and his armor-bearer. Give this army into the hands of your

Dutch Jews leaving for a concentration camp during World War II

Zealots

A Jewish sect, active during New Testament times, who favored military resistance to Roman authority. Their belief in the coming of the Messiah was strongly linked to their desire for Jewish independence.

to remove themselves from the larger community and live in isolation. Between these two extremes lies a whole spectrum of views. For example, even the Hasmonean rulers, who overthrew the Seleucids and restored the Temple, adopted some elements of Greek culture. Decorated Hasmonean minted coins and Hasmonean architecture, for example, reflected strong classical Greek influence.

We have no literature that represents the position of total compromise—that is, Jewish writings about Jews who totally abandoned their faith in order to embrace people Israel; make them ashamed of their troops and their cavalry. (1 Mc 4:30b–32)

The military option was certainly one that was available, and exercised, by some Jewish groups. Whether this philosophy was in any way related to the **Zealots**, a Jewish sect in New Testament times, is debatable. The Zealots' belief in the coming of a messiah was intimately connected with their desire to recover Jewish independence as a nation. They did not act as an organized military, but instead were more like political terrorists that killed foreigners and even Jews who were against their cause.

In any case, the military option as one to maintain Jewish identity and faith was certainly not the only option available.

Spiritual Resistance

Another way of responding to foreign rule was to focus on maintaining a strong religious commitment in spite of the political challenges. The philosophy was to resist Hellenist and other secular ideas whenever threatened with them. Jews preferred death over defilement as did the martyrs of the second Book of Maccabees (see 2 Mc 6:18–7:42), in the hope that God would witness their suffering and rescue them.

In this tradition, peacefulness was admired, and *spiritual resistance* rather than violent resistance was praised—even if it resulted in martyrdom. This tradition was clearly influenced by Isaiah:

In the days to come
the mountain of the Lord's house
shall be established as the highest of the mountains,
and shall be raised above the hills;
all nations shall stream to it.
Many peoples shall come and say,
"Come let us go up to the mountain of the Lord,
to the house of the God of Jacob;
that he may teach us his ways
and that we may walk in his paths."
For out of Zion shall go forth instruction,
and the word of the Lord from Jerusalem.
He shall judge between the nations,
and shall arbitrate for many people;
they shall beat their swords into plowshares,
and their spears into pruning hooks;
nation shall not lift up sword against nation,

neither shall they learn war any more. (Is 2:2–4 NRSV)

Recall, also, that the Book of Jonah told of the possibility of new life for former enemies who repented of their violence. The stories of Daniel 1–6 are also examples of peaceful and effective resistance. For example,

Shadrach, Meshach, and Abednego answered King Nebuchadnezzar, "There is no need for us to defend ourselves before you in this matter. If our God, whom we serve, can save us from the white-hot furnace and from your hands, O king, may he save us! But even if he will not, know, O king, that we will not serve your god or worship the golden statue which you set up." (Dn 3:16–18)

Similar passages representing the tradition of spiritual resistance are offered in much of wisdom literature. For example:

When the ways of the people please the Lord,
he causes even their enemies to be at peace
with them. (Prv 16:7 NRSV)

One who is slow to anger is better than the mighty,
and one whose temper is controlled than one
who captures a city. (Prv 16:32 NRSV)

Though the entire spectrum of resistance to foreign rulers could be found among the Jews in the first century AD, Jesus himself seemed to adopt the path of spiritual resistance. In the Sermon on the Mount, he offered an alternative justice from the Mosaic law that limited retribution to an "eye for an eye." In the following passage, read how Jesus affirms the wisdom tradition of peace, and St. Paul echoes him:

Jesus' Sermon on the Mount
You have heard that it was said, "An eye for an eye and a tooth for a tooth." But I say to you, offer no resistance to one who is evil. . . . You have heard that it was said, "You shall love your neighbor and hate your enemy." But I say to you, love your enemies, and pray for those who persecute you. (Mt 5:38–39, 43–44)

St. Paul's Letter to the Romans
Bless those who persecute [you], bless and do not curse them. . . . If possible, on your part, live at peace with all. (Rom 12:14, 18)

Section in Review

Quick View

- Some Jews adopted a posture of cooperation with foreign rulers while others supported military resistance.

- A third type of resistance supported non-violent resistance on spiritual grounds even if it meant martyrdom.

For Review

1. **Main Idea**: Describe three possible positions on the spectrum of responses to the rule of foreign powers, in general, and the process of Hellenization, in particular.

2. **Main Idea**: What response did Jesus propose to the issue of foreign domination?

3. **Critical Thinking**: Which of the three forms of resistance do you think were most successful for the Jews?

For Reflection

How can you apply Jesus' teaching to the times in your life when your faith and your secular responsibilities conflict? For example, the Church teaches that Sunday should be a day of rest and prayer, when *unnecessary* work should be avoided. Should you ask your boss not to schedule you to work on Sundays? Should you attempt to complete your homework and studying on Saturdays rather than leaving

Dorothy Day and Pacifism

Dorothy Day was a Catholic layperson of the twentieth century who is being considered for sainthood. She was founder of the Catholic Worker Movement that served the poor. She was also opposed to war and promoted pacifism throughout her life. Read more about Dorothy Day (see, for example, www.cjd.org). Find at least ten suggestions for peaceful living from Dorothy's life and the Catholic Worker Movement that can be applied to your own life. Tell how you will apply each of the ideas.

them for Sunday night even if it means missing out on some good times with your friends?

After the destruction of the Temple, the Jews became more focused on rabbinic teachings and synagogue worship.

What Happened to the Jews?

When the Romans destroyed the Temple in 70 AD the Jews had the choice of disappearing into the pages of history, or reinterpreting their religious practice without the Temple. The Sadducee and Pharisee sects disappeared and the rabbis came into prominence as spiritual leaders of Judaism.

The rabbis began to rework Temple rituals for practice outside of the Temple. Many rabbinical schools emerged, with several interpretations of how Jews should practice their religion. Over the next few centuries, a collection of rabbinical teachings called the **Talmud** was created. One set of these commentaries, called the Jerusalem Talmud, was complied in Palestine in the fourth century. The other, the Babylonian Talmud, was compiled in the Babylonian area in the sixth century. These held the highest authoritative writing after the Torah.

During the Medieval Period (ca. 638–1783 AD) the Diaspora moved farther and farther away from Palestine. Jews moved to all regions of Europe, Asia, the Arabian Peninsula, and North Africa. There was a resurgence of written commentaries on the Bible and Talmuds in this period. Rabbi Shlomo ben Itsak, a French Jew known as Rashi, wrote commentaries on the Bible and Talmud that most Jews still learn at a young age.

Synagogue Worship

With the destruction of the Temple, Jews looked for other ways to pray and worship. Some Jews maintained that righteous deeds of individuals were equivalent to Temple sacrifices. Others equated the three daily periods of prayer with three daily animal sacrifices in the Temple.

Sacred Times

While Christians have taken on Sunday as the day of worship, the Jewish Sabbath, called *Shabbat* ("cease and desist") is celebrated from sunset Friday until sunset Saturday. The Shabbat is a reminder to Jews that God rested from the work of creation on the seventh day, and they should too.

Friday evening is the Shabbat dinner. Observant Jews attend synagogue services, and study the Torah but do not work at this holiest of time. Sabbath ends at sunset Saturday. A brief ceremony called *Havdalah* consists of a lighted candle, a blessing of wine, and a box of spices to take the aroma of the Sabbath into the week, concludes the Shabbat.

While the Shabbat is a weekly event, there are other Jewish sacred times celebrated annually. The major Jewish festivals are divided into two main cycles: the *Tishri* cycle in the fall and the *Nisan* cycle in the spring. The names derive from the first month in each cycle.

Tishri begins in September or October and contains *Rosh Hashanah* (the Jewish New Year) and *Yom Kippur*, the "Day of Atonement." Besides marking the creation of humankind, Jews believe Rosh Hashanah is the day God judges individuals for his or her actions of the previous year. Yom Kippur is the holiest day of the year for Jews. It is a day when Jews ask forgiveness for both communal and personal sins. A person goes directly to the person he or she has offended, if possible, asking forgiveness.

Sukkot, the Feast of Booths or Tabernacles, begins five days after Yom Kippur and lasts for eight days. Sukkot commemorates the forty years the Jews spent in the desert when they had to protect themselves by constructing huts, or booths. This festival reminds Jews that God alone is their great protector.

Pesach is the major feast of the Nisan cycle. It is more commonly known as Passover. It celebrates the Hebrews' freedom from Egyptian slavery. *Shavuot* is celebrated fifty days after the first day of Passover. It was originally a harvest festival celebrating the first of the wheat harvest. (It was during this festival that the Holy Spirit descended on the Apostles at *Pentecost*, which means "fifty days.")

Hanukkah ("Festival of Lights") marks the military victory of Judas Maccabeus. It was not a major Jewish festival until many Jewish parents felt it was important to celebrate it more strongly to counteract the strong influence of Christmas on Jewish children, especially in the United States.

Purim ("Feast of Lots") celebrates the victory of Jews over Persian prime minister, Haman, in the fifth century BC. "Lots" refers to the lots Haman randomly drew to determine the day on which he would slaughter the Jews (see the Book of Esther).

Talmud

A collection of rabbinical teachings collected after the destruction of the Jerusalem Temple in 70 AD.

Passover and Eucharist

(*CCC*, 608, 1334, 1340, 1362–1367, 1382)

At the center of the Gospel is Christ's Paschal Mystery. The word *paschal* is taken from the Jewish word for Passover, *pasch*. The Exodus, the occasion in which God spared the firstborn children of Israel and allowed Moses to lead his people from slavery in Egypt to the Promised Land, is remembered at Passover. Jesus in the New Testament redefined this experience.

The Gospels suggest that Jesus was celebrating a Passover meal in the upper room with his disciples at the Last Supper (Mt 26:18, Mk 14:22–23, Lk 22:7–13, 1 Cor 11:24–25). At the time that Jesus celebrated this feast, the Passover meal probably included unleavened bread, wine, some herbs, and an unblemished lamb. Their ceremony would have consisted of a blessing (*berakah*) of both the cup and the bread. These elements are described in the New Testament. Yet, there is no sign of the lamb. In its place, Jesus is the Lamb of God, the unblemished paschal lamb (Ex 12:4–5) who is led to slaughter (Is 53:7). Jesus gave the Passover a new meaning. The Eucharist "fulfills the Jewish Passover" through the Paschal Mystery (*CCC*, 1340). Christ's Suffering, Death, Resurrection, and Ascension are a passing over from slavery to sin to ultimate freedom in the Resurrection of humanity.

Passover Meal	Eucharist
Bread and wine (Ex 12:15, Nm 9:11–12)	Jesus shared bread and wine with his disciples (Lk 22:19–20)
Unblemished Lamb (Ex 12:4–5)	Jesus is the Paschal Lamb, the Lamb of God (Jn 19:36, 1 Cor 5:7, 1 Pt 1:19)
None of the lamb's bones should be broken (Nm 9:12)	The soldiers did not break Jesus' bones on the Cross (Jn 19:33, 36)
Berekah ("blessing")	Jesus took the bread and said a blessing (Mt 26:26, Mk 14:22, Lk 22:19–20)
Celebrates the Hebrews passing from slavery in Egypt to freedom in the Promised Land (Ex 12)	Celebrates the passing from slavery to sin to freedom in the Resurrection, from death to new life (1 Cor 5:7–8)
Moses poured blood on the people at the establishment of the Covenant (Ex 24:8, Zec 9:11)	Jesus poured out his blood at the establishment of the New Covenant (Jer 31:31, Lk 22:20)

The synagogue became the place for Jews to worship in community.

Synagogues are constructed with a gathering space for men, women, and children, and a central chamber for the reading of the Torah and for prayer. (In Orthodox synagogues today, there is separate seating for men and women.) The Torah is kept in a large cupboard that symbolizes the Ark of the Covenant on the eastern wall. The people face the east, not only facing the Ark, but also facing toward Jerusalem.

The synagogue really has three functions: It is a House of Prayer where Jews can address God. It is a House of Study where Jews can study the Torah. And it is a House of Assembly where Jews are able to meet socially.

Jews in the Modern Era

The Age of Enlightenment began the modern era for the Jews (1738 to present). During this time, the Jews achieved social and economic equality alongside their Christian neighbors in Europe. In Germany, Reform Judaism advocated full integration where the Jews lived. This belief extended to the United States. In the United States, Conservative Judaism reacted against Reform Judaism, only modifying Jewish practice in a limited way. Orthodox Judaism is the most traditional wing of Judaism. Its members strictly follow the Torah. In the 1930s, Reconstructionist Judaism developed from Conservative Judaism. It understood Judaism as a culture, not a religion, and did not hold faith in an all-powerful God.

Also, in the late nineteenth century, Zionism, or Jewish nationalism, began as a movement to return the Jews to their homeland in Palestine. After the murder of about six million Jews by the Nazi Germans in the 1930s and 1940s, the worldwide community responded to the goals of Zionism and, with the help of the United Nations, established the State of Israel in 1948.

Originally, Jerusalem remained divided under the rule of Jordan and Israel. The Six Day War in 1967 brought the city under the control of Israel. This war, and the entire return of the Jews to Palestine, has caused the region, and the world, much tension that has yet to be resolved. But it is clear that any resolution must honor the needs and aspirations of Palestinians (both Muslim and Christian) and Jews.

Section in Review

Quick View

- After the fall of the Temple in AD 70, the Jews turned to rabbis and their teachings in the Talmud as well as synagogue worship to maintain their religion.

- Since the Age of Enlightenment, the Jews achieved relative social and economic equality with Christians in Europe.

- After the World War II Holocaust, Jewish nationalism (Zionism) led many Jews to return to Palestine to establish the state of Israel.

For Review

1. **Main Idea**: How did Jewish rabbis adapt their religion after the destruction of the Temple in 70 AD?

2. **Main Idea**: Name the three functions of a Synagogue.

3. **Main Idea**: What were the circumstances around the founding of the state of Israel in 1948?

4. **Critical Thinking**: What aspects of Old Testament Jewish history would validate the Zionist movement of the twentieth century?

For Reflection

Share an experience of meeting and knowing a Jewish person. Describe his or her religious practice and faith as you know and understand it.

Further Reflection

The study of the Old Testament for this course is nearly completed. Needless to say, the development of the Old Testament canon took many years. None of the authors of the sacred books could have imagined that what they were writing at the time would be used by generation after generation for thousands of years to come. Recall, too, that though the prophets knew they were being used as "mouthpieces" for God, their written prophecies were not recorded until years later.

At the time of King Josiah's reform following the Babylonian Exile, books of the Law were found and used as the basis for reform. This was the first time the Jews considered their writings to be sacred and God's inspired Word. From 621 BC to about 400 BC, the writings surrounding the Law of Moses grew and eventually became the Torah.

The six historical books that followed the Book of Deuteronomy helped to form the historical record of the Jews. Some of the prophetic books also came on the scene. By 200 BC these books of the prophets were considered part of Sacred Scripture. In the last stages of history prior to the birth of Christ, the wisdom literature and other post-Exilic books developed. The disputes over the canonicity of some of these books have been covered, but in any case the number of books in the Old Testament had filled out, as determined by the Church.

The early Church made constant use of the Old Testament. It would look to its pages to see how the Old Covenant prefigured the work of Salvation—only accomplished in the fullness of time in the Person of Jesus Christ, God's incarnate Son.

The opening of the letter to the Hebrews describes the climax of God's Revelation, which comes with the presence of Jesus Christ:

> In times past, God spoke in partial and various ways to our ancestors through the prophets; in these last days, he spoke to us through a son, whom he made heir of all things and through whom he created the universe,
>
> who is the refulgence of his glory,
>> the very imprint of his being,
> and who sustains all things by his mighty word.
> When he had accomplished purification from sins,
> he took his seat at the right hand of the Majesty on high
> as far superior to the angels
> as the name he has inherited is more
>> excellent than theirs. (Heb 1:1–4)

Vocabulary Review

Directions: Match the term with its definition below.

Septuagint   **Ptolemies**   **Dead Sea Scrolls**   **Hasidim**   **Pharisees**   **Essenes**

Hasmonean Dynasty   **Sadducees**   **Zealots**   **Talmud**

1. Jewish sects who favored military resistance to Roman authority.

2. Aristocratic Jews who favored strict adherence to the letter of the Torah and Temple worship.

3. The group who supported the Maccabees in their military efforts against Antiochus IV.

4. Group of Jews who valued adherence to the Law and took a separatist posture against foreign rule.

5. Group of Jews who took an extreme position of living separate from the Jewish community in the desert around the Dead Sea.

6. Rulers of Judea until 63 BC and descendants from the Maccabees.

7. Dynasty descending from Ptolemy I, general under Alexander the Great.

8. Collection of rabbinical teachings collected after the destruction of the Temple in AD 70.

9. The oldest known manuscripts of the books of the Old Testament in Hebrew.

10. This Greek translation is the oldest complete edition of the Old Testament.

Performance Assessment Project

The Jews living under Persian, Greek, and Roman rule reacted to their oppression in three different ways: cooperation, violent resistance, and non-violent spiritual resistance. Based on what you know about Jewish history during this time period, which of the three responses would be in the best interest of the Jews and why? Use historical evidence from the time period as well as Scriptural evidence (Old Testament kings, prophets, wisdom literature, or apocalyptic literature) to support your claim.

Called to Prayer

She got up, and they started to pray and beg that deliverance might be theirs. He began with these words:

> *"Blessed are you, O God of our fathers;*
> *praised be your name forever and ever.*
> *Let the heavens and all your creation*
> *praise you forever.*
> *You made Adam and you gave him his wife Eve*
> *to be his help and support;*
> *and from these two the human race descended.*
> *You said, 'It is not good for the man to be alone;*
> *let us make him a partner like himself.'*
> *Now, Lord, you know that I take this wife of mine*
> *not because of lust,*
> *but for a noble purpose.*
> *Call down your mercy on me and on her,*
> *and allow us to live together to a happy old age."*

> *—Tobit 8:5–7*

- **Reflection**: This is a common reading chosen at nuptial Masses. Tobiah and Sarah prayed this prayer together on their wedding night and received protection from God. Why is it beneficial for husbands and wives to pray together? Do you have trouble praying out loud with your friends and family?

- **Meditation**: Put yourself in Tobiah or Sarah's shoes. As Tobiah, describe your love for Sarah based on the prayer above. As Sarah, how does this prayer affect you and your appreciation for Tobiah?

- **Resolution**: Consider the way you treat people of the opposite sex. Do you treat them with respect at the level of Tobiah and Sarah? What can you do differently moving forward?

Notes

1. Among the most authoritative translations available is the following: *The Dead Sea Scrolls Translated: The Qumran Texts in English* (Second Edition), ed. Florentino Garcia Martinez, (Trans. Wilfred Watson), E.J. Brill/ Eerdmans (Grand Rapids, New York) 1996.

Epilogue

Why Should Catholics Know the Old Testament?

This question is important for reflection, although many Catholics today might answer: "We really *don't* need to know the Old Testament very well. After all, Jesus is the most important Person in the Bible, and we learn about him in the *New* Testament, not the Old Testament."

The *Catechism of the Catholic Church* teaches that this answer is hardly accurate:

> Christians . . . read the Old Testament in the light of Christ crucified and risen. Such typological reading discloses the inexhaustible content of the Old Testament; but it must not make us forget that *the Old Testament retains its own intrinsic value as Revelation* reaffirmed by the Lord himself. Besides, the New Testament has to be read in the light of the Old. Early Christian catechesis made constant use of the Old Testament. As an old saying put it, the New Testament lies hidden in the Old and the Old Testament is unveiled in the New. (*CCC*, 129; emphasis added)

In other words, understanding Christ and the mysteries of our Faith can be more fully accomplished by understanding the text and nuances of the sacred pages of the Old Testament. Several examples help to illustrate how this is so.

Understanding Jesus' Cleansing of the Temple

Jesus' "cleansing" of the Temple is described in all four Gospels. Recall Mark's version of the episode:

> They came to Jerusalem, and on entering the temple area he began to drive out those selling and buying there. He overturned the tables of the money changers and the seats of those who were selling doves. He did not permit anyone to carry anything through the temple area. Then he taught them saying, "Is it not written:

> 'My house shall be called a house of prayer for all peoples'?

> But you have made it a den of thieves."

> The chief priests and the scribes came to hear of it and were seeking a way to put him to death, yet they feared him because the whole crowed was astonished at his teaching. When evening came, they went out of the city. (Mk 11:15–19)

It was obviously a shocking display! Imagine the reaction of the crowds. Do you think the reaction of the people who originally witnessed the incident was different from how you, as a modern Catholic, react to reading the story? Unless you know your Old Testament better than many modern Catholics, the people of Jerusalem would most certainly have reacted differently from you in several ways.

First, the people milling around the Temple grounds would not have been totally shocked by what Jesus did. After all, these Jewish people knew well the stories of prophets such as Jeremiah, who often made similar public displays. Jeremiah, for instance, once went about carrying a wooden yoke across his shoulders:

> Thus the Lord said to me: Make for yourself bands and yoke bars and put them over your shoulder. (Jer 27:2)

Likewise, the prophet Ezekiel often engaged in public displays that both shocked and instructed, such as the time he shaved himself, then burned part of his hair as a symbol of coming destruction:

> As for you, son of man, take a sharp sword and use it like a barber's razor, passing it over your head and beard. Then take a set of scales and divide the hair you have cut. Burn a third in the fire, within the city, when the days of your siege are completed; place another third around the city and strike it with the sword; the final third strew in the wind, and pursue it with the sword. (Ez 5:1–3)

Christ driving the moneylenders from the Temple

Given their knowledge of these stories and other dramatic stories involving the prophets, the people around the Temple would probably not have been totally shocked by what they witnessed. Instead, they probably would have stepped to a safe distance, and then *watched and listened*! A student of the Old Testament today would likely react the same way.

Second, the Gospel reports that the Temple officials (chief priests and scribes) became so upset with what Jesus had done, that they were "looking for a way to put him to death." But why? Again, someone with little background in the Old Testament would probably think, "Because Jesus caused such a commotion—he made a mess in the Temple. That must be what upset the officials."

But think about that kind of reasoning. Tables can be set back in place and animals can be rounded up. After about forty minutes or so, it was probably "business as usual" in the Temple square. Why seek to kill someone for what amounts to a mere half hour's inconvenience? More likely, the Temple officials were so upset because

they knew their Hebrew Scriptures. What did the Temple officials hear that modern readers sometimes miss?

Jesus referred to the Temple as both a "house of prayer" and a "den of thieves." Take a deeper look at each reference. Jesus was actually quoting Jeremiah. Jeremiah stood in precisely the same place where Jesus was standing about 600 years before. In Jeremiah's famous "Temple Sermon" (see Jer 7), he blasted the sins and corruption of the people who thought that offering sacrifices could "cover over" their immoral behavior—their social injustice toward the widow and the orphans who needed help:

> Are you to steal and murder, commit adultery and perjury, burn incense to Baal, go after strange gods that you know not, and yet come to stand before me in this house which bears my name and say: "We are safe; we can commit all these abominations again"? (Jer 7:9–10)

Jeremiah added shockingly:

> Has this house which bears my name become in your eyes a *den of thieves*? (Jer 7:11; emphasis added)

At the end of this sermon, Jeremiah stated clearly that the Temple where he was standing was to be destroyed because of the sins of the people. God, he said, would treat "this house" just as he treated Shiloh, an even older shrine that was *destroyed* by the Assyrians. And, of course, Jeremiah was quite correct: Nebuchadnezzar came and destroyed the Temple.

With this information as background, it becomes clear that the Temple officials were reacting strongly because Jesus referred to the Temple and its officials as a "den of thieves." Not only was Jesus implying that the Temple officials were just as corrupt as those in the time of Jeremiah, but Jesus was also implying that the current Temple was going to be destroyed. And, like Jeremiah before him, Jesus was also quite correct. The Romans destroyed the Temple during the Roman wars against the Jews in 70 AD—barely one generation after the Death and Resurrection of Jesus.

Remember, the Temple was the source of both authority and money for these Temple officials. The Temple was also the center of collaboration with the hated Roman occupying forces and the center of the economically corrupt administration that routinely defrauded the

Jewish people. The chief or high priest was the closest thing that the Jewish people had to a leader in the Roman period. When Jesus implied that the Temple officials were corrupt, *and* that the Temple was going to be destroyed, the Temple officials knew that they could not tolerate this from a prophet whom some of the crowd already considered even greater than Jeremiah!

But that was not all. A third piece of information gleaned from reading and knowing the Old Testament relates to Jesus' use of another surprising phrase as well. Carefully read this passage:

> Let not the foreigner say,
>   when he would join himself to the Lord,
>   "The Lord will surely exclude me from his
>   people" . . .
> And the foreigners who join
>   themselves to the Lord,
>   ministering to him,
> Loving the name of the Lord,
>   and becoming his servants—
> All who keep the sabbath free from profanation
>   and hold to my covenant,
> Them I will bring to my holy mountain
>   and make joyful in my *house of prayer*;
> Their holocausts and sacrifices
>   will be acceptable on my altar,

For my house shall be called a *house of prayer* for all peoples.
Thus says the Lord God,
     who gathers the dispersed of Israel:
Others will I gather to him
     besides those already gathered. (Is 56:3, 6–8; emphasis added)

According to the prophet, God has compassion for *all* people, Jews and Gentiles alike and he is ready to receive non-Jews into the company of the People of God. The Book of Isaiah announced that God will welcome "foreigners" and then the Temple of God will be a "house of prayer for all peoples." This is, of course, the same language Jesus used.

Only with this understanding of the Old Testament can we really understand what Jesus was saying in this passage. Jesus said that the Temple was corrupt, like Jeremiah did. Jesus implied that the Temple would be destroyed, also as Jeremiah had. Finally, Jesus said that the Temple *should* be a place for *all* peoples who want to be part of the People of god, not only the Jews—just like the Book of Isaiah said!

This was too much for the Temple officials to handle. Not only was Jesus threatening the livelihood of the Temple officials and calling them corrupt, Jesus was *also* saying that God loved the Gentiles as he loved the Jews and was willing to welcome them into the Temple to worship. By

Christ preaching in the Temple

these words, Jesus was threatening everything that these Temple officials believed in: exclusivity for the Jews as a religion, along with authority and economic rights of dominance over the Jewish people. This "cleansing of the Temple" passage really points to Jesus as a *Prophetic Messiah*.

This point is only as clear to us today as it was to the first listeners if we know and understand the related passages in the Old Testament.

The Rejection of Jesus at Nazareth

Another example that can help us to understand why knowing the Old Testament is important to understanding the New Testament occurs at the beginning of Jesus' public ministry, as recorded in the Gospel of Luke. The passage in Luke 4:14–30 tells us that Jesus went to his home synagogue and read the Scriptures publicly:

Read Luke 4:14–30.

What happened in this episode? Jesus read a very popular passage from the Book of Isaiah. (Incidentally, notice how important the Prophetic Book of Isaiah is in the New Testament!) When he finished the passage, he sat down (the typical sign that a teacher was about ready to speak) and said to the congregation, "Today this scripture passage is fulfilled in your hearing" (Lk 4:21).

The passage says that "all spoke highly of him and were amazed at the gracious words that came from his mouth" (Lk 4:22). And why not? Jesus had just read one of the most powerful promises recorded in Scripture: God would liberate his people. What did the people listening to Jesus think? Well, obviously, they thought that *they* were "the poor" to whom the Spirit of God would bring "glad tidings." They also likely thought of themselves as the "captives" and the "oppressed."

But Jesus surprises them. With his next few words Jesus makes it clear that he is not referring to those in the synagogue as the captives, blind, and oppressed spoken of in the Book of Isaiah. Rather, he reminds them of the prophets Elijah and Elisha who healed *foreign* people, not Jews. The people listening to Jesus realized what he was implying: God cares for Gentiles as much as he does for Jews. This kind of talk was too much for those who heard Jesus. They rose to try to kill him, but Jesus miraculously escaped from them.

In this episode, Jesus referred directly to the Old Testament traditions of these prophets, so that his hearers would understand what he meant. Many Jews resented Jesus' message, but many accepted it. Some probably sympathized with Jesus' message, even if they were not sure who Jesus was. Today, even if they do not agree with Christians on who Jesus is, many modern Jews accept that Jesus was an important reformer. Christians, too, often display the same willingness to learn from Judaism.

Understanding the Duties of a Christian According to St. Paul

In St. Paul's letter to the Romans, he addresses a way for Christians to live in peacefulness: "Bless those who persecute [you], bless and do not curse them" (Rom 12:14). Paul continues,

> Have the same regard for one another; do not be haughty but associate with the lowly; do not be wise in your own estimation. Do not repay anyone evil for evil; be concerned for what is noble in the sight of all. If possible, on your part, live at peace with all. (Rom 12:16–18)

There is little doubt that this strong teaching is reflective of the words and actions of Jesus. However, Paul then quotes a proverb:

> Rather, "if your enemy is hungry, feed him; if he is thirsty, give him something to drink; for by so doing you will heap burning coals upon his head." Do not be conquered by evil but conquer evil with good. (Rom 12:20–21)

Re-read the prior passage. What does "heap burning coals upon his head" mean? What could this mean? Some have suggested that St. Paul was saying something like: "Let God do the dirty work. You be nice, and God will get your enemies in the end." Another view is that the best revenge is simply to treat one's enemies well. But is this really *consistent* with what St. Paul has written? He finishes this section by writing, "Do not be conquered by evil . . ." so he clearly presumes that his advice is positive, not negative. What does he *really* mean?

Paul's original readers of the letter to the Romans—mostly Jewish Christians—would have been able to put these words into context with what they learned from the Hebrew Scriptures. They would have recalled how the prophet Isaiah was made pure when God touched his mouth with a burning coal (see Is 6:7). For the prophet

A group of young people at the the Wailing Wall in Jerusalem

Isaiah, the symbol of the ember or coal from the altar actually removed his sin. It was a coal from the altar of sacrifice, which was how ancient Israelites offered sacrifice to cleanse themselves from the stain of sin. So, St. Paul's reference to "heaping burning coals" on an enemy's head most likely referred to a means of purification. The kindness of a Christian to a non-believer would purify the non-believer, that is, bring him to Christ.

Again, understanding the Old Testament helps today's reader turn a troubling image into a profound idea.

The Absolute Need for the Old Testament for Today's Catholics

These three examples discussed in the preceding sections help to prove the value of studying the Old Testament. The New Testament contains the eternal truth of God's plan for humanity. But the Church in its wisdom has accepted the *entire* Bible—Old *and* New Testament.

There is so much more to learn and appreciate about your Christian faith by continuing your journey through the Old Testament. Consider how different your view of Jesus would be if you did not know anything about the Prophets. Consider how different your view of Jesus would be if you did not know about the kings of Ancient Israel, and the idea of God's promised "Messiah."

Consider how different your view of one of the final words of Jesus, "My God, My God, Why have you forsaken me?" would be if you did not know that Jesus was quoting Psalm 22, which really is a great psalm of triumph that finally alludes to resurrection:

> For dominion is the Lord's
> and he rules the nations.
> To him alone shall bow down
> all who sleep in the earth;
> Before him shall bend
> all who go down into the dust. (Ps 22:29–30)

In summary, without the Old Testament, Catholics cannot fully and completely understand all that God has to say to us in the Sacred Scriptures. If you had a seven-page letter from your parents or a friend, would you want to throw away the first five pages of that letter and only read the last two? Don't we want to hear everything that God intends for us to hear?

You may be at the end of your journey through this textbook, but you are just getting into your stride for your journey through the Bible!

Your Next Step

Hopefully, many of you have decided that Bible study is both interesting and exciting. You may wish to know how to continue with your Bible study journey now that this course is concluding. Here are three suggestions to help you take your next step:

1. Buy a Bible *for yourself.*

The treasured "family Bible" in your home should not count as your own Bible. You need a personal copy of the Bible so that you can write notes all over the pages.

Some students think that writing in the Bible is somehow being "disrespectful," but that is silly. Writing notes means that you are studying and thinking. As you read your Bible, mark passages that are especially interesting or put question marks next to passages that you have questions about. There is nothing better than a Bible filled with notes and with pages that are heavily used. It means that a person is really taking Bible study seriously.

2. Join a Bible study at your parish.

Your parish youth ministry or religious education program may offer such a study. You may also be able to participate in an adult Bible study program at your parish. Be careful here. Some Bible studies are lead by well-meaning people with very little training or background in Scripture study or in the teachings of the Church. If you find this to be true, ask your high school teachers or pastor for advice. You can even call the religion department of the nearest Catholic college or university for information on how to further your study of the Bible.

3. Buy or borrow some extra resources to help you study the Bible.

If you are really serious about continuing to study the Bible, think seriously about acquiring some study books to help you along the way. Three really good books to put in your personal Bibles Study library are:

- A one-volume Bible Commentary like the *New Jerome Biblical Commentary*. In this book, Catholic Bible scholars have provided all kinds of fascinating information about each passage of the Bible. It is good to read the Commentary as you read your Bible. Take notes, and write in the Commentary, too.

- A Bible Dictionary. You may need to look up words or names that you are not sure about. There are many excellent Bible dictionaries, such as the *HarperCollins Bible Dictionary* or the *Eerdmans Bible Dictionary*. Make sure it is the most recent edition available, as these books are updated regularly.

- A Bible Atlas (e.g., the *Collegeville Atlas of the Bible*). An atlas will help you to locate places where Biblical events happened. A good Bible atlas will give you maps for each major time period to show you how settlements changed, how Empires changed, and how trade routes became more important.

Good luck! See you in Bible class!

Appendix: Catholic Handbook for Faith

A. Beliefs

From the beginning, the Church expressed and handed on its faith in brief formulas accessible to all. These professions of faith are called "creeds" because their first word in Latin, credo, means "I believe." The following creeds have special importance in the Church. The Apostles' Creed is a summary of the Apostles' faith. The Nicene Creed developed from the Councils of Nicene and Constantinople and remains in common between the Churches of both the East and West.

Apostles' Creed

> I believe in God,
> the Father almighty,
> Creator of heaven and earth,
> and in Jesus Christ, his only Son, our Lord,
> who was conceived by the Holy Spirit,
> born of the Virgin Mary,
> suffered under Pontius Pilate,
> was crucified, died and was buried;
> he descended into hell;
> on the third day he rose again from the dead;
> he ascended into heaven,
> and is seated at the right hand of God the Father almighty;
> from there he will come to judge the living and the dead.
>
> I believe in the Holy Spirit,
> the holy catholic Church,
> the communion of saints,
> the forgiveness of sins,
> the resurrection of the body,
> and life everlasting. Amen.

Nicene Creed

> I believe in one God,
> the Father almighty,
> maker of heaven and earth,
> of all things visible and invisible.

> I believe in one Lord Jesus Christ,
> the Only Begotten Son of God,
> born of the Father before all ages.
> God from God, Light from Light,
> true God from true God,
> begotten, not made, consubstantial with the Father;
> through him all things were made.
> For us men and for our salvation
> he came down from heaven,
> and by the Holy Spirit was incarnate of the Virgin Mary,
> and became man.
>
> For our sake he was crucified under Pontius Pilate,
> he suffered death and was buried,
> and rose again on the third day
> in accordance with the Scriptures.
> He ascended into heaven
> and is seated at the right hand of the Father.
> He will come again in glory
> to judge the living and the dead
> and his kingdom will have no end.
>
> I believe in the Holy Spirit, the Lord, the giver of life,
> who proceeds from the Father and the Son,
> who with the Father and the Son is adored and glorified,
> who has spoken through the prophets.
>
> I believe in one, holy, catholic, and apostolic Church.
> I confess one Baptism for the forgiveness of sins
> and I look forward to the resurrection of the dead
> and the life of the world to come. Amen.

Gifts of the Holy Spirit

1. Wisdom
2. Understanding

3. Counsel

4. Fortitude

5. Knowledge

6. Piety

7. Fear of the Lord

Fruits of the Holy Spirit

1. Charity

2. Joy

3. Peace

4. Patience

5. Kindness

6. Goodness

7. Generosity

8. Gentleness

9. Faithfulness

10. Modesty

11. Self-control

12. Chastity

The Symbol of Chalcedon

Following therefore the holy Fathers, we unanimously teach to confess one and the same Son, our Lord Jesus Christ, the same perfect in divinity and perfect in humanity, the same truly God and truly man composed of rational soul and body, the same one in being (*homoousios*) with the Father as to the divinity and one in being with us as to the humanity, like unto us in all things but sin (cf. Heb 4:15). The same was begotten from the Father before the ages as to the divinity and in the later days for us and our Salvation was born as to his humanity from Mary the Virgin Mother of God.

We confess that one and the same Lord Jesus Christ, the only-begotten Son, must be acknowledged in two natures, without confusion or change, without division or separation. The distinction between the natures was never abolished by their union but rather the character proper to each of the two natures was preserved

as they came together in one person (*prosôpon*) and one hypostasis. He is not split or divided into two persons, but he is one and the same only-begotten, God the Word, the Lord Jesus Christ, as formerly the prophets and later Jesus Christ himself have taught us about him and as has been handed down to us by the Symbol of the Fathers.
—From the General Council of Chalcedon (AD 451)

Understanding the Paschal Mystery

This article by Rev. Paul Turner first appeared in the Institute Resource Packet of the North American Forum on the Catechumenate (2004), pp. 14–15.

"Paschal Mystery" is the expression we use for the Suffering, Death, Resurrection, and Ascension of Christ, and for our participation in Christ through baptism and death.

On the road one day with his disciples, Jesus took the Twelve aside to explain something to them in private (Mk 10:33–34). "We are going up to Jerusalem, and the Son of Man will be handed over to the chief priests and the scribes, and they will condemn him to death and hand him over to the Gentiles who will mock him, spit upon him, scourge him, and put him to death, but after three days he will rise."

The Gospels say Jesus predicted his Passion on numerous occasions, but the significance eluded even his closest followers. Once he suffered his horrible death and stunned the world with his Resurrection, people understood his prediction.

The Resurrection of Jesus became the centerpiece of early Christian preaching. In Acts of the Apostles 13:28–30, for example, Paul announced, "Even though [the inhabitants of Jerusalem] found no grounds for a death sentence, they asked Pilate to have [Jesus] put to death, and . . . they took him down from the tree and placed him in a tomb. But God raised him from the dead."

The Paschal Mystery also promises believers a share in the Resurrection. Paul explains the benefit of faith (2 Thes 2:14): "To this end [God] has also called you through our Gospel to possess the glory of our Lord Jesus Christ." "Christ has been raised from the dead, the firstfruits of those who have fallen asleep" (1 Cor 15:20). To the Romans (6:5), he says, "If we have grown into union with him through a death like his, we shall also be united with him in the resurrection." Paul's words recall those of Jesus himself (John 14:3): "If I go and prepare a place for you, I will come back again and take you to myself, so that where I am you also may be."

Both words, *paschal* and *mystery* are important. *Paschal* refers to Passover. The annual Passover recalls the day that the angel of death passed over Israel in exile, sparing the firstborn of God's Chosen People, but visiting terror upon their enemies (Ex 12). It was at Passover when Jesus mounted the Cross at Calvary, freeing his own Chosen People from sin and vanquishing death forever (Jn 19:14).

Mystery refers to our faith. We do not understand how God will save us, or even why God loves us so. We do not appreciate the joy that awaits us in eternal life. "What eye has not seen, and ear has not heard, and what has not entered the human heart, what God has prepared for those who love him, this God has revealed to us through the Spirit" (1 Cor 2:9).

Christians face the Paschal Mystery with every baptism and every death. Baptism ushers us into the Paschal Mystery, and death transports us to the threshold of its completion. "In the sacraments of Christian initiation we are freed from the power of darkness and joined to Christ's Death, Burial and Resurrection. . . . Baptism recalls and makes present the paschal mystery itself, because in baptism we pass from the death of sin into life" (*Christian Initiation, General Introduction* 1, 6).

"In the face of death, the Church confidently proclaims that God has created each person for eternal life and that Jesus, the Son of God, by his Death and Resurrection, has broken the chains of sin and death that bound humanity" (*Order of Christian Funerals, General Introduction* 1).

The Paschal Mystery of Christ is the promise of life for Christians. This glory gives us hope and helps us face our fears.

One day long ago Jesus foretold his Death, unveiling the Paschal Mystery to the Twelve. Mark describes the experience this way: "The disciples were on the way, going up to Jerusalem, and Jesus went ahead of them. They were amazed, and those who followed were afraid."

This still describes the experience of every Christian. We are disciples, on the way—the way of the commands of Christ, the way toward our own death, our own Jerusalem. Jesus is not exactly with us. He is ahead of us. This belief makes us amazed, but we followers remain afraid. We know not what lies ahead. It is all mystery. But we believe it is paschal, and therein lies our hope.

B. Faith in God: Father, Son, and Holy Spirit

Our profession of faith begins with God, for God is the First and the Last, the beginning and end of everything.

Attributes of God

St. Thomas Aquinas named nine attributes that seem to tell us some things about God's nature. They are:

1. *God is eternal.* He has no beginning and no end. Or, to put it another way, God always was, always is, and always will be.

2. *God is unique.* There is no God like YHWH (see Is 45:18). God is the designer of a one-and-only world. Even the people he creates are one of a kind.

3. *God is infinite and omniscient.* This reminds us of a lesson we learned early in life: God sees everything. There are no limits to God.

4. *God is omnipresent.* God is not limited to space. He is everywhere. You can never be away from God.

5. *God contains all things.* All of creation is under God's care and jurisdiction.

6. *God is immutable.* God does not evolve. God does not change. God is the same God now as he always was and always will be.

7. *God is pure spirit.* Though God has been described with human attributes, God is not a material creation. God's image cannot be made. God is a pure spirit who cannot be divided into parts. God is simple, but complex.

8. *God is alive.* We believe in a living God, a God who acts in the lives of people. Most concretely, God assumed a human nature in the divine Person of Jesus Christ, without losing his divine nature.

9. *God is holy.* God is pure goodness. God is pure love.

The Holy Trinity

The Holy Trinity is the central mystery of the Christian faith and of Christian life. Only God alone can make it known to us by revealing himself as Father, Son, and Holy Spirit. Viewed in the light of faith, some of the Church dogmas, or beliefs, can help our understanding of this mystery:

- *The Trinity is One.* There are not three Gods, but one God in three Persons. Each one of them—Father, Son, and Holy Spirit—is God whole and entire.

- *The three Persons are distinct from one another.* The three Persons of the Trinity are distinct in how they relate to one another. "It is the Father who generates, the Son who is begotten, and the Holy Spirit who proceeds" (Lateran Council IV quoted *CCC*, 254). The Father is not the Son, nor is the Son the Holy Spirit.

- *The three divine Persons of the Blessed Trinity related to one another.* While the three Persons are truly distinct in light of their relations, we believe in one God. The Three Persons do not divide the divine unity. They are inseparable in what they are and are inseparable in what they do. However each Divine Person reveals his own unique personal properties in the work that is done by the whole Trinity. Above all, the divine missions of the Son's Incarnation and the gift of the Holy Spirit show forth the personal properties of the Divine Persons. The Council of Florence taught: "Because of that unity the Father is wholly in the Son and wholly in the Holy Spirit; the Son is wholly in the Father and wholly in the Holy Spirit; the Holy Spirit is wholly in the Father and wholly in the Son" (quoted in *CCC*, 255).

St. John Damascus used two analogies to describe the doctrine of the Blessed Trinity.

Think of the Father as a root,
of the Son as a branch,
and of the Spirit as a fruit,
for the substance of these is one.

The Father is a sun
with the Son as rays
and the Holy Spirit as heat.

Read the *Catechism of the Catholic Church* (232–260) on the Holy Trinity.

Faith in One God

There are several implications for those who love God and believe in him with their entire heart and soul (see *CCC*, 222–227):

- It means knowing God's greatness and majesty.

- It means living in thanksgiving.

- It means knowing the unity and dignity of all people.

- It means making good use of created things.
- It means trusting God in every circumstance.

C. Deposit of Faith

"Deposit of Faith" refers to both Sacred Scripture and Sacred Tradition handed on from the time of the Apostles, from which the Church draws. All that she proposes is revealed by God.

Canon of the Bible

There are seventy-three books in the canon of the Bible, that is, the official list of books the Church accepts as divinely inspired writings: forty-six Old Testament books and twenty-seven New Testament books. Protestant Bibles do not include seven Old Testament books in their list (1 and 2 Maccabees, Judith, Tobit, Baruch, Sirach, and the Wisdom of Solomon). Why the difference? Catholics rely on the version of the Bible that the earliest Christians used, the *Septuagint.* This was the first Greek translation of the Hebrew Scriptures begun in the third century BC. Protestants, on the other hand, rely on an official list of Hebrew Scriptures compiled in the Holy Land by Jewish scholars at the end of the first century AD. Today, some Protestant Bibles print the disputed books in a separate section at the back of the Bible.

The twenty-seven books of the New Testament are divided into three categories: the Gospels, the letters written to local Christian communities or individuals, and the letters intended for the entire Church. The heart of the New Testament, in fact all of Scripture, is the Gospels. The New Testament is central to our knowledge of Jesus Christ. He is the focus of all Scripture.

There are forty-six books in the Old Testament canon. The Old Testament is the foundation for God's self-Revelation in Christ. Christians honor the Old Testament as God's Word. It contains the writings of prophets and other inspired authors who recorded God's teaching to the Chosen People and his interaction in their history. For example, the Old Testament recounts how God delivered the Jews from Egypt (the Exodus), led them to the Promised Land, formed them into a nation under his care, and taught them in knowledge and worship.

The stories, prayers, sacred histories, and other writings of the Old Testament reveal what God is like and tell much about human nature, too. In brief, the Chosen People sinned repeatedly by turning their backs on their loving God; they were weak and easily tempted away from God. YHWH, on the other hand, *always* remained faithful. He promised to send a messiah to humanity.

Listed below are the categories and books of the Old Testament and the New Testament:

The Old Testament

The Pentateuch

Genesis	Gn
Exodus	Ex
Leviticus	Lv
Numbers	Nm
Deuteronomy	Dt

The Historical Books

Joshua	Jos
Judges	Jgs
Ruth	Ru
1 Samuel	1 Sm
2 Samuel	2 Sm
1 Kings	1 Kgs
2 Kings	2 Kgs
1 Chronicles	1 Chr
2 Chronicles	2 Chr
Ezra	Ezr
Nehemiah	Neh
Tobit	Tb
Judith	Jdt
Esther	Est
1 Maccabees	1 Mc
2 Maccabees	2 Mc

The Wisdom Books

Job	Jb
Psalms	Ps(s)
Proverbs	Prv
Ecclesiastes	Eccl
Song of Songs	Sg
Wisdom	Wis
Sirach	Sir

The Prophetic Books

Isaiah	Is
Jeremiah	Jer
Lamentations	Lam
Baruch	Bar
Ezekiel	Ez
Daniel	Dn
Hosea	Hos
Joel	Jl
Amos	Am
Obadiah	Ob
Jonah	Jon
Micah	Mi
Nahum	Na
Habakkuk	Hb
Zephaniah	Zep
Haggai	Hg
Zechariah	Zec
Malachi	Mal

The New Testament

The Gospels

Matthew	Mt
Mark	Mk
Luke	Lk
John	Jn
Acts of the Apostles	Acts

The New Testament Letters

Romans	Rom
1 Corinthians	1 Cor
2 Corinthians	2 Cor
Galatians	Gal
Ephesians	Eph
Philippians	Phil
Colossians	Col
1 Thessalonians	1 Thes
2 Thessalonians	2 Thes
1 Timothy	1 Tm
2 Timothy	2 Tm
Titus	Ti
Philemon	Phlm
Hebrews	Heb

The Catholic Letters

James	Jas
1 Peter	1 Pt
2 Peter	2 Pt
1 John	1 Jn
2 John	2 Jn
3 John	3 Jn
Jude	Jude
Revelation	Rv

How to Locate a Scripture Passage

Example: 2 Tm 3:16–17

1. Determine the name of the book.

    The abbreviation "2 Tm" stands for the Book of Second Timothy.

2. Determine whether the book is in the Old Testament or New Testament.

    The Book of Second Timothy is one of the New Testament letters.

3. Locate the chapter where the passage occurs.

    The first number before the colon—"3"— indicates the chapter. Chapters in the Bible are set off by the larger numbers that divide a book.

4. Locate the verses of the passage.

    The numbers after the colon indicate the verses referenced to. In this case, verses 16 and 17 of chapter 3.

5. Read the passage.

    For example: "All Scripture is inspired by God and is useful for teaching, for refutation, for correction, and for training in righteousness, so that one who belongs to God may be competent, equipped for every good work."

Relationship Between Scripture and Tradition

The Church does not derive the revealed truths of God from the Holy Scriptures alone. The Sacred Tradition hands on God's Word, first given to the Apostles by the Lord and the Holy Spirit, to the successors of the Apostles (the bishops and the Pope). Enlightened by the Holy Spirit, these successors faithfully preserve, explain, and spread it to the ends of the earth. The Second Vatican Council fathers explained the relationship between Sacred Scripture and Sacred Tradition:

> It is clear therefore that, in the supremely wise arrangement of God, Sacred Tradition, Sacred Scripture, and the Magisterium of the Church are so connected and associated that one of them cannot stand without the others. Working together, each in its own way, under the action of the one Holy Spirit, they all contribute effectively to the salvation of souls. (*Dei Verbum*, 10)

D. Church

The Church is the Body of Christ, that is, the community of God's people who profess faith in the risen Lord Jesus and love and serve others under the guidance of the Holy Spirit. The Church is guided by the Pope and his bishops.

Marks of the Church

1. *The Church is One.* The Church remains one because of its source: The unity in the Trinity of the Father, Son, and Spirit in one God. The Church's unity can never be broken and lost because this foundation is itself unbreakable.

2. *The Church is Holy.* The Church is holy because Jesus, the founder of the Church, is holy, and he joined the Church to himself as his body and gave the Church the gift of the Holy Spirit. Together, Christ and the Church make up the "whole Christ" (*Christus totus* in Latin).

3. *The Church is Catholic.* The Church is catholic ("universal" or "for everyone") in two ways. First, she is catholic because Christ is present in the Church in the fullness of his body, with the fullness of the means of Salvation, the fullness of faith, Sacraments, and the ordained ministry that comes from the Apostles. The Church is also catholic because she takes her message of Salvation to all people. Put another way, the Church in this world is the Sacrament of Salvation, the sign and instrument of the communion of God and men. As Pope Paul VI explained, this is so because God desires "that the whole human race may become one People of God, form one Body of Christ, and be built up into one temple of the Holy Spirit" (quoted in *CCC*, 776).

4. *The Church is Apostolic.* The Church's apostolic mission comes from Jesus—"Go, therefore, and make disciples of all nations" (Mt 28:19)—and is directed by the Holy Spirit. It is from God's love for us that we receive both our obligation and vigor to proceed in forging God's mission that all will be saved and come to a knowledge of the truth. "Salvation is found in the truth" (*CCC*, 851). It is the Church's love for Christ that spurs this mission on. The Church remains apostolic because she still teaches the same things the Apostles taught. The Pope and bishops, who are

successors to the Apostles, lead and guide the Church until Jesus returns.

The Apostles and Their Emblems

St. Andrew

Tradition holds that Andrew was crucified on a X-shaped cross, called a *saltire*.

St. Bartholomew

Bartholomew was flayed alive before being crucified. He was then beheaded.

St. James the Greater

James the Greater, the brother of John, was beheaded by Herod Agrippa. It is the only death of an Apostle mentioned in Scripture (Acts 12:2). The shell indicates James's missionary work by sea in Spain. The sword is of martyrdom.

St. James the Less

James the Less is traditionally known as the first bishop of Jerusalem. The saw for his emblem is connected with the tradition of his body being sawed into pieces after he was pushed from the pinnacle of the Temple.

St. John the Evangelist

John was the first bishop of Ephesus. He is the only Apostle believed to have died a natural death, in spite of many attempts to murder him by his enemies. One attempt included his miraculous survival after drinking a poisoned drink.

St. Jude

Some traditions have Sts. Jude and Peter martyred together. It is thought that he traveled throughout the Roman Empire with Peter.

St. Matthew

Matthew's shield depicts three purses, reflecting his original occupation as tax collector.

St. Matthias

Matthias was the Apostle chosen by lot to replace Judas. Tradition holds that Matthias was stoned to death and then beheaded with an ax.

St. Peter

Simon Peter was the brother of Andrew. The first bishop of Rome, Peter was crucified under Nero, asking to be hung upside down because he felt unworthy to die as Jesus did. The keys represent Jesus' giving Peter the keys to the Kingdom of Heaven.

St. Philip

Philip may have been bound to a cross and stoned to death. The two loaves of bread at the side of the cross refer to Philip's comment to Jesus about the possibility of feeding the multitudes of people (Jn 6:7).

St. Simon

The book with fish depicts Simon as a "fisher of men" who preached the Gospel. He was also known as Simon the Zealot.

St. Thomas

Thomas is thought to have been a missionary in India, where he is thought to have built a church. Hence, the carpenter's square. He may have died by arrows and stones. It is then thought that he had a lance run through his body.

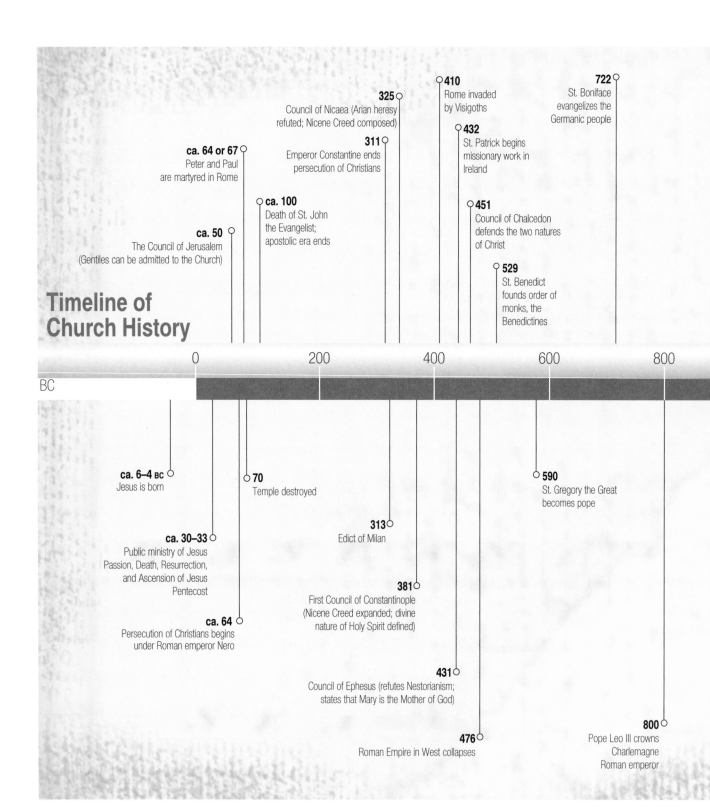

Timeline of Church History

410
Rome invaded
by Visigoths

722
St. Boniface
evangelizes the
Germanic people

325
Council of Nicaea (Arian heresy
refuted; Nicene Creed composed)

432
St. Patrick begins
missionary work in
Ireland

311
Emperor Constantine ends
persecution of Christians

ca. 64 or 67
Peter and Paul
are martyred in Rome

451
Council of Chalcedon
defends the two natures
of Christ

ca. 100
Death of St. John
the Evangelist;
apostolic era ends

529
St. Benedict
founds order of
monks, the
Benedictines

ca. 50
The Council of Jerusalem
(Gentiles can be admitted to the Church)

0   200   400   600   800

BC

ca. 6–4 BC
Jesus is born

70
Temple destroyed

590
St. Gregory the Great
becomes pope

ca. 30–33
Public ministry of Jesus
Passion, Death, Resurrection,
and Ascension of Jesus
Pentecost

313
Edict of Milan

381
First Council of Constantinople
(Nicene Creed expanded; divine
nature of Holy Spirit defined)

ca. 64
Persecution of Christians begins
under Roman emperor Nero

431
Council of Ephesus (refutes Nestorianism;
states that Mary is the Mother of God)

476
Roman Empire in West collapses

800
Pope Leo III crowns
Charlemagne
Roman emperor

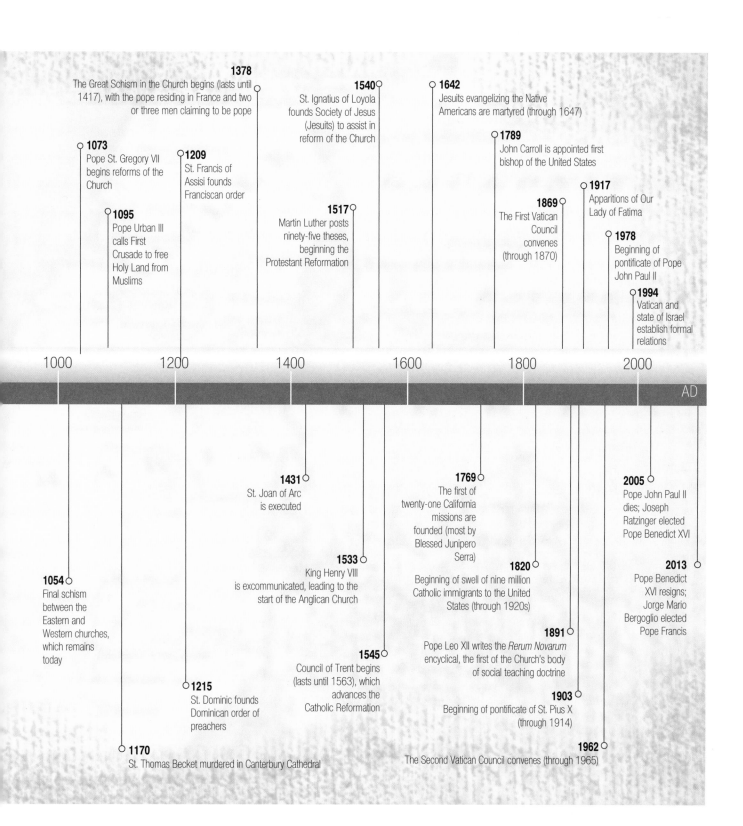

1378
The Great Schism in the Church begins (lasts until 1417), with the pope residing in France and two or three men claiming to be pope

1073
Pope St. Gregory VII begins reforms of the Church

1209
St. Francis of Assisi founds Franciscan order

1540
St. Ignatius of Loyola founds Society of Jesus (Jesuits) to assist in reform of the Church

1642
Jesuits evangelizing the Native Americans are martyred (through 1647)

1789
John Carroll is appointed first bishop of the United States

1095
Pope Urban III calls First Crusade to free Holy Land from Muslims

1517
Martin Luther posts ninety-five theses, beginning the Protestant Reformation

1869
The First Vatican Council convenes (through 1870)

1917
Apparitions of Our Lady of Fatima

1978
Beginning of pontificate of Pope John Paul II

1994
Vatican and state of Israel establish formal relations

1000 — 1200 — 1400 — 1600 — 1800 — 2000

AD

1431
St. Joan of Arc is executed

1769
The first of twenty-one California missions are founded (most by Blessed Junipero Serra)

2005
Pope John Paul II dies; Joseph Ratzinger elected Pope Benedict XVI

1054
Final schism between the Eastern and Western churches, which remains today

1533
King Henry VIII is excommunicated, leading to the start of the Anglican Church

1820
Beginning of swell of nine million Catholic immigrants to the United States (through 1920s)

2013
Pope Benedict XVI resigns; Jorge Mario Bergoglio elected Pope Francis

1891
Pope Leo XII writes the *Rerum Novarum* encyclical, the first of the Church's body of social teaching doctrine

1215
St. Dominic founds Dominican order of preachers

1545
Council of Trent begins (lasts until 1563), which advances the Catholic Reformation

1903
Beginning of pontificate of St. Pius X (through 1914)

1170
St. Thomas Becket murdered in Canterbury Cathedral

1962
The Second Vatican Council convenes (through 1965)

The Pope

The bishop of Rome has carried the title "Pope" since the ninth century. Pope means "papa" or "father." St. Peter was the first bishop of Rome and, hence, the first Pope. He was commissioned directly by Jesus:

> And so I say to you, you are Peter, and upon this rock I will build my church, and the gates of the netherworld shall not prevail against it. I will give you the keys to the kingdom of heaven. Whatever you bind on earth shall be bound in heaven; and whatever you loose on earth shall be loosed in heaven. (Mt 16:18–19)

Because Peter was the first bishop of Rome, the succeeding bishops of Rome have had primacy in the Church. The entire succession of Popes since St. Peter can be traced directly to the Apostle.

The Pope is in communion with the bishops of the world as part of the Magisterium, which is the Church's teaching authority. The Pope can also define doctrine in faith or morals for the Church. When he does so, he is infallible and cannot be in error.

The Pope is elected by the College of Cardinals by a two-thirds plus one majority vote in secret balloting. Cardinals under the age of eighty are eligible to vote. If the necessary majority is not achieved, the ballots are burned in a small stove inside the council chambers along with straw that makes dark smoke. The sign of dark smoke announces to the crowds waiting outside St. Peter's Basilica that a new Pope has not been chosen. When a new Pope has been voted in with the necessary majority, the ballots are burned without the straw, producing white smoke and signifying the election of a Pope.

Recent Popes

Since 1900 and through the pontificate of Pope John Paul II, there were nine Popes. Pope John Paul II was the first non-Italian Pope since Dutchman Pope Adrian VI (1522–1523). The Popes of the twentieth century through John Paul II with their original names, place of origin, and years as Pope:

- Pope Leo XIII (Giocchino Pecci): Carpineto, Italy, February 20, 1878–July 20, 1903.

- Pope St. Pius X (Giuseppe Sarto): Riese, Italy, August 4, 1903–August 20, 1914.

- Pope Benedict XV (Giacomo della Chiesa): Genoa, Italy, September 3, 1914–January 22, 1922.

- Pope Pius XI (Achille Ratti): Desio, Italy, February 6, 1922–February 10, 1939.

- Pope Pius XII (Eugenio Pacelli): Rome, Italy, March 2, 1939–October 9, 1958.

- Pope John XXIII (Angelo Giuseppe Roncalli), Sotto il Monte, Italy, October 28, 1958–June 3, 1963.

- Pope Paul VI (Giovanni Battista Montini): Concessio, Italy, June 21, 1963–August 6, 1978.

- Pope John Paul I (Albino Luciani): Forno di Canale, Italy, August 26, 1978–September 28, 1978.

- Pope John Paul II (Karol Wojtyla): Wadowice, Poland, October 16, 1978–April 2, 2005.

- Pope Benedict XVI (Joseph Ratzinger): Marktl am Inn, Germany, April 19, 2005–February 28, 2013.

- Pope Francis (Jorge Mario Bergoglio): Buenos Aires, Argentina, March 13, 2013–present.

Fathers of the Church

Church Fathers, or Fathers of the Church, is a traditional title that was given to theologians of the first eight centuries whose teachings made a lasting mark on the Church. The Church Fathers developed a significant amount of doctrine that has great authority in the Church. The Church Fathers are named as either Latin Fathers (West) or Greek Fathers (East). Among the greatest Fathers of the Church are:

Latin Fathers
St. Ambrose
St. Augustine
St. Jerome
St. Gregory the Great

Greek Fathers
St. John Chrysostom
St. Basil the Great
St. Gregory of Nazianzen
St. Athanasius

Doctors of the Church

The Doctors of the Church are men and women honored by the Church for their writings, preaching, and holiness. Originally the Doctors of the Church were considered to be Church Fathers Augustine, Ambrose, Jerome, and Gregory the Great, but others were added over the centuries. St. Teresa of Avila was the first woman Doctor (1970). St. Catherine of Siena was named a Doctor of the Church the same year. The list of Doctors of the Church:

Name	Life Span	Designation
St. Athanasius	296–373	1568 by Pius V
St. Ephraem the Syrian	306–373	1920 by Benedict XV
St. Hilary of Poitiers	315–367	1851 by Pius IX
St. Cyril of Jerusalem	315–386	1882 by Leo XIII
St. Gregory of Nazianzus	325–389	1568 by Pius V
St. Basil the Great	329–379	1568 by Pius V
St. Ambrose	339–397	1295 by Boniface VIII
St. John Chrysostom	347–407	1568 by Pius V
St. Jerome	347–419	1295 by Boniface XIII
St. Augustine	354–430	1295 by Boniface XIII
St. Cyril of Alexandria	376–444	1882 by Leo XIII
St. Peter Chrysologous	400–450	1729 by Benedict XIII
St. Leo the Great	400–461	1754 by Benedict XIV
St. Gregory the Great	540–604	1295 by Boniface XIII
St. Isidore of Seville	560–636	1722 by Innocent XIII
St. John of Damascus	645–749	1890 by Leo XIII
St. Bede the Venerable	672–735	1899 by Leo XIII
St. Peter Damian	1007–1072	1828 by Leo XII
St. Anselm	1033–1109	1720 by Clement XI
St. Bernard of Clairvaux	1090–1153	1830 by Pius VIII
St. Anthony of Padua	1195–1231	1946 by Pius XII
St. Albert the Great	1206–1280	1931 by Pius XI
St. Bonaventure	1221–1274	1588 by Sixtus V
St. Thomas Aquinas	1226–1274	1567 by Pius V
St. Catherine of Siena	1347–1380	1970 by Paul VI
St. Teresa of Avila	1515–1582	1970 by Paul VI
St. Peter Canisius	1521–1597	1925 by Pius XI
St. John of the Cross	1542–1591	1926 by Pius XI
St. Robert Bellarmine	1542–1621	1931 by Pius XI
St. Lawrence of Brindisi	1559–1619	1959 by John XXIII
St. Francis de Sales	1567–1622	1871 by Pius IX
St. Alphonsus Liguori	1696–1787	1871 by Pius IX
St. Thérèse of Lisieux	1873–1897	1997 by John Paul II
St. John of Avila	1500–1569	2012 by Benedict XVI
St. Hildegard of Bingen	1098–1179	2012 by Benedict XVI

Ecumenical Councils

An ecumenical council is a worldwide assembly of bishops under direction of the Pope. There have been twenty-one ecumenical councils, the most recent being the Second Vatican Council (1962–1965). A complete list of the Church's ecumenical councils with the years each met:

Nicea I	325
Constantinople I	381
Ephesus	431
Chalcedon	451
Constantinople II	553
Constantinople III	680–681
Nicea II	787
Constantinople IV	869–870
Lateran I	1123
Lateran II	1139
Lateran III	1179
Lateran IV	1215
Lyons I	1245
Lyons II	1274
Vienne	1311–1312
Constance	1414–1418
Florence	1431–1445
Lateran V	1512–1517
Trent	1545–1563
Vatican Council I	1869–1870
Vatican Council II	1962–1965

E. Morality

Morality refers to the goodness or evil of human actions. Listed below are several helps the Church offers for making good and moral decisions.

The Ten Commandments

The Ten Commandments are a main source for Christian morality. The Ten Commandments were revealed by God to Moses. Jesus himself acknowledged them. He told the rich young man, "If you wish to enter into life, keep the commandments" (Mt 19:17). Since the time of St. Augustine (fourth century), the Ten Commandments have been used as a source for teaching baptismal candidates.

I. I, the Lord am your God: you shall not have other gods besides me.

II. You shall not take the name of the Lord, your God, in vain.

III. Remember to keep holy the sabbath day.

IV. Honor your father and your mother.

V. You shall not kill.

VI. You shall not commit adultery.

VII. You shall not steal.

VIII. You shall not bear false witness against your neighbor.

IX. You shall not covet your neighbor's wife.
X. You shall not covet your neighbor's goods.

The Beatitudes

The word *beatitude* means "happiness." Jesus preached the Beatitudes in his Sermon on the Mount. They are:

Blessed are the poor in spirit, for theirs is the kingdom of God.

Blessed are they who mourn, for they will be comforted.

Blessed are the meek, for they will inherit the land.

Blessed are they who hunger and thirst for righteousness, for they will be satisfied.

Blessed are the merciful, for they will be shown mercy.

Blessed are the clean of heart, for they will see God.

Blessed are the peacemakers, for they will be called children of God.

Blessed are they who are persecuted for the sake of righteousness, for theirs is the kingdom of heaven.

Cardinal Virtues

Virtues—habits that help in leading a moral life—that are acquired by human effort are known as moral or human virtues. Four of these are the cardinal virtues, as they form the hinge that connects all the others. They are:

- Prudence
- Justice
- Fortitude
- Temperance

Theological Virtues

The theological virtues are the foundation for moral life. They are gifts infused into our souls by God.

- Faith
- Hope
- Love

Corporal (Bodily) Works of Mercy

1. Feed the hungry.
2. Give drink to the thirsty.
3. Clothe the naked.
4. Visit the imprisoned.
5. Shelter the homeless.
6. Visit the sick.
7. Bury the dead.

Spiritual Works of Mercy

1. Counsel the doubtful.
2. Instruct the ignorant.
3. Admonish sinners.
4. Comfort the afflicted.
5. Forgive offenses.
6. Bear wrongs patiently.
7. Pray for the living and the dead.

Precepts of the Church

1. You shall attend Mass on Sundays and on holy days of obligation and rest from servile labor.
2. You shall confess your sins at least once a year.
3. You shall receive the Sacrament of Eucharist at least during the Easter season.
4. You shall observe the days of fasting and abstinence established by the Church.
5. You shall help to provide for the needs of the Church.

Catholic Social Teaching: Major Themes

The 1998 document Sharing Catholic Social Teaching: Challenges and Directions—Reflections of the US Catholic Bishops—*highlighted seven principles of the Church's social teaching. They are:*

1. Life and dignity of the human person
2. Call to family, community, and participation
3. Rights and responsibilities
4. Preferential option for the poor and vulnerable
5. The dignity of work and the rights of workers
6. Solidarity
7. God's care for creation

Sin

Sin is an offense against God.

Mortal sin is the most serious kind of sin. Mortal sin destroys or kills a person's relationship with God. To be a mortal sin, three conditions must exist:

- The moral object must be of grave or serious matter. Grave matter is specified in the Ten Commandments (e.g., do not kill, do not commit adultery, do not steal, etc.).

- The person must have full knowledge of the gravity of the sinful action.

- The person must completely consent to the action. It must be a personal choice.

Venial sin is less serious sin. Examples of venial sins are petty jealousy, disobedience, "borrowing" a small amount of money from a parent without the intention of repaying it. Venial sins, when not repented, can lead a person to commit mortal sins.

Vices are bad habits linked to sins. Vices come from particular sins, especially the seven capital sins: pride, avarice, envy, wrath, lust, gluttony, and sloth.

F. Liturgy and Sacraments

The Sacraments and the Divine Office constitute the Church's liturgy. The Mass is the most important liturgical celebration.

Church Year

The cycle of seasons and feasts that Catholics celebrate is called the Church Year or Liturgical Year. The Church Year is divided into five main parts: Advent, Christmas, Lent, Easter, and Ordinary Time.

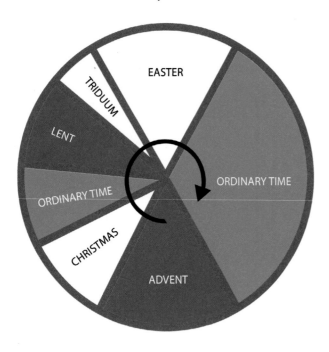

Holy Days of Obligation in the United States

1.	Immaculate Conception of Mary	December 8
2.	Christmas	December 25
3.	Solemnity of Mary, Mother of God	January 1
4.	Ascension of the Lord	Forty days after Easter
5.	Assumption of Mary	August 15
6.	All Saints Day	November 1

The Seven Sacraments

1. Baptism
2. Confirmation
3. Eucharist
4. Penance and Reconciliation
5. Anointing of the Sick
6. Holy Orders
7. Matrimony

How to Go to Confession

1. Spend some time examining your conscience. Consider your actions and attitudes in each area of your life (e.g., faith, family, school/work, social life, relationships). Ask yourself, is this area of my life pleasing to God? What needs to be reconciled with God? With others? With myself?

2. Sincerely tell God that you are sorry for your sins. Ask God for forgiveness and for the grace you will need to change what needs changing in your life. Promise God that you will try to live according to his will for you.

3. Approach the area for confession. Wait an appropriate distance until it is your turn. If you do not know the priest, it is proper to share your state in life (e.g., single or married), the time of your last confession, any difficulties you are having in leading a Christian life, and anything else by way of introduction which may help the priest to exercise his ministry.

4. Make the Sign of the Cross with the priest. He may say: "May God, who has enlightened every heart, help you to know your sins and trust his mercy." You reply: "Amen."

5. Confess your sins to the priest. Simply and directly talk to him about the areas of sinfulness in your life that need God's healing touch.

6. The priest will ask you to pray an Act of Contrition. Pray an Act of Contrition you have committed to memory (see page 267). If your memory fails, say a prayer of sorrow in your own words.

7. The priest will talk to you about your life, encourage you to be more faithful to God in the future, and help you decide what to do to make up for your sins—your penance.

8. The priest will then extend his hands over your head and pray the Church's official prayer of absolution:

God, the Father of mercies, through the Death and Resurrection of his Son, has reconciled the world to himself and sent the Holy Spirit among us for the forgiveness of sins; through the ministry of the Church may God give you pardon and peace, and I absolve you from your sins in the name of the Father, and of the Son, and of the Holy Spirit.
You respond: "Amen."

9. The priest will wish you peace. Thank him and leave.

10. Go to a quiet place in church and pray your prayer of penance. Then spend some time quietly thanking God for the gift of forgiveness.

Order of Mass

There are two main parts of the Mass, the Liturgy of the Word and the Liturgy of the Eucharist. The complete order of Mass:

The Introductory Rites

The Entrance
Greeting of the Altar and of the People Gathered
The Act of Penitence
The *Kyrie Eleison*
The *Gloria*
The Collect (Opening Prayer)

The Liturgy of the Word

Silence
The Biblical Readings (the reading of the Gospel is the high point of the Liturgy of the Word)
The Responsorial Psalm
The Homily
The Profession of Faith (Creed)
The Prayer of the Faithful

The Liturgy of the Eucharist

The Preparation of the Gifts
The Prayer over the Offerings
The Eucharistic Prayer
　　Thanksgiving
　　Acclamation
　　Epiclesis
　　Institution Narrative and Consecration
　　Anamnesis
　　Offering
　　Intercessions
　　Final Doxology
The Communion Rite
　　The Lord's Prayer
　　The Rite of Peace
　　The Fraction (Breaking of the Bread)
Communion
Prayer after Communion

The Concluding Rites

Communion Regulations

To receive Holy Communion properly, a person must be in the state of grace (free from mortal sin), have the right intention (only for the purpose of pleasing God), and observe the Communion fast.

The fast means that a person may not eat anything or drink any liquid (other than water) one hour before the reception of Communion. There are exceptions made to this fast only for the sick and aged.

Three Degrees of the Sacrament of Orders

There are three degrees of the Sacrament of Holy Orders: the ministries of bishop, priest, and deacon.

The bishop receives the fullness of the Sacrament of Orders. He is the successor to the Apostles. When he celebrates the Sacraments, the bishop is given the grace to act in the Person of Christ, who is the head of the body of the Church.

Priests are ordained as coworkers of the bishop. They, too, are configured to Christ so that they may act in his Person during the Sacraments of Eucharist, Baptism, and the Anointing of the Sick. They may bless marriages in the name of Christ and, under the authority of the bishop, share in Christ's ministry of forgiveness in the Sacrament of Penance and Reconciliation.

Deacons are ordained for service and are configured to Christ the servant. Deacons are ordained to help and serve the priests and bishops in their work. While bishops and priests are configured to Christ to act as the head of Christ's body, deacons are configured to Christ in order to serve as he served. Deacons may baptize, preach the Gospel and homily, and bless marriages.

G. Mary and the Saints

The doctrine of the communion of saints flows from our belief that we Christians are closely united as one family in the Spirit of Jesus Christ. Mary is the Queen of the Saints. Her role in the Church flows from an inseparable union with her son.

Mother of God

Mary, the Mother of Jesus, is the closest human to cooperate with her Son's work of Redemption. For this reason, the Church holds her in a special place. Of her many titles, the most significant is that she is the Mother of God.

The Church teaches several truths about Mary.

First, she was conceived immaculately. This means from the very first moment of her existence she was without sin and "full of grace." This belief is called the Immaculate Conception. The feast of the Immaculate Conception is celebrated on December 8.

Second, Mary was always a virgin. She was a virgin before, in, and after the birth of Jesus. As his Mother, she cared for him in infancy and raised him to adulthood with the help of her husband, Joseph. She witnessed Jesus' preaching and ministry, was at the foot of his Cross at his crucifixion, and present with the Apostles as they awaited the coming of the Holy Spirit at Pentecost. With her whole being, she is as she stated: "I am the handmaid of the Lord" (Lk 1:38).

Third, at the time of her death, Mary was assumed body and soul into Heaven. This dogma was proclaimed as a matter of Faith by Pope Pius XII in 1950. The feast of the Assumption is celebrated on August 15.

The Church has always been devoted to the Blessed Virgin. This devotion is different from that given to God—Father, Son, and Holy Spirit. Rather, the Church is devoted to Mary as the first disciple, the Queen of all Saints, and her own Mother. Quoting the fathers of the Second Vatican Council:

> In the meantime the Mother of Jesus, in the glory which she possesses in body and soul in heaven, is the image and the beginning of the Church as it is to be perfected in the world to come. Likewise she shines forth on earth, until the day of the Lord shall come, a sign of certain hope and comfort to the pilgrim People of God. (*Lumen Gentium*, 68)

Marian Feasts throughout the Year

January 1	Solemnity of Mary, Mother of God
March 25	Annunciation of the Lord
May 31	Visitation
August 15	Assumption
August 22	Queenship of Mary
September 8	Birth of Mary
September 15	Our Lady of Sorrows
October 7	Our Lady of the Rosary
November 21	Presentation of Mary
December 8	Immaculate Conception
December 12	Our Lady of Guadalupe

Canonization of Saints

Saints are those who are in glory with God in Heaven. *Canonization* refers to a solemn declaration by the Pope that a person who either died a martyr or who lived an exemplary Christian life is in Heaven and may be honored and imitated by all Christians. The canonization process first involves a process of beatification that includes a thorough investigation of the person's life and certification of miracles that can be attributed to the candidate's intercession.

The first official canonization of the universal Church on record is St. Ulrich of Augsburg by Pope John XV in 993.

Some non-Catholics criticize Catholics for "praying to saints." Catholics *honor* saints for their holy lives but we do not pray to them as if they were God. We ask the saints to pray with us and for us as part of the Church in glory. We can ask them to do this because we know that their lives have been spent in close communion with God. We also ask the saints for their friendship so that we can follow the example they have left for us.

American Saints

North American Jesuit Martyrs. Five French missionaries were martyred in Canada; another three in New York.

Those who were killed in New York were Saints Isaac Jogues, René Goupil, and Jean Lalande. Their shrine is at Auriesville, New York. Canonized in 1930.

St. Frances Cabrini (1850–1917). Italian immigrant who became a naturalized American citizen in 1909. Founded the Missionary Sisters of the Sacred Heart. Worked tirelessly among the American immigrants. Known as the "Heavenly Patroness of all Emigrants." Her shrine is in New York City. Canonized in 1946.

St. Elizabeth Ann Bayley Seton (1774–1821). First native-born American to be canonized a saint. Daughter of an aristocratic Episcopalian, New York family. Mother of five children. When widowed, she converted to Catholicism (1805) and founded the American Sisters of Charity (1809). Established many Catholic schools that served as the prototype of the American Catholic school system. Her order also founded many hospitals and served heroically during the Civil War. Canonized in 1975.

St. John Nepomucene Neumann (1811–1860). Native of Bohemia who served as a pioneer diocesan priest in Rochester and Buffalo, New York. Joined the Redemptorist and was named the fourth bishop of Philadelphia in 1852. Was a gentle, prayerful, faithful missionary and example to his flock. Canonized in 1977.

St. Rose Philippine Duchesne (1769–1852). French-born foundress of the Religious of the Sacred Heart. Came as a missionary to the Louisiana Territory at the age of forty-nine. Established a mission in Missouri with the first free school west of the Mississippi. Devoted her years of service to educate Native Americans, care for their sick, and combat alcoholism in the tribes. Known by the Pottawatomi Indians as the "Woman-Who-Prays-Always." Canonized in 1988.

St. Katharine Drexel (1858–1955). Called the "Millionaire Nun," Katherine Drexel inherited a fortune that she eventually used for missionary endeavors in the community of Sisters of the Blessed Sacrament, which she founded in 1891. She established sixty missions for the education of Native Americans and African Americans and founded Xavier University in New Orleans, the only Catholic university dedicated to serving African Americans. Canonized in 2000.

St. Anne-Thérèse Guérin (1798–1856). French nun who came to Vincennes, Indiana, and later helped establish the Academy of St. Mary-of-the-Woods (1841) at Terre Haute, Indiana, the first Catholic women's liberal arts college in the United States. Established schools and orphanages and engaged in many charitable works to help the poor and sick. Canonized in 2006.

H. Devotions

Catholics have also expressed their piety around the Church's sacramental life through practices like the veneration of relics, visits to churches, pilgrimages, processions, the Stations of the Cross, the rosary, religious medals, and many more. This section lists some popular Catholic devotions.

The Mysteries of the Rosary

Joyful Mysteries

1. The Annunciation
2. The Visitation
3. The Nativity
4. The Presentation in the Temple
5. The Finding of Jesus in the Temple

Mysteries of Light

1. Jesus' Baptism in the Jordan River
2. Jesus Self-manifestation at the Wedding of Cana
3. The Proclamation of the Kingdom of God and Jesus' Call to Conversion
4. The Transfiguration
5. The Institution of the Eucharist at the Last Supper

Sorrowful Mysteries

1. The Agony in the Garden
2. The Scourging at the Pillar
3. The Crowning with Thorns
4. The Carrying of the Cross
5. The Crucifixion

Glorious Mysteries

1. The Resurrection
2. The Ascension
3. The Descent of the Holy Spirit
4. The Assumption of Mary
5. The Crowning of Mary as the Queen of Heaven and Earth

How to Pray the Rosary

Opening

1. Begin on the crucifix and pray the Apostles' Creed.

2. On the first bead, pray the Our Father.

3. On the next three beads, pray the Hail Mary. (Some people meditate on the virtues of faith, hope, and charity on these beads.)

4. On the fifth bead, pray the Glory Be.

The Body

Each decade (set of ten beads) is organized as follows:

1. On the larger bead that comes before each set of ten, announce the mystery to be prayed (see above) and pray one Our Father.

2. On each of the ten smaller beads, pray one Hail Mary while meditating on the mystery.

3. Pray one Glory Be at the end of the decade. (There is no bead for the Glory Be.)

Conclusion

Pray the following prayer at the end of the Rosary:

Hail, Holy Queen
Hail, holy Queen, Mother of Mercy,
our life, our sweetness, and our hope.
To thee do we cry,
poor banished children of Eve.
To thee do we send up our sighs,
mourning and weeping in the valley of tears.
Turn then, most gracious advocate,
thine eyes of mercy toward us;
and after this our exile,
show unto us the blessed fruit of thy womb, Jesus.
O clement, O loving, O sweet Virgin Mary.

V. Pray for us, O holy Mother of God,
R. that we may be made worthy of the promises of Christ.
Amen.

Stations of the Cross

The Stations of the Cross is a devotion and also a sacramental. (A sacramental is a sacred object, blessing, or devotion.) The Stations of the Cross are individual pictures or symbols hung on the interior walls of most Catholic churches depicting fourteen steps along Jesus' way of the cross. Praying the stations means meditating on each of the following scenes:

1. Jesus is condemned to death.

2. Jesus takes up his cross.

3. Jesus falls the first time.

4. Jesus meets his Mother.

5. Simon of Cyrene helps Jesus carry his cross.

6. Veronica wipes the face of Jesus.

7. Jesus falls the second time.

8. Jesus consoles the women of Jerusalem.

9. Jesus falls the third time.

10. Jesus is stripped of his garments.

11. Jesus is nailed to the cross.

12. Jesus dies on the Cross.

13. Jesus is taken down from the Cross.

14. Jesus is laid in the tomb.

Some churches also include a fifteenth station, the Resurrection of the Lord.

Novenas

The novena consists of the recitation of certain prayers over a period of nine days. The symbolism of nine days refers to the time Mary and the Apostles spent in prayer between Jesus' Ascension into Heaven and Pentecost.

Many novenas are dedicated to Mary or to a saint with the faith and hope that she or he will intercede for the one making the novena. Novenas to St. Jude, St. Anthony, Our Lady of Perpetual Help, and Our Lady of Lourdes remain popular in the Church today.

Liturgy of the Hours

The Liturgy of the Hours is part of the official, public prayer of the Church. Along with the celebration of the Sacraments, the recitation of the Liturgy of the Hours, or Divine Office (*office* means "duty" or "obligation"), allows for constant praise and thanksgiving to God throughout the day and night.

The Liturgy of Hours consists of five major divisions:

1. An hour of readings

2. Morning praises
3. Midday prayers
4. Vespers (evening prayers)
5. Compline (a short night prayer)

Scriptural prayer, especially the Psalms, is at the heart of the Liturgy of the Hours. Each day follows a separate pattern of prayer with themes closely tied in with the liturgical year and feasts of the saints.

The Divine Praises

These praises are traditionally recited after the benediction of the Blessed Sacrament.

> Blessed be God.
> Blessed be his holy name.
> Blessed be Jesus Christ, true God and true man.
> Blessed be the name of Jesus.
> Blessed be his most Sacred Heart.
> Blessed be his most Precious Blood.
> Blessed be Jesus in the most holy sacrament of the altar.
> Blessed be the Holy Spirit, the Paraclete.
> Blessed be the great Mother of God, Mary most holy.
> Blessed be her holy and Immaculate Conception.
> Blessed be her glorious Assumption.
> Blessed be the name of Mary, Virgin and Mother.
> Blessed be St. Joseph, her most chaste spouse.
> Blessed be God in his angels and his saints.

I. Prayers

Some common Catholic prayers are listed below. The Latin translation for three of the prayers is included. Latin is the official language of the Church. There are several occasions when you may pray in Latin; for example, at a World Youth Day when you are with young people who speak many different languages. This section opens with a lesson from the Second Vatican Council on the importance of prayer.

The Importance of Prayer

The spiritual life, however, is not limited solely to participation in the liturgy. Christians are indeed called to pray with others, but they must also enter into their rooms to pray to their Father in secret (see Mt 6:6); furthermore, according to the teaching of the Apostle, they must pray without ceasing (see 1 Thes 5:17). W also learn from the same Apostle that we must always carry around in our bodies the dying of Jesus, so that Jesus' life may also be made manifest in our mortal flesh (see 2 Cor 4:10–11). That is why we beg the Lord in the sacrifice of the Mass that "receiving the offering of the spiritual victim, he may fashion us for himself as an eternal gift."

Sign of the Cross

> In the name of the Father,
> and of the Son,
> and of the Holy Spirit. Amen.

> *In nómine Patris,*
> *et Filii,*
> *et Spíritus Sancti.*
> *Amen.*

Our Father

> Our Father
> who art in heaven,
> hallowed be thy name.
> Thy kingdom come;
> thy will be done on earth as it is in heaven.
> Give us this day our daily bread
> and forgive us our trespasses
> as we forgive those who trespass against us.
> And lead us not into temptation,
> but deliver us from evil.
> Amen.

> *Pater Noster qui es in caelis:*
> *sanctificétur Nomen Tuum;*
> *advéniat Regnum Tuum;*
> *fiat volúntas Tua,*
> *sicut in caelo, et in terra.*
> *Panem nostrum cotidianum da nobis hódie;*
> *et dimítte nobis débita nostra,*
> *sicut et nos dimíttimus debitóribus nostris;*
> *et ne nos inducas in tentatiónem,*
> *sed libera nos a Malo.*
> *Amen.*

Glory Be

> Glory be to the Father
> and to the Son
> and to the Holy Spirit,

as it was in the beginning,
is now,
and ever shall be,
world without end. Amen.

Glória Patri
et Filio
et Spiritui Sancto.
Sicut erat in princípio,
et nunc et semper,
et in sae'cula saeculórum.
Amen.

Hail Mary

Hail Mary, full of grace,
the Lord is with thee.
Blessed art thou among women
and blessed is the fruit of thy womb, Jesus.
Holy Mary, Mother of God,
pray for us sinners now
and at the hour of our death. Amen.

Ave, María, grátia plena,
Dóminus tecum.
Benedicta tu in muliéribus,
et benedíctus fructus ventris
tui, Iesus.
Sancta María, Mater Dei,
ora pro nobis peccatoribus
nunc et in hora mortis nostrae.
Amen.

Memorare

Remember, O most gracious Virgin Mary,
that never was it known
that anyone who fled to your protection,
implored your help,
or sought your intercession was left unaided.
Inspired by this confidence,
I fly unto you,
O virgin of virgins, my Mother,
To you I come, before you I stand,
sinful and sorrowful.
O Mother of the word incarnate,
despise not my petitions,
but in your mercy hear and answer me. Amen.

The Angelus

V. The Angel of the Lord declared unto Mary.
R. And she conceived of the Holy Spirit.
Hail Mary . . .
V. Behold the handmaid of the Lord.
R. Be it be done unto me according to thy word.
Hail Mary . . .
V. And the Word was made flesh.
R. And dwelt among us.
Hail Mary . . .
V. Pray for us, O holy Mother of God.
R. That we may be made worthy of the promises of Christ.
Let us pray: Pour forth, we beseech thee, O Lord, thy grace into our hearts; that we, to whom the Incarnation of Christ, thy Son, was made known by the message of an angel, may by his Passion and Cross be brought to the glory of his Resurrection. Through the same Christ, our Lord. Amen.

Regina Caeli

Queen of heaven, rejoice, alleluia.
The Son whom you merited to bear, alleluia,
has risen as he said, alleluia.
Rejoice and be glad, O Virgin Mary, alleluia.
For the Lord has truly risen, alleluia.

Grace at Meals

Before Meals

Bless us, O Lord,
and these your gifts,
which we are about to receive from your bounty,
through Christ our Lord. Amen.

After Meals

We give you thanks, almighty God,
for these and all the gifts
which we have received
from your goodness
through Christ our Lord. Amen.

Guardian Angel Prayer

Angel of God, my guardian dear, to whom God's love entrust me here, ever this day be at my side, to light and guard, to rule and guide. Amen.

Prayer for the Faithful Departed

V. Eternal rest grant unto them, O Lord.

R. And let perpetual light shine upon them.

V. May their souls and the souls of all faithful departed,

through the mercy of God, rest in peace.

R. Amen.

Morning Offering

O Jesus, through the Immaculate Heart of Mary, I offer you my prayers, works, joys, and sufferings of this day in union with the holy sacrifice of the Mass throughout the world. I offer them for all the intentions of your Sacred Heart: the Salvation of souls, reparation for sin, the reunion of all Christians. I offer them for the intentions of our bishops and all members of the apostleship of prayer and in particular for those recommended by your Holy Father this month. Amen.

Act of Contrition

O my God, I am heartily sorry for having offended Thee, and I detest all my sins because of they just punishments, but most of all because they offend Thee, my God, who art all good and deserving of all my love. I firmly resolve with the help of Thy grace to sin no more and to avoid the near occasion of sin. Amen.

Prayer for Peace (St. Francis of Assisi)

Lord, make me an instrument of your peace.
Where there is hatred, let me sow love;
where there is injury, pardon;
where there is doubt, faith;
where there is despair, hope;
where there is darkness, light;
where there is sadness, joy.
O Divine Master,
grant that I may not seek so much to be consoled as to console;
to be understood, as to understand,
to be loved, as to love.
For it is in giving that we receive,
it is in pardoning that we are pardoned,
and it is in dying that we are born to eternal life.

Glossary

ancestor—Any person to whom you are related by blood who comes before you on a family tree.

angel—A spiritual, personal, and immortal creature, with intelligence and free will, who glorifies God and serves as God's messenger. Satan was at first a good angel, but he and other devils became evil through their own choices.

apocalyptic literature—A highly symbolic style of writing in which hidden truths are revealed within a narrative framework. The revelation is often delivered by an angelic or visionary being.

archaeology—The science of studying material remains of past human life and activities.

Ark of the Covenant—The portable shrine built to hold the tablets on which Moses wrote the Law. It was a sign of God's presence to the Israelites. Solomon built the Temple in Jerusalem to house the ark.

artifact—Something created by past humans, usually for a specific purpose (tools, pottery, clothing, etc.).

Asherah—The Canaanite goddess sometimes called the "Queen of Heaven." She was the consort of Baal and the goddess of fertility. The practice of sacred prostitution is connected with the worship of Asherah.

Baal—The Canaanite god of fertility, associated with storms and rain. He was the most prominent of the Canaanite gods and the one most often worshipped by the Israelites.

Bet Av—The basic social unit of the Israelite society, a patriarchal household of immediate and extended family members.

call narrative—A story that describes a person's initial awareness that God wanted him or her to do something specific. The calls of the prophet have five common elements: there is something mysterious and holy about the encounter; God acts first; the prophet resists; God reassures; God sends the prophet on his or her mission.

canon—An official list of books belonging to the Bible, both the Old Testament and New Testament.

circumcision—The surgical removal of foreskin; it was the physical sign of the covenant between God and Abraham.

civil laws—Laws dealing with the day-to-day issues that arise between people living, in the case of the Israelites, in an agrarian community such as the consequences when one person's animal injures another person, or when borders between properties are disputed.

context—The historical, cultural, social, or political circumstances surrounding an event or record.

covenant—A binding and solemn agreement between human beings or between God and his people, holding each to a particular course of action.

critical reading—A number of methods of studying the Bible that aim to discover what God is communicating—both to the people of the Bible and to people today.

Cyrus—The Persian king who allowed some of the Jews to return to Jerusalem after he conquered the Babylonians in 539 BC. This event is typically understood to mark the end of the Exile. However, many Jews remained in the Diaspora, never returning to Palestine, which remained controlled by the Persians.

David—The king of the united kingdom of Israel from 1009 to 969 BC. He conquered the Trans-Jordanian states, gaining control of the major trade routes linking Egypt and Mesopotamia. Jesus was a descendant of David.

Dead Sea Scrolls—Ancient scrolls containing the oldest known manuscripts of the books of the Old Testament in

Hebrew. They were discovered in caves near Qumran on the Dead Sea between 1947 and 1953.

deuterocanonical—A term meaning "second canon." Books included in the Catholic Old Testament but not in the Hebrew Bible. These additions are 1 and 2 Maccabees, Judith, Tobit, Baruch, Sirach, Wisdom, and parts of Esther and Daniel.

Diaspora—A group migration or flight away from the homeland into one or more other countries. The word can also refer to people who have maintained their separate identity (often religious, but occasionally ethnic, racial, or cultural) while living in those other countries after the migration.

elders—Mature, usually male, members of the Israelite community who met regularly to rule on specific disputes within the community.

eschatology—A study of the "last things," such as death, judgment, immortality, Heaven and Hell, and the like.

Essenes—A group of Jews whose resistance to foreign influence took them to the extreme position of living in entirely separate communities in the desert around the Dead Sea. It is probable that they were the ones who hid the Dead Sea Scrolls, which were not discovered until the middle of the twentieth century.

Establishment religion—A religion that tends to support the power of the ruling class over the common people. In the case of the Israelite monarchy, it joined YHWH worship with the worship of other Canaanite gods.

evolution—The scientific theory which proposes that current forms of life developed gradually out of earlier ones.

harlotry—In the Old Testament, this term refers not only to a woman's illicit sexual behavior, but perhaps even more commonly to the practice of worshipping Canaanite gods along with YHWH. Jezebel is referred to as a "harlot" in this sense, not because she was ever unfaithful to Ahab.

hasidim—A Hebrew word meaning "loyal ones." It refers to a group who supported the Maccabees in the military effort against Antiochus IV. They also were probably the core members of the later group known as the Essenes.

Hasmonean Dynasty—Descendants of the Maccabees who ruled in Judea after the ousting of the last of the Syrians in 141 BC until the establishment of Roman authority in 63 BC. John Hyrcanus was the first ruler in this dynasty and ruled until 128 BC.

Hellenistic—Relating to the culture, history, or language of Greece after the death of Alexander the Great in 323 BC.

hieroglyphic writing—An ancient form of Egyptian writing, more stylized than pictograms but not based on an alphabet.

historical psalm—A psalm recounting events from the history of Israel such as the covenant with the Patriarchs, the Exodus, or the settling of the Promised Land.

Hyksos—A group of non-Egyptians who came to power in Egypt between 1650 and 1500 BC.

Inarus Revolt—An Egyptian revolt against the Persians in 460 that had Greek support. It may have influenced Cyrus's decision to allow the Jews to return to Palestine and rebuild Jerusalem, as it would have allowed for increased military presence on the western flank of the Persian Empire facing Greece.

Jezebel—A Canaanite princess, married to Ahab, one of the kings of the northern kingdom. She orchestrated the murder of Naboth in order to gain his property for her husband.

Josiah—The last independent king of Judah, and one of only two kings to receive unmitigated praise in the Old Testament. He initiated religious reforms attempting to purify the worship of YHWH in the Temple. He was killed in a battle with the Egyptians who then established a puppet government in Jerusalem.

Jubilee—Every seventh sabbatical year (i.e., every forty-ninth year). In a year of Jubilee all debts were to be forgiven, and land that had been sold to pay a debt was to be returned to the original family. In this way, the wealth of the entire community was to be redistributed among the poor, preventing unrelieved poverty and large gaps between the rich and the poor.

Judah—The name of the southern kingdom after the splitting of the monarchy. It included the territory originally belonging to just two of the twelve tribes, Judah and Benjamin.

Judea—The Aramaic name for the place formerly called Judah. It was a name first given after the Babylonian Exile. Though the region varied over the years, it always included the city of Jerusalem.

judge—In ancient Israel, one who acted as a temporary military leader, as well as arbiter of disputes within and between tribes. Judges were also expected to remind the people of their responsibility to God.

just war doctrine—Teachings of the Church that define the moral limits of warfare.

koine—The common Greek language introduced in Palestine by Alexander the Great in 333 BC. It is the language of the Septuagint and remained the common language of Palestine until Latin replaced it in AD 500.

Lamentations—The Book of Hebrew poetry written in response to the devastation in Jerusalem by those who remained behind after the conquest of 587.

levirate marriage—The marriage of a widow to a near relative of her deceased husband. The first male child of a levirate marriage would be considered the legal son of the widow's first husband.

Magisterium—The teaching authority of the Church concerning issues of faith and morals. The Magisterium consists of the Pope and the college of bishops acting together.

major prophets—Three of the latter prophets, Isaiah, Jeremiah, and Ezekiel, whose books in the Old Testament are quite lengthy.

Marduk—The main state god of the Babylonians during the reign of Nebuchadnezzar. It was to his temple in the city of Babylon that the Temple furnishings and vessels from the Temple of Solomon were carried following the destruction of the Temple and Jerusalem in 587 BC.

messenger formula—The opening words of a prophetic speech, attributing what follows to God, as in "Thus says the Lord . . ." or "The Lord said. . . "

minor prophets—The twelve prophets of the Old Testament whose recorded sayings are much briefer than those of the major prophets: Hosea, Joel, Amos, Obadiah, Jonah, Micah, Nahum, Habbakuk, Zephaniah, Haggai, Zechariah, and Malachi.

Mishpachah—The Hebrew word for the "clans" that were associations of related Bet Av, gathered together to help with planting and harvesting, and with defense against aggressive neighbors.

"murmurings"—The stories in the Book of Exodus of the complaints of the Israelites in the desert against Moses and against God.

myths—Symbolic stories that express a spiritual truth or a basic belief about God.

nabi—The Hebrew word translated as "prophet."

natural law—The participation of man in God's eternal law that reveals what he intends us to do and avoid according to his wise and loving plan.

Neo-Assyrian Empire—A new empire in the Mesopotamian region that eventually conquered the Northern Kingdom, sending it's ruling class into exile in 722 BC.

oracle—A brief, poetic declaration preceded by the messenger formula, "Thus says the Lord," which establishes it reliably as a message from God. Pagan religions also use the word sometimes for the person who delivers the message, as was the case with the famous "oracle of Delphi."

paganism—The profession of no religion.

parallelism—A characteristic common to Hebrew poetry in which two lines express the same or opposite thoughts, one right after the other.

patriarchs—Male rulers, elders, or leaders. The patriarchs of Israel are Abraham, Isaac, and Jacob.

Pharisees—A group of Jews whose response to foreign rule was one of cultural and religious separatism. They valued adherence to the Law, and exhibited great respect for teachers and interpreters of the Torah. They were responsible for the introduction of rabbis and synagogues into the cultural life of the Jews.

pictograms—The earliest form of writing in which pictures represented words or ideas.

post-Exilic—Referring to the time after the return of the exiles to Jerusalem in 539 BC.

prehistoric—Refers to events or objects that date to a time before writing developed and written records existed.

primeval history—Stories or myths about the origins of the earth, humans, other creatures, languages, and cultures.

Psuedepigrapha—Ancient books from the same timeframe as the books of the Bible, especially the New Testament. The Church decided these books were not inspired by God and could not be included in the canon of the Bible.

Ptolemies—The dynasty descending from Ptolemy I, a general under Alexander the Great, who ruled Egypt and Palestine from 320 to 200 BC when they lost control of the land to the Syrian empire.

punitive justice—Laws that rely on punishment as a deterrent to criminal activity.

rabbi—The local leader of a community's synagogue, respected for his piety and knowledge of the Law. This is a position that came into being with the establishment of the synagogues by the Pharisees.

religious laws—Laws that govern the actions of the priests, the regulations for sacrifice, and the building and maintenance of the Temple.

remnant—The exiles and former exiles who remained faithful to YHWH during the time of captivity and who were expected to restore Jerusalem.

restorative justice—Laws that are concerned primarily with restoring community after an offense has occurred. The goal is to keep the community together, as the survival of the society depends on everyone fulfilling his or her role.

Sadducees—Originally an aristocratic group of wealthy Jews in Jerusalem who favored strict adherence to the letter of the Torah and regarded Temple worship as essential to Jewish life. They denied such doctrines as the resurrection and the existence of angels because those subjects cannot be found in the Torah.

Saul—The first king of Israel, anointed by the prophet Samuel. He was never able to fully unite the twelve tribes and organize them into a recognizable nation.

scribes—People trained to write using the earliest forms of writing before literacy was widespread.

Septuagint—The oldest complete edition of the Old Testament. It is a Greek translation of earlier Hebrew texts, probably written in Alexandria during the time of Ptolemaic rule over Palestine. The word itself, *Septuagint*, is Latin for "seventy" which refers to the traditional story that seventy scholars from the Holy Land were brought to Alexandria to accomplish the translation.

shofet—A Hebrew word traditionally translated in English as "judge" that more literally means "temporary military leader."

Showbread—The twelve loaves of bread presented on the altar every Sabbath as an offering to YHWH. The priests consumed the bread at the end of every week. (This is also sometimes spelled "shewbread" but the pronunciation does not change.)

sin—An offense against God. Sin is a deliberate thought, word, deed, or omission against the eternal law of God.

Solomon—David and Bathsheba's son, the last king of the united monarchy. He was renowned for his wisdom as well as for his wealth and his many large building projects. In addition to the king's palace and numerous walled fortresses throughout Palestine, he also built the Temple of Jerusalem to house the Ark of the Covenant.

synagogue—A meeting place for study and prayer introduced by the Pharisees to foster study of the Law and adherence to the covenant code.

syncretism—A blending of two or more religious traditions.

Talmud—A collection of rabbinical teachings collected after the destruction of the Jerusalem Temple in 70 AD.

Tradition—The living transmission of the Church's Gospel message found in the Church's teaching, life, and worship. It is faithfully preserved, handed on, and interpreted by the Church's Magisterium.

typology—The study of types of writing that have common traits. Typology in Scripture study involves reading the Old Testament in light of Christ crucified and risen.

Ugarit—An ancient city of the Canaanites that was discovered in 1928. Many texts were found there, from which scholars have learned a great deal about the Canaanite religion.

Vineyard Song—An important passage of the Book of Isaiah depicting the Chosen People as the vine of God. This image recurs in the New Testament in the words of Jesus and the writings of the Apostle, Paul.

wisdom literature—Collections of wise sayings, proverbs, and short stories that offer insights into the proper way to live. Hebrew wisdom literature began to be collected during the Exile and the post-Exilic period.

Zealots—A Jewish sect, active during New Testament times, who favored military resistance to Roman authority. Their belief in the coming of the Messiah was strongly linked to their desire for Jewish independence.

Zoroastrianism—The official religion of the Persian Empire, which understood the universe to be caught in a constant struggle between light and darkness. Jewish belief in angels and in Satan's influence can be traced to the influence of this foreign religion.

Subject Index

A

Aaron, 148

Abel, 58

Abijah, 170

Abimelech, 70

Abortion, 94

Abraham, 63, 64, 66
  asked to sacrifice Isaac, 71
  blessings and threats, 70–71
  changing name from Abram, 68, 69
  covenant with, 55, 69–70
  as father of faith, 68–71
  from Abram, 68, 69
  righteousness of, 70
  the wanderer, 68–69

Act of Contrition, 269

Adam and Eve, 55
  connection to Jesus and Mary, 59
  Original Justice, 57–58
  Original Sin, 58–60

Adonai, 3, 4, 84

Adultery, 95

Ahab, 130, 140, 160

Ahasuerus, 220

Ahaz, King, 37, 162, 170

Ai, 24

Ain Ghazal, 27

Alexander Janneus, 228

Alexander the Great, 184
  dates of, 218
  Jews living under, 221–222
  in outline of Hebrew history, 15

Alexandria, 222–223
  library of, 223, 224

Allegorical sense of Scripture, 7

Ammon, 37, 132

Amon-Re, 87

Amos, 140
  call from God, 149
  compared to Hosea, 159, 162
  as prophet, 43, 157–159

Amos, Book of, 157–159
  Amos hears call from God, 149
  concern for the poor, 151
  hope for the future, 159
  oppression by rich, 158
  warning by, 158

Anagogical sense of Scripture, 7

Anat, 129

Ancestor stories, 63–67
  Abraham, 68–71
  dating, 64
  duplication of, 64–65
  formation and arrangement of, 65–67
  importance of, 67
  Jacob, 72–74
  Joseph, 74–75
  women's role in, 64

Ancient writing, decoding, 25–26

Andrew, St., 255

Angel, 58
  angel of the Lord and call of prophets, 150
  Gabriel protecting Tobiah, 219–220

Angelus, 268

Anna, 219

Antiochus III, 223, 224

Antiochus IV, 42, 211, 212, 224–226
  defiling the Temple, 226

Scripture Index

Old Testament

Pentateuch

Genesis

Exodus

Photo Credits

Superstock
page 7, 10, 14, 15, 25, 31, 43, 44, 50, 57, 63, 66, 71, 73, 80, 88, 92, 93, 104, 109, 110, 112, 115, 119, 124, 126, 128, 130, 134, 135, 137, 139, 140, 142, 149, 157, 159, 168, 173, 175, 177, 178, 179, 180, 187, 188, 207, 211, 219, 220, 227, 230, 235, 243, 244, 246

Corbis
page 85, 232

WGBH
page 36